Advance Praise for

GENERALS AND ADMIRALS,
CRIMINALS AND CROOKS

"I couldn't put this book down. *Generals and Admirals, Criminals and Crooks* is very sobering, and it should be. I highly recommend this book to a wide audience, and most especially to the leaders of America's armed forces."

—Lieutenant General (Ret.) Joseph DiSalvo, U.S. Army

"*General and Admirals, Criminals and Crooks* should be read and discussed by military leaders at all levels. Jeff Matthews exposes the failures, not only of individuals, but often of teammates who failed to speak up, and allowed so much to go so wrong."

—General (Ret.) Joe Lengyel, U.S. Air Force, 28th Chief, National Guard Bureau

"This book should be required reading at commissioning sources, the various levels of officer professional military education, and as part of the CAPSTONE course for all newly selected generals and flag officers."

—Brigadier General Jeff Hurlbert, U.S. Air Force, Commandant, National War College

"*Generals and Admirals, Criminal and Crooks* is an engrossing, exemplary, and necessary book about leadership and the importance of character and humility."

—Tim Bakken, professor of law, U.S. Military Academy

"Jeff Matthews has provided an invaluable service in documenting the disconcerting lapses in judgment by American admirals and generals. This book should be read by every senior leader and individual aspiring to lead at high levels of command."

—Rear Admiral (Ret.) Tim Gallaudet, U.S. Navy

"Jeff Matthews's assessment of blatant criminal behavior through the nuances of loyalty to a cause or individual reveals how power, and absolute power, can influence and corrupt."

—Brigadier General (Ret.) Dave Reist, U.S. Marine Corps

"*Generals and Admirals, Criminals and Crooks* is a must read upon promotion to senior ranks and in the senior service schools. It is a sobering reminder to all senior officers that with great power comes great responsibility and that integrity is instrumental in leadership and maintaining an effective military."

—Major General (Ret.) Michael Kingsley, U.S. Air Force

"*Generals and Admirals, Criminals and Crooks* is the most necessary study for aspiring military and political leaders I have ever encountered. The book should be required reading at our nation's war colleges."

—Lieutenant General (Ret.) Stephen M. Speakes, U.S. Army

Generals and Admirals, Criminals and Crooks

This book was selected as the 2023 Giles Family Fund Recipient. The University of Notre Dame Press and the author thank the Giles family for their generous support.

Giles Family Fund Recipients

2019   *The Glory and the Burden*, Robert Schmuhl (expanded edition, 2022)

2020   *Ars Vitae: The Fate of Inwardness and the Return of the Ancient Arts of Living*, Elisabeth Lasch-Quinn

2021   *William Still: The Underground Railroad and the Angel at Philadelphia*, William C. Kashatus

2022   *An Inconvenient Apocalypse: Environmental Collapse, Climate Crisis, and the Fate of Humanity*, Wes Jackson and Robert Jensen

2023   *Generals and Admirals, Criminals and Crooks: Dishonorable Leadership in the U.S. Military*, Jeffrey J. Matthews

The Giles Family Fund supports the work and mission of the University of Notre Dame Press to publish books that engage the most enduring questions of our time. Each year the endowment helps underwrite the publication and promotion of a book that sparks intellectual exploration and expands the reach and impact of the university.

GENERALS
AND ADMIRALS,
CRIMINALS
AND CROOKS

Dishonorable Leadership in the U.S. Military

JEFFREY J. MATTHEWS

University of Notre Dame Press
Notre Dame, Indiana

University of Notre Dame Press
Notre Dame, Indiana 46556
undpress.nd.edu

Published in the United States of America

Library of Congress Control Number: 2023937449

ISBN: 978-0-268-20652-9 (Hardback)
ISBN: 978-0-268-20654-3 (WebPDF)
ISBN: 978-0-268-20651-2 (Epub)

To my mother, Margareta Matthews,
a loving mom, a lover of history,
and a dedicated military spouse.

To Peter Collins,
who lives in our hearts and minds.

To the countless generals, admirals,
soldiers, sailors, airmen, and marines
who have served our country honorably.

We promote good leadership not by ignoring bad leadership, nor by presuming it immutable. To the contrary, our only hope is to take it on, to decode and decipher it, and then to attack it as we would any disease that damages, debilitates, and sometimes even kills.

— Barbara Kellerman

CONTENTS

AUTHOR'S NOTE

In June 2017 I conducted a lengthy interview with General Colin Powell at his home in McLean, Virginia. I was then finishing my biography of the former secretary of state and chairman of the Joint Chiefs of Staff. At the conclusion of the interview, Powell asked playfully, "So Dr. Matthews, what's the subject of your next book?" I answered, "Well, sir, the working title is: *Bad Generals*!" He laughed and quipped, "I hope there will be some *bad admirals* in there too." I assured the general there would be.

Three months earlier, unbeknownst to me, Congresswoman Jackie Speier, the chair of the U.S. House Armed Services Subcommittee on Military Personnel, had written the following to Secretary of Defense James Mattis, a retired Marine Corps general:

> I am extremely concerned by the growing number of senior military leaders found to have committed misconduct, particularly as several of these cases are only coming to light years after the fact. The perception among the junior ranks of the military, the Congress, and the American public is that these senior general and flag officers more often than not avoid reprimand, and the rare instances of punishment amount to a slap on the wrist compared to what a private or a captain would receive for an identical offense. I urge you to do everything within your power to reinforce core

values amongst the senior ranks, and to ensure the fair application of military justice across the force.[1]

The phenomenon of dishonorable conduct by American generals and admirals became clear in October 2017 when the Department of Defense's Office of Inspector General reported on the misconduct of *hundreds* of senior officers and civilian executives over a four-year period. Beginning in 2019 and using court records, declassified government documents, inspector general reports, and journalistic and historical accounts, I set out to catalog and categorize the ongoing problem of criminal and unethical conduct by senior military leaders.

ACKNOWLEDGMENTS

One of the pleasures of book writing is the ability to publicly thank people who, directly or indirectly, helped to bring the project to fruition. No matter what you might hear, book work is teamwork. First and foremost, I must recognize my true love, Liz Collins. For years she endured grim stories about dishonorable generals and admirals, and most importantly, she also served as my earliest editor. Thank you, my darling Libby, for your infinite generosity. Other family members have also been tremendously supportive, including my inspiring daughters, Kate and Emily, my mother, Margareta "Nordgauer" Matthews, and my two brothers, Andy and Major General Earl Matthews, U.S. Air Force (Ret.). Moreover, the spirit of my late father, Lieutenant Colonel Cleve Matthews, U.S. Army, was always in the ether. Thanks also to my new extended family, including Keslie Watts, and all members of Clan Mettler, especially Henry, Izzie, and Samantha.

A cadre of historians were especially generous with their time and thoughts. Collectively, their sage and candid counsel improved this book immensely. I absolutely treasure their friendships. Professor Harry Laver (Command and General Staff College), Professor Emeritus Andy Fry (University of Nevada, Las Vegas), and Professor Emeritus Tom Appleton (Eastern Kentucky University), all read and commented on the entire manuscript. I am also appreciative of Professor Emeritus George Herring (University of Kentucky) for providing detailed feedback on the Johnny Johnson chapter. Professor Andrew Feight (Shawnee State University) read and commented on the Jacob Smith chapter.

Moreover, I have benefitted enormously from conversations with retired generals and admirals, most especially with Lieutenant General H. R. McMaster, Lieutenant General Steven Boutelle, Rear Admiral John Bitoff, and Brigadier General Mark Odom. I am also appreciative of the support that I have received from my students and colleagues at the University of Puget Sound, especially Rebecca Harrison (and Dean!), President Isiaah Crawford, and the faculty of the School of Business and Leadership. In addition, I must recognize the Jewett family, whose endowment continues to underwrite my research. I must also recognize George Matelich, a former university trustee, who continues to inspire and enrich the lives of so many of our students, the Matelich Scholars. Many friends have also been supportive, including the Arizona hunting boys, the racquetball gang, my Las Vegas banking comrades, and our Hawthorne Drive neighbors.

I also acknowledge a group of scholars, journalists, and retired military personnel whose research and writings were extraordinarily helpful in the construction of this book: Barbara Kellerman, Craig Whitlock, Tom Vanden Brook, Geoff Ziezulewicz, Karen DeYoung, Brian McAllister Linn, Arthur Herman, Lewis Sorley, Mark Perry, Tom Ricks, Francis Duncan, Malcolm Byrne, Robert Timberg, Gregory Vistica, William McMichael, Leonard Wong, and Paul Yingling.

Finally, I would like to recognize my dedicated teammates at the University of Notre Dame Press, especially Steve Wrinn, Eli Bortz, Rachel Kindler, Kathryn Pitts, who have supported this project from the onset, and my copyeditor Rachel Martens. Thank you.

INTRODUCTION

There are no bad soldiers, only bad generals.
— Napoleon

While the vast majority of generals and admirals serve honorably, there remains an ugly strain of criminal and unethical leadership in the upper ranks of the American military. It transcends time, race, gender, and branch of service. Since the formation of the Continental Army and Navy, the military has suffered countless bad generals and bad admirals. The earliest exemplars of malfeasance were Esek Hopkins, the first commander in chief of the Continental Navy, and Army Major General Benedict Arnold. Congress relieved Hopkins in 1777 for committing multiple transgressions, including his "most inhuman and barbarous" treatment of British prisoners.[1] Arnold, on the other hand, who had served bravely, even brilliantly, under George Washington, later betrayed the Revolution by spying for Great Britain and ultimately leading British combat troops against American forces. "Treason! Treason! Black as hell," exclaimed one Continental officer. "That a man so high on the list of fame should be as guilty as Arnold, must be attributed not only to original sin, but actual transgression. . . . We were all [in] astonishment."[2]

Two and a half centuries later, it remains bewildering that so many U.S. flag officers (term used here to describe Navy admirals and Army,

Air Force, and Marine generals), all reared on duty, honor, and country — and purportedly the best and brightest in uniform — continue to dishonor themselves and the American military profession. In a single four-year period, for example, the Defense Department documented the misconduct of "at least" five hundred senior leaders.[3] From 2013 through 2017, the unbecoming conduct of America's generals, admirals, and civilian executives varied from bribery and public drunkenness to sodomy and obstruction of justice. In its fiscal 2018 report, the Department of Defense's inspector general (DoDIG) declared that unethical conduct trends represented a top-ten "management and performance challenge" for the armed forces.[4] According to the DoDIG, there had been a 13 percent increase in complaints of "misconduct by senior officials" and the number of *substantiated* allegations jumped from 26 to 37 percent.[5] In short, the dishonorable behavior of so many flag officers contradicts the military's reputed high standards of integrity. Unfortunately, the ethics and crime problem has not abated.

Misconduct in 2017 alone resulted in the demotion of a retired four-star Air Force general, Arthur Lichte, who had coerced sex with a subordinate while still on active duty; the demotion and retirement of an Army lieutenant general, Ronald Lewis, who misused government credit cards at international strip clubs, abused alcohol, and lied about it; the relief, demotion, and retirement of two Army major generals, Wayne Grigsby and Joseph Harrington, both of whom had inappropriate relationships with women; and the arrest of a demoted rear admiral, Bruce Loveless, who was indicted for conspiring against the U.S. government and taking bribes in the form of sex workers and lavish gifts from a foreign defense contractor.[6]

In 2018, the Marine Corps reprimanded Brigadier General Rick Uribe for treating his aide-de-camp as his personal "servant" and for accepting gifts while acting as director of the Combined Joint Operations Center in Iraq. According to a DoDIG report, Uribe, a former inspector general himself, "showed a habitual pattern" of having his aide, a female officer, perform personal tasks and errands such as changing his soiled bedsheets, retrieving his laundry and meals, and drafting his unofficial correspondence. The inspector general also discovered that Uribe had violated ethics rules when he solicited and accepted gifts from subordinates and failed to reimburse them for miscellaneous expenses.[7] That same year, another inspector general investigation substantiated allegations that Robbie Asher, the recently fired adjutant general of the Oklahoma National Guard, had engaged in an inappropriate relationship with a subordinate officer and improperly accepted gifts from her. The army demoted Asher from major general to brigadier.[8] In August 2018, Major General Paul Hurley Jr. was relieved as the commanding general of Fort Lee, Virginia, and the Army's Combined Arms Support Center due to a loss in confidence in his leadership. He was reportedly under investigation for inappropriate sexual relationships. Hurley was subsequently demoted to brigadier general and forced to retire.[9] After multiple allegations of misconduct, the DoDIG also investigated Rear Admiral Ronny Jackson, the White House physician, who at the time was the Trump administration's nominee to lead the Department of Veterans Affairs. (Jackson's nomination was later withdrawn.) The inspector general's report concluded that the rear admiral had fostered a toxic command climate in which he "disparaged, belittled, bullied, and humiliated" his subordinates.[10] Jackson retired in 2019.

In April 2019, Rear Admiral John Ring was fired as commander of Joint Task Force Guantanamo because he "mishandled or directed the mishandling of classified information, made inaccurate reports, and created a poor command climate."[11] That same month, Major General Clay Garrison was relieved from his position as the assistant adjutant general of California's Air National Guard because of his inability to "maintain a positive command climate."[12] On May 1, 2019, the Army reprimanded Leon Salomon, a retired four-star general, who, while still on active duty, had committed an indecent assault against the wife of a subordinate general officer.[13] In June 2019, Rear Admiral Jeffrey Harley was removed as president of the Naval War College after numerous complaints of misconduct. He retired in December and a subsequent Naval inspector general investigation substantiated seven allegations of wrongdoing, including violations of travel, alcohol, personnel, and fundraising regulations.[14] In August 2019, the Navy fired Rear Admiral Stephen Williamson, director of industrial operations at Naval Sea Systems Command, for an inappropriate sexual relationship with a civilian subordinate.[15] In November 2019, Air Force Lieutenant General Lee Levy was stripped of his third star for creating a toxic work environment at the Air Force Sustainment Center at Tinker Airbase. One witness told investigators: "I think if he [Levy] was in the battlefield, he probably would've been shot in the back."[16] In December 2019, the commander of the Wisconsin National Guard, Air Force Major General Donald Dunbar, was forced to resign after a federal investigation concluded that his management of sexual assault and harassment investigations had violated state and federal laws over the course of ten years.[17]

In January 2020, Major General William Cooley was relieved of command at the Air Force Research Lab at Wright-Patterson Air Force Base because of suspected sexual misconduct. Ten months later, the two-star general was formally charged with the sexual assault of a civilian, his sister-in-law. Cooley's court-martial was the first ever military trial of an Air Force general. In April 2022, Cooley was convicted of abusive sexual conduct, sentenced to a reprimand, and docked five months' worth of salary.[18] In June 2020, Army Reserve Major General Miyako Schanely, commander of the 416th Theater Engineer Command in Illinois, was suspended after allegations arose that she had mishandled investigations of sexual harassment and assault. The Army substantiated the complaints and Schanely was relieved and reprimanded.[19] In the summer of 2020, Brigadier General David Hamilton, the former director of operations for NATO's Allied Rapid Reaction Corps, was demoted and retired after Army criminal investigators determined that he had groped a female soldier.[20] In October 2020, the Marine Corps relieved Major General Stephen Neary, commander of marine forces in Europe and Africa, for using a racial slur in the company of subordinates.[21]

In April 2021, the adjutant general of California's National Guard relieved Major General Gregory Jones, the commander of the state's

Air Guard, after losing "faith, trust and confidence in his ability to foster an inclusive and healthy command climate."[22] Five months later, the Army suspended Brigadier General Amy Johnston, the chief of public affairs, after a command climate survey uncovered an "overwhelmingly hostile" workplace, including sexually and racially harassing behaviors. According to her staff, Johnston created a "culture of fear" and was prone to "frequent outbursts" and to "belittling and demeaning subordinates." In February 2022, after an Army inspector general investigation, the Army reprimanded Johnston, who was immediately cleared for retirement.[23]

In May 2022, the DoDIG reported to Congress that investigators had substantiated complaints against two additional, unnamed generals. An Air National Guard brigadier general received a letter of admonishment for abusing subordinates and making them perform numerous nonofficial duties on his behalf. A Marine two-star general received a letter of counseling for failing to safeguard classified information. He had included secret government material in his autobiography, which was stored on an unclassified server.[24]

★ ★ ★ ★

Generals and Admirals, Criminals and Crooks is not an ad hominem attack on America's senior military leadership. It recognizes that a decisive majority of admirals and generals have served honorably and that all leaders, military and civilian, make mistakes — often the very same mistakes. Troublesome issues of extralegal violence, sexism, racism, toxicity, obstruction, and corruption are not unique to the armed forces. To solve such problems, all organizations (including public institutions) must dare to expose and confront their leadership failures, no matter how disconcerting or embarrassing. Candid self-examinations are crucial for the U.S. military given its vital role in our democratic society. Because of the disproportionate power and influence of generals and admirals, their misconduct can have utterly dangerous effects, eroding not only civilian faith and confidence in the military, but also trust and respect *within* the all-volunteer ranks. John Adams wrote, "Liberty cannot be preserved" unless the citizenry has "that most dreaded, and envied kind of knowledge," the truth about the character and conduct of its leaders.[25]

This book's primary objectives are to draw wider public attention to the nature of bad leadership and to illuminate specific types of unethical and criminal conduct committed by senior U.S. military leaders. Although we Americans are culturally inclined to study organizational success and good leadership, there are practical reasons to explore the failures and unseemly side as well. Most significant perhaps is that with an enhanced understanding of bad leaders (and bad colleagues and bad subordinates), we are better equipped to identify them, contest them, and hold them accountable. This is especially pertinent for leaders in government service. While the goal herein is to expose and catalog complex and pressing leadership problems, one hopes that a frank and historically grounded work such as this one will stimulate further debate and critical self-assessment within the U.S. military. Sober examinations of bad leadership can and should contribute to the positive development of good leaders. As Harvard's Barbara Kellerman writes in *Bad Leadership*, "To deny bad leadership equivalence in the conversation and curriculum is misguided, tantamount to a medical school that would claim to teach health while ignoring disease."[26] Moreover, Lord John Dalberg-Acton, the grandson of a Neapolitan admiral, was entirely correct when he argued that we historians have a professional obligation — "[a] historic responsibility" — to hold powerful leaders accountable as "power tends to corrupt and absolute power corrupts absolutely."[27]

Generals and Admirals, Criminals and Crooks employs operative definitions of good and bad leadership. Good leadership is ethical, lawful, and effective. Bad leadership is *either* unethical, criminal, or ineffective, or worse, *all three*. This book concentrates on unethical and criminal conduct by active-duty military leaders, thus setting aside the subjects of honorable but *ineffective* flag officers and the unchecked misbehavior of generals and admirals in the retired reserves. As for method, the text utilizes a case-study approach to scrutinize seven types of criminal or unethical leadership by American admirals and generals:

War Crimes
Insubordination
Moral Cowardice
Toxic Leadership
Obstruction of Justice
Sex Crimes
Public Corruption

While there are many forms of criminal and unethical behavior, the primary focus here is on serious misconduct having both historical *and* contemporary relevance. The heinous crime of treason so vividly represented by General Benedict Arnold during the American Revolution and by Generals Joseph E. Johnston and Albert Sidney Johnston during the Civil War, for example, has been excluded for insufficient modern application. Most of the book's chapters are biographical and devoted chiefly to the career of an individual flag officer, but the final two survey *groups* of wayward admirals. The chapters are organized chronologically, beginning with the Philippine-American War (1899–1902) and ending with the Navy's twenty-first-century Fat Leonard scandal.

WAR CRIMES

In late April 2004, *60 Minutes II* broadcast graphic evidence of American soldiers abusing and humiliating Iraqi prisoners of war. The captives, who were legally entitled to Geneva Convention protections, suffered systematic psychological and physical abuse while being detained at Abu Ghraib prison. After multiple investigations, only low-ranking enlisted personnel were convicted of crimes; not a single officer was *judicially* punished. The one flag officer held accountable was a reserve brigadier general, Janis Karpinski, who commanded the 800th

Military Police Brigade. She was relieved of command and ultimately demoted to colonel. While Karpinski has accepted responsibility for her failed leadership, other Army generals — equally or more complicit in the prisoner abuses — have not.[28]

> **WAR CRIME** — a willful act causing unnecessary injury or suffering during armed conflict in violation of humanitarian laws that give rise to individual criminal responsibility[29]

Chapter 1 covers the subject of war crimes by examining the long and checkered career of Army Brigadier General Jacob H. "Hell Roaring Jake" Smith. His service began heroically during the Civil War and ended disgracefully during the Philippine-American War. The latter war, though largely forgotten in the public mind, is well known to military historians for foreshadowing the counterinsurgency warfare and the race-based crimes committed against prisoners of war and civilians during the Vietnam War. General Smith personified the harshness of the U.S. campaign in the Philippines. He once ordered his subordinate commanders to "Kill and burn! The more you kill and burn the better you will please me."[30]

INSUBORDINATION

On May 22, 1977, President Jimmy Carter relieved Major General John K. Singlaub, the Army's chief of staff in South Korea. The Carter administration's new policy was to withdraw U.S. ground troops from Korea over a four- to five-year period. A few days before his relief, Singlaub, who vehemently opposed the withdrawal, unwisely granted an interview to the *Washington Post*. He told its Tokyo bureau chief, "If we withdraw our ground forces on the scheduled suggested, it will lead to war."[31] Carter viewed the statement as a "very serious breach" of military discipline.[32] The president swiftly relieved Singlaub, but did not force his retirement. That came a year later when the general again publicly criticized Carter, this time for the president's "ridiculous" policies on the B-1 bomber, the neutron bomb, and the Panama Canal.[33]

INSUBORDINATION — willfully disobeying a legitimate and lawful order, using threatening or insulting language, or behaving in a disrespectful manner toward a superior

Five-star Army General Douglas MacArthur, profiled in chapter 2, exemplifies the menace of unrestrained insubordination. From an early age, MacArthur sought to emulate his father, Arthur, an accomplished army lieutenant general who once commanded "Hell Roaring Jake" Smith and all U.S. forces in the Philippine-American War. From the beginning of his career, the younger MacArthur was bold, brilliant, and vain. His fifty-year military record is replete with extremes. In the First World War, he demonstrated daring heroics and extraordinary battlefield leadership. A quarter century later, during the Second World War, his command in the Pacific theater, including his retaking of the Philippines, captivated and inspired the American people. But throughout those many years, MacArthur also evidenced a pattern of unethical and unprofessional behavior. The general's persistent insolence and insubordinate machinations during the Korean War finally brought about his downfall. By April 1952, President Harry S. Truman had no choice but to fire that "son of a bitch."[34]

MORAL COWARDICE

During the ramp-up to the Iraq War, many American general officers had serious misgivings about the necessity of armed conflict and the adequacy of post-invasion planning. According to General Richard Myers, the chairman of the Joint Chiefs of Staff (2001–2005), "few military professionals were comfortable" with the George W. Bush administration's predictions of a peaceful stabilization after the ousting of Saddam Hussein.[35] Nevertheless, the generals — including Myers — did not muster the courage to challenge the administration's optimistic assumptions. Marine Corps commandant James Jones later admitted that the Joint Chiefs had been "emasculated" by the civilian leadership and resorted to conformity and sycophancy.[36] Candid and forthright dissent by the senior military leadership might have saved American and Iraqi lives. At an absolute minimum, by speaking up assertively, or by retiring or resigning in protest, these flag officers could have safeguarded their personal and professional honor.[37]

MORAL COWARDICE — a fear-based failure to act responsibly in defense of moral values and ethical principles

The problem of moral cowardice is examined in chapter 3 by chronicling the career of General Harold K. "Johnny" Johnson. A 1933 graduate of West Point, Johnson served under Douglas MacArthur in the Philippines during the Second World War and was taken prisoner by the Japanese in 1942. He remained in the army after his release in 1945 and served valiantly during the Korean War. Promoted to Army chief of staff in 1964, Johnson personally opposed President Lyndon Johnson's limited-war policy against communist forces in South and North Vietnam. From the onset in his role as Army chief, Johnson favored a more aggressive and comprehensive strategy.

Although legally obligated to proffer his best military advice to the Johnson administration, General Johnson and the other members of the Joint Chiefs of Staff failed to confront the president with their professional objections. Instead, they acquiesced to a warfighting strategy that they believed had little chance of success. Moreover, General Johnson remained silent when he observed the commander in chief and his defense secretary, Robert McNamara, lie to Congress and the America people about the costs of the war and the number of troops the administration would commit to it. General Johnson agonized over his complicity. In retirement, he expressed deep remorse: "My principal regret is that I was not much more forceful in attempting to deal with the Secretary of Defense and the President. . . . In retrospect, it is reasonably clear now that the Joint Chiefs of Staff did not have their wits about them when they failed to oppose the President. . . . I am now going to my grave with that lapse in moral judgment on my back."[38]

TOXIC LEADERSHIP

In October 2019, the Air Force inspector general (AFIG) concluded that Brigadier General Jennifer Grant habitually lectured, harangued, and humiliated her staff while commanding the Fiftieth Space Wing at Schriever Air Force Base. One witness compared Grant's leadership style with being in an abusive marriage or relationship: "You'll do whatever you can not to make her mad, not take another face shot. You're constantly walking on egg shells." According to the inspector general's report, Grant had fostered "an environment infused with fear and intimidation, which stilted communication and undermined the welfare and morale of her subordinates." The negative command climate that Grant cultivated was especially severe and described as "the worst the IG team had seen in 20 years."[39]

> **TOXIC LEADER** — a superior with dysfunctional personal characteristics who routinely engages in negative behaviors without regard for the well-being of subordinates and unit morale

Chapter 4 tells the story of Admiral Hyman Rickover, a prime example of toxic leadership. A 1922 graduate of the Naval Academy, he proved himself an excellent engineering officer *and* a caustic, unpopular commander.[40] One superior remarked that Rickover possessed "no outward signs of qualities of leadership."[41] Without hope of obtaining a major sea command, the antisocial, workaholic Rickover became a shore engineer. During World War II, he served effectively as the chief of the Electrical Section of the Navy's Bureau of Engineering, but his exacting standards and coercive and controlling leadership produced "whole shiploads of enemies."[42] After the war and despite his well-known "personality problems," Rickover was selected to lead the Navy's new Nuclear Power Branch and the civilian-led Atomic Energy Commission's Naval Reactors Branch.[43] Always leading with an acid tongue and iron fist — and having the support of powerful allies on Capitol Hill — Rickover oversaw the creation of the world's first nuclear fleet. His career demonstrates both the allure and the hazards of accomplished toxic leaders.

OBSTRUCTION OF JUSTICE

In 2018, the Air Force inspector general launched a multifaceted investigation into the behavior of Brigadier General Paul Tibbets IV, the grandson of Paul Tibbets Jr., who piloted the *Enola Gay* when it dropped a nuclear bomb on Hiroshima. Tibbets IV was accused of covering up the attempted suicides of four airmen, making inappropriate comments to and about women, misusing government vehicles, and improperly soliciting and accepting gifts. Despite his repeated denials of wrongdoing and conveniently poor memory when he faced questioning, investigators substantiated the charges. Tibbets had been slated for promotion to major general but was instead admonished and forced into retirement.[44]

> **OBSTRUCTION OF JUSTICE** — the commission of criminal acts, such as destroying evidence and making false statements, intended to undermine the due administration of law and justice

Chapter 5 explores crimes of obstruction committed by members of the Reagan administration during the Iran-Contra scandal, including two active-duty flag officers. Admiral John Poindexter served on the National Security Council staff for five years and became the president's fourth national security advisor. Army General Colin Powell served for three years as the senior military assistant to Defense Secretary Caspar Weinberger and later became Reagan's sixth and final national security advisor. Despite their dissimilar backgrounds, personalities, and competencies, both Poindexter and Powell were fast-rising flag officers before the Iran-Contra scandal broke in 1986. Their complicity in the illicit Iranian and Nicaraguan programs and their participation in the subsequent cover-up reveal the tragic consequences of excessive and misdirected loyalties.

SEX CRIMES

In April 2017, the Army charged retired Major General James Grazioplene (a 1971 graduate of West Point) with six counts of incest and rape while on active duty. A probable-cause hearing was held in August, but the case was dropped after a judge ruled that the military's statute of limitations had expired. Nevertheless in December 2017, Virginia prosecutors indicted Grazioplene on rape charges for crimes committed when he and his daughter lived in the state. Virginia has no statute of limitations on rape. The retired general was arrested and jailed without bond. Eighteen months later in July 2020, Grazioplene agreed to plead guilty to aggravated sexual battery. The judge gave him time served and a twenty-year suspended sentence. In June 2021 Defense Secretary Lloyd Austin demoted Grazioplene to the rank of second lieutenant, "the highest grade in which he served on active duty satisfactorily."[45]

> **SEX CRIME** — any unlawful sexual act, including indecent exposure, harassment, abusive contact, assault, and rape

Chapter 6 dissects the abhorrent sex-crimes scandal known as Tailhook '91. In early September 1991, as part of the Navy-sanctioned Thirty-Fifth Annual Tailhook Symposium, groups of drunken Navy and Marine Corps aviation officers assaulted at least eighty-three women and seven men at the Las Vegas Hilton. A majority of the assaults occurred in the hallway and hospitality suites on the third floor.

There were no immediate repercussions because Tailhook conventions were known to be seamy "annual bacchanalia."[46] When Navy helicopter pilot Lieutenant Paula Coughlin told her superior, a rear admiral, that she had been "practically gang-banged by a group of fucking F-18 pilots," his reaction was disturbingly dismissive: "That's what you've got to expect on the third deck with a bunch of drunk aviators."[47] After the sexual assaults were reported in the press, multiple investigations — and a massive cover-up — ensued. Five admirals ultimately retired early, another was demoted, and two more were relieved of command and reassigned.

PUBLIC CORRUPTION

In 2005 the Army National Guard faced a manpower shortage while supporting wars in Afghanistan and Iraq. To bolster recruitment efforts, Lieutenant General Clyde Vaughn initiated the $400 million Guard Recruiting Assistance Program (G-RAP). The program paid people, including active Guard members, for referring new recruits. These assistant recruiters were awarded $2,000 for each candidate that enlisted and even more if the recruit completed basic training. G-RAP solved the Guard's personnel problem, but poor oversight also led to a multimillion-dollar scandal with hundreds of people receiving illegal payments for soldiers they had not referred. In 2014, the Army inspector general substantiated wrongdoing by five senior leaders, including generals and civilian executives. Vaughn and Lieutenant General H. Steven Blum, the chief of the National Guard Bureau, received letters of reprimand for general mismanagement and negligent oversight. By 2016, the Army reported that more than four hundred soldiers, including many reserve officers, were convicted of crimes or suspected of defrauding the government out of an estimated $6 million.[48]

> **PUBLIC CORRUPTION** — the breach of public trust and abuse of position by self-serving government officials and their private-sector accomplices

Chapter 7 describes an epic public corruption scheme known as the Fat Leonard scandal. In September 2013, federal agents arrested Leonard Francis, a Singapore-based defense contractor, for defrauding the government out of more than $35 million. He had overcharged the Navy for husbanding services at ports throughout Asia. For two decades, Francis successfully bribed dozens of naval officers with cash, encounters with sex workers, lavish banquets, luxury goods, and free travel. In exchange, the naval officers provided Francis with classified materials, including government procurement bids and contracts, the movement schedules of Navy ships and submarines, and even law enforcement's investigations into Francis's company. "Everybody was in my pocket," Francis boasted in 2021. "I had them rolling around in my palm. I had the Navy by their balls!"[49]

As of late 2022, the Justice Department had charged thirty-four people with crimes related to the Fat Leonard corruption scandal. A large majority of those indicted elected to plead guilty, including one rear admiral who was sentenced to eighteen months in prison. The federal trial of another admiral ended with a deadlocked jury.[50] The Navy separately disciplined fifty other officers, including ten admirals. As one Pacific Command staff officer stated, "China could never have dreamt up a way to do this much damage to the U.S. Navy's Pacific leadership."[51]

★ ★ ★ ★

In trying to comprehend the persistence of bad leadership in the American military (and elsewhere in society), several overarching ideas emerge from the chapters that follow. First, as illustrated in the studies of Smith, MacArthur, and Rickover, some individuals have compromised ethical foundations and thus demonstrate undesirable behaviors — such as intemperance, insolence, dishonesty, and superciliousness — throughout their careers. Officers of this class possess "immutable fault lines" in their personal character.[52] Nevertheless, they are able to accumulate institutional power and attain high rank because of their proven ability to deliver results for their superiors and organizations. In other words, unethical, even criminal officers can succeed professionally when they are undeniably effective in their work. These officers are enabled and promoted within a culture that too often is devoted to utilitarian ethics, a philosophical canon that prioritizes ends over means — competence over character. A second type of officer, as personified by Johnson, Poindexter, and Powell, exhibits ethical virtues and competence during the course of their career, but over time or through circumstance he allows himself — consciously or unconsciously — to be corrupted. The book's final two chapters about the Tailhook admirals and the Fat Leonard scandal, respectively, further underscore how the accumulation of power and status combined with flawed institutional cultures and structures can debase ordinarily good people *and* amplify preexistent shortcomings in others.

The long, shameful, and often shocking saga of criminal and unethical leadership in the U.S. military must be recounted if we are ever to learn from it and minimize its frequency. Let us begin with Brigadier General Jacob Smith and America's war of choice in the Philippines.

CHAPTER ONE

WAR CRIMES

Jacob H. "Hell Roaring Jake" Smith

WAR CRIME—a willful act causing unnecessary
injury or suffering during armed conflict
in violation of humanitarian laws that give rise
to individual criminal responsibility

For centuries leaders have sought to protect prisoners of war and non-combatants during times of armed conflict. After thwarting an attack by a Syrian army, the prophet Elisha advised the King of Israel not to kill his Syrian prisoners, but rather to show mercy and provide for them. "You shall not slay them," he said. "Would you slay those whom you have taken captive with your sword and with your bow? Set bread and water before them that they may eat and drink and go to their master."[1] Similarly, Islamic law sought to prevent the suffering of captives and civilians. Abu Bakr, the benefactor and successor of Muhammad, commanded his soldiers: "Do not commit treachery or deviate from the right path. You must not mutilate dead bodies. Neither kill a child, nor a woman, nor an aged man. Bring no harm to the trees, nor burn them with fire, especially those which are fruitful. Slay not any of the enemy's flock, save for your food. You are likely to pass by people who have devoted their lives to monastic services; leave them alone."[2]

Two hundred and fifty years ago, the founders of the United States of America also championed basic human rights during times of war. Even before penning the Declaration of Independence, the Second Continental Congress established sixty-nine Articles of War to regulate the behavior of the Continental Army and to authorize military trials for adjudicating soldier misconduct.[3] General George Washington was especially concerned about the Revolutionary Army's treatment of civilians and prisoners of war.

★ ★ ★ ★

In September 1775, Washington ordered then-Colonel Benedict Arnold to monitor and control his soldiers after occupying Quebec, Canada. If they misbehaved, Arnold was to punish them severely. The general insisted that Arnold's officers "observe the strictest discipline and good order, by no means suffering any inhabitant to be abused, or in any manner injured, either in his person or property, punishing with exemplary severity every person who shall transgress, and making ample compensation to the party injured." As for prisoners, Washington instructed Arnold, "You will treat [them] with as much humanity and kindness, as may be consistent with your own safety and the public interest. Be very particular in restraining, not only your own troops, but the Indians, from all acts of cruelty and insult, which will disgrace the American arms and irritate our fellow subjects against us."[4]

A century later, the wartime conduct of U.S. soldiers, sailors, and marines was regulated by revised Articles of War and by General Order No. 100. The latter, so-called Lieber Code, named for its principal author Francis Lieber, was issued by President Abraham Lincoln during the Civil War. This code of military ethics consisted of ten sections and 157 articles and covered an array of subjects, including martial law, military jurisdiction, vengeful retaliation, public and private property rights, punishment for crimes against civilians, and the proper treatment of deserters, prisoners, partisans, spies, "War-rebels," and "Armed prowlers."[5]

Historians John Fabian Witt and T. Hunt Tooley have documented how the Lieber Code (also known as Lincoln's Code) could be used *against* enemy combatants and civilians as well as to *protect* them.[6] Designed to be consistent with Lincoln's emancipation of enslaved African Americans in Confederate states, the Lieber Code sanctioned the use of extreme measures against the enemy if deemed a "military necessity." In brief, General Order No. 100 codified Lincoln's utilitarian warfighting philosophy, which held that wars are waged for political objectives and "the more vigorously wars are pursued the better it is for humanity. Sharp wars are brief."[7]

Nevertheless, the Lieber Code clearly imposed restrictions on the U.S. military and provided protections for civilians and combatants. Article 60 stated, "It is against the usage of modern war to resolve, in hatred and revenge, to give no quarter." Article 68 asserted, "Unnecessary or revengeful destruction of life is not lawful." Article 71 prohibited soldiers from killing or inflicting "additional wounds on an enemy already wholly disabled" and stated further that any orders or encouragement to do so were illegal. So, while allowing for "sharp" and "vigorous" warfare, including the starvation of unarmed enemies, General Order No. 100 acknowledged that "military necessity does not admit of cruelty — that is, the inflicting of suffering for the sake of suffering or for revenge, nor the maiming or wounding except in fight nor the torture to extort confessions. It does not admit of the use of poison in any way, nor the wanton devastation of a district."[8]

The Lieber Code provided a foundation for future international agreements on the law of war, including the Hague Conventions of 1899 and 1907 and the Geneva Conventions of 1949. Among the dozens of war crimes detailed in the Geneva Conventions are murder, torture, rape, pillaging, wanton property destruction, denial of fair trials for prisoners, starvation of civilians, bombardment of undefended and strategically insignificant towns, killing or wounding a surrendered and unarmed combatant, attacks against civilians not engaged in hostilities, and declarations that no quarter will be given (no lives will be spared).[9]

★ ★ ★ ★

The bloody but often forgotten Philippine-American War was an unforeseen consequence of the Spanish-Cuban-American War of 1898. In the latter, the United States swiftly defeated Spanish land and naval forces stationed in Cuba and the Philippines. Both countries had been Spanish colonies for centuries. After the so-called splendid little war, the Spanish withdrew from Cuba and "sold" the Philippine Islands to the United States for $20 million. The William McKinley administration not only valued the archipelago's geostrategic importance, but also hoped to "educate the Filipinos and uplift them and Civilize and Christianize them."[10] Having essentially aligned themselves with the Americans against the Spanish, the Filipinos had expected political independence. After the U.S. Navy had demolished the Spanish fleet in Manila Bay, the Filipinos, under the leadership of Emilio Aguinaldo, declared their independence and formed a republican government. When President McKinley refused to recognize their sovereignty, the Filipinos rebelled against their new colonizers. As historian Paul Kramer has so convincingly argued, American imperialism in Asia — the geopolitical aims and the brutal means of conquest — was fueled in good measure by Anglo-Saxon racism.[11]

The Philippine-American War began in February 1899 with U.S. troops driving Filipino forces from the capital city during the Battle of Manila. By November and after suffering a series of battlefield defeats, Aguinaldo dispersed his army and adopted guerrilla tactics to take advantage of the home terrain, and this frustrated the American occupiers. In late spring 1900, Major General Arthur MacArthur, the U.S. military governor of the Philippines and father of future general Douglas MacArthur, offered the rebels amnesty, promising "complete immunity for the past and liberty for the future."[12] The three-month program failed to end the conflict and Filipino soldiers began to accelerate their attacks on American stations. In December 1900, MacArthur invoked the Lieber Code and launched "a new and more stringent" offensive.[13] This ruthless and effective campaign resulted in mass rebel surrenders and a general pacification by the end of spring 1901. In his final report to Washington on July 4, MacArthur declared that "the armed insurrection" in the Philippines "is almost entirely suppressed" thanks to the application of "very drastic" methods.[14]

But only two months after MacArthur's departure, Filipino insurgents sprang a surprise attack on an American outpost at Balangiga on the island of Samar. The successful ambush led to the death of forty-eight soldiers of the U.S. Ninth Infantry. The brazen rebel victory, which was widely covered in the American press, embarrassed and angered Major General Adna Chaffee, MacArthur's successor in Manila.

Prodded by President McKinley's successor, Theodore Roosevelt, Chaffee pledged to end "the soft mollycoddling of treacherous natives."[15] He deployed to Samar one of his most seasoned combat leaders, Brigadier General Jacob H. "Jake" Smith. A forty-year Army veteran, Smith appeared a sensible choice. He had fought with distinction as a battalion commander at the Battle of Santiago, Cuba, during the war of 1898 and had been fighting in the Philippines for more than two years. Smith's rapid rise in rank reflected his proficiency as a battlefield commander. He had arrived in Manila in April 1899 as a lieutenant colonel, and only thirteen months later he was promoted to brigadier general.

Smith, however, was known to be intemperate in personality and extreme in his treatment of both Filipino revolutionaries and suspect civilians. He had long before earned the sobriquet "Hell Roaring Jake," and even a cursory examination of his military record reveals an officer with notable ethical failings. For example, Smith had been convicted in 1886 of conduct unbecoming an officer and was dismissed from the army only to be reinstated because of influential political friends. General Chaffee, overtaken by a desire to exact vengeance for the "Balangiga Massacre" and pacify Samar, failed to restrain Smith, who created a command climate that encouraged brutality that exceeded the legal and moral limits of the Lieber Code. Brian McAllister Linn, a preeminent military historian of the Philippine-American War, concluded that Smith's selection to lead the Samar Campaign "must go down as one of the gravest blunders of the entire war."[16]

Six months after Smith assumed command on Samar, his favorite subordinate commander, Marine Major Littleton T. Waller, was arrested for murdering eleven Filipino prisoners. In the course of his trial, the major recounted Smith's staggering orders to take "no prisoners," to kill "all persons who were capable of bearing arms," and to "kill and burn. The more you kill and burn, the better you will please me."[17] Waller's shocking testimony led to Smith's detainment and court-martial. "Howling Wilderness Jake" (another moniker earned by Smith) was vilified in the American press by both imperialist and anti-imperialist political factions for his "disgraceful and wicked" orders. Ultimately, President Theodore Roosevelt intervened. The commander in chief punished Smith for his failed generalship, including his perverse influence on Waller, who had "sullied the American name."[18]

★ ★ ★ ★

Jacob Hurd Smith was born on January 29, 1840, in Scioto County, Ohio. He grew up along the Ohio River near Portsmouth, Ohio, and South Portsmouth, Kentucky. Smith attended public schools before entering the Collegiate and Commercial Institute, a college preparatory academy also known as the Russell Military Academy and located one mile from Yale University in Connecticut. The prep school offered classical and modern curricula along with vocational training. All students wore uniforms and the cadets participated in daily drills. Knowledge of Smith's experience at the academy is limited, though he developed notable skill at copperplate penmanship. After a year of study, he returned to his parents' home.[19]

A month before Smith's twenty-first birthday, South Carolina seceded from the Union. The Civil War broke out in April 1861. Patriotic and ambitious, Smith enlisted in the Second Kentucky Volunteer Infantry (Union) and received a commission as a second lieutenant. The Second Kentucky, attached to the Kanawha Brigade of the Department of the Ohio, first saw action on July 14 at the Battle of Barboursville in western Virginia (now West Virginia). Union forces prevailed and Smith, who suffered a slight head wound, comported himself well.[20] By early 1862, Smith earned promotion to captain after "having won his spurs by an arduous campaign."[21] His regiment was now attached to the Twenty-Second Brigade, Fourth Division of the Army of the Ohio, which was commanded by Major General Don Carlos Buell. The army was ordered to reinforce Ulysses S. Grant's forces near Shiloh, Tennessee.

As part of Major General William "Bull" Nelson's division and Colonel Sanders D. Bruce's brigade, Captain Smith and the Second Kentucky arrived at Pittsburg Landing on the evening of April 6. They had missed the first day of fighting. Smith's regiment, consisting of 799 soldiers, took a position on "the extreme left line" near the banks of the Tennessee River. On the morning of April 7, Union troops launched a major offensive. With fixed bayonets and operating under heavy fire, the Second Kentucky charged a Confederate artillery battery across the Peach Orchard. Smith recalled that "the losses were terrible and officers and men fell around and about me."[22] The rebel battery was overtaken, but only temporarily as the Louisiana Crescent Regiment counterattacked.

After pulling back to regroup, Smith and the Second Kentucky made a second assault and secured the enemy artillery. The costs were steep. Smith's lieutenant was killed, as was nearly a third of his company. Smith himself was badly wounded. A rifle bullet had ripped through the young captain's hip, causing him to fall "doubled like a closed jack-knife." Fearful of bleeding out, he pushed a silk handkerchief deep into the wound. "I stopped the outside flow of blood," he recalled, "by pushing the soft silk cloth into the entrance and exit of the bullet . . . the missile went through me."[23] Smith was then transported by boat to Evansville, Indiana. From there, a childhood friend arranged his passage to South Portsmouth, where he convalesced at his parents' home.

Unable to rejoin combat with the Second Kentucky, Smith accepted an appointment to the recently created Invalid Corps in June 1863.

The new unit employed disabled soldiers in a variety of light-duty occupations such as orderlies, nurses, cooks, and guards. Smith was posted to Louisville, Kentucky, as a recruiter and inspection officer.

During his two years in Louisville, the war hero Smith earned a reputation as an effective recruiter of freed Black men; he also earned a small fortune through illegal skullduggery. The captain came into contact with questionable East Coast agents trying to fill draft quotas for eastern municipalities. The agents told Smith that they could bolster his recruiting efforts by offering to pay each new recruit a $300 signing bonus. Unbeknownst to Smith, the agents planned to pocket for themselves an additional $400 per recruit. Smith accepted the offer and "scoured Kentucky's jails, prison pens, and workhouses" for men.[24] After finding the first ten recruits, he asked the Army Provost Marshal General to determine whether the bonus system was permissible.

Meanwhile, the East Coast agents sent Smith $92,000 in advance funds. Rather than deposit the money in a bank, Smith used the cash to start a sutler business selling wares to the Army. He also made speculative investments in whiskey, gold, and diamonds.

Ultimately, the Provost Marshal accepted Smith's ten new recruits but forbade any further bonus payments. Naturally, the agents demanded the balance of their money back. Short of cash, Smith stalled them until his investments paid off (and handsomely). The value of the captain's assets increased from approximately $4,000 in 1862 to $40,000 by the end of 1865. According to Smith, he repaid the majority of his creditors, including the agents, by the close of the war. In October 1865, at twenty-five years old, Smith was honorably discharged from the army. He and his new wife bought a farm in rural Illinois and a house in Chicago.[25]

For reasons still unknown, Smith joined the Regular Army in March 1867. Because of his "gallantry at Shiloh" he was appointed as a brevet major. Smith was assigned to the Thirteenth Infantry, which conducted operations throughout Montana. Despite or because of his short stature and small frame, the verbose and "garrulous" Smith had the habit of shouting orders and heaping "invective on his subordi-nates." For this, he acquired the nickname "Hell Roaring Jake."[26]

In 1869, Smith received a temporary appointment to the Judge Advocate Corps, the legal branch of the Army. He hoped to make the assignment permanent, but the brevet major's sordid business deal-ings in Louisville came back to haunt him. That same year, a fraud law-suit was filed against Smith and his father-in-law, and the case revealed the dramatic rise in Smith's net worth. Although he denied any malfea-sance Smith was forced to explain the entire bonus scheme saga and his related speculative investments. The damning information reached the Army. General Joseph Holt determined that Smith was "in a di-lemma full of embarrassment" and not worthy of the Judge Advocate Corps or his rank as brevet major.[27] During the next decade, the de-moted Captain Smith served with the Nineteenth Infantry at various posts in Louisiana, Colorado, and Kansas.

In the autumn of 1881, the Nineteenth was attached to the Army's Department of Texas. Smith then spent a decade on the Texas frontier, an unpleasant experience. His health deteriorated, he suffered from "ear troubles, neurological problems, and nervous prostration," and his legal and financial woes continued. In 1884, a Chicago law firm filed a lawsuit against him.[28] Even more troubling, Smith's misconduct led to two courts-martial. In 1885, he was charged with conduct unbecoming an officer and gentleman. He was accused of not paying $135 lost in a poker game at the Mint Saloon in Brackett, Texas, near Fort Clark. Smith was found guilty and sentenced to half-pay for a year during which he was not allowed to leave the fort.

Smith's misbehavior during and after his courts-martial, which in-cluded lying in his appeal to the Adjutant General, led to a second trial. In 1886, he was again convicted of conduct unbecoming an officer and was dismissed from the Army. Influential friends, however, intervened on his behalf. A collection of "Civil War comrades and political patrons" from Ohio persuaded President Grover Cleveland to reinstate Smith and reduce his penalty to a mere letter of reprimand.[29] By spring 1890, he was serving in the Army's Department of the Lakes, which encompassed a huge swath of the Midwest from Kansas and the Dakotas to Ohio and the Great Lakes. Smith was promoted to major in 1894 and served in the West until the outbreak of the Spanish-Cuban-American War.

On June 24, 1898, Smith landed on the shores of Cuba as an acting lieutenant colonel and the commander of the First Battalion, Second Infantry Regiment. As in the Civil War a quarter century earlier, he displayed courageous and resolute leadership on the battlefield. On July 1, the entire Second Regiment, consisting of eighteen officers and 601 enlisted men, were directed to the front lines. They encountered a retreating stream of wounded Americans. Smith's battalion witnessed panic among the Seventy-First New York Infantry, and to "steady" his own men and "set an example," he took the extraordinary step of drilling the battalion in manual of arms.[30] Major Smith and his First Battalion eventually secured a "prominent and wooded hill" south of a blockhouse overlooking Santiago. This position was nine hundred yards from Spanish entrenchments. During the ensuing firefight, Smith ordered his men to "hold the position at all hazards." The fighting was fierce. Around 4 p.m., while inspecting his line, Smith was shot in the chest. He remained with his troops for two hours before taking leave to see the regimental surgeon.[31]

Early in the morning on July 2, the Spanish opened fire. Smith's troops worked desperately to fortify their entrenchment. Casualties mounted and the battalion began to exhaust its ammunition. They were relieved by the Third Infantry, but returned to the front line at 7 p.m. Two hours later, the Spanish launched an offensive. Smith's commander later reported that "the firing was terrific and accompanied by artillery." Smith himself wrote that the "whole front of the line became engaged" and his position was "severely bombarded by artillery fire and well-directed volleys of infantry." After forty minutes of intense combat, the Second Infantry successfully repelled the Spanish attack.[32]

A temporary truce was called on July 3. By then the Second Infantry had suffered six deaths and fifty-two were wounded, including four officers. In a report to his superiors, Smith lauded the performance of his men who were "deserving of great praise for their conduct and soldierly bearing: standing all the hardships of heat, lack of food, etc., with fortitude, and uncomplaining to a wonderful degree." Smith's leadership earned equal praise from Brigadier General J. Ford Kent, the First Division commander. He wrote, "I can not too earnestly commend Colonel Smith for his conduct during the battles before Santiago, Cuba. Though severely wounded Colonel Smith remained with his regiment, on duty, for several days, and even executed a tour as field officer of the day. Subsequent to this I urged him to go to the hospital."[33]

Hostilities resumed in the late afternoon of July 10 with U.S. forces firing "all along the line." One of the captains in the Second Regiment was killed by Spanish cannon fire that "literally cut him in twain." The American attack, according to Smith's commander, was waged with "enormous vigor, completely overwhelming the Spaniards in their trenches."[34] The Spanish sued for peace the next day. For his valorous leadership, Smith earned promotion from "acting" to brevet lieutenant colonel and took command of the Twelfth Infantry Regiment, Third Brigade, Second Division. By the end of August most U.S. forces had returned to the United States. The war with Spain concluded officially on December 10, 1899, with the Treaty of Paris.

The end of the short Spanish-Cuban-American War begot a new, longer war in the Philippines. The Filipinos, like the Cubans, had aligned themselves with American forces against the Spanish and expected independence from colonial rule. The United States, however, purchased the Philippines from Spain and declared sovereignty over the strategically located archipelago. The Filipinos rebelled, launching a patriotic war for independence.

On February 19, 1899, two weeks after the first battle of the Philippines War, brevet Lieutenant Colonel Smith and more than a thousand soldiers of the Twelfth Infantry Regiment and elements of the Seventeenth Infantry boarded the U.S. Army transport *Sheridan* to join the fight. After sixty-four days at sea, the *Sheridan* arrived in Manila. By then, the anti-American insurrection had been raging for more than two months. The U.S. commanding general and military governor, Major

General Elwell S. Otis, controlled two Army divisions from his Manila headquarters. At this time, the First and Second Divisions, commanded by Major Generals Arthur MacArthur and Henry W. Lawton, respectively, were fighting a successful campaign forty miles north of the capital in central Luzon along the Manila-Dagupan railroad.

On June 30, the Twelfth Infantry was attached to Brigadier General Frederick Funston's First Brigade of MacArthur's Second Division, which was conducting the Malolos Campaign in the north. Smith and his men joined the First at its field headquarters in San Fernando. In July, the regiment underwent a thorough inspection. The inspector general praised Smith for delivering positive results and his exacting leadership: "The regimental commander, Lieut. Col. Jacob H. Smith, appeared to be a rigid disciplinarian and determined to hold officers and men to a strict accountability for the proper performance of duty."[35]

In early August, MacArthur organized an operation to secure his western and northern flanks. The Twelfth regiment helped take Calulut and Bacolor on August 9.[36] Several days later, Brigadier General Loyd Wheaton ordered Smith to attack enemy forces who were defending the strategic intersection and railroad terminal at Angeles City. At this time, Smith's command included 27 officers, 884 enlisted soldiers, and a small detachment of light artillery. The Filipino force he faced numbered between 1,500 and 2,500 men.

Smith's offensive began in the morning on August 16. He later described the rebel trenches outside of the city as "well located and concealed in the bamboo thickets." He noted, "The insurgent fire was very general and very heavy." Before making his assault across open rice fields, Smith bombarded the trenches and city barricades. "The insurgents were stubborn in their resistance," Smith reported, "but could not withstand the steady style of the Twelfth Infantry advance."[37] After an hour of combat, the enemy retreated to the north. The Americans occupied Angeles and took possession of three locomotives, twenty-five train cars, and a large store of unhulled rice. Smith's superiors considered the battle a "brilliant action and splendid success," but it had come with a price: four men were killed and fourteen more wounded.[38]

MacArthur ordered Smith to fortify Angeles, as it would soon become his new field headquarters. At 5 a.m. on the morning following the battle, the Filipinos attempted to retake the city. With a force of eight hundred they attacked from two directions. Smith's men were well prepared and repelled the onslaught. MacArthur reported to Otis that his capable regimental commander "resisted the attack successfully and drove the insurgents back into the mountain with no casualties on his side." He added, "Smith is safe and able to take care of himself for a few days."[39]

One of Smith's challenges was determining which civilians in Angeles were loyal to him. After learning that a prominent and seemingly respectable lawyer was in communication with the insurgents, the lieutenant colonel had him arrested and sent to San Fernando to stand trial. On August 19, one of Smith's reconnoitering patrols was ambushed. Two regimental first lieutenants were shot; one died instantly, the other survived despite a bullet ripping "through right upper jaw to middle neck."[40] The ambush enraged Smith, causing him to abandon any policy of leniency. He directed all male civilians to "prove their professed friendship" by digging trenches and cleaning streets. He ordered his soldiers "to shoot all men" who tried to pass their exterior lines and enter the town.[41]

On August 31, MacArthur appointed Joseph "Fighting Joe" Wheeler as the new commander of the First Brigade, which included the Twelfth Infantry. Like Smith, Wheeler had fought at Shiloh in 1862, but on the opposite side. Two decades after the Civil War, Wheeler had won election to Congress representing an Alabama district. His appointment as brigadier general in the Philippines, as in Cuba the year before, was politically motivated. President McKinley wanted to demonstrate the reunification of the Blue and Gray.

Always impetuous, the sixty-two-year-old Wheeler wanted to fight and to "be with the troops of the brigade which are nearest to the enemy."[42] He pleaded with MacArthur to move his First Brigade, Second Division headquarters to Angeles, where Smith and the fighting Twelfth were stationed. MacArthur balked and posted the ex-Confederate to

Santa Rita to conduct inspection duties. Throughout September, Smith engaged in skirmishes with intrepid guerrilla forces. Although technically under Wheeler's command, his combat missions were most often directed by the Second Brigade commander, Brigadier General Loyd Wheaton. Wheeler was finally allowed to join Smith and the Twelfth at the end of September, but MacArthur kept the aging southern general out of combat for another month.

In this environment, Commanding General Otis plotted a major offensive to capture or kill President Aguinaldo and destroy the insurrection. The planning led to Army leadership changes. Brigadier General Frederick Grant, son of the Union hero and former president, replaced Wheaton as commander of the Second Brigade, Second Division. Smith was promoted to colonel and given command of a dozen companies in the Seventeenth Infantry, which operated under Grant. Otis's masterplan called for "triple pincer movement" with MacArthur pushing eighty miles north along the railroad from Angeles to Dagupan, Lawton advancing northeast up the Rio Grande, and Wheaton linking up with MacArthur's Second Division at Dagupan via the Lingayen Gulf.[43]

Lawton's lead force, commanded by Samuel B. Young, began the autumn campaign on October 9. MacArthur's own advance was delayed because of sabotaged railroad lines. Young's progress had the effect of stimulating rebel attacks on the Angeles encampment. In mid-October, for eleven straight days, the rebels besieged the city late at night. Again and again, the Filipinos suffered horrific losses. The well-entrenched Second Division consisted of 300 officers and 11,000 soldiers.

MacArthur's northerly advance began on November 5. Smith's regiment, consisting of more than nine hundred soldiers, operated on the west flank. His Seventeenth Infantry engaged in "brisk action" against the enemy at Magalang.[44] Commanding superior firepower, Smith's troops routed the insurgents, who suffered nearly two hundred casualties. Smith reported eight wounded among his troops and the capture of fifty rebels and fifty water buffalo. In his account of the battle, MacArthur lauded Smith's "remarkably small loss considering the duration of the fighting and the punishment inflicted on the enemy." He praised the colonel for executing the attack "in a superior manner" and conveyed his "highest professional appreciation."[45] By the time the Second Division had taken Mabalacat three days later, Smith reported killing another sixty-five rebels, wounding more than a hundred, and capturing twenty-eight.[46]

The combat continued. On November 9 Smith overtook an enemy outpost, killing twenty-nine insurgents and taking four prisoners. The Seventeenth suffered three casualties. In the early morning of November 11, the insurgents attacked Smith's regiment near Santa Rita. While U.S. forces repelled the attack with field artillery, Smith lost two men. That same day the Seventeenth charged and then captured the insurgent stronghold at Capas without the benefit of artillery.[47] "I have made many marches in my life," Smith reported to headquarters, "and I think this is one of the most difficult I ever encountered."[48] MacArthur continued to be impressed by Smith's "great execution" even when facing most "unfavorable" circumstances.[49]

Despite dogged rebel resistance, the Second Division advanced steadily. Smith's Seventeenth and the Thirty-Sixth Regiments were engaged in heavy combat and hard marching.[50] On November 12, MacArthur's forces occupied Tarlac, which until then had served as Aguinaldo's temporary headquarters. Eight days later, MacArthur reached his destination, Dagupan, where his army joined with Wheaton's forces. Aguinaldo dispersed his army and retreated north into the mountains. On November 23, MacArthur sent a wire to Otis in Manila: "The so-called Filipino Republic is destroyed."[51]

Otis was overjoyed by the news. Thinking that the war in the north had been won, he directed the Second Division to spread out from the railroad line and occupy all towns and villages to protect the civilian population from bandits and rebel raiders. As the governor of the Philippines, Otis shifted American rule from a war footing to a more benevolent policy that promoted civilian governance, developed infrastructure, and provided healthcare and education. As part of his "pacification" instructions, Brigadier General Grant issued to Smith and other subordinate commanders strict orders "against looting, and against offending or intimidating the natives, and especially against interfering with women."[52]

Grant's brigade conducted regular police patrols scouring the countryside for insurgents who, after adopting guerrilla military tactics, were looting villages for supplies and executing civilians suspected of aiding U.S. forces. Finding the raiders was a frustrating ordeal. The terrain was inhospitable and the rebels often melded into the general population. The latter tactic was described by Americans as the "amigo dodge."[53]

In December, the *New York Times* published a front-page story featuring Smith's battlefield exploits — "DEATH FOR LUZON BANDITS: Guerrillas Caught by Col. Smith Will Be Shot or Hanged." The paper reported that American officers believed that the war in the Philippines was "worse than fighting Indians, owing to the difficulties of the country and the trouble of locating the enemy, who resort, when hard pressed, to amigo dodge and hide their guns." As a result, some soldiers wished that the army would issue a proclamation denying prisoner of war status to captured insurgents. The story detailed how Smith had tracked a band of guerrillas to a village near Malasqui, which had been "in a state of terror" for weeks. The rebels had executed twenty-five Filipino civilians for showing "friendliness to the Americans." Smith's men apprehended the "ruffians" and sent them by train to MacArthur's Bayambang headquarters for trial.[54]

Many white soldiers, Smith included, viewed the Filipinos' adoption of guerrilla warfare as unmanly and uncivilized. This perspective elevated their sense of racial superiority over their dark-skinned enemy and also provided further justification for extralegal violence. In their diaries and letters home, soldiers regularly denigrated Filipinos as "savages" and "n*****s."[55] A private in the Sixth Infantry, for example, wrote, "Just back from the fight. Killed 22 n*****s captured 29 rifels [*sic*] and 1 shotgun and I tell you it was a fight. . . . [W]e just shot the n*****s like a hunter would rabbits."[56] Soldiers wrote freely about the widespread killings of civilians. "We bombarded a place called Malabon," wrote a soldier in the Third Artillery, "and then we went in and killed every native we met, men, women, and children. It was a dreadful sight, the killing of the poor creatures. . . . we [had] orders to spare no one."[57] One army officer, who had returned stateside, recalled the frequent dehumanization of the Filipino enemy: "Our men have been relentless, have killed to exterminate men, women, and children, prisoners and captives, active insurgents and suspected people, from lads of ten up, an idea prevailing that the Filipino was little better than a dog, a noisome reptile in some instances, whose best disposition was the rubbish heap."[58]

The battlefield progress achieved by U.S. forces during November and December 1899 had resulted from some two hundred intense engagements with Filipino insurgents. Sixty-nine Americans were killed and approximately three hundred wounded. The bloody year came to a dramatic close when the rebels killed Major General Lawton, the Army's First Division commander.

Lawton's death contributed to another reorganization of U.S. forces. Smith and his Seventeenth Infantry were assigned to Brigadier General J. Franklin Bell's Fourth Brigade, Second Division. Despite the organizational shifts, Smith's command continued to police the countryside near the midsection of the Manila-Dagupan railroad. Bell described the region as being "infested" with criminal gangs and the "flotsam and jetsam from the wreck of the insurrection."[59]

On February 15, 1900, Smith and fifty soldiers "surprised a band of 30 ladrones." They killed twelve, wounded two, and captured two more.[60] On a subsequent patrol, Smith was ambushed but his troops overcame the insurgents, even capturing a number of them. Not having an adequate jail facility, Smith ordered his men to construct one from unused train rails. Frank G. Carpenter, a freelance journalist, reported on "Col. Jake Smith's Jail" for the weekly magazine *Timely Topics*. Carpenter wrote that "our soldiers have had trouble in finding quarters to incarcerate criminals," but in Bautlata he had found "one of the queerest jails of Luzon." He detailed the dimensions of the "cattle pen" — fifteen feet by thirty feet — and how "into this iron cage the insurrectos were brought. There were fifty of them in the cage when I photographed them, and a harder-looking set of Filipino brigands I have not seen."[61]

On April 7, MacArthur assumed command of the newly created Department of Northern Luzon. The department covered 30,000 square miles and contained two million Filipinos. A few weeks later when MacArthur replaced Otis as the Military Governor and Commander of the Philippines, he gave command of the Northern Luzon to Major General Loyd Wheaton. The department contained six military districts. General Bell's brigade, including Smith's regiment, was given responsibility for District Three, with headquarters in Dagupan (Pangasinan Province).

During the spring of 1900, U.S. forces achieved a series of notable victories in Northern Luzon. On April 7, in the mountains northwest of Tarlac, Colonel Smith led infantry and cavalry in a direct attack against a senior rebel general, Francisco Macabulos. Five rebels were killed and fifteen thousand rounds of ammunition were seized. The insurgents' fortified encampment included barracks for two hundred men and stored twenty tons of rice. The garrison was destroyed.[62] Macabulos escaped but his wife and several officers were taken prisoner. Later that month, Smith achieved a major coup when he captured General Antonio Montenegro and hundreds of rebels.[63] Such successes continued in May when more than two hundred insurgents surrendered to U.S. troops. General Macabulos capitulated in June, surrendering 174 men and 200 rifles.[64]

Smith's achievements led to a pivotal promotion and a substantial increase in responsibility. MacArthur had been impressed by Smith's capturing of three towns (Angeles, Magalang, and Capas) and complimented the colonel's "exacting" leadership.[65] Smith was made a brigadier general in the U.S. Volunteers on June 1, 1900, and on July 30 he replaced Bell as the military governor of the Third District, comprised of the provinces of Zambales, Pangasinan, and Tarlac in the Department of Northern Luzon. Smith's expanded command, headquartered in Dagupan, included five Regular Army regiments, two Volunteer regiments, and three cavalry troops spread out over sixty-five separate posts. In just two years, Smith had risen from the rank of brevet major to brigadier general.

During his first month of command, General Smith's soldiers engaged the enemy on seven occasions. This resulted in the confirmed killing of five insurgents, the capture of thirteen more, and the destruction of a large barracks. The Americans did not suffer any casualties.[66]

As a military district governor, Smith stirred controversy when he intervened in a religious dispute in Dagupan.[67] In September, he gave a warm reception to Placide Chapelle, the Catholic Archbishop of the New Orleans, Louisiana, Diocese. Chapelle was in the Philippines as a papal delegate seeking to protect the church's extensive property interests. American policy was to be neutral in Filipino religious matters, but U.S. military authorities found common cause in the Church's opposition to native priests who were sympathetic to the insurgents. In Dagupan, Chapelle deposed Father Adriano Garces and ordered him to leave the parish. But the popular priest resisted, supported by thousands in the congregation. The archbishop asked Smith to intervene but, with the city in "religious anarchy," the brigadier general hesitated. Chapelle returned to Manila "defeated" by the "unruly priest."[68] Later, however, when tensions lessened, Smith arrested Garces from the parish on the grounds that he was "not loyal" to the American administration. In November, Washington inquired about the controversy. MacArthur reported that the priest's removal had been "necessary [to] preserve [the] peace" but that he was no longer confined.[69]

In the autumn of 1900, the insurgents seized the initiative against U.S. forces in the Philippines. They hoped to influence the upcoming American presidential election that once again pitted McKinley and his "Imperialist" Republican Party against the anti-imperialist Democrat William Jennings Bryan.[70] On September 13 Filipino rebels captured fifty Americans of the Twenty-Ninth Infantry on the island of Marinduque. Four days later at Mavitac, they killed twenty-four troopers and wounded another nineteen. MacArthur reported to Washington that the rebels had adopted a frustratingly effective strategy of launching quick attacks "as soldiers, and immediately afterwards are within the American lines in the attitude of peaceful natives, absorbed in a dense mass of sympathetic people, speaking a dialect of which few white men and no American, have any knowledge."[71]

Contact with the enemy also intensified in Smith's Third District. During September, October, and November, four of his troopers were killed and six wounded. The rebels suffered much worse. Smith reported killing thirty-four, wounding thirty-three, and taking seven prisoners.[72] The general prodded his officers to be much more aggressive against civilians suspected of collaborating with the enemy. In early October, he instructed his commanders "not to allow their suspicions [of civilians] to be lulled to sleep by friendly association and social intercourse with the native inhabitants." Many "apparently . . . friendly" Filipinos, he declared, "are guilty of the blackest treachery."[73] On October 30, an outraged Smith reported the arrest of civilians suspected of a brutal attack on five American soldiers. "I only wish that I could have been there to have summarily dealt with them," he wrote, "but it is difficult to get Officers to take prompt measures under G.O. [General Order] 100" (the Lieber Code). He bluntly asserted, "A few killings under G.O. 100 will aid very much in making the enemy stop these assassinations."[74]

To the dismay of the Filipinos, McKinley won reelection on November 2, 1900. Earlier in the summer, MacArthur had announced an amnesty program in the Philippines, but it had failed. Now, free of American political constraints, the general decided that harsh measures were needed to fully subdue Aguinaldo and the rebels of Luzon. The War Department encouraged MacArthur and desired his plan to be "prosecuted with vigor."[75] Brigadier General Smith was eager to play his role. On November 14, he wrote to the adjutant general in Manila that "the time has arrived when punishment must be meted out to the hostiles in order that decisive actions may shorten our work in the field."[76] In December, at the cost of one American life, his soldiers killed twenty-two rebels and wounded nineteen. They also captured seven men and nearly one hundred rifles.[77]

Just days before Christmas, MacArthur alerted his departmental commanders of a "new and more stringent policy." While he cautioned against the application of "unnecessary hardships" and forbade violations of the laws of war, he emphasized that "whenever action is necessary the more drastic the application the better."[78] In Smith's District Three and throughout the Department of Northern Luzon, U.S. forces ramped up arrests, trials, and executions of civilian suspects. To further inhibit the rebels, American soldiers systematically destroyed towns, villages, food stores, livestock, and crops.[79]

Some company commanders thought MacArthur's new policy too extreme — even immoral, illegal, and counterproductive — but they found little sympathy among senior commanders. At one point, Captain William M. Swaine of the First Infantry cautioned General Smith that "there are about 3,500 people in my district who had always shown their friendship for the Americans and their hatred for the insurrectos in every possible way." "The people went to the mountains . . . ," he wrote, and they "will die there, they have nothing to eat." Although a crime in direct violation of General Order No. 100, Smith responded, "Let them die, the sooner they are all dead the sooner we will have peace."[80]

MacArthur's post-election campaign was equally brutal and effective. An Army major commanding operations in Abra reported that "the province suffered severely; every man was [labeled] an active insurrector or sympathizer. . . . whole villages had been burned, storehouses and crops had been destroyed, and the entire province was devoid of food products as was the Shenandoah after Sheridan's raid during the [C]ivil [W]ar."[81] A Republican congressman who toured the Philippines was shocked by the extralegal violence he observed: "The good Lord in Heaven only knows the number of Filipinos that were put under the ground. Our soldiers took no prisoners, they kept no records, they simply swept the country, and wherever and whenever they could get hold of a Filipino they killed him."[82]

Smith's effectiveness in subduing the insurgency was demonstrated by his willingness to establish civil governments throughout much of his district. In a report to Manila, the general said that this transition was possible in part because of three dozen captured "criminals" and "notorious insurgents" who were given "the death penalty for their barbarous crimes." On February 14, 1901, a new government was established in the Pangasinan Province where, according to Smith, "the inhabitants . . . had shown a commendable spirit in adapting themselves to American rule" and had provided "many and unquestioned evidences of their loyalty." Four days later, governance was established in the Tarlac Province. Smith was especially happy to report: "The towns are now rapidly being reorganized in accordance with the Municipal Code, and the erstwhile capital and stronghold of Aguinaldo seems to be entirely pacified."[83]

MacArthur's "more stringent" offensive in North Luzon concluded at the end of spring 1901. Aguinaldo and other influential Filipino leaders had capitulated. MacArthur believed that "the insurrection was rapidly approaching complete collapse."[84] Major combat had ceased in Smith's Third District, and in his comprehensive report of April 30, he lavished praised upon his troops, especially the officers. "The command officers of the regiments," he wrote, "have been all that the district commander could wish in their devotion to duty, energy and success in accomplishing the important and multifarious duties devolving on them. They deserve any material recognition it may be practicable for the government to bestow."[85]

By the end of May, some twenty thousand insurgents surrendered and all meaningful resistance in North Luzon had collapsed. On July 4, MacArthur reported to Washington that "the armed insurrection" in the Philippines "is almost entirely suppressed" thanks to "very drastic" military methods. He added, that in time "the Filipino people will become warmly attached to the United States by a sense of self-interest and gratitude."[86] MacArthur also boasted that during his fourteen-month term as senior commander, U.S. forces had inflicted five thousand casualties on the enemy while suffering only seven hundred. For his contributions to the victorious campaign, the brutally effective Brigadier General Smith was elevated from the Volunteers to the Regular Army. His long career had reached impressive if improbable heights.

In July 1901 Major General Adna Chaffee replaced MacArthur as the commanding general of U.S. forces in the Philippines. He inherited several hot spots of insurrection in South Luzon and on the island of Samar. In May, MacArthur had placed Samar within Brigadier General Robert P. Hughes's Department of the Visayas, instructing him to take "emergency" and "drastic measures" to quash the rebels led by General Vincente Lukban.[87] As ordered, Hughes waged a harsh campaign. He implemented a naval blockade, destroyed civilian crops, and engaged in sporadic combat against the insurgents. In August, to give Hughes more support, Chaffee sent seven companies of the Ninth Infantry for garrison duty in Samar. The next month, Hughes reported that he had pacified the island and moved his headquarters to the island of Cebu.[88] He had made a grievous error in judgment.

On September 28, a coastal garrison manned by the Ninth Infantry at Balangiga came under a coordinated surprise attack by Filipino guerrillas and local townspeople. Of the eighty-eight men of Company C, fifty-nine were killed and twenty-three wounded. Many of the bodies were mutilated. The survivors managed to escape by canoe to Basey, the nearest post, where some died of their wounds. The "massacre" at Balangiga was the most significant U.S. Army loss of the Philippine-American War. Believing that the war was essentially over, Americans at home were shocked by the defeat. A frenzied U.S. press corps compared the disaster to George Custer's slaughter at the Battle of Little Big Horn.

The American people were already in mourning. Two weeks earlier President McKinley had been assassinated. Elevated from the vice presidency, Theodore Roosevelt ordered Chaffee "in no unmistakable terms" to apply "the most stern measures to pacify Samar."[89] Angered and embarrassed by the surprise attack, Chaffee needed little prodding. In a rare conference with journalists, the commanding general announced that it was "utterly foolish" to pretend that the war was over and as a result he would punish the Filipinos who fought "in manner not in accordance with the recognized laws of war."[90] To the point, Chaffee proclaimed, "The situation calls for shots, shells, and bayonets as the natives are not to be trusted."[91]

The U.S. military response came on September 29. Up from Basey, a U.S. gunboat blasted Balangiga with cannon and Gatling gun. Troops went ashore, located the dead American soldiers, and buried them in the plaza. The town was set ablaze.

Chaffee's broader solution to the insurrection on Samar was to deploy one of his most experienced, violent, and effective commanders, Brigadier General Smith. "Hell Roaring Jake" took command of the newly formed Sixth Separate Brigade, with four thousand soldiers, and assumed responsibility for Brigadier General Hughes's First District, which included Samar and the nearby and relatively peaceful island of Leyte. On September 30, Chaffee wrote to Hughes: "General Smith, as I am told, is an energetic officer, and I hope he will prove so in command of that brigade."[92] The commanding general also wrote to the War Department, "I shall let Smith prosecute affairs vigorously in Samar."[93] There is no doubt that Chaffee ordered Smith to wage a severe campaign. "I do not propose to hamper you at all," Smith recalled him saying, "but on the contrary, give you all the assistance you need to crush the insurrection in Samar." Chaffee further directed, "The interior must be made a wilderness if that is the only remedy."[94]

Smith arrived in the First District during the second week of October and established his headquarters in Tacloban, Leyte. He immediately toured dozens of army posts that stretched across the island. The American-owned *Manila Times*, which had tracked and celebrated Smith's exploits during the war, forewarned of "dark and bloody days" and predicted that Samar "will soon have the unenviable distinction of being the bloodiest island in the annals of the insurrection."[95] Smith issued a series of coercive decrees. He ordered a tightening of the U.S. naval blockade to curtail the flow of food and supplies to Samar. Civilian municipal leaders were to surrender all arms or face deportation. Smith also established coastal concentration zones to separate untrustworthy civilians from Filipino forces operating in the island's interior.

On October 23, Smith boarded the USS *New York* to confer with Rear Admiral Frederick Rogers, the commander of all naval forces in the Philippines (also the grandson of legendary commodore Matthew Perry). The general and admiral were joined by Major Littleton Waller, a Marine

Corps battalion commander whose unit Rogers assigned to Smith. Waller would essentially serve as Smith's southern field commander.

In their meeting, the Army general made clear that Waller's region was "one of the hardest problems of the whole command" and that he and his men could not trust the civilian population.[96] *All* Filipinos were considered enemies of the United States. Smith conveyed his belief that the soldiers at Balangiga had been the victims of not only of the rebels and collaborators, but also pathetically weak U.S. leaders — namely, American officers who sympathized with the "Little Brown Brother." Smith ordered Waller to implement a "fire-and-sword policy" and to make "War Hell" on Samar."[97] In another clear violation of the Lieber Code, he illegally ordered Waller to "kill all persons capable of bearing arms." The major, no stranger to impulsive violence, asked for clarification: "I would like to know the limit of age." The general replied, "Ten years of age."[98]

The next day, Smith, Waller, Rogers, and two companies of marines cruised to Balangiga aboard the *New York*. Naval guns bombarded insurgent trenches burrowed into the hills above the war-torn town. Once ashore, the party made a grisly discovery. Wild hogs had dug up the bodies of Company C. Smith flew into a rage. He ordered his troops to rebury the marred and decaying corpses and to construct a protective fence in the plaza. He then roared at Waller and his officers, "Kill and burn! The more you kill and burn the better you will please me. I want no prisoners, do you understand?"[99]

Waller was eager to punish the Filipinos for the bloodshed at Balangiga. There is no doubt that the marines were on a mission of vengeance. Insurgents and villagers, whether sympathizers or not, would feel their wrath. Still, Waller did not intend to murder women, girls, and *young* boys. He confided to one of his company commanders, Captain David Porter, "I've instructions to kill everyone over ten years old. But we are not making war on women and children, only on men capable of bearing arms. Keep that in mind no matter what other orders you receive."[100]

Inspired by Smith's bloodlust, Waller issued harsh orders to his command, ones meant to "avenge our late comrades . . . the murdered men of the Ninth U.S. Infantry." As of October 23, he instructed his marines that their expeditions were "punitive." None of the natives on Samar were to be trusted and men who had not surrendered by October 25 should be "regarded and treated as enemies." All acts of treachery, he said, were punishable "immediately with death." Civilian rice stores, hemp stocks, and unregistered boats were to be confiscated or destroyed, and natives were to be impressed for "all manual labor as far as possible." One marine later remembered interpreting Waller's orders as: "We were not making war against women and children. We were to shoot on sight anyone over twelve years old, armed or not, to burn everything and to make the island of Samar a howling wildness."[101] Waller, it appears, believed boys became morally legitimate targets at the age of thirteen, not eleven.

The marines began their assault at the end of October. During the first ten days, they marched twenty-five miles along the coast and destroyed every village and small town that they encountered. By Waller's estimate, the marines killed 39 Filipinos, captured 18, burned 255 homes, disabled 30 canoes, slaughtered 13 water buffalo, and destroyed one ton of hemp and a half ton of rice. Waller's battalion was realizing Smith's desire "to set the entire island of Samar ablaze" and thus "probably wipe out most of its population."[102]

On November 4, the *Manila News* accurately reported that Smith, after having conquered the coastal towns and villages, would shift his campaign to the island's interior. The general had already arrested countless civilian suspects, including "Spaniards and half-breeds," and he had incarcerated them in "big stockades and kept under guard." Any natives found outside of the coastal concentration zones "would be shot and no questions asked," the newspaper noted.[103]

In mid-November, Waller and his marines turned to the interior. They targeted an insurgent stronghold on the Sohoton River, not far from Balangiga. Along the way they burned another 165 homes. The eventual assault on the Sohoton fortress, supported by American gunboats anchored in the river, was executed flawlessly. Thirty rebels were killed and forty bamboo cannons destroyed. The marines suffered no casualties. In his report to Smith, Waller boasted that his victory was "the most important of the whole campaign as far as [its] effect on the insurgents were [sic] concerned. We have proved to them that their impregnable places can be taken."[104]

Smith was elated with the marines. He wrote glowingly to Waller, "There is nothing impossible for the American fighting men, and your work in the Sohoton Province is an additional proof of that fact. Success by barefooted Americans began at Valley Forge, and I am proud to know that the same indomitable spirit that won in spite of obstacles over one hundred years ago has shown itself in Samar."[105] The Army general recommended that Waller be promoted to brevet colonel.[106]

While Waller waged his search and destroy campaign in the south, Smith and his Army forces swept through the north. Meanwhile, navy gunboats blocked any attempts by the insurgents to escape the island by watercraft. The coordination between the Army and Navy, while generally effective, was sometimes haphazard, with gunboats mistakenly shelling pro-American Filipinos. When Smith learned that the Samarian rebels were receiving food, arms, and supplies from nearby Leyte, he closed ports and halted commerce between the islands. He also allowed his subordinates, including torture expert Major Edwin Glenn, to raid the Leyte coast and kidnap civilians, who were subjected to vicious, illegal interrogations.[107] Smith declared that the people of Leyte were traitors and deserved "the same heroic treatment which is being applied to Samar."[108]

But the general had exceeded his portfolio. Leyte, which had been largely pacified, was under civilian authority and the island's American governor complained to Manila about the military's usurpation of power. Luke Wright, the vice governor of the Philippines, informed his superior, Governor William Howard Taft, that Smith possessed the "insane idea that Leyte is full of insurrectos and that arbitrary and drastic measures are the remedy for the situation." Wright recommended to General Chaffee that he relieve Smith immediately and replace him with someone "less extreme and violent."[109]

Although Chaffee refused to relieve Smith, he did compel him to accept civilian authority on Leyte and temper his most severe policies.

In a private letter, Chaffee acknowledged that "Smith has very worked hard on Samar," but not always "with good judgment."[110]

Waller meanwhile continued his assault in the south. As if he needed a reminder, Smith issued him a stark handwritten order: "The interior of Samar must be made a howling wilderness."[111] With that directive the general earned a new sobriquet: "Howling Wilderness Smith."[112] Waller was doing his best and succeeding. In December, one of his marines wrote home and informed his sister that his unit had been "hiking all the time killing all we come across."[113] At the end of the month, Waller reported favorably to Smith. The insurgents had been "so punished by the repeated hammerings and by the capture of their stronghold that they have scattered and fled."[114]

The same could be said for the entire island. From October 10 to December 31, Smith's Sixth Separate Brigade, including Waller's marines, had killed or captured 759 insurgents and destroyed 1,662 homes, 226 boats, 587 water buffalo, and tons of rice and hemp.[115] "A vigorous policy," Smith wrote, "produced good results," and he wanted more.[116]

On Christmas Eve 1901, Smith issued new orders to his station commanders. He informed them that the "great mass of evidence at hand" indicated civilians were undergirding the rebellion, especially those in the influential and wealthy class. The only course forward for the brigade, he commanded, was to "wage War in the sharpest and most decisive manner possible." The new policy was to stimulate among the entire civilian population a "burning desire" to end the war, a need "so intense," "so personal . . . and so real" that they will be impelled to switch sides and support the American occupation. Neutrality by civilians "must not be tolerated." Invoking the Lieber Code, Smith declared that "short wars, severe wars are the most humane," and he argued that "no civilized war however civilized can be carried on . . . a humanitarian basis." In carrying out the new policy, he granted subordinate commanders complete "discretion in their adoption of any and all measures of warfare" and likewise instructed them to give their younger officers "a large latitude of action and . . . discretion."[117]

Four days later, Waller and fifty-five marines, two Filipino Scouts, and thirty-three native porters undertook a final mission under Smith's command. It would prove a disaster and lead to Waller's and Smith's courts-martial. The major had hoped to discover a fabled jungle trail that connected Samar's east and west coasts. A week into the arduous and ill-conceived exploration, Waller's men had grown sick and exhausted. They were running out of food and no trail had been found. Waller selected fifteen of his healthiest men and pressed ahead to collect relief supplies. After ten grueling days, his ragtag party was rescued.[118]

The major reported to Smith's adjutants on Leyte and sent word to Rear Admiral Rodgers. Two days later, on January 8, Waller formed a relief expedition to find the rest of his men. They searched for eight days but to no avail. Waller returned to Leyte and notified Smith of his failure. Thoroughly drained and suffering from a high fever and severe ankle injury, the major retreated to his headquarters at Basey.

Back in the jungle, the marines had split into two parties. The first, commanded by Captain David Porter, made a forced march. The group, eight marines and seven Filipinos, eventually discovered some canoes and reached the safety of the coast. Four of his men, however, were too weak to hike and had been abandoned in the jungle. They were rescued later. The second party, consisting of thirty-two marines and a group of native porters, was worse off. Led by First Lieutenant Alexander S. Williams, the men were starved and exhausted. Ten died in the jungle. Desperate and scared, Williams came to believe that his native bearers, who assisted the marines by carrying their heavy rifles and ammunition, were concealing food and plotting a mutiny. According to Williams, three weeks into the failed mission, he ordered some of the Filipino porters to collect firewood. He claimed that they attacked him and ran off into the jungle. Williams's party, including all of the porters and scouts, was rescued the following day. One of the marines succumbed to his injuries after the rescue, setting the American death toll at eleven.

On January 20, 1901, Porter and Williams arrived at brigade headquarters in Tacloban. They accused one scout and the native porters of mutiny and attempted murder. The ailing Major Waller sent instructions that the shackled Filipinos be transported to Basey. Porter and Williams recommended that ten natives be executed. Waller, still bedridden, asked Sergeant John Quick, who had been on the disastrous expedition what he thought of the situation. "I would shoot them all down like mad dogs," Quick retorted. With no further questioning, let alone an investigation or a trial, Waller ordered a total of eleven Filipinos (the same number of marines who had died) executed in the post's main plaza. Their bodies were left exposed to the elements to serve as examples to other civilians. Waller's report to Smith was cold and terse: "It became necessary to expend eleven prisoners. Ten who were implicated in the attack on Lieutenant Williams and one who plotted against me."[119]

Registering no objection to the killings, Smith forwarded Waller's report to Major General Chaffee, who soon arrived in Tacloban. The commanding general wanted a briefing on Samar and a general inspection. On January 23, Chaffee asked a pointed question: "Smith, have you been having any promiscuous killings in Samar for fun?" Smith snapped, "No, sir" and claimed total ignorance. "Well," Chaffee said, "I understand that at Basey they have been killing some people over there."[120] Smith appeared unconcerned and later falsely claimed under oath that he had initiated an investigation. The general did not think Waller and the marines had done anything inappropriate. In his mind, they were gallant exemplars. The next month, when Army troops replaced Waller's battalion at Basey, Smith offered the marines a tribute: "You are as fine a group of soldiers as has ever served under my command and I have been an officer for forty years."[121]

Despite such accolades, Chaffee had ordered an inspector general investigation into the "promiscuous killings" at Basey. The general came to believe that Waller had in fact violated the Lieber Code and the Articles of War by assuming command authority that only Smith possessed and that he had willfully and tragically executed innocent people who had helped to save marines from dying in the jungle.[122] When Waller reached Manila en route home to the United States, Chaffee had him arrested for murder.

Waller stood before a military tribunal on March 17, accused of "willfully and feloniously and with malice aforethought, murder and kill 11 . . . natives of the Philippines Islands."[123] He admitted to ordering the executions but entered a plea of not guilty. Four days later, he testified that his actions were wholly consistent with Smith's directions. In other words, he was just following orders. Waller said that his decision to execute the eleven Filipinos was "absolutely inspired" by his superior.[124] He further assured the court that he had acted with a sound mind despite his weakened physical state at the time. When Captain Porter took the stand, he fully supported the major's contention that he was following Smith's orders. Porter testified that Waller had "absolute authority" in the Samar's southern district. Asked if Waller's general orders of October 23 exceeded Smith's intentions and instructions, he answered, no. "They did not," he said, "go as far."[125] Porter was asked whether Smith had delegated to Waller the "power of life and death over unarmed and defenseless prisoners." Porter replied, yes, that "was the impression that he gave me, decidedly." He added that Smith's declaration that "we want no prisoners" presented more evidence of Waller's command authority.[126]

The prosecution called Brigadier General Smith to Manila as a rebuttal witness. Upon hearing that news, General Chaffee remarked to his wife, "It looks as if Jake Smith is going to be in the soup too."[127] On April 7, Smith admitted to the court that he had ordered subordinate commanders to punish Filipino treachery, and severely. But in an attempt to protect himself, Smith committed perjury. He denied ever directing his officers to give no quarter and to engage in summary executions.

Smith testified that he never exceeded the limits of the Articles of War or General Order No. 100. All charges of treachery, he said, must be referred "to a military commission." He insisted that he "never told any officer, in confidence or otherwise, that I would sustain him in treating prisoners in any way but the manner prescribed by the laws of war."[128] When asked if he had granted Waller "the power of life and death over unarmed and defenseless prisoners," Smith replied, "No, sir. I had no such authority myself and could not delegate any authority I did not have." Despite giving testimony that squarely refuted Waller and Porter's, the Army general extolled the marines' performance during the Samar Campaign: "The Marines did good work, magnificent work, equal to that of any soldiers that ever fought anywhere." He said Waller in particular had done "extraordinarily fine work, had acted with vigor and proved a fine officer."[129]

Waller was unmoved by the praise. Angry, he rose from his courtroom chair and questioned Smith directly. He asked pointedly, did not the general "order treachery to be punished summarily by death?" Smith answered reverently, "No, sir." Astonished by the flagrant lie, Major Waller snapped, "You did not?" At this point the president of the court intervened. He instructed Waller to show Smith, his superior officer, "a certain attitude of respect, both in tone and gesture." The marine apologized and continued his questioning. Smith testified that Waller's October orders to his marines were too severe, that he should have adhered to the Lieber Code. Waller should not have ordered his men to "punish treachery summarily with death," but rather "punish treachery as prescribed by the laws of war."[130]

Waller, stunned by Smith's shamelessly dishonest testimony, took the stand again on April 8 to refute the general's falsehoods. He informed the court that in all his discussions with Smith, his commander never once invoked the restrictions of the Lieber Code. Waller then reiterated a list of the general's harsh orders: "I want no prisoners," "there would be no quarter," "I wish you to kill and burn. The more you kill and burn, the better you will please me." The latter order, Waller testified, was given to him "not once only, but several times. I think every officer there heard him." Moreover, Waller swore that Smith wanted "all persons killed who were capable of bearing arms," including "all over ten years of age," and that "the interior of Samar must be made a howling wilderness."[131]

Closing statements were delivered on April 11 and 12. The prosecutor argued that Waller had failed in his legal duty to investigate the treachery charges against the native bearers. If he had, the major would have discovered that the Filipinos did not deserve the death penalty. In fact, "much of their conduct was deserving of the highest commendation." Moreover, the prosecutor contended that Waller's poor leadership during the failed expedition had "brought disaster upon those soldiers of the Marine Corps."[132]

In his defense, Waller claimed that the summary execution of prisoners was not unusual in war, especially when facing a vile enemy. He had personally witnessed the British kill prisoners of war in Egypt and the Europeans conduct executions in China. Waller admitted that his campaign in Samar had been motivated by vengeance and that he and his men wanted to kill "savage, treacherous" Filipino "devils" for what they had done to American soldiers at Balangiga. As for the native bearers on his imprudent jungle expedition, he said, "I ordered the eleven men shot" because they had "attempted to murder my officers and men. I shot them." He concluded on a note of rectitude, "I honestly thought I was right then. I believe now that I was right."[133]

The jury panel, which consisted of thirteen Army and Marine Corps officers, deliberated for less than thirty minutes. By a vote count of eleven to two, they acquitted Waller of all charges.[134] He was free to go. Later, when he returned to the United States, Waller was baldly honest with reporters about how he and General Smith approached the war: "You can't stop the revolution in the Philippines unless you take the severest measures. . . . I received both verbal and written orders from Gen. Smith to kill all insurrectos who were caught armed or refused to surrender. It was the only thing that could be done, and I never questioned Gen. Smith's orders." He exclaimed, "I left Samar a howling wilderness."[135]

On April 16, at President Theodore Roosevelt's urging, Secretary of War Elihu Root cabled Chaffee in Manila, directing him to investigate whether Smith had given Waller such severe and brutal orders. If substantiated, the directives represented "violations of law and humanity" and Chaffee must place General Smith on trial by court-martial. Chaffee was warned that no matter how abhorrent the Filipino enemy had behaved, "nothing can justify the use of torture or inhuman conduct of any kind on the part of the American Army." Root also emphasized that

Roosevelt wanted a full and honest investigation with "nothing being concealed and no man being for any reason favored or shielded."[136]

Chaffee believed that Waller's acquittal had been a "miscarriage of justice" because war crimes had been committed, and responded to Root immediately.[137] The commanding general reported that he had detained Smith and would arrange for his trial in Manila. Still, Chaffee was sympathetic to Smith and informed Root that he wanted his field general to be saved from any "injustice." He posited further that the president could not "fully comprehend" that Smith's application of "serious measures" had been absolutely critical to the successful campaign in Samar. "Some officers," Chaffee conceded, "have doubtless failed in [the] exercise [of] due discretion, blood grown hot in their dealings with deceit and lying, hence severity [in] some few occasions." But the commanding general did not believe General Smith should be held responsible for the misconduct of his subordinate officers.[138]

Chaffee could not prevent Smith's trial, but he could influence it, and did so materially. Despite the fact that Smith's orders were indeed "violations of law and humanity," Chaffee did not charge him with issuing illegal orders to commit war crimes (including unnecessary killing), for which he could have faced the death penalty if he had been convicted. Instead the major general charged his brigade commander with the lesser crime of "conduct to the prejudice of good order and military discipline" evidenced by issuing dramatic orders such as: "I want no prisoners (meaning thereby that giving of quarter was not desired or required)."[139] Moreover, the jury was populated with senior officers, including Major General Loyd Wheaton and Brigadier General J. Franklin Bell, who were not only sympathetic to Smith's plight, but had long practiced severe tactics against Filipino insurgents and civilians.

Smith's notorious court-martial began on April 25. To nobody's surprise, he pled not guilty, but the general startled everybody in the courtroom by allowing his lawyer to stipulate that Waller's testimony had been in large part accurate. Smith had indeed given the marine drastic orders such as "kill and burn," make the interior of Samar "a howling wilderness," kill "all persons . . . capable of bearing arms" above the age of ten, and not to "burden himself [Waller] with prisoners."[140] It was an astonishing admission and the prosecutor pounced. He called Waller and other marines to the stand. They reiterated Smith's orders and his unmistakable directive for a most severe campaign. Under cross-examination, however, Waller proved helpful to Smith's defense. The major said he did not think Smith actually wanted him to kill women and children, and he reminded the court that he, in fact, did not kill any women or children. Waller also said that he did not believe Smith's orders violated the laws of war.

News of Smith's shocking admissions reached the United States a day after the trial began. Even stalwart supporters of the war and the Roosevelt administration condemned the Army general. The *New York Times* editorial board forecast Smith's swift demise, writing "these orders are bloody and cruel to a degree which the American people will not believe to be justified even against the most treacherous savages," and "We should suppose that the result of the court martial would terminate the military career of Gen. Jacob H. Smith." Whatever the verdict, the newspaper asserted that the central issue at hand was morality, not legality: "What a court might say in legal or technical justification of Gen. Smith's orders is not now the question. He will fail in the moral justification before the American people and, we believe, before the President and Secretary of War."[141]

Back in Manila, Smith's defense witnesses included an array of officers and enlisted soldiers who had experienced the hardships of the Samar Campaign. One after another they testified in graphic detail about the brutality and treachery of the Filipino people. One of the survivors of Balangiga, Sergeant Clifford Mumby, recounted how some of his fellow troopers "had been cut across the body, and the cuts filled with jam taken from the issue commissary." Consistent with the Lieber Code, Smith's attorney argued that the general's "sharp, relentless plan" for Samar merely sought to bring a speedy conclusion to the war and his "humane campaign" was reminiscent of Union forces in the Civil War.

"You," the counsel said to the panel of judges, "who marched with Sherman from Atlanta to the sea, know how your routes were marked by clouds of smoke by day and [pillars] of fire by night. And that was war."[142]

In the end, the biased jury found Smith only partially guilty as charged. His leadership had indeed been prejudicial to good order and military discipline. But the panel was careful to exclude from its guilty verdict the extreme allegation of Smith giving an illegal "no quarter" order. Moreover, the judges determined that Smith's broad order to Waller was *not* to kill all Samarian Filipinos who were "capable of bearing arms," but rather to kill only those capable of bearing arms *and* "in actual hostilities against the United States."[143] With these mitigating findings, the panel recommended an exceedingly light punishment: a written reprimand. The judges explained their twisted reasoning while ignoring many facts in the case: "The court is thus lenient in view of the undisputed evidence that the accused did not mean everything that his unexplained language implied; that his subordinates did not gather such a meaning, and that the orders were never executed in such sense, notwithstanding the fact that a desperate struggle was being conducted with a cruel and savage foe."[144]

Chaffee, who had prodded Smith to undertake a severe campaign in Samara, was most pleased. But the high-profile trial's soft verdict had domestic political considerations. President Roosevelt intervened as the court's reviewing authority. His final judgment would come after receiving the trial records and transcripts. The president was fully supportive of the war effort in the Philippines, but he had been troubled by Waller's summary execution of the Filipino porters and his courtroom acquittal. "The shooting of the native bearers by orders of Major Waller," he wrote, "was an act which sullied the American name." If Waller was not held accountable for his criminal conduct reasoned the ole Rough Rider, then perhaps his superior should be. Roosevelt had learned of Smith's oft intemperate language, including his boasting of "shooting n*****s" in the Philippines. The president believed that the severity of Smith's illicit orders must have inspired Waller to execute the helpless prisoners.[145]

Meanwhile, politicians from both parties and imperialist and anti-imperialist newspapers continued to lambast Smith. Republican congressman Joseph C. Sibley of Pennsylvania, a reliable ally of the Roosevelt administration, decried Smith as "a disgrace . . . to every man who ever wore the uniform of the United States, and a blot and a disgrace to our present civilization."[146] Republican Senator Henry M. Teller of Colorado declared that "in the records of all the great wars since the Middle Ages, you cannot find such a disgraceful and wicked order as that issued by General Smith."[147] Washington State's Republican senator George Turner pronounced Smith "a monster in human form."[148] Even Republican Senator Henry Cabot Lodge of Massachusetts and the pro-Roosevelt *New York Times* professed "shock" and "regret" over "General Jacob H. Smith's admission that he issued the orders to burn and kill."[149]

Secretary of War Root received Smith's trial materials in June, including a detailed analysis from Army Judge Advocate General George Davis. Davis regretted that Smith had only been charged with the crime of conduct prejudicial to good order and discipline and not "the real offense" of ordering war crimes. Davis concluded that Smith's instructions to take no prisoners represented "a substantial departure from the laws of war" as he had incited "revengeful feelings" and thus induced Waller's marines to commit illegal "acts of cruelty and harshness in retaliation for the treatment to which our own troops had been subjected." But because Smith had not been charged with "serious" crimes, Davis concluded that he had little choice but to concur with the jury's verdict.[150]

In his written review of the records completed in July, Secretary Root condemned the viciousness of General Smith's orders to Waller. He characterized the directives as "unjustifiable" and "intemperate, inconsiderate, and violent expressions, which if accepted literally, would grossly violate the humane rules governing American armies in the field." Root concluded that Smith had "signally failed" in his duty as a general officer to lead his men properly and thus deserved a punishment beyond a written reprimand. Yet Root, like the biased military jury, refused to draw any connection between Smith's extreme orders and Waller's killing of the defenseless Filipino bearers. The secretary wrote to Roosevelt, "Fortunately, they [Smith's verbal instructions] were not taken literally and were not followed. No women or children or helpless persons put to death in pursuance of them."[151]

Root also defended Smith's harsh campaign on the island, arguing that it was allowable under the Lieber Code. The general's "written and printed orders and the actual conduct of military operations in Samar, were justified by the history and conditions of the warfare and the cruel and treacherous savages who inhabited the island." He claimed the conduct of U.S. forces "were wholly within the limitations of General Orders, No. 100, of 1863, and were sustained by precedents of the highest authority."[152] Still, Root concluded that Smith deserved a material punishment. He recommended to Roosevelt that the general be admonished *and* forced to retire. "It is no longer for the interest of the service [the Army]," he wrote, "that Gen. Smith should continue to exercise the command of his rank. His usefulness as an example, guide, and controlling influence for the junior officers of the Army is at an end."[153]

On July 16, as Smith was steaming home aboard the army transport ship *Thomas*, the Roosevelt administration announced that he had been reprimanded and cashiered from the army. Newspapers across the country published the entirety of Roosevelt's written review of the general's prosecution. In it, he chastised Smith for intemperate and injurious leadership during a time of war. Unlike Root, the president linked Waller's abhorrent executions to Smith's issuance of severe and illegal orders:

> [T]he very fact that warfare is of such character as to afford infinite provocation for the commission of acts of cruelty by junior officers and the enlisted men, must make the officers in high and responsible position peculiarly careful in their bearing and conduct, so as to keep a moral check over any acts of an improper character by their subordinates. . . . [T]here have been instances of the use of torture and of improper heartlessness in warfare on the

part of [American] individuals or small detachments. In the recent campaign ordered by General Smith, the shooting of the native bearers by the orders of Major Waller was an act which sullied the American name. . . . It is impossible to tell exactly how much influence language like that used by General Smith may have had in preparing the minds of those under him for the commission of the deeds which we regret. Loose and violent talk by an officer of high rank is always likely to excite to wrongdoing those among his subordinates whose wills are weak or whose passions are strong. . . . [I]t is deeply to be regretted that he [Smith] should have so acted in this instance as to interfere with his further usefulness in the Army. I hereby direct that he be retired from the active list."[154]

Smith did not learn of his dismissal until after landing at the San Francisco pier on August 1, 1902. The warrior-general was met by a group of soldiers who cheered his return. Major General Chaffee worried about Smith's reaction, fearing that he would talk "absurdly unwise" and "act like an unbalanced lunatic."[155] But he initially refused to speak with reporters and took a room at the Occidental Hotel. Two days later, the chastened general emerged and fielded queries from an eager press corps. Smith admitted his surprise at being retired by the president, but "Hell Roaring Jake" showed uncharacteristic restraint and he refused to complain. "I am a soldier," he said, "and take what is coming to me."[156] Asked about his use of force on Samar, the general acknowledged that his tactics against the enemy were indeed harsh, but insisted that his methods were not excessive: "Some of those in Samar are nothing but savages, and, of course, cannot be treated like civilized people."[157]

Smith then boarded a train, the first of several, en route to see family in Portsmouth, Ohio. The press hounded him. When he arrived home on August 11, he was given a hero's welcome and greeted by three thousand townspeople, a triumphant band, and cannon salutes. Two units from the Ohio National Guard accompanied Smith's horse-drawn carriage to his sister's home. Before dispersing, the Guard soldiers let out three enthusiastic cheers. A local journalist expressed surprise by the general's appearance, writing, "He is a small man, rather slim, and is very bald. He is a neat dresser and in his citizens clothes did not look like the fierce fighter who had carried terror to the hearts of the most savage tribes in the Philippines islands."[158] After dinner that evening, Smith spoke freely with reporters. He justified his severe campaign on Samar on the grounds that the Filipinos were "savages of the most degraded kind" who failed to recognize the rules of civilized warfare.[159]

A week later, Smith was lionized at a men-only banquet at the Washington Hotel. The event was organized by local Civil War veterans and the Portsmouth mayor. The decorated hall featured prominent images of Presidents Washington, Lincoln, Grant, and McKinley. The absence of Roosevelt's picture was conspicuous, "noted by all who viewed the scene."[160] Wearing his dress uniform, Smith delivered a patriotic and prideful address. He highlighted his decades of service, the selflessness of soldiering, and his controversial leadership in the Philippines. He said,

> Whether on the Southern battlefields or the great plains of the West, on the Isle of Cuba, or in the tropical jungles of the Philippines we tried to do our duty to the United States and our flag. For the humble part which I took in bringing into subjection the tribes of Samar I am aware that there has been much criticism, but to take criticism is part of a soldier's training. I have already had occasion to say that he must take what comes to him without complaint, and let his country say whether he has acted the part of a soldier or not.[161]

After the banquet, Smith was celebrated at a public reception that attracted "great throngs" of people who lined up to clasp "the hand of the old warrior."[162]

The *New York Times* editorial board applauded the "taste and temper" of Smith's address, but underscored its support of Roosevelt's decision to relieve the general. "The uncontested fact," the board wrote, "was that Gen. Smith had issued a truculent order, disgraceful to his position as a general officer of the United States Army." Like Roosevelt, the *Times* linked Smith's illegal orders to kill, burn, and take no quarter to Waller's wanton killing of the Filipino scout and porters. "[I]t was clearly shown," the board asserted, that one of Smith's commanders had taken his orders literally and that subordinate "even pleaded an excuse for what was clearly an atrocity."[163]

Jacob Smith lived in relative obscurity until his death on March 1, 1918. The *New York Times* was generous in its obituary stating that news of his passing had "brought recollections to army officers of the picturesque career of the old fighter, who became celebrated in the Philippine campaign as 'Hell Roaring Jake.'" Many civilians had been "astounded at the severity of [his] measures. But he cleared out the nest of outlaws who had kept the province in a continual state of insurrection and he received the hearty approval of his fellow officers, who knew the problem."[164] Smith was buried with military honors at the Arlington National Cemetery near Washington, DC.

★   ★   ★   ★

In the two-hundred-fifty-year history of the U.S. military, General Jacob Smith is the only flag officer ever court-martialed for giving orders that constituted a war crime. By creating a "kill and burn" and "no quarter" command climate in Samar, the general was culpable for the atrocities committed by his subordinates, including Waller's summary execution of eleven defenseless Filipinos. The command responsibility, however, did not start and stop with Smith. The president, the secretary of war, and the commanding general of the Philippines were equally eager to exact a harsh and bloody revenge for the Balangiga massacre and to forcibly subdue all of the inhabitants of Samar. The ruthless, racist, and effective Smith was their means to that end.

Major General Chaffee, under orders from Washington to take "the most stern measures to pacify Samar," selected Smith to lead the Samar Campaign because of his known "propensity for violent extralegal action."[165] Chaffee gave Smith unambiguous and unfettered orders: "crush the insurrection in Samar. . . . The interior must be made a wilderness if that is the only remedy."[166] Chaffee also kept the Roosevelt administration and the public informed of his intentions. He cabled Washington that "I shall let Smith prosecute affairs vigorously in Samar" and told the press, "The situation calls for shot, shells, and bayonets as the natives are not to be trusted."[167] It is no wonder that Chaffee was unenthusiastic about Smith's court-martial and not surprising that he would abuse his command authority by charging Smith with a relatively minor offense and by allowing a jury to be stacked with biased senior officers. Chaffee's conduct amounted to a dereliction of duty for which he was never held accountable. "After Balangiga," historian Brian McAllister Linn writes, "it was clearly Chaffee's military and moral responsibility to emphasize exactly what would be tolerated, and to caution Samar's new commander [Smith] against letting either his own emotions or his troops' behavior get out of hand. . . . [I]t is almost certainly true that he urged Smith to employ the harshest methods."[168]

The military's relatively mild treatment of general officers suspected of direct or indirect roles in the commission of war crimes was repeated seven decades later during the Vietnam War. In their reviews of the infamous case of the My Lai massacre, which featured "individual and group acts of murder, rape, sodomy, maiming, and assaults on noncombatants and the mistreatment and killing of detainees," the Army's Criminal Investigation Division and the Peers Commission both determined that Americal Division Commander Major General Samuel Koster and his senior deputy, Brigadier General George Young, had wittingly directed a cover-up of the horrific crimes. As the senior commanders they were ultimately responsible.[169] Both generals were charged with dereliction of duty and a failure to obey lawful regulations. The charges, however, were dropped before trials were convened on the grounds of insufficient evidence and no "intentional abrogation of responsibilities."[170] This occurred despite the fact that two field grade officers had testified in a related trial that they had told General Young about the war crimes. Nevertheless, the Army demoted Koster, issued letters of censure to him and Young, and rescinded both of their Distinguished Service Medals. But without military trials, the extent of their derelict conduct went undisclosed for decades.[171]

Simultaneously, Brigadier General John Donaldson, who had served in the same Americal Division, was charged with murdering six Vietnamese civilians and the unlawful assault of two others. Donaldson had a grisly, racist reputation as "a d*nk hunter" and "a g**k hunter" who was "obsessed with having a good kill ratio and a good body count."[172] The Army Criminal Investigation Command identified thirteen occasions when Donaldson shot or ordered others to shoot "unarmed and unresisting" Vietnamese women and men.[173] In its page-one coverage of the case, the *New York Times* noted that "the last general formally accused of war crimes was Brig. Gen. Jacob H. Smith" who, during the Philippine-American War, gave orders that "no prisoners should be taken," that the island of Samar be made "a howling wilderness," and that "all persons above the age of 10 years should be killed."[174] As with Koster and Young, the charges against Donaldson were dropped before trial. According to an Army investigator, key eyewitnesses had been coerced into changing their testimony and thus the legal case crumbled. Unlike Koster and Young, Donaldson was not subjected to any punishment whatsoever.[175]

Thirty years after the Vietnam War, on April 28, 2004, *60 Minutes II* broadcast graphic evidence of American soldiers humiliating and abusing Iraqi prisoners of war. The prisoners were clearly entitled to Geneva protections, but the psychological and physical abuse of detainees at the Abu Ghraib prison was systematic. Many Iraqis were tortured and at least one murdered. The military spokesman in Iraq, Brigadier General Mark Kimmitt, exclaimed, "This is wrong. This is reprehensible."[176] Defense Secretary Donald Rumsfeld offered to resign over the controversy. After multiple extensive investigations, however, the only soldiers convicted of crimes were low-ranking enlisted personnel who claimed they had been merely following orders from their superiors. Not a single officer was judicially punished. The colonel in command of military intelligence and interrogations at the prison never faced criminal prosecution, although he was reprimanded and fined. His deputy, a lieutenant colonel who directed the prison's interrogation and debriefing center, was acquitted of charges connected to prisoner mistreatment. The one flag officer held accountable for the scandal was a reserve brigadier general, Janis Karpinski, who commanded the 800th Military Police Brigade. She was responsible for all detention facilities in Iraq but *not* the interrogations at Abu Ghraib. The general was relieved of command and demoted to colonel, although she was not subjected to a court-martial for dereliction of duty and command responsibility for the crimes committed by her soldiers.

Some, including Karpinski, argue persuasively that she was scapegoated and that other general officers (and civilian executives) in the chain of command were also culpable for the crimes committed by U.S. soldiers against Iraqi prisoners. Karpinski has taken responsibility for her leadership failures and even admitted to violating the Geneva Conventions while working at the behest of Brigadier General Barbara Fast, the senior intelligence officer in Iraq who was directing interrogations, and Lieutenant General Ricardo Sanchez, the commander of coalition ground forces.[177] Specifically, Karpinski admits to following extralegal orders to detain certain "ghost" captives without assigning them prisoner of war numbers or in any way acknowledging their apprehension. "We all knew it was contrary to the Geneva Conventions," she later confessed.[178]

Major General Geoffrey Miller, the gung-ho commander of the terrorist detention facility at Guantanamo Bay, bears responsibility for the abuses that occurred there and also at Abu Ghraib. In late summer 2003, he and his "tiger team" were detailed to Iraq by Secretary Rumsfeld to advise Sanchez, Fast, and Karpinski on how to "Gitmo-ize" Iraq and make prisoner interrogations more productive.[179] One of Miller's recommendations was for Karpinski's military police to "soften up detainees between interrogations" and create "the conditions for the successful exploitation of internees."[180] At one briefing, the major general instructed Karpinski and others: "Look, the first thing you need to do is treat these prisoners like dogs. If they ever get the idea they're anything more than dogs, you've lost control of your interrogation."[181] Sanchez approved Miller's recommendations and the implementation of "exceptionally tough tactics."[182] After the Abu Ghraib scandal broke and Karpinski was ousted, Major General Miller was not reprimanded. Instead, the *effective* albeit ethically challenged general was elevated and put in charge of all detainee facilities in Iraq. He reported directly to Sanchez.

In a detailed examination of the law doctrine of *command responsibility*, William Peters, a professor of criminal justice and former Army Judge Advocate General officer, has illuminated the "troublesome problem" of the U.S. military not thoroughly investigating generals and admirals *suspected* of direct or indirect culpability for war crimes.[183] He demonstrates how in Vietnam, Iraq, and Afghanistan, "senior U.S. military commanders have repeatedly and systematically avoided courts-martial and formal adjudication of serious war crime allegations."[184] Because of the military's failure to effectively police its most senior ranks, Peters recommends that Congress use its authority to regulate the armed forces and create a civilian office of special prosecutor for war crimes. With a government department that ensures the adjudication of war crimes allegations, perhaps generals like Miller, Sanchez, Fast, Chaffee, and Smith would be held fully accountable for violating the laws of war.

CHAPTER TWO

INSUBORDINATION

Douglas MacArthur

INSUBORDINATION — willfully disobeying
a legitimate and lawful order, using threatening
or insulting language, or behaving in
a disrespectful manner toward a superior

Leaders of high-performing organizations encourage independent critical judgment among subordinates and create cultures that allow for honest and loyal dissent. Critical thinking and morally courageous expression are the prerogatives of leaders and followers alike. Problems can arise, however, when subordinates are insubordinate — when they disrespect or threaten leaders and when they disobey legitimate, lawful instructions. There are, of course, degrees and frequencies of insubordination, ranging from the innocuous to the severe and from the infrequent to the habitual. As a consequence, penalties for insubordination vary. Harshly punishing someone who has committed a relatively harmless offense can have unintended negative consequences, such as depressing morale and suppressing valuable dissent. On the other hand, material and unjust insubordination warrants stark punishment, such as demotion, termination, and even legal recourse. Lesser reprimands would have the effect of sanctioning and encouraging insubordination. Leaders have an obligation to respond to insubordinate conduct and punish proportionally.

From the time of its founding, the United States armed forces have been regulated by congressional articles that expressly prohibit insubordinate behavior. In times of war, officers and enlisted personnel who disobey lawful orders can be sentenced to death. For the officer corps, especially admirals and generals, two regulations have proven particularly relevant: the prohibition of "reproachful or provoking speeches or gestures" and "disrespect" toward civilian superiors.[1] The enforcement of these punitive regulations is integral to maintaining order and discipline within the ranks and for preserving the constitutional principle of civilian control of the military.[2]

During the Civil War, President Abraham Lincoln relieved two impertinent and obstinate major generals, John C. Fremont and George B. McClellan. In late July 1861, Fremont, the legendary explorer and former Republican presidential nominee, assumed command of the important Department of the West, headquartered in St. Louis. A month later and without consulting his superiors in Washington, Fremont issued an audacious proclamation. He declared martial law in Missouri and directed the confiscation of property, including enslaved people, from Missourians who actively supported the Confederate cause. Stunningly, the edict asserted that all confiscated slaves were to be freed. Lincoln, deathly afraid of losing crucial slaveholding border states to the Confederacy, asked Fremont in confidence to strike the emancipation clause and otherwise conform to the new Confiscation Act. The truculent general, who had a history of insubordination, refused, arguing that he had made his bold declaration after "full deliberation, and upon the certain conviction that it was a measure right and necessary, and I still think so."[3] Understandably, Lincoln was furious. On September 11, he drafted a public letter of rebuke, demanding that

Fremont amend the proclamation. The next month, after the Army adjutant general documented Fremont's "wholly incompetent and unsafe" management of the Western Department, Lincoln fired the great "Pathfinder of the West."[4]

Much better known is Lincoln's dismissal of George McClellan, who had taken command of the Army of Potomac when Fremont assumed control of the Western Department. Immediately upon reaching Washington, DC, 34-year-old McClellan clashed with his direct superior, Winfield Scott, the 75-year-old general-in-chief of the Union army. The arrogant and ambitious "young Napoleon" openly criticized Scott's war strategy and his "entirely insufficient" preparations to defend the capital.[5] McClellan shared his criticisms with Lincoln. In letters to his wife, the general denigrated Scott as a "dotard," "a perfect imbecile," and possibly "a *traitor*."[6] McClellan isolated Scott, repeatedly excluding him from high-level communications with Lincoln and the cabinet. Suffering from such "persistent neglect and disobedience," the aged general was inclined to remedy the situation "by arrest and trial before Court Martial."[7] Instead the old lion surrendered, choosing to retire from active duty. Ironically, decades earlier, then-Captain Scott had been convicted of insubordinate "unofficer-like conduct" at court-martial, and as a brigadier general he had campaigned to oust a newly appointed commanding general whose authority he refused to recognize.[8]

Although Lincoln elevated McClellan to general-in-chief of Union forces, the president himself soon became the target of the vain general's derisions and snubs. McClellan privately disparaged Lincoln as a "baboon," as "the *original gorrilla* [sic]," and as a country hick "ever unworthy" of the presidency.[9] On multiple occasions, McClellan forced Lincoln to wait for *him* before holding meetings on the war. The insolent general also derided Secretary of War Edwin Stanton as "the most unmitigated scoundrel I ever knew."[10] Most galling to Lincoln and Stanton was McClellan's extraordinary reluctance to go on the offensive against the Confederate army. A near breaking point came in August 1862 when McClellan was ordered to join his Army of the Potomac with Major General John Pope's Army of Virginia, which was under attack.

McClellan opposed the plan and his willful, disobedient delays contributed to Pope's defeat in the Second Battle of Bull Run. Lincoln and Stanton were irate. The president considered the general's behavior "shocking" and "unpardonable," and the secretary of war wanted McClellan court-martialed for his "disobedience to superior orders."[11] However, seeing no good senior leadership alternatives, the president stuck with his overly cautious general until November when he finally relived McClellan for not aggressively pursuing the Confederate army in the weeks after it had retreated from the Battle of Antietam.

In the twentieth century, Army Brigadier General Billy Mitchell offered a textbook illustration of intemperance and insubordination. A highly decorated pilot and brilliant commander of air combat units in the First World War, Mitchell became the Assistant Chief of the Air Service in 1921. He was a fervent and outspoken advocate of air power and labored tirelessly to prove that low-cost bombers could easily destroy expensive battleships. Mitchell's sharp and often excessive critique of national security policy, especially naval power, and his advocacy for an air force independent of and equal to the Army and Navy rankled not only his senior military leaders, but also the secretary of war and the president.

In extensive testimony before two Congressional committees in 1924–1925, Mitchell assailed Navy leadership for discounting the strategic significance of air power and exaggerating the importance of the surface fleet. He brazenly asserted that "surface ships are a thing of the past."[12] The general furthermore accused the War Department of silencing fellow officers who shared his views. As a celebrity war hero, Mitchell's strident commentary was covered in the national press. Incensed by his insubordination, Secretary John Weeks condemned Mitchell for being "so lawless, so contrary to . . . an efficient organization, so lacking in reasonable teamwork, so indicative of a personal desire for publicity . . . that his actions render him unfit for a high administrative position."[13] Backed by President Calvin Coolidge, Weeks held Mitchell accountable by refusing to reappoint him as the assistant chief of the Army air branch. This automatically triggered his demotion to colonel, and he was banished to Fort Sam Houston in Texas as an air officer with the Thirteenth Corps.

The admonishment failed to quell Mitchell's rebelliousness. In September 1925, he seized upon two naval air disasters to amplify his disapproval of Navy, Army, and civilian military leadership. In San Antonio, Mitchell gathered a group of newspaper reporters and delivered a scorching rebuke. His nine-page statement read in part: "These accidents are the direct result of the incompetency, criminal negligence and almost treasonable administration of the national defense by the navy and the war departments. . . . I can stand by no longer and see the disgusting performances by the navy and war departments at the expense of the lives of our people [military air crews], and the delusion of the American public."[14]

The Army immediately relieved Mitchell of command and Coolidge sanctioned his court-martial. Accused of insubordination and conduct unbecoming an officer, Mitchell used his trial to renew the argument for an independent air force and to rehash his critique of air policy, which, he said, was being "dictated by non-flying officers of the army and navy who know practically nothing about it."[15] The well-publicized court-martial lasted more than six weeks and featured more than one hundred witnesses. The outcome, however, was never in doubt. Mitchell was found guilty. While he was not discharged from the army, Mitchell was suspended from duty and rank without pay for five years. Coolidge lessened the penalty by granting half-salary, but Mitchell rejected the compensation and resigned from service.

There have been other cases of flagrant flag officer insubordination. Beginning in 1947, for example, Rear Admiral Dan Gallery, a World War II hero, made public speeches and published controversial articles that not only promoted strategic naval aviation, but also disparaged the so-called atomic blitz strategy of the new U.S. Air Force. In the *Collier's* article "If This Be Treason," the contemptuous Gallery attacked the Truman administration for its overreliance on Air Force bombers and its diminution of the Navy's offensive warfighting capabilities. Like Mitchell, whom the admiral praised as a truth-telling martyr, Gallery condemned his civilian and military superiors for silencing and even purging flag officers who disagreed with the "new and desperately dangerous" national security policy.[16] For his insubordination, Gallery was reprimanded and sent unceremoniously to sea, assigned to an inconspicuous research group in the Atlantic. Although he remained on active duty until 1960, the Navy refused to promote the "tempestuous" Gallery.[17]

Decades later, Army Major General John Singlaub, Air Force Major General Harold Campbell, Admiral William Fallon, and Army General Stanley McChrystal were all relieved of duty and forced into retirement for public comments deemed disrespectful of the Carter, Clinton, Bush, and Obama administrations, respectively. (These cases are discussed later in this chapter.) In 2010, Brigadier General Greg Stroud, commander of the 162nd Fighter Wing in Tucson, Arizona, was relieved for defying a superior's instructions not to intervene in an ongoing sexual harassment investigation.[18] Two years later, Stroud's former superior, Brigadier General Michael Colangelo, the commander of Arizona's Air National Guard, was himself fired after he sent a "blatantly disrespectful" email to Major General Hugo Salazar, the Adjutant General of the state's National Guard.[19] Still, there remains no more striking example of insubordination than that of Douglas MacArthur.

★ ★ ★ ★

On June 25, 1950, Communist North Korean forces unexpectedly invaded the Republic of (South) Korea. Supported by the Soviet Union and Communist China, the North Korean blitzkrieg was a supreme test of the Truman administration's national security policy. As the first U.S. president during the Cold War, Harry S. Truman sought to defend America's global interests and allies and contain the spread of communism, all without igniting a third world war.

From the outset of the Korean crisis, Truman and his advisors determined that North Korea's aggression could not be appeased.

Prompted by Washington, the United Nations Security Council issued a hurried resolution that authorized the use of force against North Korea. The U.N. mandate was to repel the communist offensive and push North Korean forces back across the 38th parallel.[20] In one of the most fateful decisions of the early Cold War and in American military history, Truman appointed General Douglas MacArthur as the commander of U.S./U.N. forces in Korea. MacArthur had spent the majority of his Army career in Asia and had become a national hero as a victorious Pacific commander during World War II. After the war, Truman had contained the general's presidential ambitions by appointing him commander of all U.S. forces in the Far East and as the supreme commander for Allied powers in occupied Japan.

At the time of MacArthur's Korean appointment, some observers registered prescient misgivings. *New York Times* columnist James Reston worried about the risks of a broader war in Asia because of the general's legendary hubris and penchant for autonomous action. Reston described MacArthur as "a sovereign power in his own right, with stubborn confidence in his own judgment" and as a commander with an "old habit of doing things in his own way without too much concern about waiting for orders from Washington."[21] Dwight Eisenhower, who had served under MacArthur for seven years, thought it highly imprudent of Truman to select "'an untouchable' whose action you cannot predict and who will himself decide what information he wants Washington to have and what he will withhold."[22]

Indeed, less than a year after MacArthur assumed his new command, he was ingloriously fired by Truman for "open insubordination."[23] During those turbulent ten months, the five-star general violated multiple provisions of the Articles of War. His transgressions included willful disobedience, provocative gestures, disrespect toward the president, and conduct unbecoming a military officer.[24] MacArthur's misconduct during the Korean War was singularly notorious, but an examination of his illustrious career reveals a pattern of unprofessional and unethical behavior that was often enabled by his superiors.

No general appeared better prepared than Douglas MacArthur to lead the campaign against North Korean aggression. The highly decorated commander had been absorbed into martial life since his birth in 1880 at the Army's barracks in Little Rock, Arkansas. MacArthur's father, Arthur, was a genuine American war hero who as a *teenager* led Union volunteer soldiers against Confederate forces on Missionary Ridge (Tennessee, 1863), on Kennesaw Mountain (Georgia, 1864), and at the Battle of Franklin (Tennessee, 1864). Arthur survived bullet wounds to the wrist, chest, knee, and shoulder, and was eventually awarded the Medal of Honor. By the end of the Civil War, just shy of twenty years old, he had risen to the rank of lieutenant colonel in Wisconsin's Twenty-Fourth Volunteer Infantry Regiment.

After Appomattox, Arthur MacArthur joined the Regular Army and participated in the western campaign against the Apaches and famed warrior Geronimo (birth name Goyahkla). More than two decades later, Arthur rose to prominence once again while commanding U.S. soldiers in the Philippine-American War. MacArthur's celebrated exploits inspired young Douglas's army career, and the father bequeathed to his son not only a "prickly sense of honor" but also an antipathy for civilian leadership and a willingness to exceed orders.[25] Douglas learned a lifelong precept from his father's professional success: "It's the orders you disobey that make you famous."[26]

For much of his career, Douglas sought to equal his father's storied achievements. His quest began at the U.S. Military Academy, where, according to a fellow cadet, young MacArthur "often wondered if he would be as great a man as his father—and thought if hard work would make him so, he had a chance."[27] MacArthur's ambition, discipline, and talent led to quick success, and he proceeded to compile one of the most brilliant records in the history of the institution.

MacArthur's independence and self-assuredness were evident early at West Point. On one occasion, he refused to take a special mathematics examination along with the lowly "goats" of his class.

Cadet MacArthur, insulted by the association with low-achieving cadets, believed that his high marks on previous exams had earned him an exemption. His instructor, however, insisted on the exam because MacArthur had missed taking prior tests due to health problems. Unaffected, the brash cadet informed his superior, "Sir, I will not take the test." MacArthur explained himself to another cadet, "I know it is an order, but it is an unreasonable one."[28] Ultimately, the instructor yielded, perhaps because MacArthur's father was gaining glory in the Philippines as a major general. Douglas MacArthur graduated from the academy in 1903 — first in his class academically and at the top rank of First Captain.

On his father's advice, MacArthur began his Army career with the Corps of Engineers, which in peacetime promoted officers faster than the Infantry. As a junior officer, MacArthur performed well in the Philippines and Japan, and then at Fort Leavenworth, Kansas. He was promoted to captain in 1911 and soon afterward earned a prestigious assignment on the General Staff in Washington, DC.

In 1914, the Army chief of staff sent MacArthur on a special assignment to Veracruz, Mexico, which was occupied by American forces. There he engaged in a covert intelligence operation that resulted in gunfire. MacArthur demonstrated courage under fire and a fellow captain recommended that he be nominated for a Medal of Honor. A nomination was put forward but the medal was not granted. The rejection enraged MacArthur. Feeling disrespected, he crafted a memorandum to the Army chief and the secretary of war. In it, he assailed the "rigid narrow-mindedness" of the decorations board.[29] As a consolation prize, the Army promoted the upstart captain to major.

After the United States declared war on Germany in April 1917, the War Department sought to expand the army to 500,000 soldiers. Still on the General Staff, MacArthur alone advocated for the mobilization and deployment of the National Guard. Other staff officers, including the Army chief, recommended that the Guard protect the homeland while the Regular Army train raw recruits for battle in France. In the end, MacArthur "indiscreetly endorsed" the General Staff's report to

Secretary of War Newton Baker, but could not resist adding a terse note of dissent: "I completely disagreed with its conclusion, but would not attempt to detail my reasons, as I felt no one would give them the slightest attention."[30] As MacArthur later confessed, "It was a discourteous remark," disrespectful of the Army chief. But Secretary Baker and President Woodrow Wilson came to agree with the independent-minded major and they overruled his uniformed superiors.[31] Baker then gave MacArthur an accelerated promotion to colonel and appointed him the chief of staff for the newly organized Forty-Second Infantry Division, which consisted of dozens of National Guard units from across the country. "I could only think of [my father and] the old 24th Wisconsin [Volunteer] Infantry," MacArthur recalled in his memoirs.[32] The ambitious young colonel and his national patchwork "Rainbow Division" landed on French shores in November 1917.

MacArthur first entered into combat in February 1918. Acting on his own accord, he volunteered to join a French reconnaissance patrol. When the patrol was discovered by a German sentry, a firefight ensued. The engagement resulted in the capture of a number of German soldiers, including an officer. The French commander awarded MacArthur the Croix de Guerre medal for his contributions. Although the colonel's "crazy stunt" had not been authorized by his American superior, he still received a Silver Star for valor. It was the first of many.[33]

A few weeks after this initial brush with danger, MacArthur accompanied Iowa's 168th Infantry in a hazardous and successful advance against German defenses. He earned a Distinguished Service Cross for bravery. Over the next several months, the Rainbow Division engaged in frequent combat and suffered some two thousand casualties. Often acting without orders, MacArthur, a staff officer, participated in many of the unit's daring raids.

On the field of battle, MacArthur directed troops but brandished no weapons, save for a riding crop. The doughboys labeled him "the Fighting Dude," a byproduct of his fearlessness and unorthodox attire. In violation of Army dress regulations, MacArthur shunned the standard uniform and helmet. Instead, he outfitted himself in riding breeches, cavalry boots, a grey West Point turtleneck, and a knitted scarf, all topped by a soft-visored barracks cap, which crumpled because he had removed the steel lining. Famed Army aviator Billy Mitchell, a MacArthur family friend from Wisconsin, admired the cap and adopted the look.[34]

In June 1918, MacArthur, at thirty-eight years old, was promoted to brigadier general, making him the youngest general in the U.S. Army.[35] The next month he earned a second Silver Star for leading counterattacks against a German onslaught at Souain, where some 750 Americans were killed. He won two more Silver Stars a few weeks later and was placed in command of the Eighty-Fourth Brigade after its brigadier was dismissed for a lack of daring.

MacArthur's inspiring combat leadership continued during the Meuse-Argonne Offensive of October 1918. In the bloody battle for Cote de Chatillon, he and his men exploited a gap in the German lines and overran the enemy's position. Tank commander George S. Patton described the young general as "the bravest man I ever met."[36] For the Chatillon victory, MacArthur earned a second Distinguished Service Cross and a recommendation that he be promoted to major general. By November, the German army had surrendered and "the war to end all wars" ended.

After a short stint in occupied Germany, MacArthur and his depleted division returned home. Secretary Baker hailed his protégé as the war's "greatest American field commander."[37] In a show of respect, the surviving soldiers of the Forty-Second Division gave their Fighting Dude a gold cigarette case marked with an engraving: "Bravest of the Brave."[38] In less than two years, Douglas MacArthur had transformed himself from an upstart major to a genuine war hero general. These wartime experiences reinforced his independence, self-confidence, *and* inclination to be insubordinate.

In the interwar years, MacArthur's professional achievements were comparatively inconsequential, although he did receive promotion to major general in early 1925. For three years beginning in 1919, he served as superintendent of West Point, where his progressive reform agenda encountered fierce resistance. Thereafter, he twice served in the Philippines, once as the commander of the Military District of Manila and then as the commander of the Philippine Department. His stateside duty stations included Fort McPherson (Atlanta) and Fort McHenry (Baltimore). In the latter posting, MacArthur served as one of thirteen judges in the court-martial of his friend and fellow maverick, Billy Mitchell. MacArthur characterized the judicial appointment as "one of the most distasteful orders I ever received."[39] While Mitchell's court-martial was a low point in MacArthur's career, an unusual highlight came in 1927 when he was named temporary president of the U.S. Olympic Committee. Americans won an unprecedented twenty-four gold medals at the 1928 Netherlands games.

During the early throes of the Great Depression, MacArthur received most welcome news. President Herbert Hoover had chosen him — over six senior major generals — to become Army chief of staff, a position of four-star rank. The president wanted "younger blood."[40] MacArthur was elated; a quarter century prior, his father had been passed over for the pinnacle position. Douglas relished the authority and independence that accompanied the rank: "I had been in military service for thirty-one years, years of receiving orders and following policies I had not promulgated. . . . Now the responsibility of making the decisions and giving the order was mine."[41] MacArthur's seventy-eight-year-old mother prodded him to be bold. She remarked that his late father would be "ashamed" if he showed timidity.[42]

Unfortunately for MacArthur, the nation's economic calamity meant that his tenure as Army chief would be marked by steep declines in army budgets and a deterioration in preparedness. His top priority became preserving a force structure and officer corps capable of leading the army's eventual reconstruction. MacArthur's championing of the National Guard, ROTC (Reserve Officer Training Corps), and West Point met with marginal success. Even historian Michael Schaller, one of the general's harshest critics, concludes that under the bleak circumstances of the Depression, "MacArthur probably did as good a job as any Chief of Staff could have."[43]

The nadir of MacArthur's leadership in Washington, DC, came with Hoover's response to First World War veterans who marched on the capital in 1932. In May, some 20,000 impoverished vets and their families, the so-called Bonus Expeditionary Force (B.E.F.), began erecting makeshift encampments in and around the city. The unemployed veterans demanded early payment of World War I "adjusted compensation certificates," which were not scheduled to be paid until 1945. Hoover believed that the march on Washington by the B.E.F. was a communist provocation encouraged by his Democratic opponents in an election year. MacArthur shared the president's perspective and advocated for a declaration of martial law. The general prepared for a domestic conflict by readying infantry, tanks, armored vehicles, and the Third Cavalry, whose executive officer was none other than Colonel George Patton. No timidity there.

On July 28, two veterans were killed in a scuffle with district police. While refusing to declare martial law, Hoover decided to "drive the veterans out of the city."[44] MacArthur placed Brigadier General Perry L. Miles in charge of the operation, but he could not resist joining the action. Dwight Eisenhower, MacArthur's de facto military secretary, recalled telling him that it was "highly inappropriate" for the chief of staff to participate in such an operation. But the general dismissed Ike's counsel because "incipient revolution was in the air."[45] MacArthur compounded this poor decision by wearing a uniform with row upon row of medals, badges, and ribbons; he also sported pristine riding boots and jangling spurs.[46]

MacArthur was determined to rout the veterans. Patton's saber-drawn cavalry cleared Pennsylvania Avenue, and then the masked and bayonetted infantry tossed tear gas grenades at the protestors. The vets eventually fled across the Eleventh Street Bridge to their families at the Anacostia Flats encampments. The chaotic and violent scene worried Hoover. Secretary of War Patrick Hurley sent two separate instructions ordering MacArthur not to pursue the veterans across the bridge to where hundreds of women and children were camped. Nevertheless, on the night of July 28, cavalry and infantry crossed the river. Amid a haze of tear gas, soldiers chased off the civilians and set ablaze their shanty-town. Hoover could see the fire and smoke from the White House.

The military action against American citizens was widely covered in the press. Many Republicans lauded MacArthur's forceful leadership, but much of the country was appalled by his harsh treatment of downtrodden veterans. For the first time, his reputation suffered a serious blow. Moreover, a question arose as to whether MacArthur had exceeded or disobeyed orders regarding the Anacostia camp. According to General Miles, new instructions had reached MacArthur but "too late to abandon the operation, that the troops were committed."[47] In his memoirs, MacArthur admitted that he had received new orders while on the bridge but falsely claimed that he "halted the command" after completing the crossing.[48] Eisenhower's remembrances were incriminating. He recalled telling MacArthur that an officer had arrived at the scene with new orders, to which the Army chief barked, "I don't want to hear them [the orders] and I don't want to see them [the orders]. Get him [the officer] away."[49]

Feeling triumphant at the time, MacArthur met with a group of eager journalists. He boasted that he had put down a most treacherous "insurrection." He asserted that the protesters "were about to take over in some arbitrary way either the direct control of the Government or else control it by indirect methods."[50] MacArthur praised Hoover's decisiveness and assured reporters that had the president "not acted with the force and vigor, which he did, it would have been a sad day for the country tomorrow."[51] For good measure, the general speculated, "There were, in my opinion, few veteran soldiers in the group that we cleared out today; few indeed."[52]

Hoover was anything but triumphant. He was upset with Mac-Arthur and dressed him down at the White House. The president thought his army chief had been insubordinate, disobeying his instructions not to cross the bridge to the Anacostia camp. "Certain of my directions . . . were not carried out," the president later wrote.[53] Hoover was further incensed by MacArthur's press conference in which he detailed political justifications for the military operation.

Taken aback by the president's anger, MacArthur offered to resign but was unapologetic. The president, who deflected the gesture, knew full well that the Bonus March debacle further diminished his chances for reelection. Decades later, Eisenhower harshly criticized MacArthur's role in the affair: "I told that dumb son-of-a-bitch he had no business going down there. I told him it was no place for the Chief of Staff."[54]

Few were surprised when Franklin Delano Roosevelt (FDR) trounced Hoover in the 1932 presidential election. But the new president astonished many when he retained MacArthur as Army chief of staff. After all, in the wake of the Bonus March crackdown, it was FDR who had characterized the flamboyant, heavy-handed general as "one of the two most dangerous men in America." (The other most dangerous man being Huey P. "the Kingfish" Long Jr., the populist Democratic governor turned senator from Louisiana.) Yet Roosevelt also believed that he could "tame" such tigers to suit his political purposes.[55] Indeed, early in the Democratic administration MacArthur embraced FDR's decision to have the War Department oversee the implementation of the Civilian Conservation Corps (CCC), a cornerstone of the liberal New Deal.

Although he collaborated on the CCC, MacArthur did not hesitate to challenge the president on the Army's dwindling budget. On this topic, the general's self-righteous and impetuous nature led to a sorry display of professional insolence.[56] In March 1933, MacArthur, Secretary of War George Dern, and two other generals met with Roosevelt at the White House. The president's fiscal plan was to slash the Army's budget by half, the National Guard's by a quarter, and the Reserves' and ROTC's by a third. Dern, backed by the generals, calmly argued against the drastic cuts on the basis of safeguarding national security, especially in light of worrisome developments in Italy, Germany, and Japan. But facing the ongoing economic crisis at home, FDR was unreceptive and lashed out at Dern. MacArthur, who described the president as "a scorcher when aroused," felt compelled to interject himself. "I felt it my duty to take up the cudgels," he later wrote. "The country's safety was at stake and I said so bluntly." But MacArthur's emotional outburst was beyond blunt; he was contemptuous. He admonished the president on the danger of defense cuts, exclaiming that when the country loses "the next war and an American boy, lying in the mud with an enemy bayonet through his belly and an enemy foot on his dying throat, spits out his last curse, I want the name to be Roosevelt, not MacArthur!"[57]

Incensed by the general's reproach, Roosevelt snapped, "You must not talk that way to the President!" MacArthur grasped the magnitude of his mistake. Disrespecting the commander in chief was a direct violation of the Articles of War, an offense punishable by dismissal from the service. Sensing that his career might have reached a dramatic end, MacArthur offered his resignation. Roosevelt regained his composure, however, and with a "cool detachment which so reflected his extraordinary self-control," he reassured his army chief. "Don't' be foolish, Douglas," he said, "you and the budget [office] must get together on this." MacArthur was comforted, ashamed, and nauseated. After the meeting, he vomited on the White House steps.[58]

In the end, FDR compromised on the Army's budget and the reductions were not as severe as originally proposed. Nevertheless, these were exceedingly lean years for military appropriations. A turning point did not arrive until the 1936 budget, which, to MacArthur's delight, represented the first marked increase in military spending in more than a decade. While he knew the U.S. Army remained woefully under-resourced and underprepared for major combat, he had saved it from an even worse fate.

MacArthur served as Roosevelt's Army chief of staff for nearly three years. Afterward, rather than retire, he swallowed a mandatory reduction in rank to major general and assumed a new and appealing position as the first military advisor to the Commonwealth of the Philippines. The assignment was equally pleasing to FDR, who was happy to have a potential political rival stationed eight thousand miles from Washington, DC.

MacArthur arrived in Manila in October 1935. In his unique role, he was accountable to Manuel L. Quezon, the newly elected Filipino president, and to General Malin Craig, the new U.S. Army chief of staff.

MacArthur had negotiated from Quezon a generous supplemental salary and a bonus scheme that far exceeded his Army pay. MacArthur also requested and received the unprecedented rank of field marshal of the Philippine army. His ostentatious title was matched by an unconventional and colorful uniform, one that "made him look like the headwaiter at an Army and Navy Club."[59]

MacArthur's field marshal status notwithstanding, there was no substantive Philippine army apart from the respected "Scout" regiments attached to the U.S. Army's garrison. MacArthur's assignment was to build a national defense force, one capable of defending the seven-thousand-island archipelago. The long-term project was a tremendous undertaking and progress came at a glacial pace. Despite MacArthur's inexplicable optimism, which his aide Eisenhower derided as the "purple splendor," the enterprise proved impractical because of the meager financial resources supplied by the Philippine and American governments.[60]

In January 1938, when the prospects for the fledgling Philippine army looked exceedingly dim, MacArthur made a desperate decision. He ordered his American staff to organize a military parade in Manila to show off their accomplishments to date. Eisenhower viewed the parade as a terrible waste of scarce financial resources. Quezon soon learned about MacArthur's plan. Horrified, the Filipino president confronted the general, who proceeded to blame his staff for the idea. This infuriated Eisenhower, who immediately requested a transfer. He told MacArthur in no uncertain terms, "General, all you're saying is that I'm a liar, and I am not a liar. So I'd like to go back to the United States right away."[61]

Although he persuaded Ike to stay on, MacArthur's mission in the Philippines was doomed; his distinguished career was fading. Late in the previous year (1937), the War Department, seeing no purpose in continuing the Philippine army project, had ordered the general to return home. However, rather than assume a new command, MacArthur chose to retire from the army. For the next several years, he soldiered on as a well-heeled foreign military advisor overseeing a "very weak outpost" in the distant Pacific.[62] A military press officer stationed in Manila observed that, MacArthur "cut[s] no more ice in this U.S. Army than a corporal."[63]

But MacArthur's career was resurrected in July 1941, when Roosevelt's third Army chief of staff, George Marshall, recalled him to active duty. Europe had been at war for nearly two years and the Germans had recently invaded Russia. Moreover, Japanese aggression in the Pacific was becoming increasingly intolerable. Appointed to the rank of lieutenant general, MacArthur was made Commanding General, U.S. Armed Forces in the Far East. Marshall promised to send him all the soldiers and aircraft he could spare, hoping that a demonstration of force would deter Japan. If that failed, MacArthur would have to defend the Philippines.

In late November 1941, MacArthur received a secret cable warning of a possible "surprise aggressive movement" against the Philippines or Guam.[64] Two weeks later, in the early morning of December 8 (December 7 in Washington, DC), he learned that Pearl Harbor was under attack. Manila was the next likely target. MacArthur's command had failed to adequately prepare its defenses, which included a reinforced air corps with fifty B-17 Flying Fortress bombers. Later that day, in what was called a second Pearl Harbor, Japanese planes breached Filipino air space and destroyed or debilitated twelve U.S. bombers and thirty-four new P-40E fighters that were on the ground at Clark Field. Due to an abysmal failure of generalship, the Americans and Filipinos lost two-thirds of the American Far East Air Force inventory and suffered more than one hundred casualties.[65]

The United States immediately declared war on Japan. Soon after, the Japanese invaded the Philippines, causing MacArthur and his eighty thousand soldiers to beat a hasty retreat to defensive positions on the Bataan Peninsula and Corregidor Island. During the next several months, the American press portrayed MacArthur not as a failed general on the run but rather as a heroic leader of a brave resistance army. After five months of conflict, U.S. and Filipino forces surrendered. The capitulation of these malnourished and sick men represented the greatest mass surrender in U.S. military history and marked the beginning of the gruesome Bataan Death March.

Roosevelt had foreseen that the Philippines would collapse, so weeks before the surrender he ordered MacArthur's evacuation to Australia. The general departed Corregidor in March 1942, but not before accepting a $500,000 bonus payment from President Quezon (an estimated $9 million in 2022).[66] After reaching safe harbor in Melbourne, MacArthur declared his intention to personally liberate the Philippines, declaring, "I shall return." He was named supreme commander of the Allied Forces Southwest Pacific Area, one of two major theater commands in the Pacific.

The immediate priority was to shield Australia and then reverse the Japanese advance. MacArthur effectively deployed the Australian and American forces under his command. He waged a long, hard-fought campaign to secure New Guinea and other Pacific islands. An early turning point came in November 1942. After relieving the battlefield commander in New Guinea, MacArthur ordered Lieutenant General Robert L. Eichelberger to "take Buna, or not come back alive."[67] Eichelberger succeeded in capturing the northern outpost in January, but Allied casualties were steep. The costly victory foreshadowed MacArthur's bloody slog during the next year.

Throughout, MacArthur railed against Roosevelt's "Europe First/ Germany First" war strategy and complained bitterly about the inadequacy of resources dedicated to the Pacific theater. The general, who was lionized in the national press, had long entertained the idea of becoming president. Should he be swept into office by popular demand in 1944, he could finally prosecute the war on his terms. MacArthur confided to Eichelberger, the "only reason I want to be President . . . is to beat that S.O.B. Roosevelt."[68]

MacArthur did not make his political ambitions public, but he did encourage an "undercover movement" for the presidency. He directed loyal Army officers to communicate directly with sympathetic politicians and Republican donors, including Senator Arthur Vandenberg, Congresswoman Claire Boothe Luce, and businessman and retired brigadier general Robert Wood.[69] In June 1943, Eichelberger wrote in his diary: "My Chief talked of the Republican nomination — I can see he expects to get it. And I sort of think so too."[70]

In spring 1944 with the war still raging and after dozens of MacArthur-for-President clubs had sprouted across the country, the supreme commander of the Southwest Pacific made a bold gamble. He allowed his name to appear on select state ballots for the Republican presidential nomination. MacArthur placed third in Wisconsin and won in a landslide in Illinois, where he attracted 550,000 votes. A national Gallup poll ranked him second among all GOP contenders. By not campaigning overtly or criticizing Roosevelt publicly, MacArthur considered his politicking wholly honorable.

MacArthur's utter disloyalty became public in April 1944, when Republican Congressman Arthur L. Miller released to the press his correspondence with the general. Miller's letters were harshly critical of Roosevelt and the New Deal. The Nebraskan wrote that MacArthur "owe[d] it to civilization and the children yet unborn [to] be our next president." The general needed to "destroy this monstrosity" and the "monarch" who was threatening "our American way of life." In his replies, MacArthur expressed his unreserved agreement with "the complete wisdom and statesmanship of your comments." He also declared that such criticisms of Roosevelt would "arouse the thoughtful consideration of every true patriot" in the country.[71]

The publication of these partisan letters not only undercut MacArthur's chances of winning the Republican nomination, but also instilled in him a fear that he would be relieved of command. He had clearly violated the Articles of War, which prohibit any disrespect of the president. In an act of self-preservation, MacArthur drafted a public statement and gathered reporters at midnight. His purpose was to "entirely repudiate the sinister interpretation that they [his letters] were intended as criticism of any political philosophy or any personages in high office."[72] Remarkably, he did not rule out his willingness to be drafted at the Republican convention. Two weeks later, with the controversy still roiling, MacArthur finally declared that he would not accept the Republican nomination.[73]

All of this political wrangling occurred just months before Mac-Arthur and FDR were to meet in Hawaii. There, they would discuss war plans for the Pacific theater. The two men had not seen each other for nearly a decade. The intervening years had done little to inspire MacArthur's deference to his commander in chief. Unlike Admiral Chester Nimitz, who greeted Roosevelt immediately upon his arrival at Pearl Harbor, MacArthur enjoyed "a leisurely bath" and made the president wait for *him*. Nimitz, who led the Second Allied Command in the Pacific, was shocked by the general's indecorous habit of addressing the president as "Franklin."[74]

On the evening of July 27, 1944, the trio, along with Admirals William Leahy and William "Bull" Halsey, engaged in an hours-long debate over the best strategy for defeating the Japanese. Nimitz championed a campaign that would first take Chinese Formosa (Taiwan) and then Iwo Jima and Okinawa. MacArthur, on the other hand, promoted the reconquest of the Philippines. He argued that Luzon, the largest and northernmost island, provided the integral base from which "to clamp an air and naval blockade on the flow of all supplies from the south to Japan, and thus, by paralyzing her industries, force her to early capitulation."[75]

MacArthur both cautioned and coerced the president. First, in an obvious reference to FDR's broken promises in 1941–1942 to send reinforcements to Bataan and Corregidor, MacArthur said that the Filipinos "look on America as their mother country. Promises must be kept."[76] He then argued against the Nimitz plan on moral grounds, insisting that Roosevelt could never justify the liberation of Chinese Nationalists on Formosa while at the same time abandoning a U.S. protectorate with tens of thousands of Allied prisoners of war (POWs).[77]

After lunch the next day, MacArthur secured a private meeting with FDR. He doubled down on his "Philippines First" strategy and threatened the commander in chief. "Mr. President, the country has forgiven you for what took place on Bataan. You hope to be reelected . . . but the nation will never forgive you," he exclaimed, "if you approve a plan which leaves 17 million Christian American subjects to wither in the Philippines under the conqueror's heel." He insisted, "Politically it will ruin you."[78] Roosevelt's reaction remains unknown, but later he requested extra aspirin from his doctor, saying, "In all my life nobody has ever talked to me the way MacArthur did."[79]

In the end, the president, secretary of war, and Joint Chiefs of Staff (JCS) approved a two-pronged Pacific strategy, one that included a campaign to retake the Philippines. MacArthur orchestrated a successful amphibious landing in October 1944, and after five months of bloodletting on Leyte and Luzon, he rescued Manila. At the Bilibid prison, he told a famished American POW, "I'm a little late, but we finally came."[80] Even Eisenhower, a frequent critic of the "big baby" MacArthur, confessed that the general's magnificent New Guinea and Philippine campaigns "have no equal in History."[81]

Two weeks after MacArthur's return to the Philippines, the American people elected Roosevelt to an unprecedented fourth term. He promptly promoted MacArthur to the rank of general of the Army with a fifth star. But Roosevelt, the longest serving American president, died of a stroke in April 1945. Even on that somber occasion, MacArthur demonstrated a lack of grace. In public he snidely noted how FDR had "greatly changed and matured over the decades."[82] In private he cut deeper by telling an aide, "So, Roosevelt is dead: a man who never tells the truth when a lie would serve him just as well."[83]

After securing Manila and much of the Philippines, MacArthur focused on the planned invasion of Japan. He did not learn about the Manhattan Project until July 1945. The next month atomic bombs obliterated Hiroshima and Nagasaki. The Japanese surrendered, thus concluding the Second World War.

For all his disrespect of FDR, MacArthur despised his new commander in chief, Harry S. Truman. He believed the former vice president to be an unintelligent, uninformed, second-rate politician. The general complained, "And now we're even worse off with that Jew in the White House. Truman. You can tell by his name. Look at his face."[84] That Truman was not Jewish was beside the point.

To be sure, the antagonistic feelings were mutual. Truman considered the flamboyant and egotistical MacArthur "a play actor and a bunco man" who should have been left at Corregidor in 1942 to suffer the same fate as his men, not elevated to high command. Truman derided the general of the army as "Mr. Prima Donna, Brass Hat, Five Star McArthur [sic]." He once railed that MacArthur was "worse than the Cabots and the Lodges. They at least talked with one another before they told God what to do. Mc tells God what to do right off."[85]

Still, Truman, like Roosevelt, made a calculated political decision regarding the maverick general. After the war, he appointed Mac-Arthur as supreme commander for the Allied powers in Japan. In addition to his Far East command, the general would oversee the Japanese occupation. Truman wanted to win the presidency in his own right in 1948; keeping the popular hero general in Asia mitigated the risk of MacArthur barnstorming for the White House.

MacArthur was intellectually and temperamentally suited for many of the herculean tasks that lay before the vanquished Japanese people. Acting as a near-proconsul, he successfully implemented the Pentagon's postwar policies in short order, including Japan's demilitarization and democratization. And while some early economic reforms such as breaking up oligarchic companies failed to rejuvenate the economy, MacArthur facilitated a remarkable political transformation of Japanese society, including the emancipation of women and the guarantee of civil liberties. These were historically significant triumphs.

Nevertheless, MacArthur remained an ambitious and supercilious subordinate. He twice rejected invitations from the president to return home for consultations. While still on active duty in 1947–1948, Mac-Arthur again encouraged "the movement" for the Republican presidential nomination. In October 1947, he wrote to a wealthy Republican supporter, "Should the movement become more expressive . . . and take on the character of popular will, I should be left no alternative but to consider it a mandate which I could not in good conscience ignore."[86] In March 1948, MacArthur issued an audacious *public* statement: "I would be recreant to all my concepts of good citizenship were I to shrink . . . from accepting any public duty to which I might be called by the American people."[87]

But a presidential run was not to be. MacArthur was crestfallen when he failed to win a single primary. He fell further into depression in November when "Give 'em Hell Harry" upset Republican nominee Thomas E. Dewey. Had MacArthur retired then at the age of sixty-four, he would be remembered primarily for his distinguished service in two world wars and for his transformative leadership in postwar Japan. But the general had no intention of retiring and thus his misconduct in the coming Korean War would forever exemplify his deficiencies as a flag officer.

North Korean forces crossed the 38th parallel in June 1950. Seoul fell quickly, MacArthur acted without approval from Washington and provided South Korea with P-51 Mustangs, artillery, and other weaponry. The general did not expect his commander in chief to show much resolve against the communist incursion. MacArthur declared, "If Washington only will not hobble me, I can handle it with one arm tied behind my back."[88] But Truman surprised the general. He retroactively authorized MacArthur's weapons shipment to South Korea and, to prevent "a general Asiatic war," he ordered the Seventh Fleet to position itself between the Chinese Nationalists on Formosa (Taiwan) and the Communist Chinese mainland.[89] Truman also rallied the United Nations Security Council. On June 30, MacArthur requested the deployment of U.S. ground forces. Truman approved two divisions and three tank battalions. The deployment allowed the general to establish a defensive perimeter around the southern port of Pusan.

On July 8, as American airpower slowed the North Korean advance, MacArthur was officially appointed commander in chief of the United Nations Command. In a message of appreciation, the general pledged his "complete personal loyalty" and his "absolute devotion" to Truman and the U.N. mission.[90] As mentioned, although the White House and the Pentagon approved of MacArthur's elevation, others thought it unwise. Eisenhower was wary of MacArthur's unpredictability, autonomous decision making, and political machinations.[91]

The new U.N. commander's capriciousness soon became apparent. On July 31, MacArthur flew to Formosa (Taiwan) to confer with Generalissimo Chiang Kai-shek, who had offered Truman 33,000 troops in the fight against communist North Korea. Truman had declined the offer, fearing that Communist China would respond by entering the war. After a two-day conference, Chiang announced to the press that "an agreement" had been reached with General MacArthur and that the "foundation for a joint defense of Formosa and for Sino-American military cooperation" had been laid.[92] MacArthur, who was upset with Truman for declining Chiang's troops offer, planned to send the generalissimo three squadrons of F-80 jet fighters.

Truman and his advisors were furious. MacArthur's freewheeling attempt to make policy might provoke Communist China. Washington had not approved a new defense pact with Chiang nor the deployment of U.S. aircraft to Formosa. Defense Secretary Louis Johnson sent MacArthur a pointed message reminding him that only the president makes foreign policy and that "the most vital national interests requires that no action of ours precipitate general war or give excuse to others to do so."[93] Truman dispatched presidential advisor Averell Harriman to Tokyo to settle the matter with the general. In his report back to Washington, Harriman conveyed MacArthur's pledge, "As a soldier, I will obey any orders I receive from the President." But Harriman remained uneasy because he "did not feel that we came to full agreement . . . on Formosa and with the Generalissimo." Moreover, the general "has a strange idea that we should back anybody who will fight communism."[94]

Despite Truman's affirmed policy on China, MacArthur was adamant that the United States should ally itself with the Chinese Nationalists. In a brazen act of insubordination, he took his case public. On August 10, 1950, he released a press statement complaining that "persons 10,000 miles away" were advocating "a policy of defeatism and appeasement in the Pacific."[95] Shortly thereafter, he composed a similar message to be read at the annual meeting of the Veterans of Foreign Wars (VFW). Before the convention, he shared his written remarks with the sympathetic editor of *U.S. News & World Report*, but not with his superiors in Washington. The magazine quickly published MacArthur's statement: "Nothing could be more fallacious than the threadbare argument by those who advocate appeasement and defeatism in the Pacific that if we defend Formosa we alienate continental Asia." It concluded with a warning that Asian nations will "respect and follow aggressive, resolute and dynamic leadership [but] turn on a leadership characterized by timidity or vacillation."[96]

MacArthur had publicly rebuked his commander in chief's "appeasement" policy in China. Chairman of the Joint Chiefs of Staff Omar Bradley characterized the shocking statement as representing "the height of arrogance."[97] Secretary of State Dean Acheson described MacArthur's "effrontery" as being born out of "incredible arrogance and vanity."[98] Truman was furious and contemplated firing the general. The situation in Korea, however, remained too precarious. Instead, the president demanded that MacArthur withdraw the VFW message before it was read aloud. "[Its] various features with respect to Formosa," Truman communicated, "are in conflict with the policy of the United States."[99]

Relieving MacArthur, while constitutionally and militarily justifiable, would have been a fraught political decision. The general remained immensely popular with the American people and Congressional Republicans. Truman's favorability rating, on the other hand, had plummeted to 35 percent. More important, the U.N. commander was on the threshold of a daring counteroffensive in Korea.

Drawing on his experience with the amphibious campaigns in New Guinea and the Philippines, MacArthur prepared to land a large army behind enemy lines at Inchon, a seaport near Seoul. From there, he planned to cut off North Korean supply lines, block their retreat from the south, and call forth from Pusan the U.S. Eighth Army. "I will, on the rising tide of the fifteenth of September," he proclaimed dramatically, "land at Inchon and between the hammer of this landing and anvil of the Eighth Army, I will crush and destroy the armies of North Korea."[100]

The Joint Chiefs resisted the risky operation, but MacArthur's powers of persuasion ultimately brought them around. With Truman's approval, the general launched a spectacular invasion against an unsuspecting enemy. The operation reversed the early course of the war. By the end of September, in just two weeks, MacArthur's forces had liberated Seoul and routed much of the North Korean army, whose remnants fled back north across the 38th parallel. Truman pronounced the campaign a "brilliant maneuver."[101] Newly appointed Secretary of Defense George Marshall characterized it as a perfect operation, and Eisenhower wrote to MacArthur, "You have again given us a brilliant example of professional leadership."[102] Even Omar Bradley, who had been skeptical, admitted that the sudden triumph was "mind-boggling" and that MacArthur deserved to be "canonized as a 'military genius.'"[103]

The Inchon victory had the effect of further inflating MacArthur's massive ego. It also chastened his Pentagon superiors, who grew even more reluctant to oppose his judgments in the field. In hindsight, Army Chief of Staff Lawton Collins confessed that the general's public stature became so "overpowering, that the Chiefs hesitated thereafter to question later plans and decisions of the general, which should have been challenged."[104] With considerable despair, Secretary Acheson concluded, "there's no stopping MacArthur now."[105] Indeed, when the Joint Chiefs ordered MacArthur not to preside over a *political* ceremony reinstating the South Korean government in Seoul, he did so anyway and without repercussion.

MacArthur's success in the south led to a new, expansive, and perhaps impossible U.N. mission. He was ordered to go north across the 38th parallel to destroy the North Korean forces. This was to be accomplished without drawing the Soviets or Chinese into the war. His orders read, "Under no circumstances will your forces cross the Manchurian or USSR borders of Korea and, as a matter of policy, no non-Korean ground forces will be used in the northeast provinces bordering the Soviet Union or in the area along the Manchurian border."[106] The U.N.'s ultimate goals were Korean unification and democratization, but not at the cost of starting World War III.

In this battlefield context and with mid-term Congressional elections approaching, Truman flew seven thousand miles to Wake Island in the Pacific to meet with his winning field commander. Secretary Acheson warned Truman that the "difficult" general already possessed "the attributes of a foreign sovereign" and "it did not seem wise to recognize him as one."[107] The president did not need the reminder. "I have a whale of a job before me," Truman wrote to a confidant. "Have to talk to God's right-hand man."[108] The politically motivated trip, which included a planeload of reporters, was reminiscent of the Roosevelt-MacArthur-Nimitz conference in Hawaii six years prior.

As with the Roosevelt conclave, MacArthur hated being used as a political prop — especially for a Democrat, and most especially for Truman. At Wake Island, the general made his displeasure obvious with discourteous slights. Rather than stand waiting for Truman at the bottom of the president's plane ramp, MacArthur sat in a jeep parked some twenty-five yards away. Only when the president started down the ramp did the general approach. In front of the press corps, MacArthur was determined to be on a literal equal footing with his superior. Furthermore, instead of properly saluting his commander in chief, the general, with his shirt unbuttoned, grabbed Truman and shook his hand.

On October 15, MacArthur and the president met privately for an informal conversation, thereafter joining a larger group that included Army Secretary Frank Pace, JCS Chairman Omar Bradley, Assistant Secretary of State Dean Rusk, and others. Neither the president nor MacArthur wanted the meeting to be drawn out. Truman and the others peppered the general with questions, and his answers were most often brief.

Smoking a briar pipe, MacArthur provided updates on various topics, including his war plans for North Korea. He predicted that major combat in Korea would be concluded soon, "by Thanksgiving." When Truman and Rusk reiterated the need to avoid Soviet and Chinese involvement, MacArthur explained that he would deploy South Korean troops, not U.S. or other U.N. forces, to the border provinces near China and the Soviet Union. The South Koreans, he said, would serve as "the buffer." When Truman asked what the chances of Soviet or Chinese intervention were, MacArthur said assuredly, "Very little. . . . We are no longer fearful of their intervention." If China did intervene, "only 50,000 to 60,000 could be gotten across the Yalu River," and those forces would suffer "the greatest slaughter."[109]

This main meeting at Wake Island was completed in just ninety minutes. Thereafter, standing before the press, Truman awarded MacArthur another Distinguished Service Medal, the fifth of his career. The president invited him to join a prescheduled lunch, but the general declined, preferring to return to his command headquarters in Tokyo. JCS Chairman Bradley, whom MacArthur rather casually called "Omar," viewed the lunch declination as disrespectful. Regardless, Truman was satisfied with the trip and happily boarded his plane for Washington.[110] He would never see MacArthur again.

For more than a week after the meeting at Wake, U.N. forces routed the North Korean army and moved rapidly toward the Yalu River bordering China. Despite his commitment to only utilize South Korean "buffer" troops in the border regions, MacArthur ordered *all* troops to "drive forward with all speed and full utilization of their forces."[111] The Joint Chiefs were astonished and grew increasingly anxious about fast-advancing U.S. forces. They informed MacArthur, "Your action is a matter of concern here."[112] Nevertheless, they and Truman permitted the hero of Inchon to command the field.

On October 25, nearly two hundred thousand Chinese Communist forces launched a devastating two-week assault on U.N. troops. MacArthur, who had always considered himself a master of the "Asian mind," was caught completely off guard. Truman's fear of a wider war had just been realized. If not managed adroitly, China's intervention might mark the beginning of another world war.

MacArthur's leadership was reactionary. Without contacting Washington, he ordered his air commander, Lieutenant General George Stratemeyer, to begin a massive new bombing campaign. He told him to destroy the bridges linking North Korea and China and to lay waste to every "factory, city, and village" between the U.N. line and the Yalu.[113] The extremity of the orders worried Stratemeyer. Recognizing the danger of U.S. bombers accidentally straying into Chinese territory, he telephoned the Pentagon. Upon hearing the news, the Joint Chiefs overrode MacArthur's order and forbade any bombing within five miles of the Chinese border.

MacArthur rebelled. He insisted that the Joint Chiefs inform the president of his views because "your instructions may result in a calamity of major proportion for which I cannot accept the responsibility without his [Truman's] personal and direct understanding of the situation." MacArthur claimed that the Chinese offensive threatened "the ultimate destruction of the forces under my command" and warned that the Pentagon's bombing restrictions would "be paid for dearly in American and other United Nations blood."[114] Fearing that MacArthur might be correct, the president, the secretary of defense, and the Joint Chiefs capitulated. They approved an utterly devastating air offensive trusting and hoping that their battlefield commander knew best. It was a grave mistake.

"We committed the worst possible error," Bradley later reflected. "[W]e sensed something was badly wrong. MacArthur had exceeded his authority in ordering the bombing of the Sinuiju bridges and had first tried to do it without Washington clearance. It was an indication that he was going off willy-nilly on his own in defiance of established policy. . . . Right then — that night — the JCS should have taken firmest control of the Korean War and dealt with MacArthur bluntly."[115]

MacArthur's bombing offensive lasted for several weeks. The Chinese withdrew as suddenly as they had appeared and the U.N. commander sensed that final victory was near. On November 24, MacArthur seized the initiative by ordering a major ground attack. Within earshot of reporters, he said, "I hope to keep my promise to the G.I.s to have them home by Christmas."[116] MacArthur's boldness and optimism were misplaced. The Chinese responded to his offensive with some three hundred thousand troops. Their counterattack, made in combination with sixty-four thousand North Korean soldiers, sent U.N. forces reeling to the south.

Embarrassed by the debacle, MacArthur defended himself publicly and hyperbolically, shifting the blame to his superiors, whose supposed battlefield restrictions, he said, were "an enormous handicap, without precedent in military history." Rather than relieve MacArthur over the battlefield setback and his public outburst, Truman issued a gag order requiring all military officers to have their public statements preapproved by the Defense Department.[117]

At the Pentagon, Army Lieutenant General Matthew Ridgway was astounded that the Joint Chiefs did not exercise tighter control over MacArthur, who he thought was acting perilously like George Custer at the Battle of the Little Big Horn. On December 3, after meeting with the secretaries of State and Defense, the Joint Chiefs, and others, Ridgway asked his old friend Hoyt Vandenberg, the Air Force chief, "Why don't the Joint Chiefs send orders to MacArthur and *tell* him what to do?" Vandenberg shook his head and said, "What good would that do? He wouldn't obey the orders. What can we do?" Flabbergasted, Ridgway became emotional and pushed back: "You can relieve any commander who won't obey orders, can't you?!" Vandenberg simply walked away looking "puzzled and amazed."[118]

Fearing further humiliation on the battlefield, MacArthur demanded from Washington a new policy direction: a much-expanded war with China. He proposed bombing the mainland, blockading its coastline, and deploying Chinese Nationalist troops on Formosa to both North Korea and China. Moreover, he demanded "ground reinforcements of the greatest magnitude."[119] Without this drastic change in strategy MacArthur predicted the defeat of U.N. forces and a dramatic evacuation to Japan, an American Dunkirk. President Truman, Defense Secretary Marshall, and the Joint Chiefs rejected the radical proposal, to which MacArthur gave an ominous reply: "Under the extraordinary limitations and conditions imposed upon the command in Korea . . . its military position is untenable."[120] Bradley agreed with Secretary Acheson and viewed MacArthur's obstinacy as "incurably recalcitrant" and "basically disloyal." Bradley also found himself incredulous that "Washington was thus being placed in a position of *convincing* a subordinate commander that our orders should be carried out." MacArthur, he believed, "was skating on very thin ice indeed."[121]

Despite MacArthur's dire warnings, conditions in Korea shifted measurably and positively in late December when Ridgway left Washington to assume command of the Eighth Army. MacArthur gave him free rein to attack, and soon the Chinese counteroffensive stalled. By the end of February 1951, the Eighth Army and other U.N. forces were actually pushing Chinese forces back north toward the 38th parallel. Truman and his advisors agreed that "General Ridgway alone was responsible for this dramatic change." His exceedingly effective leadership provided them with an opportunity for peacemaking.[122]

Truman, Marshall, and the JCS decided that the best policy was to pursue an armistice with China and North Korea rather than reinvade the north. MacArthur was informed of their decision on March 20. Four days later, the general deliberately scuttled the president's plans for a peace initiative. In a preemptive *public* pronouncement, MacArthur lambasted China's "complete inability to accomplish by force of arms its conquest of Korea" and warned that a U.N. expansion of the war to the Chinese mainland "would doom Red China to the risk of imminent military collapse." He then offered to personally negotiate a peace by "confer[ring] in the field with the Commander-in-Chief of the enemy forces."[123]

This brazen act brought Truman to his breaking point. Secretary Acheson described the general's statement as "defiance of the Chiefs of Staff, sabotage of an operation of which he had been informed, and insubordination of the grossest sort to his Commander in Chief." Deputy Defense Secretary Robert A. Lovett declared that MacArthur "must be removed and removed at once."[124] Truman agreed. "I could no longer tolerate his insubordination," he wrote, because the general "was in open defiance of my orders as President and Commander-in-Chief."[125]

Still, MacArthur's removal had to be managed thoughtfully. The general was a persistent political threat and the presidential primaries were only one year away. Because of the war, Truman's approval rating had sunk to a dismal 26 percent. In firing the general, Truman wanted the explicit support of Marshall and the Joint Chiefs of Staff. In early April, as Marshall and the senior military leadership deliberated on the matter, more evidence of MacArthur's insubordination surfaced in the House of Representatives.

On April 5, House Minority Leader Joseph W. Martin Jr., a Massachusetts Republican, read into the congressional record a March 20 communication from MacArthur. In the letter, the general expressed support for a speech by the congressman who had called for opening "a second front" in Korea. Martin wanted the intervention of Chinese Nationalist troops, exclaiming, "If we are not in Korea to win, then this administration should be indicted for the murder of American boys." MacArthur concurred. "As you pointed out," the general wrote, "we must win. There is no substitute for victory."[126]

While Truman had already decided that "our Big General in the Far East must be recalled," Martin's "political bomb" cemented the decision for Marshall and the Joint Chiefs.[127] Marshall was "revolted" by the revelations. And while the Pentagon leadership sought to avoid "God forbid! — a Billy Mitchell-type court-martial," they agreed with the president that MacArthur must be relieved.[128] The JCS articulated four justifications: "He was not in sympathy with the policy to limit the war to Korea; that he had disobeyed the 'gag order' and had undercut the president's peace initiative; that it was difficult to coordinate plans with him as they never knew if he would obey orders; and that failure to relieve him would damage civilian control."[129]

On April 11, 1951, Truman relieved that "son of a bitch" of all his military commands.[130] The president's official statement explained that the general, "one of our greatest commanders," was relieved due to his inability to give "his wholehearted support" to the expressed policies of the United States and the United Nations. While Truman acknowledged that a "full and vigorous debate on matters of national policy is a vital element in the constitutional system of our free democracy," he insisted that "military commanders must be governed by the policies and directives issued to them."[131]

MacArthur's five-decade career was coming to a swift close. Far from feeling humiliated, the general remained defiant. He assumed the role of a patriotic martyr *and* his unbecoming conduct continued.

Upon returning to the United States, MacArthur was welcomed by massive crowds. On April 18, half a million people cheered his arrival in San Francisco. Another five hundred thousand Americans greeted him in Washington, DC, where he addressed a joint session of Congress.

Thereafter, millions of New Yorkers hailed the legendary general with a nineteen-mile tickertape parade. Perhaps the Republican presidential nomination was finally within his grasp.

In his famous "old soldiers never die" speech to Congress, MacArthur was careful not to criticize Truman by name and claimed to not be "partisan." Yet standing at the lectern, he proceeded to condemn the administration for refusing his repeated calls for "a drastic revision of strategic planning" — in short, a much-expanded war against Communist China. "War's very object is victory," he bellowed, "not prolonged indecision. In war there can be no substitute for victory." MacArthur also claimed, falsely, that the Joint Chiefs "fully shared" his views, but others in Washington had "forbade victory," preferring instead to "appease Red China."[132] His thirty-seven-minute address was interrupted by applause no fewer than fifty times.

In May and June 1951, the Senate Armed Services Committee held hearings on the Korean War, including the issue of MacArthur's dismissal. The general testified first. As before, he was dishonest, claiming that his strategy for an enlarged war with China had been supported by the Pentagon. MacArthur asserted that his proposals were "practically identical" to and "in complete accord with the military recommendations of the Joint Chiefs of Staff."[133] He argued therefore that he had not been insubordinate to his *military* superiors. With all seriousness, he professed, "No more subordinate soldier has ever worn the American uniform." Moreover, MacArthur avowed that he could not have been insubordinate to *civilian* leadership because in his mind once a war begins "the military takes over, you must trust the military" and "there should be no *non-professional* interference in the handling of troops in a campaign."[134]

When George Marshall and the Joint Chiefs testified at the hearings, they corrected the record. The defense secretary made clear that he and the Joint Chiefs fully supported Truman's decisions and policies. "From the beginning of the Korean conflict down to the present moment," Marshall said, "there has been no disagreement between the President, the Secretary of Defense, and the Joint Chiefs of Staff that I am aware of." The secretary also criticized MacArthur's proposal to widen the war with China. To implement the proposal would have risked "an all-out war with the Soviet Union," he declared, and "expose Western Europe to attack by . . . millions of Soviet troops."[135]

As for MacArthur's dismissal, Marshall said it was absolutely necessary because the general had gone public with his harsh criticisms of Truman's policies. What brought about "the necessity for General MacArthur's removal," he testified, "is the wholly unprecedented situation of a local theater commander publicly expressing his displeasure at and his disagreement with the foreign and military policies of the United States. It became apparent that General MacArthur had grown so far out of sympathy with the established policies of the United States that there was grave doubt as to whether he could any longer be permitted to exercise the authority in making decisions that normal command functions would assign to a theater commander. In this situation, there was no other recourse but to relieve him."[136]

Led by Omar Bradley, the Joint Chiefs also provided damning testimony against MacArthur. As for MacArthur's advocacy of an enlarged war with China, the chairman said that the JCS agreed that this misguided strategy would "involve us in the wrong war, at the wrong place, at the wrong time, and with the wrong enemy." As for MacArthur's forced removal, Bradley asserted that it was essential because the general's "actions were continuing to jeopardize the civilian control over military authorities."[137]

Before the hearings were concluded, MacArthur embarked on a nationwide lecture tour underwritten by wealthy Republicans, including Texas oilmen. The general, still robed in uniform, harangued the Truman administration on both domestic and foreign policies. In Seattle, he disparaged the president's "diplomatic blunders abroad and reckless spendthrift aims at home." In Jackson, Mississippi, before twenty-five thousand people, he charged the Democratic Party with leading the country "toward a Communist state with as dreadful certainty as though the leaders of the Kremlin were charting the course."[138] Speaking before the Massachusetts legislature in July 1951, MacArthur made the most astonishing statement of his tour. He disavowed the military's obligation to obey the lawful orders of civilian superiors. "I find in existence," he said, "a new and heretofore unknown and dangerous concept that members of our Armed Forces owe primary allegiance and loyalty to those who temporarily exercise the authority of the executive branch of the Government. . . . No proposition could be more dangerous."[139]

Despite his personal popularity, MacArthur's contemptuous rhetoric had limited appeal among voters. By the time of the Republican National Convention in 1952, the best that he could hope for was a vice presidential nomination. But even that was not to be. Dwight Eisenhower, a more temperate and less controversial war hero general, was nominated for president. He chose Senator Richard Nixon from California as his running mate. The MacArthur era was over.

★　★　★　★

Douglas MacArthur's career is a study in extremes. As one subordinate commander attested, "The best and worst things you hear about him are both true."[140] There is no doubt that MacArthur possessed superb soldiering skills. His battlefield leadership and heroics during the First World War were truly extraordinary. His postwar reforms of West Point and his efforts to halt the bloodletting of the Army budget were commendable if not always successful. MacArthur's command in the Pacific during World War II, especially his successful New Guinea campaign and the retaking of the Philippines, instilled in the American people hope and confidence in ultimate victory over Japan. After the war, MacArthur oversaw a remarkable reconstruction of Japanese society, including its demilitarization and democratization. His brilliant amphibious landing at Inchon reversed the course of the Korean War, forcing an unprepared enemy to retreat north of the 38th parallel.

Equally striking were MacArthur's ethical failings, which were often tolerated by his superiors. In his heavy-handed treatment of the beleaguered B.E.F., he willfully disregarded orders to halt the assault. His rout of the veterans caused a national outcry. President Hoover's anger led MacArthur to offer his resignation. Less than a year later, during a military budget meeting, the general was so utterly disrespectful of President Roosevelt that he again offered to resign. Even in the Philippines, MacArthur proved willing to lie to President Quezon and betray his own staff in the process.

MacArthur's unseemly behavior continued during World War II and the occupation of Japan. At the Hawaii conference, the egomaniac general made "Franklin" wait for *him* and, worse, he had the audacity to threaten the president with political ruin if he did not order the recapturing of the Philippines. Indeed, as a theater commander, MacArthur conducted a surreptitious presidential campaign in 1944: he plotted to oust his own commander in chief! Truman received similar abuse. MacArthur rebuffed the president's invitations to return to Washington to consult on the Japanese occupation. In 1948, the general issued a *public* statement declaring that it would be his "public duty" to accept the Republican nomination for president.

Then there was the Korean War. MacArthur publicly criticized Truman's policies on Formosa (Taiwan) and China. He assailed the administration's supposedly timid, vacillating, and appeasing leadership. At the Wake Island summit, the general continued his personal affronts toward the president. After the meeting, MacArthur ignored his superiors' instructions not to deploy U.S. forces near the Chinese-North Korean border. When he later received permission to do so, his U.N. troops were overrun by Chinese forces. Embarrassed, the general openly and dishonestly blamed Truman for restricting his army's freedom of movement. Thereafter, MacArthur became even more brazen. In March 1951, he intentionally scuttled the president's plans for a peace initiative with North Korea and China. This extreme insubordination led to his relief from command. As biographer Geoffrey Perret writes, "Like the tragic heroes of the theater, he [MacArthur] would finally be brought down not by his enemies but by an immutable fault line that ran through the bedrock of his character."[141]

MacArthur's pattern of disobedience and disrespect challenged the crucial precept of civilian authority over the military. In firing the vainglorious general, Truman safeguarded a primary tenet of the

American constitution. In retirement, the former president reflected on this core leadership principle: "If there is one basic element in our Constitution, it is civilian control of the military. Policies are to be made by the elected political officials, not by generals or admirals. Yet time and again General MacArthur had shown that he was unwilling to accept the policies of the administration. By his repeated public statements he was not only confusing our allies as to the true course of our policies but, in fact, was also setting his policy against the President's." Truman concluded, "If I allowed him to defy the civil authorities in this manner, I myself would be violating my oath to uphold and defend the Constitution."[142]

Truman's Republican successor agreed that MacArthur's firing had been a constitutional necessity. Eisenhower wrote that most generals honor the "clean-cut line" between civilian authority and the uniformed military, but "if General MacArthur ever recognized the existence of that line, he usually chose to ignore it."[143] Ike warned: "When the day comes that American soldiers can in war successfully defy the entire civil government then the American system will have come to an end."[144]

It is crucial not to conflate flagrant disobedience with appropriate dissent. All leaders, including presidents, benefit from independent-minded subordinates who have the moral courage to voice reasoned concerns and objections. In fact, over the years, MacArthur's divergent views had received fair hearings from his military and civilian superiors, and he often won them over to his side. These debates were evidence of loyal dissent and as such merit commendation. But MacArthur's central failing as a flag officer was his inclination to bypass the chain of command and take his disagreements public. This type of dissent was disloyal and intolerable. If MacArthur believed his superiors were making shockingly dangerous decisions — ones he could not in execute in good conscience — he should have retired or resigned in protest.

MacArthur's gross insubordination and controversial relief cast a long shadow over the upper ranks of the U.S. military. As described earlier in the book's introduction, not until a quarter century later did another flag officer dare to publicly challenge the policy of a sitting president. In May 1977, President Jimmy Carter fired John Singlaub as the Army chief of staff in South Korea (of all places) after the major general told the *Washington Post* that the administration's policy of gradually withdrawing U.S. ground troops from the peninsula would lead to another war in Asia. A year later, Carter had little choice but to force Singlaub into retirement after the insolent general again publicly criticized the president's national security policies.

Such brazen contempt did not surface again until 1993. In May, Major General Harold Campbell, a highly decorated Vietnam War pilot, then serving as the deputy chief of staff for plans and programs of the Air Force Material Command, gave an address to American military personnel and their spouses at Soesterberg Air Base in the Netherlands. In his speech, Campbell disparaged President Bill Clinton as a "draft-dodging," "skirt-chasing," "gay loving," "dope smoking" commander in chief.[145] Word of the major general's astonishing rebuke reached Washington in short order and the Air Force immediately began to investigate. On June 19, only four weeks after the speech, the Air Force announced that Campbell had indeed committed a military crime by "uttering disparaging remarks about the President."[146] The major general escaped a court-martial but was issued an official letter of reprimand, docked $7,000, and forced to retire. General Merrill McPeak, the Air Force chief of staff, felt compelled to hold a press conference to express his support of Campbell's punishment and to underscore the constitutional subservience of the U.S. military to civilian leadership. "This is not a trivial matter," he contended. "There should be no doubt about the lesson learned. The chain of command has to be almost pollution-free."[147]

American wars in Iraq and Afghanistan led to the forced retirement of several outspoken flag officers as well. In January 2004, Lieutenant General John Riggs, leader of the Army's Objective Force Task Force, became "a persona non grata" after granting an interview to the *Baltimore Sun* in which he warned that the Army was being stretched dangerously thin and needed to be substantially expanded.[148] Riggs's public warning contradicted Defense Secretary Donald Rumsfeld's position on the appropriate army force size. The newspaper interview infuriated Rumsfeld's senior deputy, Paul Wolfowitz, who proceeded to chastise General George Casey Jr., the Army vice chief of staff. Casey, in turn, telephoned Riggs and ordered him to "stay in [his] lane." He also inquired about the three-star's plans for retirement. Riggs recognized the "handwriting on the wall" and submitted his retirement papers in March. The next month, the day before retiring, Casey informed Riggs that he was being demoted one star. The official justification was not his public contradiction of Rumsfeld, but rather an entirely unrelated "minor, minor" administrative admonishment he had received a year earlier. However, it was common knowledge that Riggs had been demoted for his public criticism of Rumsfeld's policy.[149]

Four years later in March 2008, Defense Secretary Robert Gates announced the resignation of Admiral William "Fox" Fallon, who was overseeing U.S. military operations in the Middle East. The CENTCOM commander's recall and early retirement stemmed from a series of public statements he made on television and in print that suggested he opposed the Bush administration's hardline approach to Iran and China, and also its slow withdrawal from Iraq. Fallon's candid comments created the "perception he had a different foreign policy than the president."[150] The straw that broke the back of the admiral's career was a lengthy, fawning profile in *Esquire* magazine, which noted that President Bush "is not accustomed to a subordinate who speaks his mind as freely as Fallon." The article depicted Fallon — "a man of strategic brilliance" — as a wise, courageous, and patient diplomat-warrior who served as *the* bulwark against the rash, hawkish, and ill-considered policies of the Bush administration.[151]

Army General Stanley McChrystal failed to learn from Fallon's experience. In spring 2010, as commander of U.S. and NATO Coalition Forces in Afghanistan, McChrystal allowed a freelance journalist, Michael Hastings, to embed himself with the general's staff officers. Reflecting their commander, the self-named "Team America" staff took pride in their "can-do attitude" and "disdain for authority." Indeed, the previous autumn, President Barack Obama was compelled to chastise McChrystal. He had publicly dismissed Vice President Joe Biden's recommendation for a new, less troop-heavy counterterrorism strategy in

Afghanistan.[152] "When it came to observing the formalities of civilian control," writes Andrew Bacevich, "the general turned out to be either spectacularly arrogant or stunningly obtuse."[153]

In June 2010, *Rolling Stone* magazine published Hastings's eight-page feature article on his embedded experience. It was released to the press on June 21 and made available online the next day. The wide-ranging profile documented McChrystal and his staff's open disdain for senior officials in the Obama administration. The general and his coterie did not conceal their lack of respect for Biden nor their annoyance with Obama's special representative in Afghanistan, Richard Holbrooke, who was characterized as a "wounded animal" and "dangerous." Hastings also detailed McChrystal's antagonistic relationship with Karl Eikenberry, a retired Army three-star and the U.S. ambassador in Kabul. National Security Advisor James Jones, a retired Marine four-star, was derided by staff officers as a "clown" who remained "stuck in 1985." Moreover, there was scant respect for Obama himself. According to his aides, McChrystal had determined early on that the president was uncomfortable with and intimidated by flag officers. Furthermore, he experienced Obama as being more interested in a photo-op with a field commander than a serious discussion on warfighting in Afghanistan.[154]

The *Rolling Stone* essay — titled "The Runaway General" — ignited a political firestorm in Washington. When McChrystal learned of its damning contents, he called Biden to apologize personally and issued a public apology that read in part: "I have lived by the principles of personal honor and professional integrity. What is reflected in this article falls far short of that standard."[155] The general also apologized to Defense Secretary Robert Gates, who shouted through the telephone: "What the fuck were you thinking?"[156] The vice president, in turn, called Obama, who summoned McChrystal to the White House. Obama had come to respect the general's "rebel spirit" and while he thought McChrystal and his staff had shown "atrocious judgment," the president's first impulse was to let the general off with a strongly-worded reprimand.[157] But while McChrystal was in transit from Kabul to Washington, Obama's thinking shifted to the larger issue of civil-military relations. The commander in chief concluded that "accountability and discipline" in the military were vital to sustaining a representative democracy wherein civilian authorities must have unfettered control over the armed forces.[158] The chain of command must be pollution free. On June 23, in the Oval Office, Obama unhappily accepted McChrystal's offer to resign.

One year later, in November 2011, the Army fired Major General Peter Fuller, deputy commander of the NATO Training Mission in Afghanistan. His offense was not criticism of the Obama administration, but rather a public disparagement of the Afghan government, particularly President Hamid Karzai. Fuller retired the next year.[159] Three years hence, Army Lieutenant General Michael Flynn, a McChrystal protégé, was relieved as director of the Defense Intelligence Agency (DIA) and forced into retirement. Flynn's leadership was erratic, autocratic, and divisive, and his uncompromising attempts to radically restructure the large agency were resisted by subordinates and superiors, alike. In the end, the hard-charging three-star was terminated for "insubordination" and the "erosion of morale" at DIA.[160]

Despite Flynn's poor leadership and his reputation as s "loose cannon," President Donald Trump appointed him as his first national security advisor in January 2017.[161] The retired general, however, was fired after only twenty-four days in office, the shortest tenure in the history of the office. He had lied to Vice President Mike Pence, to White House officials, and to the FBI about illicit telephone conversations with the Russian ambassador, Sergey Kislyak. In December 2017, Flynn pleaded guilty to criminal charges that he "willfully and knowingly" made "false, fictitious, and fraudulent statements" to federal agents regarding his communications with the Russian diplomat. Trump pardoned Flynn before a judge could sentence him.[162] Nevertheless, Flynn's troubles with the law continued. In January 2021, the Pentagon inspector general determined that Flynn had violated the Emoluments Clause of Constitution by receiving money from the Russian government without the required authorization from U.S. Army and the State Department. The Defense Department announced that it would withhold the general's retirement pay until it had recouped the funds.[163]

CHAPTER THREE

MORAL COWARDICE

Harold K. "Johnny" Johnson

MORAL COWARDICE—a fear-based failure
to act responsibly in defense of moral values
and ethical principles

When ordered into harm's way, soldiers, sailors, airmen, and marines are expected to be physically courageous. Cowardly conduct before the enemy may be the definitive breach of the Uniform Code of Military Justice. But comparatively little attention is given to the parallel concepts of moral courage and moral failure. In his seminal work *The Mystery of Courage*, William Ian Miller describes moral courage as the "*lonely* courage" and "the capacity to overcome the fear of shame and humiliation in order to admit one's mistakes, to confess a wrong, to reject evil conformity, to denounce injustice, and also to defy immoral or imprudent orders."[1] In times of war and peace, admirals and generals are far more likely to confront situations begging for acts of moral, not physical courage. Illegal orders must be disobeyed, but what is a senior officer to do when working for a deceitful leader or when given immoral and dangerously irresponsible orders — especially in a time of war? Dissent internally? Dissent publicly? Retire quietly? Resign in protest?

There are many inhibitors to morally courageous behavior. Perhaps none is more powerful than the inclination for self-preservation and the fear of consequences that will ensue for doing the right thing. Loyalty or misplaced loyalty is also an impediment to ethical action. Generally speaking, loyalty to one's organization, superiors, colleagues, and subordinates is a virtuous trait, but ethical dangers arise when strict fealty is prioritized over other core values such as honesty, compassion, fairness, and independent judgment. To safeguard one's conscience, moral autonomy, and the general welfare, William Felice writes, "Loyalty must be balanced with other equally important behavioral norms and values."[2] And yet another all-too-familiar obstacle to moral courage is rationalization. Rather than take personal responsibility and act courageously, people seek psychological solace in justifying their unethical inaction with false yet seemingly logical rationales.

Many U.S. flag officers have been justly criticized for lacking moral courage during the run-up to the Iraq War. Despite having serious misgivings about the necessity for war and also about the adequacy of post-invasion planning, they did not assert themselves to contest the George W. Bush administration's optimistic assumptions and sanguine forecasts of a quick victory and rapid drawdown. Moreover, Defense Secretary Donald Rumsfeld cast aside the Powell Doctrine of projecting overwhelming military power against an enemy.[3] Instead he deployed a relatively small invasion force equal to less than half of the Allied commitment in the Gulf War. General Charles Wald, who served as commander of Central Command (CENTCOM) Air Forces and deputy commander of European Command, recalled that "The civilians at OSD [Office of the Secretary of Defense] believed strongly that it was going to be a cakewalk; we had proven it in Afghanistan, it was going to be simple and it wasn't going to cost very much. You didn't need allies or the U.N. for this."[4]

The military's apprehension about insufficient planning and preparation for the Iraq War was well known to the Joint Chiefs of Staff (JCS) and to senior civilian leaders within the Bush administration. General Richard "Dick" Myers, the chairman of the JCS, acknowledged that "few military professionals were comfortable" with the administration's predictions of an easy Iraqi stabilization after Saddam Hussein's ouster.[5] But neither Myers nor his deputy, Marine General Peter Pace, or CENTCOM commander Tommy Franks forcefully expressed the military's trepidations to President George W. Bush or the National Security Council. Behind the scenes, some flag officers derided Chairman Myers's timidity and pliability, labeling him "limp Dick."[6]

Several factors account for the ultra-deference and moral failing of so many American generals and admirals. Contextually, the Bush administration was justifying the invasion of Iraq as part of the larger post-9/11 war against terrorism. Therefore, speaking out against it ran the risk of appearing naïve, insubordinate, or worse, unpatriotic. Among other contributing factors were Rumsfeld's near-tyrannical leadership of the Defense Department and his insistence that his office, not the JCS, control the Iraq War planning effort. Marine Corps commandant James Jones admitted that Rumsfeld had effectively "emasculated" the Joint Chiefs.[7] The predominance of conformity and sycophancy also inhibited the moral courage of those generals closest to Rumsfeld — Myers, Pace, and Franks.[8] "Secretary Rumsfeld wanted yes-men around him," observed Army Major General John Batiste, "and that's what he got."[9]

One leadership lesson from Iraq is clear: senior military officers possess an inalienable responsibility, especially in times of war, to speak out against imprudent warfighting policies that unnecessarily risk the lives of fellow citizens. "If we hold that soldiers and leaders remain moral agents on the battlefield," Lieutenant General James Dubik argues, "we must also hold their seniors equally responsible for decisions and actions taken in higher headquarters or in the capitol."[10] To remain silent or to be easily cowed at a time when people's survival is at stake is cowardly, and the rationalization that one should quietly follow orders is morally bankrupt. To avoid unethical complicity and salvage one's integrity, moral courage is best demonstrated by speaking out, and in extreme circumstances retiring or resigning in protest. Such acts of principled dissent do not challenge the authority of one's superiors, but rather contests the *prudence* of their thinking and directives.

Two revered American generals provide support for the notion of principled resignation. After Abraham Lincoln's assassination, President Andrew Johnson wanted to file treason charges against Robert E. Lee and other ex-Confederate general officers. Commanding General Ulysses S. Grant objected vehemently and threatened to resign in protest. Fully aware of Grant's influence and popularity, Johnson dropped the drastic idea. Moreover, General George C. Marshall, long the Army's paragon of virtue, publicly acknowledged that principled resignation may be appropriate for a senior military officer. Testifying before a Senate committee in 1951, he was asked by Senator Styles Bridges of New Hampshire what he would have done if he and President Franklin D. Roosevelt had "an absolute difference of opinion, where you thought the best interests of the country were not being served by the President or his administration?" Marshall replied matter-of-factly, "I probably would have resigned as [Army] chief of staff."[11] Indeed, in January 1942 Marshall had informed Roosevelt that he would resign if a proposed civilian-led Munitions Assignment Board, which was to allocate armaments and munitions, was not placed under the authority of the joint American-British military command. Although it meant breaking a personal promise to Winston Churchill, a "shaken" Roosevelt sided with Marshall, whom he regarded "as far too important to the war effort and the presidency to risk his resignation."[12]

★ ★ ★ ★

By the summer of 1964, twenty years after World War II and a decade after the Korean War armistice, the United States had intensified its commitment to defend South Vietnam from a communist insurgency backed by the government of North Vietnam. When the American ambassador in Saigon, Republican Henry Cabot Lodge Jr., announced his intention to resign and campaign for president, President Lyndon B. Johnson (LBJ) approved a series of changes in U.S. Army leadership that reflected his determination to "save" South Vietnam. He selected World War II hero General Maxwell D. Taylor, the chairman of the Joint Chiefs of Staff, to become the new ambassador and elevated Lieutenant General William C. Westmoreland from deputy commander to commander of U.S. Military Assistance Command, Vietnam. The president also appointed General Earle G. "Bus" Wheeler as his new JCS chairman and selected Lieutenant General Harold K. "Johnny" Johnson as Wheeler's replacement as the Army's chief of staff. Westmoreland and Johnson were promoted to four-star rank.

Of all the personnel shifts, Johnny Johnson's elevation was the most surprising. At fifty-two, he was the youngest Army chief since Douglas MacArthur and the second youngest ever. Even among *three-star* generals Johnson lacked seniority. He had never commanded a division, much less a corps. But as commandant of the Command and General Staff College (CGSC) from 1960 to 1963, Johnson's dedication, intellect, and temperament had impressed both Defense Secretary Robert S. McNamara and Army Secretary Cyrus Vance. Moreover, Johnson had won the confidence of General Wheeler while serving as his deputy chief of staff for military operations at the Pentagon. Although his promotion was unexpected, Johnson was well known within army ranks. During the Second World War he had endured the Bataan Death March, survived three harrowing years as a Japanese prisoner of war (POW), and was a decorated battalion and regimental commander in the Korean War. "From those experiences," Secretary McNamara later reflected, "he [Johnson] had developed an iron will, extraordinary toughness of mind and spirit, and a fierce integrity."[13]

Johnson's ethical code (grounded in Christianity) was central to his compassionate leadership and unimpeachable reputation. Perhaps he prized honesty and intellectual independence above all. He detested bureaucratic politics and sycophantic yes-men. "I have always believed," a friend wrote to Johnson, "that you were too intellectually honest and not enough a politician to become Chief of Staff."[14] As a leader of soldiers, Johnson sought to emulate the principled George Marshall, and bristled at megalomaniacs like MacArthur. As the CGSC commandant, he frequently cited Bible verses and questioned his student officers with scriptural references: "Am I my brother's keeper?" Yes, he instructed them, because "of all the things we have in the Army, our most treasured possession is the integrity of the Army as a whole, and each of these instances that we let somebody skip by is an erosion of this integrity."[15]

Throughout his tenure as Army chief of staff from 1964 to 1968, a time when the Vietnam War was Americanized, Johnson believed that the U.S. policy of *gradual* escalation against communist forces in the south and the north was inadequate for winning the war and preserving South Vietnam's independence. From the beginning, he favored a large, comprehensive, fast-tempo campaign as the best means for achieving victory and shortening the war's duration. In early 1965, General Johnson recommended and fully expected President Johnson to declare a national emergency, mobilize the reserves, and galvanize the country to crush the communist insurgency in South Vietnam and curtail North Vietnam's involvement. The new Army chief stated publicly that he subscribed to the warfighting philosophy of Confederate General Nathan Bedford Forrest: "Get there first with the most."[16]

President Johnson, however, refused to mobilize the country for war. Instead, he pursued a policy of incremental escalation. This decision caused Johnny Johnson tremendous personal and professional distress. He doubted that a limited war could succeed in Vietnam, and believed that a prolonged war would cause unnecessary casualties and degrade the Army that he loved. Again and again, more than any other member of the Joint Chiefs of Staff, Johnson contemplated resigning in protest.[17] How could he in good conscience support a deleterious war strategy? Instead of resigning, however, Johnson remained at his post, believing that he could change the administration's Vietnam policy. This was a rationalization that he came to regret. The decision not to resign pained the general until his death in 1983.

In retirement, Johnny Johnson expressed deep remorse to confidants and military groups. One of his stories became legendary. He told

Army Brigadier General Albion Knight, a Vietnam War veteran and or-dained priest in the United Episcopal Church: "I remember the day I was ready to go over to the Oval Office and give my four stars to the Presi-dent and tell him, 'You have refused to tell the country they cannot fight a war without mobilization; you have required me to send men into battle with little hope of their ultimate victory; and you have forced us in the military to violate almost every one of the principles of war in Viet-nam. Therefore I resign and will hold a press conference after I walk out of your door.' [Instead] I made the typical mistake of believing I could do more for the country and Army if I stayed in than if I got out. I am now going to my grave with that lapse in moral courage on my back."[18]

★ ★ ★ ★

Harold Keith Johnson was born on February 22, 1912, in the sparsely populated town of Bowesmont, North Dakota. His grandparents had emigrated from Canada to the Dakota Territory decades before. In 1930, Johnson and his parents relocated to Grafton, North Dakota, where his father managed a lumberyard. Religion played an important role in family life. Young Johnson learned to memorize and recite Bible verses and joined a small Methodist congregation. He was also influ-enced by the mission and comradery of the Boy Scouts. The Scout Handbook and the Bible became his lifelong companions. Johnny Johnson inherited a pioneer work ethic and spent his summers at the farms of extended family members. During his final year in high school, he worked three jobs and developed a reputation for parsimony. John-son graduated from Grafton High School in 1929 and secured an ap-pointment to West Point. He said that the military academy in New York "seemed like an exciting thing to do for a boy from North Dakota who had never been very far from home."[19]

On the eve of the Great Depression, Johnson and 469 other young men entered the U.S. Military Academy. From the outset, he struggled academically. More than a hundred of his peers fell out. But Johnson persevered. Known as an avid reader, he kept busy with various extracurricular activities including work as the sports editor for the *Howitzer* yearbook and the equipment manager for the varsity football team. Although Johnson abandoned the Methodist church because it "preach[ed] pacifism," he remained stoutly religious throughout his life.[20] Johnny was well-liked by classmates and the plebes placed under his command. One cadet later remembered Johnson's "gentle, fatherly voice" and his encouragement "to follow the paths of righteousness."[21]

Johnson graduated from West Point in the lower half of his class, ranking 232 out of 347. By then the Depression had upended the U.S. economy. As a consequence, the Army's budget was slashed and President Herbert Hoover and other Republicans were routed in the 1932 elections. The keynote speaker at Johnson's 1933 commencement ceremony was none other than General Douglas MacArthur, who had graduated from West Point thirty years earlier. The Army chief painted a somber and even cataclysmic picture for the academy's newest graduates. He warned, "The security of the United States is imperiled by politics, pacifists and retrenchment in national defense program."[22] Eight years later, when the Japanese attacked Pearl Harbor, Johnson was in the Philippines serving under MacArthur's command.

After West Point, Johnson joined the infantry and excelled in the Depression-era army. His first four years were spent with the Third Infantry at Fort Snelling, Minnesota. He held various positions including a stint with the Civilian Conservation Corps and, despite his low rank and lack of seniority, he commanded both a rifle company and a machine-gun unit. Johnson was viewed by superiors and subordinates as an unusually competent and committed soldier and a natural leader of men.[23] He was promoted to first lieutenant in 1936 and the following year was transferred to Fort Benning, Georgia, to attend the Infantry School. He completed the one-year course as superior graduate and for the remainder of the decade served with the Twenty-Eighth Infantry in northern New York.

In the summer of 1940, Johnson received orders to report to the Fifty-Seventh Infantry, Fort William McKinley, in the Philippines. His unit, known as the Philippine Scouts, consisted largely of Filipino soldiers led by American officers. Johnson took command of Company L, Third Battalion. Despite Japanese aggression in Asia and the ongoing war in Europe, now-Captain Johnson discovered "a pretty lax atmosphere" in the Philippines, where horseback riding and polo matches were routine. In spring 1941, Johnson was elevated to Regimental S-3, making him responsible for planning, training, and operations. His contemporaries were impressed by his performance and praised his "quick and agile mind, his keen wit, his positiveness, his impatience with inefficiency and sloth, his knowledge of tactics and techniques, and his ability to stimulate those who worked for him and those he worked for."[24]

With tensions escalating between the U.S. and Japan in 1941, President Franklin D. Roosevelt called General Douglas MacArthur back into active duty and appointed him commander of all forces in the Philippines. Five months later, Japanese aircraft bombed the archipelago just hours after devastating Pearl Harbor. When Japanese ground troops invaded from the north they easily overwhelmed Filipino defenses. Johnny Johnson's regiment was ordered south to the Bataan Peninsula where he was promoted to major. Under siege, MacArthur ordered all of his forces to withdraw to Bataan for a final stand.

The Japanese attacked the Fifty-Seventh Infantry on January 10, 1942. After several days of intense fighting the enemy pivoted to the west. U.S.-Filipino forces withdrew farther south nearing the coast. On February 2, Regimental Commander Colonel Edmund Lily and his operations officer, Johnny Johnson, led a three-battalion offensive near the southwest coastline. After three weeks of combat, which became known as the Battle of the Points, the Japanese retreated to ships at sea and waited for reinforcements. The U.S. victory rang hollow as Lily and Johnson could not count on reinforcements of their own. Moreover, their troops had been living on half-rations for a month and suffered from a paucity of medical supplies. There had been a failure of military leadership at the highest levels in the Philippines and it upset Johnson to see his troops in such dire straits.

On April 9, having just been promoted to lieutenant colonel, Johnson learned that friendly forces had begun to surrender to the Japanese.

Two days later, he and his men were ordered to submit in their sick, starving, and outnumbered state. As Johnson later quipped, he spent the rest of the war as "a guest of the Japanese."[25] That inhospitable saga began with the infamous Bataan Death March. Approximately twelve thousand Americans and sixty thousand Filipinos who were already suffering from malnourishment and disease were force marched sixty-five miles north to Camp O'Donnell. Thousands died along the way; many were summarily executed.

Johnson was imprisoned for three and a half years and suffered throughout. By 1944, the lieutenant colonel had been reduced to ninety-two pounds. Known as a person of immense integrity, Johnson held crucial positions while imprisoned, including that of commissary officer overseeing the acquisition and distribution of food. "They needed the most honest man in the camp," a fellow prisoner later recalled. "There was only one choice — Johnny Johnson."[26] The war ended in August 1945 and Johnson and other surviving prisoners were rescued by the Seventh Infantry Division.

Johnson's compassion for soldiers and his religious faith sustained him as a POW. "Sometimes the reservoir of energy and determination was close to empty," he said. "[But] God was close and very real in those hours."[27] Despite his own weakened condition, Johnson had routinely sacrificed for fellow soldiers. At one point, he brokered a trade with a Japanese guard, exchanging his prized West Point ring for water and a can of salmon. Johnson gave the meager provisions to others. "It was a small amount of food and a small amount of water," an American soldier remembered, "but it was distributed with perfect integrity on his part."[28] Years later, another former POW wrote to Johnson: "You exercised what I considered to be great leadership under the most abysmal of adverse conditions, and again at Fukuoka where you saved my life by forcing me to eat when I had neither the will nor the energy to do so."[29]

Once stateside, Johnson recuperated rather quickly and, like many other POWs, was gradually integrated back into the army. To brush up on their training, repatriated officers enrolled in military schools at five different posts starting with the Armor School at Fort Knox,

Kentucky. Beginning in September 1946, Johnson attended the Command and General Staff College at Fort Leavenworth, Kansas. After graduating in the top five percent of his class, he joined the faculty at Leavenworth's School of Combined Arms, where he remained for two years. In February 1950, eager to rejoin the regular troops, he assumed command of the Third Battalion, Seventh Infantry, at Fort Devens, Massachusetts. The Korean War broke out four months later.

In August 1950, Johnson's battalion was ordered to South Korea as part of the Eighth Cavalry assigned to the First Cavalry Division. The battalion immediately joined Allied forces defending the Pusan Perimeter and within days was engaged in heavy combat against the North Korean army. Johnson led his troops by example, personally directing mortar fire from a forward observation post. For his heroic leadership he was awarded the Distinguished Service Cross. Two weeks later, while MacArthur was executing a brilliant amphibious landing at Inchon, Johnson's unit pressed north with great effectiveness. By mid-October the Allies were near Pyongyang. According to an Army citation, Johnson had "fearlessly led his troops in a spearhead drive through 123 miles of enemy territory."[30] The tremendous gains, however, had come with a bloody cost. Johnson's Third Battalion, consisting of 703 men, suffered 400 casualties. He wrote to his mother, "This is a terribly grim game."[31]

Lauded by his superior as a "great combat leader who should progress to general officer grade," Johnson was elevated to regimental commander of the Fifth Cavalry.[32] At this juncture in the war, Chinese Communist forces launched a massive surprise attack across the Yalu River and trapped Johnson's former battalion. The Fifth Cavalry attempted a rescue, but failed, suffering 350 casualties in the process. Demoralized, Allied forces withdrew to the south. Johnson noted, "About all there is to do is hang on and pray each day."[33]

In December 1950, Johnson, about to be promoted to colonel, took command of the decimated Eighth Cavalry Regiment. The unit was replenished with poorly trained reservist troops. One of those soldiers recalled Johnson's inspiring leadership, describing him as an officer of remarkable "courage, morality, and fortitude."[34] In January 1951, the Eighth joined General Matthew Ridgway's winter offensive, but Johnson's participation was short-lived as he became the assistant chief of staff for operations (G-3) of I Corps. He served in that capacity until October, when he shipped home.

Johnson spent the next four years on the East Coast, first at Fort Monroe, Virginia, then at the National War College in Washington, DC, and finally on the Army staff at the Pentagon. He excelled at each station and was promoted to brigadier general in January 1956. Elmer Almquist, a peer at the time who retired as a lieutenant general, remarked, "Of all the senior officers I've known, he [Johnson] represented about the highest level of integrity. He addressed everything at the *highest* ethical plane."[35]

As a one-star, Johnson was made assistant division commander of the Eighth Infantry Division, which was relocated from Colorado to West Germany. A visible leader among his troops, he led with compassion and preached the importance of moral integrity. He remained abroad for four years, becoming the chief of staff for the Seventh Army and for NATO's Central Army Group. The much-respected, workaholic Johnson was promoted to major general in the autumn of 1959.

The following year, Johnson returned to Fort Leavenworth as the commandant of the Army's Command and General Staff College. According to biographer Lewis Sorley, "it was the ideal assignment. By this time, he was known throughout the Army as a man of iron will, deep religious faith, unlimited appetite for work, and exemplary character."[36] At Leavenworth, Johnson's constant refrain to student officers was: "Challenge the assertion."[37] He wanted them to develop intellectual independence even to the point of questioning superior officers. In 1962, while serving as commandant, Johnson completed a study on the use of tactical nuclear weapons for Defense Secretary Robert McNamara and became friends with Army Secretary Cyrus Vance.

In late February 1963, Johnson rejoined the Army staff at the Pentagon, serving as the assistant deputy chief of staff for military operations. On July 1, he was promoted to lieutenant general and was made the deputy chief, working directly for Army Chief of Staff General

Earle Wheeler. As was Johnson's habit, he emphasized to his staff the indispensability of professional integrity and unbridled candor: "We must be honest."[38] Johnson continued his call for independent critical thinking and demonstrations of moral courage. "There may be occasions when you will be given a directed solution to a given problem," he said. But the general cautioned his subordinates not to accept direction without critical assessment. "I want you to talk back," Johnson exclaimed. "Yes-men are no good. If I needed yes-men around, I wouldn't need you at all. When the going begins to get tough, you talk up."[39]

Johnson's return to Washington, DC, coincided with McNamara's oversight of major Defense Department reforms that emphasized cost-cutting efficiencies and the consolidation of decision-making power under civilian bureaucrats — the so-called Whiz Kids. One army staff officer described the prevailing Pentagon atmosphere as a "confrontation between the military professionals and McNamara's cold-blooded analysts."[40] Johnson, who worked twelve-hour days, six days a week, and half-days on Sunday, detested the arrogance of the civilian leadership and began to wonder if he ought to retire after thirty years of dedicated service. He confided to a friend, "There is little latitude any more for the [military] Services with a tremendous [civilian] centralization in Defense. One wonders sometimes whether he should remain with the resistance group or hang up his spurs and observe from the sidelines."[41]

As General Wheeler's chief of operations, Johnson regularly attended the thrice-a-week meetings of the Joint Chiefs of Staff chaired by General Maxwell Taylor. At that time, Secretary McNamara joined the flag officers during their Monday sessions. In the summer and fall of 1963 the war in Vietnam, which by then included more than twenty thousand American combat advisors, became a heightened priority at the Pentagon and the White House. In September, President John F. Kennedy (JFK) publicly reiterated America's determination to support South Vietnam's government (led by Ngo Dinh Diem) in its efforts to defeat a communist insurgency. "That is why some 25,000 Americans have traveled 10,000 miles," the president said at a press conference, "to participate in the struggle. What helps to win the war, we support;

what interferes with the war effort, we oppose. . . . We are not there to see a war lost."[42] In private, Kennedy worried that Diem, who repressed his political and religious opponents and rebuffed American advice, was insufficiently committed to the war and might cut ties to the U.S. and seek a negotiated settlement with the communists. As a consequence of these doubts and with the Kennedy administration's tacit approval, Diem was overthrown and his regime replaced on November 1. Three weeks later, JFK was assassinated in Dallas, Texas.

By allowing a bloody coup in Saigon, the United States had assumed responsibility for the war in Vietnam at a time when it might have justifiably extricated itself from that troubled country, which lacked a credible and effective democratic government. Instead, as historian George Herring writes, JFK "bequeathed" to his successor, Lyndon B. Johnson, a crisis "eminently more dangerous" than the problem he had inherited from Dwight Eisenhower in 1961.[43] And while the political and military situation in South Vietnam was deteriorating, the new American president could ill-afford a communist victory in Southeast Asia when he was only twelve months away from his next election. The U.S. objective in South Vietnam remained the same: establish a stable and secure noncommunist government in Saigon as a bulwark against communism. Moreover, General Johnson wrote in his Joint Chiefs meeting notes that JCS Chairman Taylor and the Johnson administration viewed the war as "a laboratory" for fighting communist insurgencies around the world.[44] "If we can have victory in Vietnam," President Johnson wrote to Ambassador Henry Cabot Lodge in Saigon, "there will be praise enough for all of us."[45] By the end of 1963, two hundred Americans had been killed in Vietnam.

In January 1964, the Joint Chiefs drafted a memorandum for Secretary McNamara advocating a "more aggressive program" to achieve victory in the war in South Vietnam.[46] The senior military advisors wanted to bomb Communist North Vietnam, place mines near North Vietnamese harbors, and launch intelligence flights over Cambodia and Laos. According to General Johnson, Air Force Chief of Staff Curtis LeMay frequently remarked that the United States should simply bomb North Vietnam "back into the Stone Age."[47] The Chiefs also warned McNamara that combat troops, not just advisors, would ultimately be needed to win the war. With the U.S. presidential election campaign on the horizon, neither McNamara nor LBJ wanted to undertake an overtly belligerent escalation. Instead, Johnson approved covert military operations against North Vietnam and adopted a policy of "graduated response," which General Johnson described as "a wait until the enemy reacted before you added your next element of force."[48]

In the spring of 1964, the military situation in South Vietnam worsened. General Johnson made his first of ten visits in late March. There he received overly optimistic assessments from the command staff. He did not sense impending doom, but did come away with a more measured understanding of the complex problems facing South Vietnamese society. He was convinced that a comprehensive strategy was necessary to save Vietnam, that "the application of military force alone will not solve all the problems of a country facing subversive insurgency."[49]

Fearing a pre-presidential election military defeat in South Vietnam, LBJ ordered a change to U.S. policy. "We're not getting it done," he complained to McNamara. "We're losing. So we need something new."[50] The president insisted that the Joint Chiefs "start stepping that thing up and do some winning."[51] The service chiefs, excluding Chairman Taylor, preferred "a sudden sharp blow" upon the South Vietnamese insurgents and against ninety-one targets in North Vietnam.[52] Realizing that such an all-out attack was not politically feasible, the service chiefs, again excluding Taylor, recommended to McNamara three phases of increasingly intense "graduated *overt* pressures" on the ground and from the air.[53] Neither McNamara, LBJ, nor Taylor — who often suppressed the service chiefs' most aggressive advice — wanted an explicit policy shift. Instead, they chose a milder program of applying graduated pressure, which, writes historian and Army Lieutenant General H. R. McMaster, was designed to avoid an all-out war and yet still "compel the North Vietnamese to the negotiating table and exact from them a favorable diplomatic settlement."[54]

In the early summer of 1964, LBJ approved personnel changes in army leadership that significantly impacted the war in Vietnam. General Taylor resigned to become the new American ambassador in Saigon; General Wheeler replaced him as chairman of the Joint Chiefs of Staff; Lieutenant General Johnson was promoted to four stars and elevated to Army chief of staff; and William Westmoreland, also newly promoted to general, took command of U.S. Military Assistance Command, Vietnam (MACV). At the time, Taylor was the president's most trusted military advisor, and he arrived in Vietnam with extraordinary authority. Wheeler's selection as chairman stemmed from his reputation as a politically savvy and skilled administrator and a loyal "team player."[55] Westmoreland had been serving as the deputy commander in Vietnam. Johnny Johnson's selection to be Army chief was the single biggest surprise of the general officer shuffle. Although widely respected, the survivor of the Bataan Death March had leaped over dozens of senior ranking generals. Nevertheless, he had long ago impressed McNamara and was trusted by Wheeler.

Johnson's confirmation hearing before the Senate Armed Services Committee transpired without contention and lasted a mere eighteen minutes. Known as an officer of unshakeable integrity, the general informed the committee that as an American soldier he considered it a solemn duty to defend the nation and to answer all congressional inquiries fully and truthfully. "I hold the view that my first obligation," he testified, "is to the defense of my country, that when I appear before this committee or any committee of the Congress, it is incumbent upon me to be completely honest . . . and to respond to any question that I am competent to answer."[56] He recounted that he had already delivered that same message to Secretary McNamara. Johnson's nomination was confirmed by the full Senate on July 2, 1964.

General Johnson's promotion and swearing-in ceremony were performed the next day. He said a few prayers, asking for "strength, courage, and wisdom," and quoted from the Scout Oath: "On my honor I will do my best to do my duty to God and my country." Johnson also announced that he planned to be a supportive and demanding chief. "I intend to be the Army's staunchest defender," he said, "and its severest critic. I intend to be both nourisher and pruner somewhere along the line."[57] For Johnson, ethical conduct and strict accountability were pillars of professional military leadership. At Fort Leavenworth, he had lectured the student officers: "When you don't have integrity in the Army you don't have an Army."[58] As Army chief of staff, Johnson set the example immediately. He relieved two major generals, one for having an inappropriate relationship with a subordinate's wife and another for making misleading if not blatantly false statements during an Inspector General investigation.[59]

Johnson held himself to the highest standards of conduct. Honesty was his calling card. As chief, Johnson routinely encouraged his staff to be independent-minded and to have the moral courage to challenge assumptions and assertions. Moreover, he urged them to solve "whatever problems confront you from the point of view of what is good for the country."[60] When Johnson found himself in conflict with McNamara and Army Secretary Stephen Ailes over the size of a proposed army salary increase, he decided to air their differences in his testimony before the House Armed Services Committee. "The heck with it," he concluded. "I am the spokesman for a million and a half men and I can't let them down now."[61] Johnson, alone among the Joint Chiefs, managed to convince the committee that a material pay raise was merited. After hearing Johnson's testimony, Congressman Mendel Rivers of South Carolina told the general that he had delivered "the truest from-the-heart statement in defense of the American soldier I've ever heard."[62]

Johnson knew full well that disagreeing with one's superiors, especially in public, presented a professional hazard. In fact, he had been sufficiently worried before his testimony that he called upon retired five-star Army General Omar Bradley for friendly counsel. Johnson explained "that if I could not support the policies of the [Johnson] administration I really had no part — I had no place — being in that administration." He asked Bradley if he should "request relief and resign or retire?" The former chairman of the JCS advised Johnson not to resign or retire, but to "fight your battle and you continue to fight it to the best of your ability inside." Bradley discounted the benefits of resigning in protest, saying that Johnson would be portrayed as "a disgruntled general" and "you'll be a headline for one day, and then you'll be forgotten." Johnson adopted Bradley's viewpoint, but remained determined to "speak up on the pay issue" because it was in the "[best] interests of the people in the Army."[63]

Nor did General Johnson shrink from expressing candid views in debates with colleagues on the Joint Chiefs of Staff. Early on as Army chief, Johnson locked horns with the legendary General Curtis LeMay, the Air Force chief since 1961. LeMay opposed while Johnson supported Westmoreland's request for more *Army* planes and helicopters in South Vietnam. LeMay saw the request as an encroachment on the Air Force's turf. According to Johnson's operations deputy, the dispute reached "bitter proportions" with LeMay challenging the Army chief to an air duel. "Johnson, you fly one of those damned Huey's," LeMay roared, "and I'll fly an F-105 and we'll see who survives. I'll shoot you down and scatter your peashooter all over the goddam ground." Johnson, with his customary calm, stated a willingness to learn how to fly and take-up the challenge, but for now recommended that they deliberate on Westmoreland's request.[64] Johnson won the debate. Westmoreland, however, wanted more than aviation assets. On July 21 the president also agreed to send 4,200 advisors and support troops to South Vietnam.

A monumental turning point in the Vietnam War came two weeks later on August 2 when the Joint Chiefs learned that North Vietnamese torpedo boats had attacked the U.S. destroyer *Maddox* while on patrol in the Gulf of Tonkin. The boats were easily repelled. With the U.S. presidential election only three months away, LBJ withheld an overt counterattack, but authorized more destroyer patrols and clandestine operations. The attack on the *Maddox* had been a response to previous U.S. covert assaults against North Vietnam. Two days later when informed — mistakenly — that a second attack on U.S. ships occurred, the president appeared on national television to announce retaliatory airstrikes against North Vietnam. As before, LBJ promised the

American people that "we still seek no wider war," but portrayed the counterstrikes as necessary to discourage further "open aggression on the high seas."[65] General Johnson and the Joint Chiefs supported the American reprisal, which was comprised of sixty-four Navy sorties. In fact, the flag officers had recommended an even more robust projection of power. On August 7, Congress passed the Gulf of Tonkin Resolution, which authorized the president to take all necessary measures to repel aggression and maintain peace and security in Southeast Asia.[66]

The Gulf of Tonkin incident further strengthened LBJ's presidential election campaign. His opponent, Republican Senator Barry Goldwater, had advocated a more aggressive prosecution of the war. Unaware that the United States had been conducting covert attacks on North Vietnam for six months, Congress and the public were largely content with Johnson's seemingly measured and responsive approach. After the Tonkin crisis, approval of the president's policy soared from 43 to 71 percent.[67]

As for the Joint Chiefs, they were divided on the optimal approach to saving South Vietnam from a communist takeover. LeMay favored a devastating air campaign against North Vietnam. General Johnson believed that massive bombing would have only marginal impact on North Vietnam's support of the indigenous insurgency and feared that it might actually increase Hanoi's resolve to keep fighting. Moreover, an intensified air campaign might spur the intervention of Chinese forces, which had happened during the Korean War. The Army chief thought that the primary levers to victory in South Vietnam were stabilizing the government, providing aid and security to the civilian population, and forcibly quelling the insurgency.

On September 8, the Joint Chiefs provided McNamara with a working paper outlining various "unconnected proposals" for progressing the fight in Vietnam.[68] Wanting to appear united, the Joint Chiefs obscured their sharp differences of opinion. The paper, for example, included General Johnson's advocacy for a pacification program in the south but not his apprehensions regarding a major air campaign against North Vietnam. For the first but not the last time,

Johnson violated his own ethical mantra that military officers had an obligation to report to their superiors with total honesty.

Two months before the election, LBJ continued to oppose overt escalations in the war, but he assured Chairman Wheeler that he would take action after November.[69] This private assurance came despite the president's public messaging that an escalation of the war, as called for by Goldwater, would "result in our committing a good many American boys to fighting a war that I think ought to be fought by the boys of Asia to help protect their own land."[70] He was being deceitful and his Republican opponent knew it. On September 29 at a campaign rally in Cincinnati, Ohio, Goldwater asked pointedly, "Why does he [LBJ] put off facing the question of what to do about Vietnam? Does he hope that he can wait until after the election to confront the American public with the fact of total defeat or total war in Asia?"[71]

By later October and with the military and political situation in South Vietnam deteriorating, General Johnson agreed to support a new JCS recommendation to destroy the "will and capability" of North Vietnam and to expand operations against the insurgency in the south.[72] The Chiefs did not provide a comprehensive strategy to the president and defense secretary, but rather a long list of incremental military actions beginning with improved pacification efforts and ending with a massive air and land campaign. McNamara and LBJ, however, adhered to their more limited military tack. General Johnson grew increasingly cynical about the policy of graduated escalation and for the next six months lobbied his colleagues to advise the president to "either get into this thing and win, or not go in at all."[73]

After campaigning for months as the temperate peace candidate, LBJ trounced Goldwater in the November election. For the time being, he continued his "kinda war" policy of supporting the South Vietnamese government against the insurgency and gradually applying military pressure against the North Vietnamese.[74] The president boasted that he was "going up old Ho Chi Minh's leg an inch at time." Speaking for the Joint Chiefs, General LeMay howled, "you can't get a little bit pregnant."[75] By the end of 1964, 416 Americans had died in Vietnam.

February 1965 brought major turning points in the escalation and Americanization of the Vietnam War. On the seventh of that month, Viet Cong guerrillas attacked a U.S. helicopter base in Pleiku. Eight Americans were killed, 126 wounded, and ten aircraft destroyed. Without public announcement or consultation with Congress, LBJ responded forcefully by approving not just a retaliatory strike but a sustained bombing campaign against North Vietnam. "If I don't go in now and they [Republican war hawks] show later that I should," Johnson blurted, "then they'll . . . push Vietnam up my ass every time."[76]

Ambassador Taylor, who had replaced Lodge in Saigon, knew that this was a fateful decision; the president had "crossed the Rubicon."[77] Americanization of the war evolved further on February 26 when LBJ committed two marine battalions to defend the U.S. airbase at Danang. Taylor saw the ground troops as "the nose of the camel" and believed you could not "take that nose [out of the tent] once you landed those Marines."[78] A few weeks earlier General Johnson had made headlines at a press conference when he warned, "The war in Vietnam could last as long as ten years before a victory is won for the free world."[79]

The last thing LBJ wanted was a long, drawn-out war in Vietnam. Skeptical of airpower as a decisive force in winning the war, he sought a ground plan to defeat the growing insurgency in the south. On March 4, the president summoned General Johnny Johnson to the family quarters of the White House; he wanted the Army chief to provide solutions. General Johnson was excited about the meeting as it was a rare opportunity to explain his "growing hesitation" with the administration's limited-war policy. Unfortunately, Johnson encountered the president in a foul and snarling mood.

President Johnson lambasted General Johnson for nearly an hour. He complained bitterly that the Joint Chiefs were not providing acceptable advice on Vietnam. "Bomb, bomb, bomb. That's all you know," LBJ bellowed. "Well, I want to know why there's nothing else. You generals have all been educated at the taxpayers' expense, and you're not giving me any ideas and solutions for this damn little pissant country. . . . I want some solutions. I want some answers."[80] The Army chief was dumbfounded and embarrassed by the president's tirade, which occurred in front of the general's staff. LBJ snapped again, "You don't have any answers, do you?" When the stunned Army chief hesitated, the president pointed his finger and said, "Well, go [to Vietnam and] get some."[81] Afterward the two men entered the White House elevator. The president thrust his finger into the general's chest and commanded: "Get things bubbling!"[82]

Within hours General Johnson was on a plane to Saigon, his third visit. His mission from the president was "pretty clear" to him: figure out how to "keep Vietnam free" from communism and do it without triggering the intervention of Chinese or Russian forces.[83] Although taken aback by the president's disrespectful diatribe, the Army general felt emboldened. LBJ wanted his assessment of the situation and specific recommendations for winning the war. Moreover, Secretary McNamara cabled Ambassador Taylor and instructed him to "assume no limitations on funds, equipment or personnel." The administration was "prepared to act immediately and favorably on any recommendations you and General Johnson may make."[84]

General Johnson toured South Vietnam for a week. In Saigon, he met with Taylor and commanders from the U.S. and South Vietnamese armed forces. He also held candid talks with officers in the field. The news was bad. Viet Cong insurgents were routing the South Vietnamese army and taking control of the countryside. Worse, North Vietnamese troops had crossed the demilitarized zone into the Central Highlands. "I saw a pretty desperate nation, and a pretty disconsolate group of leaders," Johnson recalled. "The word would be 'despairing' rather than 'disconsolate.' And they were on the verge of collapsing."[85] In a meeting in Saigon that was restricted to general officers, Johnson announced: "Gentlemen, as you know, I don't come as the Army Chief of Staff. I am here as a representative of the President of the United States. Mr. Johnson asked me to come, and to tell you that I come with a blank check. What do you need to win the war?"[86] The generals wanted more ground troops and more firepower. Assessing the situation as desperate, Johnson concurred. He, like Ambassador Taylor, believed blanket security at the hamlet level, "the root of the tree," was essential to winning the war.[87]

General Johnson's bleak outlook echoed the prevailing view of his staff. A month before this trip, the general had dispatched Lieutenant General Bruce Palmer, his operations deputy, to South Vietnam for a frank assessment. Palmer had reported back that the military situation was dire and recommended that the United States either deploy a sizeable ground force or withdraw from Vietnam entirely. Johnson's staff determined that at least five divisions were needed to defeat the insurgency.[88]

Johnny Johnson returned to Washington on March 12. His written report detailed the austere situation and recommended immediate action, including an intensification of bombing and covert operations against North Vietnam and the deployment of U.S. combat troops to the south. "It is clearly evident," he wrote, "that the situation in Vietnam has deteriorated rapidly and extensively" and that without providing security the South Vietnamese people will never "commit" to the war or to the Saigon government.[89] Johnson recommended the fast deployment of one army division — some sixteen thousand troops — to avert an immediate disaster. He knew that a single division was not "militarily sufficient" to truly stabilize the situation, much less carry the war, but he thought that it represented "the maximum action which is politically feasible within the U.S. at this time."[90]

On March 15, General Johnson and the other Joint Chiefs went to the White House to brief LBJ and McNamara on the situation in South Vietnam. Disturbed by their dire assessment, the president demanded that the Chiefs "kill more Vietcong" and to start providing him with weekly kill counts.[91] General Johnson seized the opportunity to give candid counsel on winning the war. In his estimation, the United States would need to deploy five hundred thousand troops and fight for five years. According to McNamara, the general's stark forecast "shocked" both him and the president. "None of us," the defense secretary later wrote, "had been thinking in anything approaching such terms."[92]

Four days later, the Joint Chiefs formally recommended that three divisions, one U.S. Army, one U.S. Marine, and one South Korean army, be deployed immediately to Vietnam. LBJ rejected their proposal. Instead, he clung to his policy of gradual escalation. To placate the Joint Chiefs, he agreed to send two Marine battalions (two thousand troops). More significantly, the president also approved a change in mission for the marines from airbase defense to proactive "counterinsurgency combat operations."[93]

LBJ's decisions to slowly escalate and further Americanize the war were largely and purposefully kept secret from the public and Congress. Again and again, the president lied about significant changes in American policy, from the systematic bombing of North Vietnam to the commitment of combat troops. At a March 20 press conference, LBJ insisted, "Our policy in Viet-Nam is the same as it was 1 year ago, and to those of you who have inquiries on the subject, it is the same as it was 10 years ago."[94] Twelve days later, after the Joint Chiefs had lobbied for the deployment of two U.S. combat divisions, he told journalists, "I know of no far-reaching strategy that is being suggested or promulgated."[95] General Westmoreland characterized the president's deceptiveness as "a masterpiece of obliquity."[96] By not speaking out or taking any action, Westmoreland, Johnny Johnson, and the other Joint Chiefs were party to the administration's deceit.

There was, however, one senior member of the Johnson administration who decided that he could no longer support the president's shrouded and incremental approach to the war in Vietnam. CIA director John McCone, a wealthy industrialist and former chairman of the Atomic Energy Commission, had been appointed by President Kennedy after the Bay of Pigs fiasco. A Catholic and a Republican, McCone was known as an exacting and independent-minded administrator, perceived by some in government as "an outsider and a bit of a moralist."[97] Like General Johnson and the Joint Chiefs, McCone was a staunch anticommunist who fully supported the objective of "saving" South Vietnam. But McCone's loyalty to the president's policy had limits; he had reached a point where he refused to be complicit in a limited-war strategy that he believed would fail. McCone was deeply concerned about sending additional ground troops to Vietnam, fearing "we will find ourselves mired down in combat in the jungle in a military effort that we cannot win, and from which we will have extreme difficulty in extracting ourselves."[98] Like LeMay, he advised the president that any further deployment of soldiers and marines must be coordinated with more intensive and widespread bombing of North Vietnam. "We must hit them harder," he wrote on April 2, 1965, "more frequently, and inflict greater damage."[99] McCone was also frustrated with LBJ's disregard for the CIA's intelligence analysis, which illuminated the deteriorating conditions in South Vietnam and the ineffectiveness of the restricted bombing campaign in North Vietnam. In his letter of resignation on April 28, McCone wrote: "I remain concerned . . . over the limited scale of air action against North Vietnam. . . . By limiting our attacks . . . we signal to the Communists that our determination to win is significantly modified by our fear of widening the war." McCone further warned that without an instant and significant military escalation "world opinion will turn against us," communist propaganda will become "increasingly effective," and domestic support for the war will dissipate.[100]

Tired of McCone's pessimism and his critique of the administration's Vietnam policy, LBJ welcomed his resignation. But the president did fear a MacArthur-like uprising among the military leadership. In an April meeting with the Joint Chiefs, LBJ tried to rally his senior military advisors by acknowledging that the war was going badly but promising there was still time to win it. "Now, I am like a coach I used to know," he told the flag officers, "and you're my team; you're all Johnson men. We played the first half of the game and the score is now 21-0 against us. . . . You're graduates of the Military Academy and you should be able to. . . . tell me how we are going to kill more Viet Cong."[101] LBJ asked them what was needed to defeat the Viet Cong. Wheeler renewed the Joint Chiefs' March 20 recommendation for the deployment of three divisions. The president said that was not feasible politically. He asked General Johnson for his view. The general agreed with Wheeler, saying a minimum of three divisions was required. In the end, the president made a meager compromise and authorized the deployment of the Army's 173rd Airborne Brigade, some five thousand soldiers.[102]

Among the Joint Chiefs, Johnny Johnson was the most adamant that the war in Vietnam could not be won without a full military mobilization, including the activation of the reserves. He wanted the president to declare a national emergency and rally the American people, whom he believed would support an expanded war effort. Johnson wanted to "get in, win, and get out."[103] In May, he drafted a proposal that was endorsed by Wheeler and the other Chiefs. Their recommendation for an all-out war was given to LBJ at the White House. Following General Johnson's presentation, an unhappy president said, "General, you leave the American people to me. I know more about the American people than anyone in this room."[104] The flag officers were dismissed.

The Joint Chiefs did not give up on "the [General] Johnson plan," designed to greatly — and publicly — escalate the war effort. During June and into July, they labored to convince McNamara of the plan's merits, hoping he could persuade the president. The defense secretary came to support a major escalation. In a July 10 meeting with the Joint Chiefs, McNamara informed them that the president was likely to approve thirty-four battalions for deployment to Vietnam but they were to keep it "out of the news."[105] On July 14, McNamara and Wheeler flew to Saigon for consultation with Westmoreland regarding current and future manpower needs. While there the defense secretary received a much-welcomed cable from his deputy, Cyrus Vance, who reported that the president had formally authorized the thirty-four battalions and that he was "favorably disposed to the call-up of reserves and the extension of tours of active duty personnel."[106] General Johnson's war plan was finally coming to fruition.

Meanwhile, amid the unpublicized escalation, the Joint Chiefs met with congressional members of the Policy Subcommittee of the House Armed Services Committee (HASC). The informal gathering was held in the office of Mendel Rivers, the HASC chairman who believed that Congress should exercise its Constitutional prerogatives related to the military. The Congressmen summoned the Chiefs to obtain their "comprehensive estimate" on the troop levels needed to win the war. At that time there were approximately seventy-five thousand U.S. forces in Vietnam. General Johnson, who had concluded that a minimum of five hundred thousand troops and as many as seven hundred thousand were required "to guarantee a free and independent South Vietnam," was not forthright with the congressmen.[107] Fearing that such blunt honesty would upset his mercurial president, the general willfully misled members of Congress. When asked about the necessary troop levels, Johnson first replied that he "really didn't know" what the requirement was "now or in the future." When pressed harder to give his professional estimate, the general lied. He said approximately two hundred fifty thousand troops were necessary and refused to say whether he recommended mobilizing the reserves. When the Chiefs were asked why the military was not bombing fuel storage targets in North Vietnam or mining Haiphong Harbor, they obfuscated.[108]

HASC Chairman Rivers grew frustrated with the flag officers' evasiveness. He told them that they were required to be forthcoming, as they were "creatures of the Congress and therefore have a duty to them [the people's representatives] as well as the Executive Branch." General Johnson, who during his confirmation hearing had pledged to tell Congress the truth, pushed back. He declared that his primary loyalty was to the president and reminded the politicians that the National Security Act specified that the Joint Chiefs were the principal military advisors not to Congress but to "the president, the National Security Council, and the Secretary of Defense." The meeting adjourned with the congressmen in a "fit of frustration." The Chiefs, on the other hand, were "astounded" by how little the representatives actually knew about the ongoing escalation in Vietnam and the probability of a protracted land war.[109]

On Thursday, July 22, LBJ met with McNamara, the Joint Chiefs, the service secretaries, and other senior advisors to discuss Vietnam. McNamara reported that the situation in South Vietnam was desperate. He and General Johnson called for a major deployment of ground forces and the mobilization of the reserves. LBJ interjected, "Isn't this going off the diving board?" McNamara admitted that it was. "This is a major change in policy," the secretary said. "We have relied on South Vietnam to carry the brunt. Now we would be responsible for [a] satisfactory military outcome."[110] The president turned to General Johnson and asked outright whether the United States should just withdraw from Vietnam and "make our stand somewhere else." The Army chief said no. The optimal path was to rally the American people and win the war by fully mobilizing the reserves. Johnson compared three options for the president: "The least desirable alternative is getting out. The second least is doing what we are doing. Best is to get in and get the job done."[111]

Visibly angry, LBJ asked Johnson, "What is your reaction to Ho's [Ho Chi Minh's] statement he is ready to fight for twenty years?" The general replied matter-of-factly, "I believe him."[112] The president then asked what level of force would be ultimately required to win in Vietnam. Speaking for the Chiefs, Marine Commandant Wallace Greene called for blockading North Vietnam, mining Haiphong Harbor, and intensifying air strikes. He also reiterated General Johnson's March assessment that five hundred thousand ground troops were needed for a five-year fight.[113] LBJ asked if that might cause China to deploy troops to South Vietnam. General Johnson, the decorated veteran of the Korean War, said, "No, I don't think they will." The president snapped, "MacArthur didn't think they would come in either."[114] Throughout the meeting, it was General Johnson who "bore the brunt of Lyndon Johnson's cold stares."[115]

Although the meeting had been contentious, the Joint Chiefs still believed that they and McNamara had finally persuaded LBJ to implement a new, large-scale war policy. General Johnson felt as if he had been locked in "a test of wills" with the president.[116] Wheeler directed the Army chief to prep the reorganized First Air Cavalry for near-immediate deployment to South Vietnam and to prepare the Army for a massive engagement. Johnson called Major General Harry Kinnard, commander of the First Air Cavalry, and told him: "Get ready. You're going to Vietnam" as "the point unit of a major American mobilization."[117]

But President Johnson changed his mind; he decided against a full mobilization. On Saturday, July 24, McNamara explained the president's decision to the Joint Chiefs and the service secretaries. LBJ had agreed to deploy at least one hundred thousand more combat troops, half immediately, including the First Air Cavalry Division. However, he would not declare a national emergency, mobilize the reserves, or extend the tours of duty for those already serving. The president was holding steadfast to his policy of gradual escalation, including restrictive bombing in North Vietnam. He would announce his decision publicly on July 28. The Joint Chiefs were astonished by these reversals. Reeling from the news, they barely registered a word of protest. General Johnson, who knew escalation without the reserves would severely degrade the Army's ability to perform its duties around the world, did speak up. "Mr. McNamara," he said, "I can assure you of one thing, and that is that without a call-up of the reserves that the quality of the Army is going to erode and we're going to suffer very badly. . . . it will be relatively soon. . . . [and] relatively widespread."[118] McNamara did not respond.

General Johnson stewed over the president's decision, which he considered catastrophic. He later recalled: "It came as a *total* and *complete* surprise and I might say a *shock. Every single contingency plan* that the Army had that called for any kind of an expansion of force had the assumption in it that the reserves would be called."[119] On July 25, he approached a sympathetic Wheeler to underscore that he was "totally opposed to the commitment without mobilization."[120] At home that night, General Johnson could not sleep. The more he thought about the army's predicament, the more he became "very determined . . . to resign."[121] As a military officer, Johnson valued loyalty to the commander in chief, but his sworn oath was to the Constitution and the American people. This was, as H. R. McMaster writes, "the ultimate test" of the Joint Chiefs' fealty to the president.[122] The next day at the White House, LBJ told his military advisors that he would not call up the reserves. McNamara expressed his support of this decision. Rather than proffer honest dissent, General Johnson and his fellow flag officers sat in "shocked silence." In other words, "the Chiefs did not disappoint the president."[123]

The following evening Wheeler joined LBJ and McNamara to discuss the war with a group of congressmen. Like his military colleagues, the general wanted to call up the reserves "to make sure that the people of the U.S. knew that we were in a war and not engaged at some two-penny military adventure."[124] Yet he remained stoic when the president and defense secretary lied about the war in Vietnam, which was escalating rapidly and without a known limit. As McMaster writes, with Wheeler at their side, the president and McNamara willfully misrepresented to members of Congress "the scale of Westmoreland's request, understated the funds they needed by approximately ten billion dollars, and argued that mobilization, from a military perspective, was not only unnecessary but undesirable."[125]

The lies and deceptions continued on July 28. At noon, LBJ announced on television new troop deployments to Vietnam, but there was no declaration of emergency or a sense of urgency. He stated that he was sending fifty thousand additional forces and that more would be needed later, but did not disclose that one hundred thousand troops were already scheduled for deployment. The president repeated the false claim that there had been no changes in U.S. policy. He was dishonest when he denied that U.S. forces were engaged in offensive combat operations. Moreover, while LBJ did say that the draft call would be increased "over a period of time," he gave assurances that it was militarily unnecessary to call reserve units into service.[126]

Johnny Johnson and others at the Pentagon watched LBJ's performance with disbelief. The general was desperate, appalled by the president's warfighting policy and his ongoing public deceptions. He decided that the only honorable choice was to resign in protest. Moreover, he planned to convene his own press conference to explain his objections to the president's approach to the war. Johnson closed the door to his office and changed into his dress uniform replete with combat decorations from two wars. He ordered his driver to retrieve his government-issued sedan. Johnson informed his staff that he was going to the White House. In the backseat of the black Ford, the general unpinned the four stars from the epaulets on his shoulders; he would hand them to the president. Keeping with his principle of expressing total honesty, Johnson planned to speak sharply: "You have refused to tell the country they cannot fight a war without mobilization; you have required me to send men into battle with little hope of their ultimate victory; and you have forced us in the military to violate almost every one of the principles of war in Vietnam. Therefore, I resign and will hold a press conference after I walk out of your door."[127]

As the general's car approached the gates of the White House, anguish rushed over him. He could not go through with it. Perhaps recalling his conversation with General Omar Bradley, he again rationalized that he could best serve the troops and the nation by working from within the administration. "The more I thought about it," Johnson recalled, "the more I came to believe that I could not walk away from the Army and the soldiers we were sending to Vietnam. I finally concluded that I could do more good by staying in the job."[128] It was a fateful decision, one that he came to regret, deeply. He would characterize it as a severe "lapse in moral courage."[129]

The negative effects of LBJ's July 1965 decisions were felt immediately by the likes of Army Lieutenant Colonel Harold G. "Hal" Moore, a battalion commander in the First Cavalry Division. On the verge of deploying to Vietnam, his unit's combat readiness, like that of many others, suffered acutely from the president's refusal to declare a national emergency and extend the duty tours of officers and soldiers who were nearing the end of their enlistments. "We were sick at heart," Moore recalled. "We were being shipped off to war sadly understrength, and crippled by the loss of almost a hundred troopers in my battalion alone. The very men who would be the most useful in combat — those who had trained longest in the new techniques of helicopter warfare — were by this order taken away from us. It made no sense."[130] In retirement, Lieutenant General Moore wrote about General Johnson's distress on the day of LBJ's televised address: "On that day, convinced that the President's escalation without a declaration of emergency was an act of madness, General Harold K. Johnson, Chief of Staff of the U.S. Army, drove to the White House with the intention of resigning in protest. . . . [But] General Johnson faltered in his resolve. . . . This decision haunted Johnny Johnson all the rest of his life."[131]

In the summer and fall of 1965, the Joint Chiefs continued their call for widespread strategic bombing of North Vietnam, believing it was one of the keys to winning the war in the south. Knowing the president would oppose the escalation for fear of Chinese intervention, Secretary McNamara kept the flag officers at bay as long as possible. The matter came to a head in early November when the Joint Chiefs were granted an opportunity to make their pitch to the president. It was, according to one aide-de-camp, "make or break time for the Chiefs."[132]

General Wheeler and the Navy and Air Force Chiefs led the presentation in the Oval Office. They called for aerial bombing of communication lines and additional military targets, and for the mining and blockading of Vietnamese harbors. McNamara had previously told the president that he personally opposed the Joint Chiefs' plan. LBJ, initially calm and attentive, started to seethe. He turned his gaze and asked Generals Johnson and Greene, who were standing back, whether they fully supported this aggressive proposal. When they both answered in the affirmative, the president unleashed a fury upon them. "You goddam fucking assholes," he screamed. "You're trying to get me to start World War III with your idiotic bullshit — your 'military wisdom.'" The president derided them as "shitheads, dumbshits, pompous assholes." The nation's senior military advisors stood in bewildered silence. LBJ then asked them what they would do if they were president. When each spoke in favor of overt escalation, the president "erupted again, yelling and cursing, again using language that even a Marine seldom hears." LBJ terminated the meeting by shouting, "Get the hell out of here right now!"[133]

General Johnson's thoughts about the excruciating episode are unknown, but Chief of Naval Operations David McDonald's reaction was captured by his aide who had been in the Oval Office holding up a large map of Vietnam. "Never in my life," McDonald confessed to his subordinate, "did I ever expect to be put through something as horrible as you just watched from the president of the United States to his five senior military advisers."[134] The president and defense secretary had clearly lost confidence in the Joint Chiefs. Still, the flag officers soldiered on, tolerating personal abuse and professional degradations. Nobody spoke up, nobody retired, nobody resigned in protest. "It was a sign in the decline in the quality of the nation's military leadership," writes Thomas Ricks, "that none of those present in that November 1965 meeting did so."[135]

Less than two weeks after LBJ's humiliating treatment of the Joint Chiefs, Lieutenant Colonel Hal Moore's First Cavalry battalion engaged three regiments of the North Vietnamese army in the Ia Drang Valley. It was the first major battle of the Americanized Vietnam War. After three days of ferocious fighting, the North Vietnamese army withdrew, having suffered more than six hundred dead and one thousand wounded. Moore's battalion sustained 79 deaths and 121 wounded. General Johnson viewed the Battle of Ia Drang as "a turning point" that cemented the U.S. commitment to defend South Vietnam. He cabled congratulations to the First Cavalry, which Moore read aloud to the battered battalion.[136] A week later, Westmoreland requested a massive increase in manpower that would bring the total commitment to 410,000 troops. In late November, General Johnson, McNamara, and General Wheeler flew to South Vietnam to assess the situation and were briefed by Moore.[137] Johnson returned to Vietnam the next month to spend Christmas with the troops; by then more than two thousand Americans had been killed.

Six months earlier, General Johnson had organized a task force to analyze how the war was being executed in South Vietnam. Influenced by Indochina expert Bernard Fall, the Army chief concluded that Washington needed "a broader look" at the situation, a multidimensional review that would "require a good deal of thought and some breakaway from rather stereotyped thinking."[138] A staunch advocate of pacification and counterinsurgency, Johnson feared that Westmoreland's strategy of attrition and attendant body counts, search and destroy missions, indiscriminate bombing, and "big bashing of the North Vietnamese Army" would be insufficient to save South Vietnam from a communist takeover.[139] He had long believed that "control is the object beyond the battle and the object beyond the war. Destruction is applied only to the extent necessary to achieve control and, thus, by its nature, must be discriminating."[140]

General Johnson's views solidified during his 1965 Christmas trip to Vietnam when he gathered a group of colonels and asked for candid assessments of the situation. One of those officers, Edward C. Meyer, who later became Army chief of staff, remembered that meeting well. "It was clear," he recalled, "that General Johnson was not happy about how the war was being fought. He looked at that huge base camp at An Khe. He said that was not what he envisioned — a third to half of the division tied up on camp security. He had wanted the forces to be dispersed throughout the area of operations. That troubled him."[141]

Back at the Pentagon, General Johnson assembled a diverse team of educated and experienced army officers to conduct the war review. Most of the group, which included one woman, had served in Vietnam. They came from various army branches and had varying educational specialties from history and politics to cultural anthropology and economics. General Johnson did not want the study "to take a dialectical form." Instead, he ordered the researchers "to address specific problems *and* specific actions that are designed to alleviate specific problems."[142] The task force worked long hours for eight months, engaging in research at home and abroad and in the analysis of hundreds of surveys completed by officers with service in South Vietnam.

General Johnson's nine-hundred-page study, "A Program for the Pacification and Long-Term Development of South Vietnam" (PROVN), was published in March 1966; it contained 140 recommendations and was a vivid reflection of the general's professional perspective. The report underscored that pacification was mission critical and that future military operations, especially those of the South Vietnamese army, should prioritize the protection of the civilian population from the Viet Cong insurgency. The report's summary stated, "The critical actions are those that occur at the village level, the district and provincial levels. This is where the war must be fought; this is where the war and the object which lies beyond it must be won."[143]

PROVN warned against a military strategy that prioritized winning conventional battles against the Viet Cong or the North Vietnamese at the expense of pacification and counterinsurgency: "At no time should

U.S. Free-World operations shift the American focus of support from the true point of decision in Vietnam — the villages. Victories over extraneous . . . Main Force battalions . . . must not be allowed to generate false optimism. Such battle wins are not indicative that this enemy is ready to quit or that he has been touched in his prime operating dimension."[144]

PROVN also called for a unification of all pacification efforts, military and civilian, under a single American leader, preferably the U.S. ambassador. It recommended that the United States assume more responsibility for overseeing the public services provided by the South Vietnamese government, which needed transformational reforms. The report stated, "Today, our eagerness to do the killing for the Government of [South] Vietnam must at least be matched by U.S. determination to force Government of [South] Vietnam action on critical 'people-oriented programs.'"[145] Furthermore, the report censured the South Vietnamese army, condemning, for example, its destructive unobserved harassment and interdiction fire which alienated the civilian population. In sum, the researchers wanted to consolidate, enhance, and Americanize the pacification programs in Vietnam.

The PROVN study proposed radical shifts in military-political policy in South Vietnam and was briefed at the highest levels of the Defense Department, including by Secretary McNamara, the Joint Chiefs, CINCPAC (Commander in Chief Pacific) Headquarters in Hawaii, and MACV Headquarters in Saigon. While the report accurately identified many problems hindering the war effort in the south and offered wide-ranging solutions, it did not immediately influence U.S. policy. President Johnson, in fact, was never briefed on PROVN. Perhaps the most significant point of resistance to PROVN was its recommendation that the United States thoroughly impose itself upon the Saigon government. For many, such a strategy was fraught, even antithetical to the war's objective of a free and independent South Vietnam.

Moreover, there was little desire among American military leadership (Westmoreland included) to embrace PROVN's explicit and implicit criticisms of the war's current strategy and tactics. With Westmoreland's blessing the report was soon *"reduced primarily to a conceptual document*."[146] Phillip Davidson, who served as Westmoreland's chief intelligence officer in Saigon, later wrote: "The study deserved more mature consideration. Its executioner was General Westmoreland." According to Davidson, the general's "reasons for throttling it are obvious. PROVN forthrightly attacked his search and destroy concept. . . . proposed taking considerable military authority away from him . . . and giving it to the ambassador." Moreover, Johnson's report had recommended "a deeper United States involvement in the GVN [South Vietnamese government] administrative affairs (which Westmoreland thought was unwise)."[147]

General Johnson grew increasingly troubled by Westmoreland's management of the war. His disillusionment was apparent when he learned from William Woolridge, the sergeant major of the Army, that battlefield reports regularly contained falsified information to demonstrate that the war was being won. The sergeant major told General Johnson that "from battalion to MACV level" the army was knowingly inflating numbers on enemy force size and the quantity of their casualties. Wooldridge remembered the general becoming "obviously upset" and declaring, "that things like this happen when you are following a policy that is not working and such actions are the result of trying to justify that false policy."[148]

The Johnson administration's ongoing dishonesty with Congress and the American public left General Johnson further disheartened. According to several officers on the Joint Staff, Johnson despised the administration's "habit of putting the best face on the war" and was "so disenchanted that he was openly calling the Department of Defense the Department of Deceit."[149] In February 1966, he again pressed McNamara to have the president declare a national state of emergency, call up the reserve forces, and request the necessary funding from Congress. The general again argued that this would finally demonstrate to North Vietnam, China, and the American people "our determination to see this war through."[150] McNamara rejected the advice.

General Johnson was granted only one private meeting with LBJ in all of 1966. Again and again, he contemplated resignation. He knew full well that he was complicit in the administration's deceptions yet he continued to rationalize his involvement. Just as leaders in the field were falsifying enemy casualty numbers, General Johnson and others in the Pentagon were submitting dishonest budgets to Congress. In retirement, the general regretted his support for annual budgets that failed to disclose or financially account for troop deployments already approved by the president. He said:

> I can recall vividly, vividly, when we were formulating the Fiscal Year 1967 budget . . . knowing [that] the money we were asking for was inadequate to the tasks that we saw ahead. Now, then, I have to ask myself, "What should my role have been?" I'm a dumb soldier under civilian control who supports or doesn't support the budget that's advanced. I could resign, but what am I? I'm a disgruntled general for forty-eight hours, and then I'm out of sight. Right? Or, I can stay and try to fight and get the best posture that we can during this time.[151]

Johnson's daily "fight" sought to raise, train, and maintain the U.S. Army, which was not only waging a war in Vietnam but also operating critical duty stations across the globe. Not able to utilize the reserves or extend the enlistments of trained and experienced soldiers, Johnson had to rely on inexperienced recruits and draftees. He faced the daunting reality that every month some thirty thousand soldiers completed their two years of service and left the army. General Johnson confessed to a military audience, "I come somewhat out of breath because for the last year and a half or so I have found myself in the position of trying to keep a bathtub filled with the plug out."[152] The work was exasperating. According to Lieutenant General Charlie Corcoran, the commanding general of I Field Force in Vietnam, "This weighed on Johnny more than anything I ever saw on him, trying to expand the Army under the restrictions laid on by LBJ and McNamara. His feeling was that the way the Army had been forced to expand was a disaster."[153]

Despite Johnson's exhaustive efforts, which included stripping U.S. forces stationed in Europe and depleting the Army's strategic reserve, he was still wittingly sending ill-prepared troops — officers and enlisted personnel — into a deadly war zone. "You will have problems in the months ahead," he wrote to Lieutenant General Arthur S. Collins Jr., the new commander of the Fourth Infantry Division, "simply because I have permitted the resources of the Army to be spread desperately thin."[154] By the end of 1966, more than six thousand Americans had been killed in Vietnam. General Ferdinand J. Chesarek, the Comptroller of the Army, stated the obvious. "The Army was in real bad shape."[155]

Presiding over a substantially degraded U.S. Army aggrieved General Johnson personally and led to his recurring thoughts of retirement or resignation. The death count in Vietnam had risen to the point that he could no longer hope to send personal condolence letters to suffering families. The general's deputy chief of staff for personnel recalled his anguish: "I remember Johnny expressing these feelings about possibly resigning on many different occasions and on several issues. I remember him saying, 'Every night I go home, and I wonder if I should resign. They're asking me to do things that frighten me. But if I resign, they'll just put somebody in who will vote the way they want him to.'"[156]

In March of 1967, the Joint Chiefs again asked for a full mobilization that would include two hundred thousand additional troops. They also requested an expansion of the land war into Laos and Cambodia and a widening of bombing targets in North Vietnam. McNamara strongly opposed the military's recommendations. He had become disillusioned with Vietnam, believing that the war was "acquiring a momentum of its own that must be stopped" to prevent "a major national disaster."[157] As was his pattern, LBJ took a middle course. In July, while still refusing to mobilize the reserves, he approved the deployment of fifty thousand troops. He also refused to expand the war into Cambodia and Laos, but did sanction a small increase in bombing targets.

The administration's policy of graduated escalation continued to frustrate Johnny Johnson and the Joint Chiefs. The flag officers were not alone. Members of the Senate Armed Services Committee (SASC) learned that LBJ and McNamara had again rejected the Joint Chiefs' recommendation to greatly expand the bombing campaign against

North Vietnam. Led by Democratic Senator John Stennis of Mississippi, the SASC's Preparedness Investigating Subcommittee (hereafter Stennis committee) "went on the warpath" and scheduled seven days of hearings to provide "the military commanders a platform to air their grievances over the civilian-imposed strategy of gradualism and bombing restrictions."[158] In August, McNamara, the Joint Chiefs, and other military leaders were called to testify. Stennis's pro-military position was clear from his opening statement: "The question is growing in the Congress as to whether it is wise to send more men if we are going to just leave them at the mercy of the guerrilla war without trying to cut off the enemy's supplies more effectively. . . . My own personal opinion is that it would be a tragic and perhaps fatal mistake for us to suspend or restrict the bombing."[159]

Chairman Wheeler and the new Air Force Chief, John McConnell, were among the first to appear before the Stennis committee. They both criticized the Johnson administration's strategy of gradual escalation and the limited bombing of North Vietnam. The generals wanted to apply "heavy pressure relentlessly" in the north and the south. Wheeler and McConnell also underscored that from the beginning of the war the Joint Chiefs had recommended "a much sharper type of attack" against North Vietnam, "a sharp sudden blow which would have . . . done much to paralyze the enemy's capability to move his equipment around and to supply people in the south."[160] Wheeler emphasized that the Chiefs currently opposed any reduction in bombing as it would be evidence of "continuing weakness and wavering on our part." He and McConnell argued that the air war had not fully succeeded because of "misguided civilian interference, graduated escalation, and the failure to attack available and lucrative targets," including storage facilities, assembly plants, bridges, harbors, and airfields.[161]

McNamara testified on August 25 with General Johnson scheduled to testify three days later. The defense secretary realized that he was entering a political snake pit in which "the Chiefs and Committee were against me."[162] He later characterized his appearance as "an extraordinarily trying ordeal" and "one of the most stressful episodes of my life."[163] In his testimony, McNamara contradicted key assertions and recommendations made by Wheeler and McConnell. The air war in North Vietnam, he testified, had demonstrated only marginal effectiveness and that more bombing would not improve the situation. "Short of annihilating the North and its people," he asserted, an expanded air campaign, including attacks on Haiphong Harbor, would not stop North Vietnam from effectively supporting the Viet Cong.[164] "To pursue this objective," he contended, "would not only be futile, but would involve risks to our personnel and to our Nation that I am unable to recommend."[165] All of this McNamara believed to be true, but then he stated something that he did not believe: that the current policy of limited war would eventually lead to victory in Vietnam. "I think it will be a successful war," he said, "if we maintain our pressure and our patience."[166]

The Stennis committee bore down on McNamara. Democratic Senator Strom Thurmond of South Carolina rejected the secretary's defense of gradual escalation and characterized the administration's Vietnam policy as one of "placating the Communists. It is a statement of appeasing the Communists. It is a statement of no-win."[167] Noting that McNamara had long opposed the Joint Chiefs' recommendations for a more intense air war, Democratic Senator Howard Cannon of Nevada asked the secretary if he had lost confidence in the flag officers. McNamara was defensive and reminded the senator that LBJ, a civilian, is the commander in chief and that the Constitution did not "intend that he would exercise that [duty] by following blindly the recommendations of his military advisors."[168] Democratic Senator Stuart Symington of Missouri continued Cannon's line of inquiry, asking the secretary if he was disturbed by the "running disagreement" between the civilian leadership and the nation's senior military advisors. McNamara, in another blatant lie, testified that there was no "gulf between the military leaders and the civilian leaders in the executive branch."[169]

The Joint Chiefs, especially General Johnson, were appalled by McNamara's testimony. They were particularly upset with his falsehoods about there being a consensus on how to fight the war and that gradual escalation would ultimately achieve victory. Late that afternoon, General Johnson, McConnell, and the new Navy chief, Thomas Moorer, gathered in Chairman Wheeler's office. No staff aides were allowed and no telephone calls were to be answered unless it was the president himself. Furthermore, Wheeler forbade the Joint Chiefs from taking meeting notes and made them swear an oath of secrecy. They discussed in detail McNamara's "bad-faith defense of a clearly discredited strategy" and how they should proceed. General Johnson complained bitterly that the military was being scapegoated for an unsuccessful war over which it had been given "little control."[170] The flag officers eventually broached the topic of a joint resignation. Johnson was "the most outspoken proponent" of a public protest. After three hours of deliberation, the chiefs agreed that they would hold a press conference the next day and resign in unison.[171]

The next morning at 8:30 a.m., the flag officers reconvened in Wheeler's office. The chairman had lost his resolve. "We can't do it," he told his colleagues. "It's mutiny."[172] General Johnson held firm. He argued that the civilian leadership was not only ignoring their best, professional military advice, but had also lied to the public about the war in Vietnam. He protested, "If we're going to go to war, then we had better be honest with the American people."[173] Wheeler resisted. He reiterated that their resignation would be mutinous and he further rationalized that resignation would have no influence on policy. "If we resign," he said, "they'll just get someone else. And we'll be forgotten. Twenty-four hours from now there will be new guys sitting in our places and they'll do what they're told." All too familiar with such rationalizations, General Johnson continued to object, warning that the war was "being lost" by their civilian superiors and that the military would be blamed for "the fall."[174] In the end, however, Johnson capitulated. No one resigned.

Over the ensuing years, Johnson, Moorer, and even Wheeler broke their silence about the contentious episode, confiding details to close aides, family, and friends.[175] Wheeler's widow told Lewis Sorley, General Johnson's biographer, "Johnny was the one who first talked about it. [But] they changed their minds."[176] Lieutenant General Bruce Palmer wrote that Wheeler and Moorer had both told him about the resignation meetings and that Johnson had discussed the matter with him on multiple occasions.[177] General Johnson later revealed the ordeal when speaking to a veterans' group after having concluded, "The story needed to come out."[178]

General Johnson appeared before the Stennis committee on August 28. He described his and the Joint Chiefs' long-held opposition to the administration's strategy of gradual escalation in Vietnam. "The major point of contention," he told James Kendall, the committee's chief counsel, "has been the rate at which pressures have been increased, and I think that the military commanders have chafed continually under a relatively low rate of increase of the pressure."[179] Senator Symington cited the recent Six Day War in the Middle East and asked Johnson what the outcome would have been had the Israelis adopted a "graduated attack policy against the Arab nations." The general stated, "They would not have a victory under their belt."[180] Symington inquired further, asking if any war had been won through a policy of gradual escalation. General Johnson answered no, positing that victory is only achieved when power is "applied faster and in greater quantity."[181]

General Johnson's critique of the limited-war strategy extended to the restrictions on bombing in North Vietnam. Republican Senator Margaret Chase Smith of Maine asked if the general supported the administration's policy of "gradually increasing pressure" on Hanoi. General Johnson testified that he had strongly opposed that policy for two years and advocated instead a much more aggressive tack, including the bombing of Haiphong Harbor. "The most effective way to employ airpower in the north," he claimed, "was as heavy a blow as possible over as short period of time as possible."[182] Republican Senator Jack Miller of Iowa asked if the current policy had prolonged the war unnecessarily. Johnson replied yes, and that a more comprehensive campaign would "shorten the war" and "result in fewer casualties." He asserted that gradualism and restricted bombing "permits the enemy to accommodate and this is not the most effective use of power."[183]

Notwithstanding his consistent criticism of gradualism and limited bombing, General Johnson believed that some progress had been achieved in the war and victory was still attainable. Any assessment, he argued, must be viewed broadly as being "integrated militarily, geographically, politically, psychologically, and socially." From a military perspective, he insisted, U.S. forces had "saved South Vietnam from certain defeat" and were "producing progressively more favorable results."[184] As for the air campaign, he said, it had "contributed significantly" in the north but "cannot by itself achieve our objectives in the south."[185] According to Johnson, the deployment of additional troops in the south and the expansion of bombing targets in the north would lead to further gains. An intensification of the war, he testified, "will increase the momentum of progress that is evident throughout much of the country."[186]

In other words, General Johnson's solution for an ultimate victory in Vietnam was the application of unremitting force. "It is something like the repetitive strokes of a jackhammer," he testified. "At some point the concrete begins to break up . . . it is this continuing and unrelenting pressure that will eventually bring us to a conclusion. . . . I think that the answer is to increase the pressure more."[187] He told Senator Symington, "I think that we have to bring pressure to bear on every single aspect and every single element of this war and that the combination of these pressures eventually is going to bring us to a point of success."[188]

Johnson's testimony, which lasted nearly three hours, reflected his view that the conflict in South Vietnam was not a civil war but a pivotal battle in the global Cold War. The communist insurgency in the south, he maintained, was being "directed from Hanoi" and was receiving material aid from not just Russia and China, but "the entire Communist bloc, East and West."[189] He noted, for example, that East Germany had donated five thousand bicycles to the North Vietnamese, who utilized them with remarkable effectiveness to transport supplies south. He agreed completely with Senator Thurmond, who stated at the hearing that Vietnam was "a war by the Communists to take over the world." Johnson offered further that the communists' strategy was "to test the patience of the American people to the extent that they will withdraw support of South Vietnam. To do this becomes a test of perseverance."[190]

McNamara and LBJ were furious with Johnson and the Joint Chiefs for airing their disagreements before Congress. Any illusion of consensus had been shattered. The president exclaimed that General Johnson and his colleagues had "almost destroyed us with their testimony before the Stennis Committee. We were murdered in the hearings."[191] The defense secretary took exception with the Joint Chiefs who had "hammered at what they considered the central problem in the way we were fighting the war — meddling by the civilians in Washington."[192] The *New York Times* editorial board, which favored a bombing pause, sympathized. The board assailed General Johnson for participating in an "insurrection" that raised "serious issues of civilian vs. military control of defense and diplomatic policy."[193]

President Johnson clung to his gradual escalation strategy throughout 1967. And while he agreed to increases in select bombing targets in North Vietnam, he continued to rebuff General Johnson and the Joint Chiefs' recommendations for faster and fuller escalation. "[President] Johnson's decisions of 1967," writes historian George Herring, "even more than those of 1965, were improvisations that defied military logic and did not face, much less resolve, the contradictions in American strategy."[194] Disenchanted with his pessimistic secretary of defense, LBJ arranged for McNamara's ouster by appointing him as president of the World Bank.

Army leadership changes were also afoot in early 1968 after the Viet Cong launched a massive coordinated offensive against South Vietnam's largest cities, including Saigon. In response to the January Tet Offensive, Westmoreland, Wheeler, and the Joint Chiefs had recommended the deployment of another 206,000 troops, thus forcing a mobilization of the reserves. More than 1,400 Americans were dying every month. But in the aftermath of Tet and amid increasing domestic opposition to the war, LBJ and Defense Secretary Clark Clifford rejected their familiar counsel. On March 23, 1968, President Johnson announced that Johnny Johnson would retire that summer and Westmoreland would be nominated to replace him as Army chief. A week later, LBJ informed the American people that he himself would not seek reelection.

General Johnson took the news of his pending retirement in stride. Lacking influence on Vietnam policy, the idea of remaining in his position or even becoming chairman of the Joint Chiefs held little appeal. He wrote to a friend: "If the senior commander were in a position to influence the course of events somewhat more than is now the case, I would probably have a different outlook. However, I see little change in the offing and since this is the case I believe that I should be fully honest with myself and my superiors and step aside."[195] General Johnson spoke to the Army staff on July 2, 1968, his final day at the Pentagon. He implored them to safeguard, at all costs, their independent judgment and moral principles. "One of the things that I am going to take away with me at noon today," he said, "is that I think that I am still my own man. I have not been captured. I have been manipulated, perhaps, a little bit, but not too much. You must not permit this. Sometimes it is awfully hard — awfully hard. Sometimes you will suffer. But this is just one of the hazards. So I want to leave this injunction with you: draw your truth line up there, and keep your toes on it — always on it — and maintain that integrity."[196]

★ ★ ★

For the next fifteen years, Johnny Johnson was tormented, not by the memory of three years in Japanese captivity, but by the Vietnam War and his four years as the Army chief of staff. Ethical leadership had been the hallmark of his thirty-five-year career. Unfailingly, he had taught his subordinates to question the assertions of their superiors and to safeguard their personal moral integrity. But time and again as Army chief, with thousands of Americans dying in Vietnam, the self-aware Johnson recognized that he was betraying his own principles. He had supported a deceitful president's disastrous policy of incremental warfare, an approach he had opposed from the outset. General Johnson believed that limited warfare bolstered the enemy and caused unnecessary casualties, and he seriously doubted that the president's policy would defeat the insurgency in South Vietnam.

Still, every time Johnson wrestled with his conscience and his inclination to resign in protest, he recoiled, satisfying himself with the rationalization that he could do more for the country by staying in uniform. In retirement, Johnson came to a different conclusion: he had made the wrong decision; he had indeed been captured by the Johnson administration. General Johnson recognized that in becoming a witting accomplice to a dishonest president's failed policy, he had surrendered his independent judgment and moral autonomy upon the altars of misguided thinking and misplaced loyalty. In hindsight, the extremely loyal Johnson wished he had taken the principled path of CIA Director John McCone, who had resigned from the administration rather than support a fateful policy that placed the country "in a military effort that we cannot win."[197]

With time, Johnson came to accept that honest, open dissent at the highest levels of government — even principled public resignation in extreme situations — is fundamentally an act of patriotism and professionalism. American military officers do not sacrifice their moral independence while serving and, by design, they do not swear oaths to the president or secretary of defense. Ultimately, for the good of the country, officers must maintain their personal integrity and defend the Constitution. In *How Do I Save My Honor?*, William Felice writes, "The key issue for citizens, civil servants, and military personnel is to have personal integrity and to act ethically in every circumstance. This means being honest to one's personal moral convictions while carrying out the government's orders, and when the two conflict, often one's personal moral convictions should carry the day. The tremendous pressure to loyally support the state in a time of war must be balanced with other virtues, including maintaining one's voice and moral autonomy. A patriotic defense of the public good in a time of war demands nothing less."[198]

As a means of rectifying his guilty conscience, General Johnson spoke out in retirement about the many times he had contemplated resigning as Army chief of staff. He also discussed his ultimate reasons for not quitting and the weight of his remorse. "I made the typical mistake," he would say, "of believing I could do more for the country and the Army if I stayed in than if I got out. I am now going to my grave with that lapse in moral courage on my back."[199] Johnson told a fellow officer, "I should have taken off my stars. I should have resigned. It was the worst, the most immoral decision I've ever made."[200] Ironically, by admitting his moral failing and having overcome any associated fear of shame or humiliation by doing so, the general was indeed exemplifying moral courage.

Although Johnny Johnson remains a tragic (and some would argue sympathetic) figure in American military history, Major General John Batiste took the lesson of his example to heart by demonstrating the moral courage to dissent honorably while in and out of uniform. Batiste commanded the Army's First Infantry Division in the Iraq War, arriving in Tikrit in December 2003. Before long he realized firsthand that the Bush administration had not deployed sufficient ground troops and other resources to secure the divided, war-torn country. Moreover, Batiste viewed the civilian leadership's decision to disband the Iraqi army as perilously short-sighted. He "freely and forcefully" expressed his concerns about the "shitty war plan" up the chain of command to headquarters and even to Defense Secretary Donald Rumsfeld's deputy, Paul Wolfowitz.[201] The deputy defense secretary, who knew Batiste well, "listened, but, clearly nothing changed." Despite his disillusionment with the Pentagon's leadership, Batiste loyally soldiered on, adhering to the principle that active-duty flag officers "don't air our differences in public."[202]

In April 2005, Batiste was offered a plum assignment, deputy commander of the V Corps under Lieutenant General Ricardo Sanchez. Although the position might earn him a third star, Batiste vacillated. He disliked the idea of working under the ineffectual Sanchez who refused to take responsibility for the Abu Ghraib prisoner abuse scandal. Moreover, Batiste remained disenchanted with Rumsfeld's strategy and questioned the Iraqi people's commitment to democracy. In the end, the general surprised many in the Defense Department by declining the promotion and choosing retirement. "How can I look myself in the mirror if I take this job?" Batiste thought. "I didn't sleep for nights," he later recounted. "But I was not willing to compromise my principles for one more minute."[203] He admitted that he had been "haunted" and ultimately inspired by the ghost of General Johnny Johnson.[204]

In April 2006, five months after retiring, Batiste broke ranks with the Pentagon and began a very public campaign criticizing the Bush administration's rush to war and its failed prosecution. He boldly called for Rumsfeld's resignation. Batiste felt morally obliged to speak up. "If I don't speak out," he said, "who the hell else will?"[205] On September 25, 2006, before a U.S. Senate panel, Batiste testified that he had forgone a promotion to three stars and retired after the "gut-wrenching realization" that he could do more for his soldiers "out of uniform." He further asserted that Rumsfeld was an incompetent, arrogant wartime leader who "browbeat subordinates" and "dismissed honest dissent." The defense secretary, Batiste said, had surrounded himself with "like-minded and compliant subordinates who do not grasp the importance of the principles of war, the complexities of Iraq, or the human dimension of warfare."[206]

TOXIC LEADERSHIP

Hyman G. Rickover

TOXIC LEADER—a superior with dysfunctional
personal characteristics who routinely engages
in negative behaviors without regard for
the well-being of subordinates and unit morale

The U.S. armed forces have long acknowledged the detrimental effects of toxic leadership. An expert on the subject, Colonel George E. Reed, U.S. Army retired, characterizes toxic leaders as those who willfully abuse and bully their subordinates as a means to self-interested ends and who, as a result, create unhealthy work climates. In *Tarnished: Toxic Leadership in the U.S. Military*, Reed laments, "It is not hard to find toxic leadership. Most military personnel have experienced it." Furthermore, its frequent occurrence "represents a violation of the un-written contract with the American people about how their sons and daughters should be treated while in service to the nation."[1]

The Pentagon has issued a multitude of regulations to curb overbearing toxic leaders in all branches of service. In 1993, for example, Secretary of Defense Les Aspin approved Joint Ethics Regulation (JER) as a single source of standards of ethical conduct and guidance for military leaders. Among the primary ethical values set forth in the JER were "caring" and "respect" for fellow Defense Department employees. Demonstrating compassion and kindness and treating people with dignity were also touted as essential acts of ethical and effective military leadership. According to the JER, considerate and empathetic leaders "help ensure that individuals are not treated solely as means to an end" and serve as a counterweight to the "temptation to pursue the mission at any cost."[2]

Nevertheless, toxic leadership proliferated. In 2003, Army Secretary Thomas E. White, a retired brigadier general, asked the Army War College to investigate the ongoing problem of "destructive" military leaders. The qualitative study, based on findings from focus groups, revealed that an overwhelming number of officers had experienced abusive and self-centered superiors who lacked concern for the welfare of subordinates and who willfully soured the workplace.[3] Five years later, a quantitative study of students at the Army War College revealed that every officer surveyed had dealt with a toxic superior at the rank of colonel or higher. In addition, more than half of the respondents had seriously considered leaving the profession of arms because of bad leadership. The War College students further reported that 11 percent of general officers and civilian executives were perceived "unfavorably" and that 8 percent were absolutely "toxic." The officers' personal experience with destructive leaders did *not* vary significantly by gender, race, or service branch.[4]

The Army War College survey was replicated in 2009 by consulting 167 active-duty Army majors attending the Command and General Staff College in Fort Leavenworth, Kansas. Eighteen percent of the respondents said that their superiors — lieutenant colonels and colonels — had "toxic" leadership styles, and, like the War College students, more than half of the majors had contemplated leaving the service because of tyrannical superiors. The authors of the study predicted that toxic leadership would persist because powerful "cultural norms," including blind loyalty and a chain of command that dissuades officers from offering constructive feedback to superiors and other authorities. Moreover, speaking hard truths to power risks retribution and career derailment.[5]

Toxic leadership in the army, even at the flag level, has persisted. In 2012–2013 alone, Lieutenant General Patrick J. O'Reilly, Brigadier General Eugene L. Mascolo, and Brigadier General Scott F. Donahue (all U.S. Army) were found guilty of toxic leadership and in violation of Defense Department and Army conduct regulations. O'Reilly regularly belittled and berated his senior staff, many of whom only escaped his harassment via transfers. The general was described as "condescending, sarcastic, [and] abusive." He was a hostile commander who practiced "management by blowtorch and pliers."[6] Similarly, Mascolo was known to become "unhinged" and ruled his staff through "intimidation and fear." His profanity-laced tirades and intimidating rants were experienced as "group beat downs."[7] Like O'Reilly and Mascolo, Brigadier General Donahue created a toxic command climate. The Army Inspector General (AIG) *twice* substantiated allegations that the general's approach to leadership was "expressing anger and moodiness, bringing people to tears" and "raising his voice or yelling, dominating discussion, exhibiting paranoia, and creating a tense work environment."[8] Similarly, in 2014, the Army Surgeon General suspended Brigadier General John Cho from his leadership position in the Western Regional Medical Command. Cho was subsequently reassigned after an inspector general investigation concluded that he had demeaned and belittled subordinates and failed to treat them with "dignity and respect."[9]

As recently as February 2022, the Army suspended Lieutenant General Duane Gamble, the deputy chief of staff for logistics, after the AIG completed a sixteen-month investigation. The three-star was accused of creating "a toxic and racist" command climate in which he routinely degraded others in public with "much of his ire" directed at African American general officers. In April 2022, Gamble was relieved of command, reprimanded, and demoted to major general for display-ing "counterproductive leadership."[10]

Toxic leadership is not limited to the army. In 2003, the superin-tendent of the Naval Academy, Vice Admiral Richard J. Naughton, re-signed after an inspector general investigation concluded that he had demeaned, berated, and intimidated his subordinates. On one occa-sion, the IG wrote, the admiral had even used "unlawful force" during an altercation with a young Marine sentry. This was not new leader-ship behavior for Naughton, who, after being formally counseled, re-tired at the two-star rank.[11] A decade later, Rear Admiral Charles M. Gaouette was fired as commander of the Stennis Carrier Strike Group after the inspector general received a complaint about his leadership. In 2013, a Navy investigation concluded that the admiral's problematic leadership, including his disrespect of other senior officers, had vi-olated three service regulations. Gaouette received a nonpunitive letter of caution, apologized for his misconduct, and then retired.[12]

That same year, it became public knowledge that Air Force Major General Stephen D. Schmidt regularly and publicly demeaned his sub-ordinates, screamed profanities, and called them idiots. In a one-year period, he "ran through" six aides-de-camp and executive officers. He also allowed his "very rude, demanding, and authoritarian" spouse to send "bullying emails" to staff. In 2013, the Air Force inspector general concluded that Schmidt's leadership was "cruel and oppressive" and characterized his conduct as "abusive and otherwise unwarranted, un-justified, and unnecessary for any lawful purpose and it resulted in mental suffering."[13]

In 2017, Army Chief of Staff Mark A. Milley issued an expanded leadership policy that formally recognized toxic leadership as a strain of destructive behavior that demoralizes subordinates, poisons the work climate, impedes mission accomplishment, and compromises mission effectiveness. According to the new policy, toxic leader conduct includes "bullying . . . abusing authority . . . poor self-control (loses temper), withholding encouragement, unfairness, unjustness, showing little or no respect, talking down to others, [and] behaving erratically." The policy specifically warned against "insensitive driven achievers" and "toxic self-centered abusers" who often achieve impressive results but at unacceptable costs to personnel. While often intelligent, dedicated, and goal-oriented, these leaders create a "frenzied, micromanaged climate" and are "inattentive to the morale of their organization." Toxic leaders exhibited neither self-awareness nor introspection.[14]

A year after the new Army policy was introduced and nearly a quarter century after the first Defense Department JER, the Pentagon expanded its sexual harassment policy to include hazing and bullying. The new joint policy, designed to prevent toxic work environments, prohibited the "berating of another person with the purpose of belittling or humiliating." Bullying was defined as "acts of aggression" toward other service members with the intent of harming them, either physically or psychologically. In brief, the new defense policy forbade demeaning, degrading, and threatening behavior.[15]

Toxic leadership remains a scourge in the military and, as Colonel Reed has eloquently written, American service personnel merit better treatment: "Our Nation entrusts its military leaders with the most precious resource it has to offer — its sons and daughters who selflessly volunteer to serve, often at great personal hazard. Such patriotism deserves the very best leadership that we can muster."[16]

★ ★ ★ ★

One of the most notorious cases of toxic leadership dates back to the early Cold War and the development of nuclear technology. In January 1947, less than two years after the United States dropped atomic bombs on Hiroshima and Nagasaki, Japan, the American government transferred control of the nation's nuclear energy program, including the personnel and laboratories associated with the Manhattan Project, from the military to the new civilian-led Atomic Energy Commission (AEC). While the AEC was charged with developing peaceful applications of nuclear energy, its instant priority in the context of the nascent Cold War was stockpiling the nation's atomic weapons arsenal.

That same year a maverick Navy captain, Hyman G. Rickover, an electrical engineer who had worked briefly at the Oak Ridge atomic laboratory in Tennessee, drafted an audacious white paper arguing for the development of a nuclear navy with a special emphasis on submarines. Going outside the chain of command, he circulated the document to senior military leaders, including Admiral Chester W. Nimitz, the chief of naval operations (CNO). Fortunately for the upstart captain, Nimitz, a submariner, was receptive to the radical concept and persuaded the Truman administration to develop the world's first atomic reactor and construct a uranium-fueled submarine. In 1948, Captain Rickover was charged with establishing and leading the Navy's new Nuclear Power Division within the Bureau of Ships. He was *also* assigned as director of the civilian AEC's new Naval Reactors Branch within the Division of Reactor Development.

With his unique, dual-hatted military and civilian responsibilities, the intense and single-minded Rickover created, led, and championed the Naval Nuclear Propulsion Program, also known as Naval Reactors. "[H]ere was a captain," *Time* magazine noted, "with power that few admirals dreamed of."[17] Absolutely dedicated to his mission, Rickover delivered remarkable results. In June 1952, President Harry S. Truman presided over a grand ceremony in Groton, Connecticut, where the keel of the *Nautilus* submarine was laid. Soon thereafter the secretary of the Navy awarded Rickover the Legion of Merit, declaring that the fifty-two-year-old captain was leading "the most important piece of development work in the history of the Navy."[18] The next year, the AEC made two stunning announcements. First, the prototype reactor for the *Nautilus*, which was being built and tested in Idaho, had "gone critical," meaning it was successfully generating substantial power. Second, the AEC would soon begin building a large, land-based reactor to supply electricity to civilians under Rickover's leadership.[19]

On January 21, 1954, the fully constructed *Nautilus* slid down the ramp at Groton boatyard into the Thames River near the Atlantic Ocean. Sea trials commenced immediately. The technical achievement was revolutionary: a gigantic stride toward the radical transformation of America's maritime force. Rickover's triumph, declares Admiral James Stavridis, was as important as the Navy's historic transitions "from sail to coal and from coal to oil."[20] Rear Admiral Dave Oliver, a submarine commander who worked for Rickover, asserts that "the technical break-through he [Rickover] oversaw was so significant and the cultural change he imposed was so vast that a few years after the submarine *Nautilus*'s first underway in 1955, nuclear power had transformed an auxiliary war-ship of World Wars I and II into a stealth platform that ruled the oceans and unbalanced the Cold War."[21] The extraordinary achievement, Oliver mused, was as if American pilots in World War I had exchanged their propeller-driven biplanes for Stealth F-117 Nighthawks.[22]

However, for all of his visionary brilliance and managerial and engineering competency, Rickover's leadership style amounted to a cult of toxic personality. Because he consistently delivered revolutionary submarines and surface ships, he accumulated unrivaled political power on Capitol Hill and, as the unencumbered czar of Naval Reactors, wielded his authority like an angry butcher dismembering sows in record time. Over many decades, Rickover proved a caustic, temperamental egomaniac who took pleasure in intimidating, threatening, bullying, and humiliating anybody — superiors, subordinates, and peers — who crossed his path. For thirty years, Admiral Stavridis writes, "[Rickover] kept the nuclear Navy in perpetual fear of his explosive temper."[23] Elmo R. Zumwalt, the chief of naval operations during the early 1970s, once quipped that the Navy's two greatest enemies were "the Soviet Union first and Rickover second."[24]

Today, Hyman Rickover looms as an American antihero. "He was a national asset," one contemporary declared, and also "a human failure."[25] Or to borrow an old expression, Rickover both "shines and stinks."[26] His bountiful talents and numerous flaws were discernable from the very beginning of his storied career.

★ ★ ★ ★

Hyman George Rickover was born Chaim Godalia Rykower in Russian Poland on December 24, 1899. Shortly thereafter, his father, Abraham, a tailor and Russian army deserter, left his Jewish village and immigrated to the United States, where he made preparations in New York City for his destitute family. In 1906, Hyman and his mother, Rachel, and his older sister, Fannie, escaped the anti-Semitic pogroms of the First Russian Revolution. They traveled by wagon across Germany as refugees, and made their way to Belgium. There they boarded the steamship *Finland* bound for America. Fannie later remembered that her anxious brother cried when he glimpsed the enormous ships docked at the Port of Antwerp. "The boats were so big," she said, "they frightened him."[27]

The "Rickovers" became American citizens, living first in Brooklyn and later on the west side of Chicago. Because of the family's meager finances, Hyman worked part-time while attending grammar school. Family life centered on work and subsistence, not warm and loving interactions. While a student at John Marshall High School, young Rickover secured full-time employment as a messenger at the Western Union Telegraph Company, where he mastered Morse code. Hyman graduated from high school with honors in early 1918 at the height of the First World War. In June, after passing rigorous entrance examinations, he entered the United States Naval Academy at Annapolis, Maryland. He stood a mere five feet six inches tall and weighed less than one hundred and thirty pounds. The bookish, stubborn, and antisocial teenager had been attracted to the academy's free tuition as much as romantic notions of ships at sea and a swashbuckling martial life.

Because of the war, Rickover and his fellow midshipmen were placed on active duty. Thus began his sixty-four-year career, the longest active service in the history of the American military. The academy for him was an unpleasant experience that forever colored his view of the institution. Like everybody at Annapolis, he was subjected to hazing, but being a poor Jewish immigrant, he "got more than the average." On at least one occasion, Rickover admitted that he "got the hell beat out of me."[28] He resented the mistreatment and long remembered his tormentors at "that lousy boys' school." Many decades later in a *60 Minutes* profile, Rickover recounted that some of those academy "bastard[s]—came around and asked me for favors for them, those who had treated me that way. I wouldn't do it."[29]

To soothe his acute social anxiety and his abject fear of failure, Rickover focused exclusively on academic work and shunned team sports, communal events, and leadership opportunities. Dr. Paul R. Schratz, a retired captain and submariner, later wrote that the maladjusted and abrasive Rickover was known as a loner and a "grinder," someone who "sacrifices athletics, girls, and other normal leisure pursuits to devote all his energy to academics." As a consequence, he was "resented as a cutthroat" trying to climb over others in class standing.[30] In the end, he graduated in the top 20th percent of his 1922 class.

From the beginning of his historic career, the independent-minded and interpersonally challenged Rickover was an outcast. That "sense of isolation and detachment from the larger naval profession," writes Admiral Stavridis, engendered lifelong bitterness and anger.[31]

Rickover's first two duty assignments, lasting from September 1922 to April 1927, were aboard surface warships. On the four-stacker destroyer *La Vallette*, his initial responsibilities included supply, watch, and commissary officer. He worked tirelessly and effectively and was soon elevated to engineering officer, which provided his first major leadership opportunity. Overseeing three dozen sailors, Rickover proved an "intense" taskmaster who pushed hard. While many subordinates disliked his no nonsense approach, he delivered excellent results to an appreciative commander.[32]

In his second assignment, Rickover was one of thirty-five ensigns aboard the battleship *Nevada*. He led the gunnery department's Fire Control Division and was later elevated to watch officer and leader of the Electrical Division. His superb performance earned him laudatory fitness reports and quick promotion to lieutenant, junior grade. Rickover's superior, Captain David W. Todd, praised him as "an exceptionally able and capable officer" who was "thoroughly honest and painstaking in all his work." Todd, however, did question his subordinate's leadership and command presence, writing presciently that while Rickover gets excellent results, he possessed "no outward signs of qualities of leadership."[33] Moreover, as at the academy, Rickover's antisocial nature and obsession with work isolated himself from his peers. He was

gaining a reputation as "an extremely able" but "taciturn and unconge-
nial, young officer."[34]

Rickover later wrote about his nonconformist approach to life. "I
value my own self-approval far more than I do the approval of others,"
he conceded. "I cannot create false impressions, even in small matters;
such would have devastating effect upon my character with the consequence that my individuality would be submerged. These many years I
have refused to conform, combating continually the natural tendency
to become engulfed in the ordinary."[35]

After nearly five years at sea, Rickover was accepted for postgraduate
work in engineering and returned to Annapolis for a year to study fundamentals. After receiving promotion to full lieutenant in 1928, he moved
to New York City to attend Columbia's School of Engineering. "Columbia," Rickover later said, "was the first institution that encouraged me to
think rather than memorize."[36] He earned a master's degree with distinction in electrical engineering. Professor Morton Arendt, a battery expert
who worked closely with the hyper-diligent lieutenant, wrote in a letter
of recommendation that, "This young officer is one of the most earnest
of men whom I have met in 37 years of engineering work."[37]

After Columbia, Rickover received approval to train as a submariner, which he believed offered both professional development and the
surest path to command. He served very briefly on the submarine *S-9*
before reporting to submarine school in January 1930. Rickover came
to loathe his instructors, whom he considered too inexperienced to
teach. He was also dismissive of his classmates, whom he perceived as
being exclusively focused on advancing their careers. After graduating
fourth in a class of thirty-seven officers, Rickover joined the diesel sub
S-48 as the engineer and electrical officer.

Rickover quickly advanced to executive officer, second in command on the *S-48*, but clashed with his doctrinaire superior, Lieutenant Olton R. Bennehoff. That their submarine suffered from end-
less battery and motor problems only exacerbated the situation.
Rickover's frequent confrontations with Bennehoff jeopardized the executive officer's aspirations for command. William D. Irvin, the chief

engineer on the *S-48* who later became a decorated sub commander in World War II, recalled that both men were "brilliant" but also inordinately rigid; they "argued constantly." Irvin also remembered his own disagreements with the irascible Rickover, who could make him "mad as hell." Rickover would invariably say, "Now look, Bill, I've heard what you have to say but shut up and do what I said."[38]

Rickover applied for submarine command but was rejected by the Navy's Bureau of Navigation. Word had spread that he was despised by his crew, characterized as "a despot who could never be satisfied" and an "unpleasant goader of men instead of a leader."[39] Instead, in July 1933, the thirty-three-year-old lieutenant was assigned to shore duty at the Office of Inspector of Naval Material in Philadelphia, Pennsylvania. Although deeply disappointed, Rickover came to enjoy his new station, which focused on improving the design and capabilities of submarines. Having taught himself German at Columbia, Rickover began to translate a seminal submarine text written by German Admiral Hermann Bauer. The book, *Das Underseeboot*, bore the all-inclusive subtitle that translates as: *Its importance as part of a fleet. Its importance in international law. Its employment in war. Its future.* Rickover's translation was subsequently published by the Naval War College's Department of Intelligence.[40]

Despite a positive efficiency report from Rear Admiral Richard M. Watt, Rickover was again denied submarine command and was assigned as assistant engineer on the recently modernized battleship *New Mexico* anchored in Los Angeles Harbor, California. He reported for a two-year tour of duty in April 1935. Delegated significant responsibility by the younger chief engineer, Rickover led 280 men with a heavy hand. Most memorably, he launched a drastic ship-wide fuel efficiency campaign in hopes of winning the Navy's annual battleship engineering competition. His uncompromising zeal won him few friends as his crusade demanded strict and uncomfortable restrictions on hot showers, indoor heating, and electric lighting. The indomitable Rickover even rebuked his captain, Charles C. Soule, for "setting a bad example" when the skipper dared to turn on the heat in his personal quarters.[41]

In the end, the *New Mexico* won two engineering competitions and Rickover was selected for promotion to lieutenant commander in 1937. The year prior he had requested a momentous shift in career lanes from sea command to shore engineering. He had rightly concluded that his prospects for a major ship command were bleak. Captain Frank Fletcher, Rickover's superior on the *New Mexico*, was fully supportive of the transition. He viewed Rickover as brilliant and exceptionally dedicated, but not an inspiring leader of sailors. In a 1937 fitness report, Fletcher wrote, "This officer is more than any one man responsible for the *New Mexico* winning the engineering competition two years in succession. Has untiring energy, unusually keen intelligence and is devoted to his profession. I consider he is exceptionally well qualified for engineering duty *only*."[42]

While waiting to hear about his shore engineering application, Rickover was assigned to the U.S. Asiatic Fleet where the newly promoted lieutenant commander suffered an embarrassing professional setback. In July 1937, he was given command of the "decrepit rust bucket" USS *Finch*, a minesweeper and tug operating in Chinese waters.[43] Rickover felt disrespected by the assignment and "swore terribly," but at least he had gained control of a ship.[44] He set out to overhaul the unsightly old vessel, which suffered from severe corrosion and constant engine malfunction. Rickover's rigid standards and obvious impatience soured the crew on his leadership. They "resented the new strong hand" who was pursuing "an enormous, almost quixotic, task."[45] Worse, Rickover "caught hell" from Fleet Commander Harry E. Yarnell after the lieutenant commander dangerously stored fifteen hundred gallons of excess gasoline on the *Finch*'s open deck and then pulled the minesweeper alongside the admiral's heavy cruiser, the *Augusta*.[46] The entire episode solidified the view that the lieutenant commander was ill suited for sea command.

Fortunately for Rickover, the Navy approved his application for engineering duty. He was temporarily transferred to the Cavite Navy Yard in the Philippines before reporting to the Bureau of Engineering in Washington, DC. While at Cavite, he was in charge of ship maintenance and repair. Rickover's tireless commitment and exacting standards won praise from his superior, but his caustic manner produced "whole shiploads of enemies."[47]

Lieutenant Commander Rickover reported to the Bureau of Engineering in August 1939, only weeks before the outbreak of World War II. He was made the assistant chief of the electrical section and took over as chief the following year. The section included both military and civilian personnel, and the position allotted Rickover extensive engagement with defense contractors. He was as demanding of civilians as he was of sailors, regardless of title or rank.

While assigned to the electrical section, Rickover's "differences" with others frequently "swelled into bitter personal disputes." His tack was primarily one of coercion. "Listen," he once warned executives at General Electric and General Motors, "you boys are going to do this. You're going to develop these generators." He added, "If you don't get to work on it, we will have to find ways to force you to do it."[48] He threatened another electrical contractor this way: "I want you to manufacture panels to those specifications. If you won't, the Navy will cancel all future orders for control panels and work with someone who will."[49]

In January 1942, a month after the Japanese attack on Pearl Harbor, Rickover was promoted to the rank of commander. Thereafter, he flew to Hawaii to inspect progress on the salvage work being conducted on the damaged battleships. The successful restoration of both the *California* and the *West Virginia* gained Rickover considerable notoriety in the Navy. During the war, his section grew exponentially, to more than three hundred people, the largest division within the Bureau of Ships. "Throughout the war," journalist Robert Wallace wrote, "Rickover worked to cram the Navy's ships with the best available equipment, driving his men to exhaustion, snarling at boobs, wrestling like Laocoon with the serpent of red tape."[50]

In accomplishing his mission, Commander Rickover never hesitated to exceed his authority and encroach upon the responsibilities of other Navy section chiefs. "He was tough, abusive, and abrasive," writes biographer Francis Duncan, and his peers and many defense contractors "would not forget or forgive his high-handed ways or insulting manners."[51]

Nevertheless, Rickover's superiors admired his expertise, tenacity, and resourcefulness. One commander wrote, "It is considered that he has made as great a contribution to the successful preparation for the carrying on the war as any officer of the Navy's Shore Establishment. The value of his contributions to the improvement of our ships is inestimable."[52]

Rickover, who had been promoted to captain in 1943, was dispatched to the Pacific late in the war to construct a massive ship-repair base on Okinawa, Japan. Almost immediately he clashed with his boss, Commodore Fred D. Kirtland, the commander of the naval operating base. The two engaged in a public and "violent disagreement" over a personnel decision.[53] Rickover carried the day, but Kirtland was later unforgiving in his performance evaluation. He viewed the defiant captain as power-hungry and insular. The commodore rated Rickover deficient in his "ability to command," deficient in the "use of ideas and suggestions of others," and deficient in his inability to "effectively delegate responsibility."[54] With this rebuke, the captain's promotion to rear admiral was highly improbable.

After the war, in the spring of 1946, forty-six-year-old Rickover and six lower-ranking naval officers were attached to the Army's Manhattan Engineer District (the Manhattan Project) at Oak Ridge, Tennessee. They, the so-called Naval Group, joined discussions on experimental nuclear power reactors. Along with the other sailors, Rickover began making the case for the Navy's adoption of nuclear power. In November, they produced "a bold and provocative" report that predicted the Navy could develop its first nuclear-fueled vessel in five to eight years.[55] The document was submitted to Vice Admiral Earle W. Mills at the Bureau of Ships and forwarded to the chief of naval operations, Admiral Nimitz.

After a year at Oak Ridge, Rickover was reassigned to Washington, DC, as a nuclear power advisor to Vice Admiral Mills. He commenced "his hard-sell" campaign for a nuclear navy but found only a few like-minded zealots.[56] In December 1947 he crafted a "carefully worded letter" arguing that national security demanded "a submarine with unlimited endurance at high speed submerged" and "only nuclear power could meet that need."[57] He recommended that the Bureau of Ships oversee a revolutionary development program and projected that an atomic submarine could be constructed in seven years. Mills endorsed the audacious proposal, as did Admiral Nimitz and Secretary of Navy John L. Sullivan.

During the next six months, Rickover maneuvered to gain responsibility for the proposed nuclear development program. And, despite the captain's well-known "personality problems," his ambitions were realized in 1948.[58] He was named the head of the Nuclear Power Branch in the Navy's Research Division and also assigned to the civilian Atomic Energy Commission as the director of the Naval Reactors Branch in the Research Development Division. The nascent joint military-civilian program became known as Naval Reactors, and for the next three decades Rickover ruled over it with an iron fist inside an iron glove. One AEC official later said of Rickover, "He is not just an ordinary empire builder. He's a complete autocrat."[59] Leveraging his civilian position with AEC, the now forty-eight-year-old captain gained complete control over the selection and training of all naval nuclear personnel, and because the Naval Reactors research and development funding came from the AEC he was often able to bypass his Navy superiors. Flouting his newfound independence, the admiral routinely shed his navy whites for civilian garb.

Rickover set an audacious goal of constructing the world's first nuclear submarine by January 1, 1955. In the first two years of development, he recruited thirty-six professionals to his staff, half military and half civilian. Rickover's meetings with government and industry scientists and engineers were frequently "loud and stormy." His "fierce arguments" with Lawrence R. Hafstad, his civilian superior at the AEC, were legendary.[60] One business executive informed a reporter, "Now don't misunderstand me. I don't dislike Rickover. I hate him."[61]

Nevertheless, the Navy captain's explicit candor, obvious expertise, and indomitable can-do spirit won him powerful allies on Capitol Hill, especially with members of the Joint Committee on Atomic Energy. In a *Life* magazine profile, Robert Wallace wrote, "Unlikely as it may sound, Rickover is a superb politician. He has an acute understanding of the congressional mind and of the pressures upon it." Wallace concluded,

"Rickover has always given Congress a straight, if sometime horrifying, answer. As a result he enjoys enormous prestige in the Capitol."[62]

In charge of a critical national security program, Rickover expected to be promoted to rear admiral despite having accrued so many enemies over the years. He was so confident of promotion that he hand-picked his successor from within Naval Reactors, Captain Robert L. Moore Jr. Rickover, however, was denied promotion by a board of admirals. Naturally, he was furious. When he learned that Moore had been discussing changes that he would make as the future head of Naval Reactors, Rickover exercised his fury and banished the once-favored captain from the program.[63]

A positive turning point for Rickover came on June 14, 1952, when before ten thousand people in Groton, Connecticut, President Truman presided over the keel laying of the *Nautilus*, which in a few years would become the first nuclear-powered submarine. Navy Secretary Dan A. Kimball told the crowd that nuclear energy was "the greatest advance in propulsion since the Navy shifted from sail to steam" and that nobody was playing a more central role in its development than "Captain H. G. Rickover."[64]

In July, Kimball decorated Rickover with a gold medal for having "held tenaciously to a single important goal through discouraging frustration and opposition."[65] The ceremony was widely covered in the press. The resolute and irascible captain was becoming a known figure beyond the Navy and Capitol Hill. The day after the ceremony, a Navy selection board convened to select those captains who would be promoted to rear admiral. Rickover, the "obstinate, egotistical, and abrasive" non-conformist, was passed over yet again.[66] He faced mandatory retirement in one year. The news shocked people outside of the Navy.

An extensive outcry ensued from the press, the public, and political allies. A concerted campaign was waged to salvage Rickover's career and cement his leadership of Naval Reactors. Congressman Sydney Yates of Chicago took to the House floor and attacked the Navy selection board for having "disposed of a naval officer who would not conform, an officer who is perhaps the Navy's outstanding specialist in the field of atomic energy."[67] In July 1953, the first year of the Eisenhower administration, a special Navy board voted six to three to promote Rickover to rear admiral. The three officers voting no were all fellow engineers.

Meanwhile, Rickover was overseeing tremendous progress at Naval Reactors. In June 1953, the Mark I, the *Nautilus*'s prototype atomic plant in Idaho, had safely generated substantial power. And while construction of the submarine continued in Groton, Rickover personally selected and supervised the training of its inaugural crew. The sailors received a rigorous academic education in physics, mathematics, and reactor engineering, as well as practical training in Idaho under a dedicated team of scientists and engineers. Finally, on January 21, 1954, fifteen thousand people gathered at the Westinghouse Electric Boat Company shipyard in Groton to witness the launching of the world's first atomic submarine. First lady Mamie Eisenhower christened the *Nautilus* with a silver-cased bottle of champagne. The submarine was an incredible achievement, a revolutionary technology that would revolutionize national defense strategy.

Rickover had only just begun to realize his bold vision of a nuclear navy. The *Nautilus* was his stark proof of a radical concept. During the ensuing decades, the White House, the Defense Department, and Congress proved more than willing to underwrite the construction of a great fleet of nuclear submarines and surface ships. To meet the critical demand, Rickover aggressively and successfully expanded his Naval Reactors empire, and influential allies in Congress ensured his promotion in rank despite objections from the Navy brass. "I am a creature of Congress," he would testify, "because, had it not been for Congress, I would not be here today."[68]

By 1972, the nuclear fleet included more than a one hundred ships and the vice admiral had overseen the training of 4,000 officers — interviewing and selecting nearly every one of them — and 22,500 enlisted sailors.[69] The next year, President Richard M. Nixon presided over Rickover's promotion to four-star admiral. Nixon proclaimed, "[T]he greatness of the American military service, and particularly the greatness of the Navy, is symbolized in this ceremony today, because this man, who is controversial, this man, who comes up with unorthodox ideas, did not become submerged by the bureaucracy, because once genius is submerged by bureaucracy, a nation is doomed to mediocrity."[70] By June 1985, three years after Rickover's retirement, the Navy had commissioned a total of 146 nuclear vessels (mostly submarines, but also nine cruisers and four aircraft carriers).[71]

Rickover had in effect built a nuclear navy within the Navy. Along with it he established a subculture that was fully dedicated to technical excellence with a fixation on safety. He devised and oversaw a quality-focused managerial system that featured precise processes and procedures, and also promoted innovation and continuous improvement. Attention to detail and stringent personal responsibility were lived mantras at Naval Reactors. To create a "culture of engineering excellence," Rickover also required every officer who wanted to command a nuclear submarine to qualify as an engineer. This controversial decision created a "new pecking order," elevating engineers over weapons, navigations, and operations officers.[72] The fact that the U.S. Navy, unlike the Soviet's, never suffered a reactor accident is testament to the effectiveness of Rickover's management systems and priorities. By the time of Rickover's death in 1986, it was estimated that America's nuclear navy had logged "40 million miles and . . . accumulated the equivalent of 30 centuries of operating time without a death or serious accident attributed to nuclear propulsion."[73]

★ ★ ★ ★

Rickover's record of accomplishment at Naval Reactors was extraordinary, truly historic. Yet, his leadership and treatment of people — his means for achieving that success — was ethically objectionable. Admiral Ralph K. James, once Rickover's superior, rightly characterized him as highly effective but deeply unethical: "an expediter, a person who knew how to twist people's tails and get the maximum out of them by threatening, more than leadership."[74] Chief of Naval Operations Elmo Zumwalt viewed Rickover as a ruthless autocrat who ruled and defended a "totalitarian mini-state" within the Navy.[75] Admiral James Stavridis recently described Rickover as "endlessly temperamental and unpredictable," a fearsome commander who "used anger like a kind of psychological rain" to coerce subordinates and others.[76]

Rickover routinely demeaned and humiliated sailors and civilians. Those subordinates he thought were overweight were ordered to write "fat letters" to their loved ones promising to lose weight.[77] Throughout his career, Rickover willfully abused his authority and embarrassed military officers by putting them under the command of their subordinates, even enlisted personnel, when he thought the lower-ranking sailors demonstrated superior competency.[78] On one occasion, Rickover punished a commander by making him wear his secretary's wig for an entire day.[79] In 1953, the admiral hired a female officer, who possessed no education in science or engineering, and gave her substantial responsibility for secondary system chemistry and heat exchangers. Rickover ordered her boss at Naval Reactors, Jim Cochran, *not* to change her assignment. "Most of us," writes former Navy chemical engineer Theodore Rockwell, "figured he [Rickover] had probably done this to humiliate Cochran because he was presumably unhappy with how chemistry was being handled."[80]

Rickover's renowned foul-mouthed tirades were meant to intimidate subordinates, civilians, and sailors. Journalist Robert Wallace described his persona as "clear meat-ax disposition all the way through."[81] Admiral Dave Oliver observed, "His cursing frightened some [subordinates] so much they froze and couldn't adequately explain themselves, and it caused others to unnecessarily back down, rather than hold their ground. It produced an environment not conducive to the free flow of information."[82] Whenever Rickover appeared at a work site, fear reverberated throughout. News of his arrival caused all hands to "tense and quicken as a slight, spare human tornado whirls through the shop. Few jobs are done fast enough or well enough to suit . . . Rickover. . . . His passage leaves a boiling wake of lacerated egos."[83]

Nor did Rickover spare reporters from his acid tongue. In a 1984 *60 Minutes* interview, he told Diane Sawyer, "No, I never thought I was smart. I thought the people I dealt with were dumb . . . including you." When she responded that he had said something similar to legendary journalist Edward R. Murrow, Rickover recalled, "Oh yeah . . . I told him he was asking stupid questions."[84]

Rickover's abusiveness, ego, and rigidity limited his ability to maximize the performance of countless Defense Department personnel. "For all his accomplishments," wrote Admiral Oliver, "there is no evidence that Rickover sought to alter his personal management style to accommodate the wide range of personalities working for him." Rickover "appears never to have been sufficiently at ease and confident to experiment with altering his management and leadership style. He thus had difficulty getting more from the less-capable individuals who make up the bulk of every organization."[85]

Controlling, suspicious, and paranoid, Rickover did not countenance challenges to his authority. Admiral James recalled in an oral history that "anyone who began to challenge him [Rickover] . . . wasn't long for the program. He's arranged for the transfer out of the program . . . any number of senior engineering-duty officers who had tremendous technical capability, greater by many measures than Rickover ever possessed." These potential successors, James asserted, also possessed the ethical and interpersonal leadership skills that Rickover so clearly lacked. James surmised that these superb officers "might have carried on the [Naval Reactors] program with equal, if not greater, success because they wouldn't have been so brutal and wouldn't have achieved their pinnacle of success by stepping over the recumbent bodies of their associates, which was typical of the Rickover approach."[86]

Rickover's notorious interviews with nuclear engineer candidates revealed his bizarre, insulting, and demeaning approach. Even Marc Wortman, the admiral's most recent and admiring biographer, writes: "Rickover could also prove simply cruel. At time he took malicious glee in hazing interviewees mercilessly with demonstrations of his absolute control over their future lives."[87] For example, the admiral sawed several inches off the front legs of a wooden chair and made many candidates undergo his stressful interrogations while trying not to slide off a slick seat. "It was difficult," Rickover acknowledged, "because . . . it was a shiny chair and they kept sliding off. So . . . they had to maintain their wits about them while they were asked these questions."[88] Some candidates were ordered out of the interview room and into a storage closet, where they stood for hours before returning to face Rickover all over again. The admiral justified his unprofessional behavior by claiming that the candidates brought it upon themselves. "Well, they came in, they gave stupid answers. So I thought I'd give them a chance to think. I'd put them in there [the closet] for a couple hours, three hours, and it gave them plenty of time to think."[89] Rickover recalled that one civilian engineer came to the interview sporting long hair. The admiral wanted to hire him but insisted that the man get a haircut. The young man refused. Rickover thought, "Fine. That was the end. The little son of a bitch should have . . . cut it all off and gotten a wig."[90]

Commander Elmo R. Zumwalt Jr., who later became chief of naval operations, wrote a thirteen-page transcript of his wrenching 1959 interview with Rickover. At the time, Rickover was a vice admiral and Zumwalt was a candidate to command a nuclear destroyer or become the executive officer of a nuclear cruiser. At 5 p.m. on a Friday, Zumwalt was told to sit and wait for his interview with Rickover. Two and a half hours later, he was informed that the admiral had left the building long ago; they were rescheduled to meet the following day. On Saturday, Zumwalt waited and waited until late in the afternoon, when he was informed that the interview was postponed indefinitely without explanation.

Weeks later, Zumwalt, at work on the executive staff of an assistant secretary of the Navy, received a sudden telephone call. Rickover wanted to conduct the interview immediately. Zumwalt gained permission from his boss to rush over. The admiral started the interview by accusing the commander of being overly cautious and without imagination or initiative. Surprised by the criticism, Zumwalt said he needed a few moments to respond. "This is no charge, God damn it," Rickover snapped. "You're not being accused of anything. You are being interviewed and don't you dare start trying to conduct the interview yourself. You are one of those wise Goddamn aides. You've been working for your boss so long you think you are wearing his stars." The admiral ordered Zumwalt out of the room, growling, "And when you come back in here, you better be able to maintain the proper respect."[91]

Zumwalt was recalled thirty minutes later. Rickover asked if Zumwalt had worked while attending high school aside from summers. The commander began to answer by saying he did work during the summer months, but Rickover interrupted. "Listen to my questions, God damn it," the admiral shouted. "You've been an aide too long. You're too used to asking the questions. You are trying to conduct this interview again." Rickover then asked about Zumwalt's extracurricular activities. The commander talked about being a debater and an admirer of attorney Clarence Darrow, who could effectively argue both sides of an issue. The admiral shouted, "You are absolutely wrong. I warn you here and now you better not try to talk to me about anything you don't know anything about. I know more about anything than you do." Rickover ordered Zumwalt out of his office, again saying, "Get him out of here. I'm sick of talking to an aide that tries to pretend he knows everything."[92]

Zumwalt returned to the interrogation chair an hour later. Rickover asked what reforms he would make to the Naval Academy's curriculum. The commander said he would curtail history and English courses in favor of more science and mathematics. "Thank God you are not the superintendent!" Rickover bellowed. "It's just the kind of stupid jerk like you who becomes superintendent . . . . Do you mean you would graduate illiterate technicians?" In truth, Rickover agreed with Zumwalt about the curriculum. Nevertheless, the incessant grilling turned to the subject of Plato's *Republic*, which ultimately caused the admiral to say, "I'm getting sick of this guy."[93] He ordered Zumwalt out for a third time.

After waiting forty-five minutes, Zumwalt retook his seat before Rickover. The admiral inquired about his first assignment after graduating from the academy. Zumwalt said he had been an assistant engineer aboard a destroyer in the Pacific. Rickover snapped, "You weren't the assistant engineer. You were just a flunky. There you go again, trying to act like an aide again. Trying to impress me." He then asked what Zumwalt would tell people at the Pentagon about this interview. Zumwalt answered, "I'm going to say it was the most fascinating experience of my life." The admiral snarled, "Now you're being greasy. Get out of here."[94] The interview was finally over.

Zumwalt was certain that he had failed, but Rickover wanted him in the nuclear Navy. He was offered a position as the executive officer aboard the *Long Beach*, a nuclear-powered, guided-missile cruiser. The thirty-eight-year-old commander declined, and instead assumed command of the USS *Dewey*, a new but conventionally powered guided-missile frigate. Eleven years later, after serving as Commander Naval Forces Vietnam, Zumwalt became the chief of naval operations, the youngest ever, and Rickover's superior.

In *Against the Tide*, a book about Rickover's leadership, Rear Admiral Dave Oliver recounted his cohort's 1977 training experience as prospective atomic sub commanders. Their three-month course culminated in extensive written and oral examinations and a final group interview with Rickover. The four-star admiral, who was then approaching eighty years old, entered the room and paced back and forth. At one point he said to the ten officers, "I understand genetics," and "If you make a mistake with my nuclear plant . . . it's because your mother was a street whore who trawled for tricks with a mattress on her back."[95] Oliver inadvertently laughed out loud. In doing so, he had broken a cardinal rule: "Never relax around a badger or an admiral." A furious Rickover leaped onto Oliver's desk and jerked his tie toward the ceiling.[96]

Oliver's memory was vivid. "I simultaneously became aware of two things," he writes. "First, there was a seventy-seven-year-old man who had suffered at least two heart attacks standing on my desk. Second, I was terrified, a bit sad for someone who liked to think of himself as a battle-hardened warrior."[97] Clearly shaken, Oliver explained to Rickover that he had heard the admiral's strict safety message many times but never in such an entertaining fashion. According to Oliver, the red-faced admiral shot "a long unblinking stare" and then "dropped my tie, jumped down directly from my desk (without touching anything), and walked wordlessly from the room."[98] Interview over. Oliver became a nuclear submarine commander.

The next year, some two hundred fifty midshipmen from Annapolis interviewed at Rickover's Naval Reactors headquarters in Arlington, Virginia. One chronicled his startling experience. After waiting for two hours, he sat in front of Rickover with a navy commander sitting behind him. The admiral unleashed a tirade about the midshipman's choice of oceanography as his major at the academy. "How can it possibly help the Navy?" he asked. The midshipman stated he possessed valuable knowledge about currents and underwater sound. The commander sitting behind the young man began yelling. Rickover left the room saying, "You're worthless to me."[99] The commander shouted over and over that the midshipman was worthless.

When Rickover returned he echoed the refrain. He asked how many oceanographers were in the entire Navy. The midshipman answered that there were enough to fill the allotted billets. Rickover "exploded" in foulmouthed anger. When he repeated the question, the midshipman asserted that there were "probably 2,000 oceanographers in the Navy." The admiral exploded again, and again, and again. After asking the candidate how many oceanographers had served in World War II, Rickover himself answered, "Goddamn it. You son of a bitch. There were only two in the whole goddamn war." The admiral then pivoted, asking the midshipman if he was engaged and planned to have children. He responded yes and said they planned to have three kids. Rickover gave a bewildering response: "Well, you could tell her to have triplets twice or twins three times or she could have a litter of six — a litter of six."[100] The midshipman was summarily dismissed. Like Oliver, he joined Rickover's nuclear Navy.

President Jimmy Carter, a Naval Academy graduate, recalled his own stressful interview with Rickover. The meeting was conducted in a large room and lasted two hours. The admiral let the young lieutenant select the subjects of their conversation. Carter clung to his strengths, including naval electronics, gunnery, tactics, music, and literature. Rickover asked a barrage of thoughtful and penetrating questions, which caused Carter to realize how limited his own knowledge actually was. "He [Rickover] always looked right into my eyes," Carter remembered, "and he never smiled. I was saturated with cold sweat." Toward the end of the interview Rickover gave the lieutenant a chance to redeem himself. He asked if Carter had given his best effort while at the academy. Carter started to answer in the affirmative but decided to admit that he could have learned more. "I finally gulped," Carter writes, "and said, 'No, sir, I didn't *always* do my best.'" Rickover gave him a long icy stare. He then finally asked, "Why not?" Mentally and emotionally drained, Carter simply froze. "I sat there for a while, shaken," he recalled, "and then slowly left the room."[101]

After being accepted into the nuclear engineering program, Carter was shocked by Rickover's callous and exacting leadership. "[H]e demanded total dedication from his subordinates," Carter recounted. "We feared and respected him and strove to please him. I do not . . . remember his ever saying a complimentary word to me. The absence of a [negative] comment was his compliment; he never hesitated to criticize severely."[102] Carter continued, "As a matter of fact, all the time I worked for him he never said a decent word to me. . . . If he found no fault, he simply looked, turned around and walked away. However, if I made the slightest mistake, in one of the foulest and most obnoxious voices I ever heard, he would tell the other people in the area what a horrible disgrace I was to the Navy."[103] When asked if he ever hated Rickover, Carter admitted, "There were a few times, yeah, when I hated him."[104]

Rickover continued to coerce and micromanage subordinates even after they passed intensive screening and training. Every workday he engaged in at least sixteen prearranged telephone calls. He also demanded continuous reporting in the form of "Dear Admiral" letters that detailed problems at Naval Reactors. "Share good news with your spouse," he barked. "All I care about is the problems."[105] Rickover's development of "the Pinks" management system further demonstrated his extreme determination to control people and information. In an era before photocopy machines, typists used carbon paper to make simultaneous copies, including pink ones. Laboring "under threat of expulsion," each typist at Naval Reactors headquarters was required to send Rickover the pink copy of every single document — correspondence, memorandum, and reports — whether partial drafts or final versions.[106] "Dammit," he once scolded his secretary, "I want *everything* that's typed in here."[107] Historian Francis Duncan underscored that "under no circumstances was a section chief or a project manager allowed to intercept or alter a pink."[108] The stacks of daily pinks enabled Rickover to scrutinize, question, and criticize the work of civilian and military personnel.

Rickover's rigid and contemptuous personality was on display to the bitter end of his career. In late 1981, Defense Secretary Caspar Weinberger and Navy Secretary John F. Lehman Jr. convinced President Ronald Reagan that the eighty-one-year-old admiral had to go. On November 13, Lehman announced that Rickover would retire in favor of a younger four-star officer. Lehman conceded to reporters that the cantankerous admiral preferred to "stay on." An accompanying press release noted, "The president feels that this is the proper time to plan and carry out an orderly transition."[109]

Against Weinberger's best judgment, Lehman arranged a meeting at the White House. He wanted the president to thank Rickover for six decades of service and to offer him a position in the administration as a nuclear science advisor. The meeting on January 8, 1982 went awry before it began. When Lehman arrived at the White House reception room, Rickover was waiting. He snapped, "What the hell are you doing here? You have a hell of a nerve after you fired me!"[110] According to Lehman, Rickover "launched into a stream of vituperation against me that left me only slightly less stunned than the receptionist."[111] The official meeting in the Oval Office proved an unmitigated disaster.

After press photographers vacated the room, Reagan began to express his appreciation for Rickover's historic accomplishments. Before long, however, the admiral interrupted, asking the president why he was being fired. Rickover then broadsided Lehman, calling him an ignorant "piss-ant" and "a goddamn liar."[112] The president was not spared from Rickover's wrath. "Are you a man? Can't you make decisions yourself? What do you know about this problem? . . . They say you're too old, and that you're not up to the job either."[113] In the face of this gross insubordination, Reagan remained calm. He told the supercilious admiral that he was not being fired and that he hoped he would join the administration in a civilian capacity. Rickover interjected, "Aw, cut the crap!"[114] At the admiral's request, Reagan agreed to speak in private. Lehman, Weinberger, and National Security Advisor Bill Clark moved to an adjacent office. "This may give you some idea of what we in the navy have had to put up with from Rickover over the years," the weary Lehman told the pair.[115] Three weeks later, Rickover was retired. "The once invincible Admiral," biographer Theodore Rockwell wrote, "was now history."[116]

★ ★ ★ ★

Hyman Rickover's career demonstrates both the allure and the hazard of toxic leadership. In the context of the Cold War and the arms race with the Soviet Union, Rickover's revolutionary vison and successful development of a nuclear navy significantly bolstered U.S. national security and helped to allay existential fears of conflict and survival. In times of crisis and uncertainty, people and organizations are often attracted to confident and decisive leaders. When those leaders, like Rickover, deliver remarkable achievements people are willing to tolerate and even condone leader misbehavior, including acts of narcissism, toxicity, and authoritarianism. In such circumstances, utilitarian ethics reign supreme; effective ends justify malfeasant means. A senior civilian engineer once asked Rickover if the ethical leadership of personnel was important to him. The admiral snapped, "Not if it interfered with getting the job done."[117] But in the profession of arms within a democratic society, mission accomplishment cannot be the sole operating principle. The means of achievement, including the treatment of defense personnel — fellow citizens — must be as ethical as the aims. In the end, a critical character test of powerful leaders is how they treat the less powerful.

As is common with organizations that enable toxic leadership, Rickover's rigid and caustic management of people engendered immediate and long-lasting problems for the Navy. Not surprisingly, many subordinate nuclear commanders followed their cutthroat admiral's example and emerged as toxic leaders themselves. "Basically, it was a world of negativism," one nuclear submariner told the *Washington Post* in 1981. Nuclear officers are "always looking for something wrong. . . . finding and correcting a mistake" made by a fellow seaman who was then subjected to "a lightning bolt out of the sky." In short, the technocratic and coercive management of Rickover's nuclear program disregarded the critical "element of humanism" in the leadership equation.[118] Decades after the admiral's retirement, submariners still complained about the lasting effects of his culture of toxicity, which had "permeated throughout the ages."[119]

The negative leadership within the nuclear navy contributed to systematic retention problems.[120] In 1988, former Navy Secretary John Lehman wrote that it was common for 60 percent of nuclear officers to quit the service after completing their "first obligated tour." He quoted a representative commander who left the Navy years earlier to signal "the alarming attrition rate" resulting from "Admiral Rickover's mistreatment of nuclear submarine officers."[121] Twelve years later, Vice Admiral N. R. Ryan, Chief of Naval Personnel, testified before a subcommittee of the Senate Armed Services Committee that "retaining the right quantity and quality of nuclear-trained officers remains the primary challenge for the community."[122] The retention problem has continued into the twenty-first century.[123]

In *Sailing True North*, a 2019 treatise on leadership and character, Admiral Stavridis concludes that Rickover's unremittingly combative style and use of anger as motivational technique was a professional moral failure, one that was counterproductive for the Navy. Stavridis writes, "Anger violates the basic tenets of civility, creates either slavish subjugation or internally hidden reserves of resentment that will ultimately play out. It opens up a chain of behavior that pays forward all the wrong moral cues and leads so often to a cycle of bad behavior."[124] Stavridis rightly praises Rickover for pulling and piloting the sometimes hidebound Navy into the nuclear era, but he also correctly condemns the admiral as "a harsh, toxic leader" who possessed an alarming "character flaw that he could not control."[125]

Unfortunately, the vexing problem of toxic leadership endures in the U.S. military — even at the flag-officer rank. Take the disturbing case of Brigadier General Norman Cooling, who in July 2017 assumed a new post as the congressional assistant to the commandant of the Marine Corps. Over the next six months, personnel at the Office of Legislative Assistant (OLA) and Senate staffers witnessed a pattern of misconduct that included Cooling's abusive tirades and demeaning, sexist commentaries. In February 2018, the Senate Armed Services Committee filed a complaint with Defense Secretary James Mattis. Cooling, who had been recommended for promotion to major general, was immediately suspended from OLA and subsequently reassigned to Marine Corps headquarters.

The Defense Department inspector general (DoDIG) conducted a fourteen-month investigation that included thirty-seven witness interviews and the examination of ten thousand emails. In the final May 2019 report, the inspector general substantiated most of the allegations of abuse and derision. Cooling had consistently devalued women — stating, for example, that they were "just naturally better at being secretaries and doing work like scheduling." He also asserted that the introduction of "inferior" women into combat had "burdened men with picking up the slack." Cooling once told a young female Marine who aspired to become a pilot that he "would rather have his daughter work in a brothel than be a female Marine pilot." The DoDIG concluded that such misogyny had evidenced "a lack of leadership, responsibility, and restraint, especially as a general officer."[126]

A majority of witnesses interviewed agreed that Cooling was "an equal opportunity offender"; he berated and abused women and men alike. On one occasion when a staff member provided the general with a list of new Marine Corps congressional fellows, Cooling erupted in anger. "You're giving it to me at the last second?" he screamed. "Are you trying to fuck me?" He then turned to another staff officer who had just returned from authorized leave. "And where the fuck," he growled, "have you been? What the fuck is this? This is bullshit." On another occasion, Cooling threatened to "castrate" a staff member who he suspected was withholding information from him. And the day before the senate committee filed its formal complaint with Secretary Mattis, Cooling humiliated a female officer during a department meeting. He told his staff that she "is a bad officer. Don't ever do anything like her." When the officer attempted to defend herself, Cooling shouted, "I don't fucking care."[127]

The inspector general's overall assessment of Cooling's leadership was unsparing. His abusive and intimidating leadership had created a toxic, undignified command climate that clearly violated military standards. "In sum, we [the DoDIG] substantiated the allegation that BGen [Brigadier General] Cooling's overall course of conduct disparaged, bullied, and humiliated subordinates, devalued women, and created a negative OLA work environ that led to a general distrust of his impartiality and leadership."[128] Investigators pointed to this representative comment from a subordinate: "His leadership was not effective here because he was just killing the weakest in the herd, and we were all eventually the weakest in the herd."[129]

Unfortunately, Cooling's is not an isolated contemporary case. In 2019–2020, the Air Force Inspector General substantiated allegations of toxic leadership against multiple female general officers. Brigadier General Brenda Cartier demeaned and bullied subordinates while commanding the Fifty-Eighth Special Operations Wing at Kirtland Air Force Base. According to the Air Force inspector general (AFIG), her "profane and disparaging language" was both "pervasive and personal." The AFIG cited a squadron commander who had attempted to provide Cartier with constructive feedback. "I don't think she realizes," the commander said, "how toxic or how abrasive she can be."[130]

Likewise, in April 2019 Brigadier General Kristin Goodwin was relieved as the Commandant of Cadets at the Air Force Academy amid allegations of misbehavior, including toxic leadership. The general was perceived by subordinates and colleagues as a cold, caustic, self-serving taskmaster who demoralized others; this caused distrust in her leadership. After conducting an investigation, the inspector general concluded that Goodwin had indeed fostered an unhealthy command climate and cited one senior subordinate who asserted that the general had created "the most bizarrely toxic and mistrustful organization I've ever been part of."[131]

As with Goodwin and Cartier, the Air Force inspector general determined that Major General Dawn Dunlop had created a toxic command climate. In May 2019, Dunlop, the military's highest ranking female fighter pilot, was fired as director of the Pentagon's top secret Special Access Programs Control Office. She was known to frequently berate and insult her "idiot" subordinates, often scolding them in public. According to a January 2020 inspector general investigative report, Dunlop's "dictatorial" and "indecorous" leadership fostered "a toxic work environment" that demoralized and intimidated subordinates and compromised her standing as a general officer.[132]

The examples of Dunlop, Goodwin, Cartier, and Cooling vividly demonstrate the ongoing presence of toxic leadership in the U.S. military — and the need to expunge it. The moral responsibility rests with *all* Defense Department personnel, and the early detection of workplace toxicity is critical to eradicating such bad leadership. Most crucially, commanders need to actively monitor and regulate *how* subordinate commanders and their personnel are accomplishing missions. If subordinate commanders are suspected of toxic behavior, then senior commanders must confront them and, if the allegations are substantiated, help them change under the threat of relief or permanent dismissal. Peers and subordinates also have ethical obligations. They possess a duty to provide poorly behaving colleagues and superiors constructive feedback, and if need be, muster the moral courage to blow the whistle to higher authorities. "[D]ealing with toxic leaders is not for the faint of heart," writes leadership scholar Jean Lipman-Blum. "The costs of *inaction*, however, may be even greater."[133]

CHAPTER FIVE

OBSTRUCTION OF JUSTICE

John M. Poindexter and Colin L. Powell

OBSTRUCTION OF JUSTICE—the commission of
criminal acts, such as destroying evidence and
making false statements, intended to undermine
the due administration of law and justice

Obstruction of justice—whether impeding government investigators
or destroying evidence—is an all-too-common federal crime and one
that has frequently rocked the White House. Perhaps the most infamous obstruction case remains Watergate. In 1974, President Richard
Nixon resigned from office after the House Judiciary Committee approved three articles of impeachment, including one for the obstruction of a federal investigation into the Watergate office break-in.[1]
Nixon's attorney general, John Mitchell, chief of staff, H. R. Haldeman,
and domestic affairs advisor, John D. Ehrlichman, were all convicted of
lying to government investigators and conspiring to obstruct justice.
Fourteen years later, President Bill Clinton was impeached for perjury
and obstruction related to his sexual affair with a White House intern.[2]

In 2007, Lewis "Scooter" Libby Jr., an assistant to President George W. Bush and the chief of staff for Vice President Dick Cheney, was convicted of giving false statements, perjury, and obstruction of justice. He had lied about his role in leaking the identity of a covert CIA agent.[3]

In 2008, Vice Admiral John "Boomer" Stufflebeem was abruptly fired from his position as the Director of the Navy Staff after the Department of Defense inspector general (DoDIG) investigated allegations of an inappropriate relationship with a civilian government employee. The DoDIG concluded that years earlier, while working as a presidential aide at the White House, Stufflebeem had indeed committed adultery. The inspector general further determined that the admiral had willfully lied during the investigation hoping to protect himself. In fact, the DoDIG stated that Stufflebeem had provided extensive "false and misleading testimony," which violated the Joint Ethics Regulation on honesty, and two Uniform Code of Military Justice (UCMJ) articles pertaining to false official statements and false swearing. After a nonjudicial disciplinary hearing, Stufflebeem was demoted to rear admiral and forced into retirement.[4]

A decade later, President Donald Trump fired his first national security advisor, retired Army Lieutenant General Michael Flynn, for lying about his contact with Russian ambassador Sergey Kislyak. Flynn subsequently pleaded guilty *twice* to making false statements to the FBI.[5] In 2018, Trump's former campaign chairman, Paul Manafort, pleaded guilty to conspiracy to obstruct justice and defraud the United States.[6] The next year, the "Mueller Report" chronicled recurrent attempts by Trump himself to obstruct Special Counsel Robert S. Mueller's investigation of Russia's interference in the 2016 presidential election. The obstruction included the president's firing of FBI Director James Comey and his attempt to fire Mueller.[7] In a related 2020 case, Trump's longtime friend and political advisor Roger Stone — a close Manafort associate — was convicted of seven felonies, including witness tampering and obstructing a congressional investigation.[8]

U.S. military officers, commissioned and noncommissioned, have also willfully impeded the administration of justice despite their solemn oath to honor and "bear true faith" to the Constitution. Service personnel accused of obstruction can be tried in either federal court or at a military court-martial. U.S. Code 1503 defines obstruction of justice as an act that "corruptly or by threats or force, or by any threatening letter or communication, influences, obstructs, or impedes, or endeavors to influence, obstruct, or impede, the due administration of justice."[9] Historically, military officers court-martialed for obstruction were charged with discrediting the armed forces and damaging good order and discipline, a violation of General Article 134 of the Uniform Code of Military Justice. The Military Justice Act of 2016 repositioned obstruction under Article 131, Perjury. While Article 131a covers the subordination of perjury, Article 131b governs "obstructing justice," with maximum punishment up to dishonorable discharge, forfeiture of allowances and pay, and five years of confinement.[10] Perhaps the most notorious cases of military obstruction occurred during investigations into the 1968 My Lai massacre. Lieutenant General William Peers, the senior investigator, ultimately reported on a massive Army cover-up, writing: "Efforts were made at every level of command from company to division to withhold and suppress information concerning the incident at [My Lai]."[11]

Since 2010, the most notorious obstruction cases in the military have been soldiers accused of murdering foreign civilians and attempting to cover up the crimes. In summer 2011, Army Staff Sergeant Calvin Gibbs, a squad leader with the Fifth Stryker Brigade, Second Infantry Division, was accused of being the ringleader in a criminal conspiracy that resulted in the sport killing of unarmed civilians in Afghanistan. Three separate murders occurred. Gibbs falsely cast the killings as occurring during legitimate combat. In 2011, after a nine-day court-martial, he was convicted on fifteen counts, including three specifications of premeditated murder and two specifications of obstruction of justice. Gibbs was given a life sentence.[12]

Two similar cases arose in 2013. Army Sergeant First Class Michael Barbera, a former team leader with a reconnaissance regiment of the Eighty-Second Airborne, was accused of murdering two deaf Iraqi teenagers. He was further charged with "lying to his commanders, directing fellow soldiers to lie to military investigators," and threatening the wife of a journalist who was about to expose the killings.[13] The convening authority ultimately dismissed the murder charges without prejudice, but not the obstruction and threat charges. In a negotiation with prosecutors, Barbera pleaded guilty to threatening the reporter's wife, and the Army dropped the obstruction charge. He was demoted and ordered to forfeit $10,000 in salary.[14]

Also in 2013, First Lieutenant Clint A. Lorance was convicted of soliciting a false statement, obstruction of justice, and two counts of second-degree murder. On July 1, 2012, while serving in Afghanistan with the Fourth Brigade Combat Team of the Eighty-Second Airborne, the overzealous platoon leader had ordered one of his marksmen to fire into a populated village without evidence of local hostile intent. Afterward, Lorance asked a sergeant at the tactical operations center to falsely report that his squad had been taking incoming fire. On patrol the next day, Lorance ordered his platoon to shoot three Afghan men who were riding on a motorcycle even though they were non-threatening. Two of the men were shot dead. Lorance falsely reported that he had been unable to conduct post-battle damage assessment because villagers had removed the corpses immediately after the shootings. Ultimately Lorance was found guilty at his court-martial and sentenced to nineteen years in federal prison.[15]

While not as morbid as the Afghan killings or as infamous as Watergate, one of the most remarkable cases of military obstructionism occurred during the Reagan administration's Iran-Contra scandal. The international fiasco entangled a Marine Corps lieutenant colonel, the secretary of defense, and flag officers in the Army, Navy, and Air Force.

★ ★ ★ ★

When Ronald Reagan won the 1980 presidential election, America's geopolitical influence appeared to be losing ground to the Soviet Union. Five years earlier, South Vietnam, Laos, and Cambodia had all become communist states. Developments in 1979 were even more alarming. First, U.S.-backed governments in Iran and Nicaragua were overthrown by anti-American revolutionaries, then the Soviet Army invaded Afghanistan and installed a government loyal to Moscow. The Reagan administration was determined to roll back such communist advances and defeat the Soviets in the Cold War, which was viewed as "the struggle between right and wrong and good and evil."[16]

Because of Nicaragua's proximity to the United States, the Soviet-supported Sandinista regime seemed especially threatening. In March 1981, the president authorized the CIA to covertly assist anti-Sandinista forces — the so-called Contras — in their nascent campaign to topple the government in Managua. A political backlash ensued when Reagan's secret war became public the following year. Through the Boland Amendment, Congress barred the administration from supporting *any military* operations designed to unseat the Sandinistas. Undeterred, the president directed the Pentagon to aid the CIA's program to bolster the Contras. Moreover, in early 1984, Reagan approved the mining of Nicaragua's harbors. When the mining operations were reported in the press, further backlash erupted.

By the time Congress passed a second, more restrictive Boland Amendment in October 1984, Reagan's extralegal war against the Nicaraguan government was being managed by National Security Advisor Robert McFarlane and his deputy two-star Admiral John Poindexter, and their action officer, Marine Lieutenant Colonel Oliver North. The latter worked closely with CIA Director William Casey and Richard Secord, a recently retired Air Force major general turned international arms dealer. For the next two years and with Reagan's blessing, McFarlane, Poindexter, and North secretly endeavored to finance, equip, and train the Contra rebels. Congress was left in the dark.

McFarlane and company also spearheaded Reagan's eventual approach to Iran's clerical government, which was at war with Iraq. The latter was a client of the Soviet Union. Although Iran's 1979 revolutionaries had ousted American ally Shah Mohammad Reza Pahlavi and held U.S. embassy personnel hostage for 444 days, Reagan wanted to weaken

Soviet influence in the Middle East. Complicating matters, however, were Iranian-sponsored terrorists in Lebanon who began kidnapping U.S. citizens in 1984, including the CIA station chief in Beirut.

In spring 1985, National Security Advisor McFarlane proposed a bold new Iran policy, one that included the active participation of the Israeli government. He recommended that the United States open a dialogue with Iranian moderates and, as a display of good faith, allow Israel to sell them U.S.-made missiles. McFarlane predicted that this action would draw Tehran away from Moscow and lead to the release of hostages in Lebanon. If implemented, however, the Iranian initiative would violate the administration's expressed policy of never negotiating with terrorists, the State Department's policy of opposing all international arms shipments to Iran, and the federal Arms Export Control Act (1976), which forbade weapons transfers to nations supporting terrorists or engaging in terrorism. Defense Secretary Caspar Weinberger and his senior military assistant, Army Major General Colin Powell, thought McFarlane's proposal was "absurd."[17]

Nevertheless Reagan approved the illicit Iranian program because of the prospect of rescuing American hostages. Between August 1985 and October 1986, the United States and Israel sold Iran 2,008 TOW (Tube-Launched, Optically Tracked, Wire-Guided) missiles, 18 HAWK (Homing All the Way Killer) missiles, and crates of HAWK spare parts. Powell personally oversaw the transfer of one thousand missiles. In the end, three hostages were released, two others were murdered, and another three Americans were kidnapped.

The Iranian and Contra operations became inextricably linked in April 1986. Poindexter, who succeeded McFarlane in late 1985 and was promoted to vice admiral, approved Lieutenant Colonel North's "neat idea" of overcharging the Iranians and illegally funneling millions in "profits" to the Nicaraguan rebels.[18] In autumn 1986 both clandestine programs were exposed; an epic scandal and mass obstructionism followed.

In November 1986, Reagan met with his senior advisors to create a "unified" if fictitious version of events pertaining to the Iran initiative. Vice Admiral Poindexter took the lead in the discussion. He concocted the narrative that there was no arms-for-hostages program and that Israel, without U.S. knowledge, had shipped missiles to Iran the previous year. No one objected to the fabrication. Reagan, Poindexter, and Weinberger repeated the lies to Congress and the public. Ahead of looming federal investigations, Poindexter deleted thousands of incriminating emails and North shredded mounds of documents. Their misguided loyalty went unrewarded. Attorney General Edwin Meese decided that someone must be held accountable for the supposedly "rogue" operations.[19] North was fired and Poindexter resigned.

In December 1986, the Justice Department named former federal judge Lawrence Walsh the "Independent Counsel of Iran-Contra Matters." He was to investigate suspected criminal conduct. In 1988, Walsh indicted Poindexter, North, and Secord for theft, conspiracy, and obstruction of justice. The next year, Secord pleaded guilty to one felony count of lying under oath to congressional investigators. In 1990, North was found guilty of three felonies, including the falsification and destruction of government documents. That same year a jury convicted Poindexter on five charges, including lying to Congress and destroying evidence. In 1992, after discovering a trove of new documents, Walsh indicted Weinberger on five counts of perjury, making false statements, and obstruction of justice. The former defense secretary's most trusted aide, General Powell, narrowly escaped indictment even though the independent counsel concluded that his false and misleading testimony during the long investigation amounted to an obstruction of justice.

★ ★ ★ ★

John Moran Poindexter and Colin Luther Powell were born within eight months of each other, the former in the summer of 1936 and the latter in spring 1937. Their childhoods had notable similarities. Both were raised in stable, loving homes, and from an early age each radiated an affability that attracted friends. Poindexter and Powell also grew tall, topping six feet, but neither exhibited significant athletic skill. Despite the parallels, the boys also had marked contrasts as they grew up eight hundred miles apart.

Poindexter was raised in rural, ethnically homogeneous white, southwestern Indiana; his father, Marlan, was an ambitious small-town banker. Early on, young Poindexter demonstrated a notable earnestness and a superior intellect that earned him the nickname "Brain" from his classmates. He excelled especially in mathematics and graduated as class valedictorian. Poindexter enjoyed camping and photography, and managed the local movie theater. He exuded confidence and displayed effective leadership as a Boy Scout.[20] Poindexter's approach to leading others was mature and nurturing. According to his cousin and fellow scout leader, John worked conscientiously with the tenderfoots (very junior Scouts). He taught them how to study the Scout manual and how a Scout is "trustworthy, loyal, thrifty, brave, clean, and reverent."[21] Poindexter's mother, Ellen, remarked affectionately that her son was "never a little boy. He was born an old man. . . . He was not mischievous. . . . He took life seriously."[22] An exceptional "self-starter," Poindexter seemed destined for success beyond the confines of Odon, Indiana.[23]

Powell, on the other hand, was raised in New York's ethnically diverse South Bronx. His parents were working-class Jamaican immigrants who secured employment in the garment district. His mother, Arie, worked as a seamstress, and his father, Luther, as a shipping department foreman. Young Powell's academic performance was mediocre at best. He admitted to not being "one of the burning lights of this extended family."[24] Colin easily lost focus and reneged on certain commitments. He ran track for a season but quit. Faking a back injury, he abandoned the church basketball team. Unlike Poindexter, Powell's stint in the Boy Scouts was brief. But ever amiable, Powell was popular with other kids and demonstrated a reliable work ethic as an acolyte at St. Margaret's Episcopal Church and as a part-time employee at Sickser's furniture and toy store. Years later, one high school classmate remembered Colin as "a friendly, always respectful gentleman," but added that she "never figured him as destined for national prominence."[25]

Neither Powell nor Poindexter's parents graduated from college, but the elders valued higher education and insisted that their sons attend university. The smart, adventurous, and landlocked Hoosier needed little prodding. Poindexter was nominated for and accepted into the Naval Academy in 1954. From the get-go he excelled at Annapolis; and as a plebe his company won top honors in the annual brigade competition. Unlike his classmate, future senator John McCain, Poindexter maintained a clean conduct record, earned superior grades, and shined on the debate team. Poised and cerebral, the pipe-smoking Poindexter was respected and popular among the midshipmen. "Poins" never flaunted his brilliance and generously helped others with their studies. "He was everybody's friend," a fellow midshipman recalled. "If you had a problem with a class, he was there to help you. He did a lot of that. People admired and respected that because he was so selfless."[26]

Peers also detected in Poindexter a simmering ambition and a subtle forcefulness. His quiet confidence and obvious intellect had a powerful effect on others. "John was so sure of his intellectual capability," classmate Whit Swain remembered, "that he knew that the decision he arrived at was correct. So when he approached you with 'Let's do it this way,' . . . You just bought it." Regarding Poindexter's determination and need for achievement, Swain commented, "John likes power and he knows how to use it and he knows how to get it. . . . He gravitated towards poles of power because it interested him, it was food and drink to him, it was what he wanted to do."[27]

Poindexter fulfilled his potential at the Naval Academy. As a senior in the 1958 winter term, he was appointed brigade commander of all midshipmen, the top leadership position. News of his appointment, including his photo, appeared on the cover of the *Washington Post*. Later in the spring of 1959, Poindexter graduated first in his class, earning a half-dozen awards and a bachelor's degree in engineering. He was eager to begin his naval career. President Dwight D. Eisenhower attended the Annapolis graduation and presented John with a sheepskin diploma, telling him, "Congratulations, I hope it won't be too much of a burden for you."[28] An inscription in the 1958 yearbook read,

"John's record here bordered on the legendary. . . . His success, as always, is a forgone conclusion."[29]

Before graduating, Poindexter wrote down the keys to his success at the academy: organization, hard work, leadership, and initiative. He also cited his ethical conduct and obedience to authority. For four years he had "kept out of trouble" and did "exactly" what he was told. Poindexter's stated career goal was to "climb to the very top," to become a senior admiral and serve as the chief of naval operations (CNO).[30]

In stark contrast to Poindexter, Powell had no burning motivation to attend college. He lacked initiative and intellectual inquisitiveness. "I went to college for a single reason," Powell later confessed to students at his high school alma mater. "My parents expected it. I don't recall having any great urge to get a higher education."[31] At seventeen, he enrolled at City College of New York, which accepted most applicants and charged a token, ten-dollar tuition. At the direction of his mother, Colin declared an engineering major. Soon overwhelmed by a mechanical drawing course, he quickly switched to geology, reputed as the least rigorous major on campus. Powell struggled academically for all four years.

Powell's saving grace was discovering City College's Army Reserve Officer Training Corps (ROTC). Colin discovered a professional passion and a second home in ROTC, with its well-established hierarchy and clearly articulated values and expectations. He later recalled, "The discipline, the structure, the camaraderie, the sense of belonging were what I craved. . . . If this was what soldiering was all about, then maybe I wanted to be a soldier."[32] Powell dedicated himself completely and his performance in military service was exceptional. He eventually rose to company commander and in the summer of 1957, spent six weeks at Fort Bragg, North Carolina, participating in a national ROTC encampment. Because of his superb Army coursework, marksmanship, physical fitness, and leadership ability, Powell was named Best Cadet of Company D and selected the second-best cadet overall.

While Powell's academic performance back at City College paled by comparison, it did not prevent him from graduating. His mediocre C-cumulative grade point average had been propped up by superior marks in ROTC courses. The latter not only allowed him to exit university as a Distinguished Military Graduate of the Class of 1958, but also to enter the army with a regular (not reserve officer) commission. Powell's white ROTC commander warned him about the harsh realities of racism in the military and advised him to comply, conform, and eschew controversy. Powell, who was elated to be joining the armed forces, appreciated the well-intended counsel. Compared to Poindexter's dream of becoming chief of naval operations, Powell's aspirations were especially modest: become a field grade officer. He was told, "If you do everything well and keep your nose clean for twenty years, we'll make you a lieutenant colonel."[33]

$\star$ $\star$ $\star$ $\star$

From the vantage point of 1958, Poindexter, not Powell, seemed destined for a superlative military career. First in his class and brigade commander at the Naval Academy, he seemed likely to attain flag rank. Poindexter's career began with a one-year stint on a small destroyer, the *Holder*, in the Atlantic. Immediately thereafter he differentiated himself by becoming a Burke Scholar, a new Navy academic program that allowed a select few officers to pursue doctoral studies in science, technology, or engineering. By 1964, after five years of intense study, Poindexter had successfully defended his dissertation before a faculty panel that included two Nobel Laureates. He graduated from the California Institute of Technology with a doctorate in nuclear physics. Poindexter's thesis advisor, German physicist Rudolf Mossbauer, later characterized him as smart and detail-oriented, "not brilliant in . . . foaming with new ideas," but intellectually sharp, absolutely organized, and extremely reliable.[34]

The erudite junior lieutenant seemed the perfect candidate to join Admiral Hyman Rickover's rapidly expanding nuclear program, but the last thing Poindexter wanted was another year of study. He desired sea duty. For the next two years, he served happily and effectively as chief engineer on the large destroyer *Pratt* operating in the Mediterranean and Atlantic. He was promoted to full lieutenant. At the age of twenty-eight,

Poindexter was assigned to the Office of the Secretary of Defense in 1966. As one of Robert McNamara's famed "Whiz Kids," he worked diligently if quietly in the Manpower Directorate of the Systems Analysis section. A Navy colleague recalled that Poindexter was "a typical academic pipe smoker"; he relished solving complex problems requiring deep concentration.[35] For three years, Poindexter impressed his civilian and military superiors. They rated him as an excellent staff officer who stood "head and shoulders above the others" and thus was "pegged for flag rank."[36]

During the 1970s, the staid but ambitious Poindexter continued his swift rise in the Navy with alternating assignments on land and at sea. On the water, he served as executive officer aboard the guided-missile destroyer *Lawrence* whose skipper concluded that "Lieutenant Commander Poindexter is the most outstanding officer I have met in the naval service."[37] At the rank of full commander, he skippered the cruiser *England* and, in his fifth sea tour, Captain Poindexter took over Destroyer Squadron Thirty-One, a battle group operating in the Western Pacific, South Pacific, and Indian Ocean. Both commands were successful.

Poindexter's performance was no less impressive when stationed on terra firma. At the Pentagon he earned a reputation as a consummate staff officer. For three years, he served on the personal staff of three Navy secretaries: John Chafee, John Warner, and J. William Middendorf. All praised Poindexter as an "absolute model naval officer" and as someone who seized the initiative and exercised sound judgment.[38] Chafee later remembered Poindexter as "a loyalist and when he embarks on a project, he gets the position from his commanding officers and follows out on it with vigor and enthusiasm. But [also] calmness."[39] For his managerial skill in "rationalizing this process, streamlining that one, [and] computerizing a third," Secretary Middendorf awarded the Hoosier the Legion of Merit.[40]

In 1976, the CNO Admiral James L. Holloway III selected Captain Poindexter over Captain Frank Kelso (a future CNO) as his new executive assistant. It was a highly coveted assignment yet also a stressful one. Holloway and Poindexter worked diligently and effectively together for three years. In the process, they became confidants, like father and son. Laboring for long hours and under immense pressure, Poindexter, according to one Pentagon colleague, "was never ruffled, just Mister Cool, a real pro."[41] Admiral Holloway lauded his principal and principled aide as a superior military professional, one "whose loyalty and judgment were second to none."[42]

In 1980, after working for Holloway and having commanded Destroyer Squadron Thirty-One, Poindexter was promoted to rear admiral. He was the second person in his Annapolis class to join the admiralty. Poindexter's ultimate goal of becoming CNO seemed increasingly realistic. "He was doing well on the sea duty side, he was doing well on the Pentagon side," noted Vice Admiral Staser Holcomb, "[and] everybody wanted him." That included senior officials at the White House.[43]

Like Poindexter, Powell's first two decades in the military alternated between command and staff assignments and included several years of classroom study. The glaring difference in their records was Powell's two tours of duty in Vietnam; Poindexter never saw combat. After intensive training as an Army airborne ranger, Powell's first assignment was in West Germany in early 1959 as a platoon leader with the Forty-Eighth Infantry, Third Armored Division. His competency and dedication impressed his commander, who wrote that "Lt Powell is one of the most outstanding young Lieutenants I have seen."[44] The superlative evaluations continued at Fort Devens, Massachusetts, where his superior exclaimed that Powell was "a truly outstanding officer in every respect and attribute of leadership. This officer is so unique in manner and performance that he could well be classified the 'Model Officer.'"[45] Promoted to captain, Powell arrived in Saigon in late 1962 assigned as a senior tactical adviser to an infantry regiment of the South Vietnamese army. The American demonstrated consummate skill and courage under fire as his unit conducted counterinsurgency operations in the contested A Shau Valley near the Laotian border. Powell was wounded when a punji spike pierced his foot from bottom to top. He was awarded a Purple Heart and Bronze Star.

After returning stateside, Powell was stationed at Fort Benning, Georgia, for nearly four years. He finished the Pathfinder airborne ranger course at the top of his class and graduated from the officers advanced course rated as the best officer from the infantry branch. Powell also successfully completed two staff assignments, leading a superior to remark that his "performance in duty, inherent abilities and extremely high potential are the finest I have observed in my service."[46] In 1967, Powell left Benning to attend the Command and General Staff College in Kansas. He graduated second in a class of more than a thousand officers, most of whom were senior in age, rank, and experience.

Major Powell returned to Vietnam in 1968. He became a staff officer in the Eleventh Infantry Brigade of the Twenty-Third Infantry Division (known as the Americal Division). While he did not lead soldiers in combat, he did earn the prestigious Soldier's Medal for heroism after rescuing a general and other officers from a crashed helicopter. Powell's competence and utter dedication earned the highest accolades from multiple commanders. Colonel Oran Henderson wrote, "MAJ Powell is an outstanding officer in every respect."[47] Colonel John W. Donaldson praised him as "the finest Major I have known."[48] Major General Charles M. Gettys declared Powell *the* most outstanding staff officer and best briefer, and stated, "I am certain that he will be a general officer, that he possesses the necessary qualifications, and time and experience will develop his demonstrated potential."[49]

Powell entered the 1970s as one of the army's most talented and dutiful field grade officers, and his star continued to rise. He returned to Washington, DC, for four years. There he earned a master's of business administration at George Washington University and participated in the prestigious White House Fellows program, which included a service assignment in the Office of Management and Budget. Thereafter, Lieutenant Colonel Powell successfully transformed a once-troubled infantry battalion in South Korea and repeated that performance while commanding an underperforming air assault infantry brigade of the 101st Airborne at Fort Campbell, Kentucky. One of Powell's superiors, the colorful Lieutenant General Henry E. "The Gunfighter" Emerson, recalled that the colonel's achievements in both assignments were "out-fucking-standing." He remembered thinking, "Goddamn, this son of a bitch [Powell] can command soldiers. . . . I put on his report this guy should be a brigadier general as quick as the law allows."[50]

In between the Korean and Kentucky assignments, Powell had attended the National War College and was selected a distinguished graduate of the Class of 1976. The next year he returned to the Pentagon, where Rear Admiral Poindexter was already serving as a senior assistant to CNO Holloway. During the next four years, Powell worked as the military assistant to three deputy defense secretaries: Carter Democrats Charles Duncan and W. Graham Claytor Jr., and Reagan Republican Frank Carlucci. Like Poindexter, Powell emerged as an elite staff officer with an outstanding reputation among civilian and military leaders. In 1979, at the age of forty-two, he had become the youngest general officer in the U.S. Army. Two years later, just before Powell's posting as an assistant division commander at Fort Carson, Colorado, Carlucci predicted that his outgoing military assistant "will become one of America's most valuable four stars."[51]

★ ★ ★ ★

In 1981, as Brigadier General Powell was heading west to join the Fourth Infantry Division (Mechanized), Rear Admiral Poindexter was assuming his new position at the White House. Although the admiral would never return to sea command, his advance through the ranks was unabated. In June, he joined Ronald Reagan's National Security Council (NSC) staff as a military assistant. National Security Advisor Richard V. Allen tasked the technologically adept admiral with revamping the antiquated Situation Room. Allen later described Poindexter's position as a liaison on "a mechanical, administrative level with the Pentagon. He was not an analyst of foreign policy."[52]

After only a year, Reagan replaced Allen with a longtime friend, Judge William P. Clark Jr., who had been serving as the deputy secretary of state. Clark brought along his State Department counselor, Robert McFarlane, to serve as his deputy. Clark and McFarlane approved Poindexter's new proposal to create a $14 million state-of-the-art Crisis

Management Center for the NSC. In addition, the admiral, working with IBM, installed a new internal electronic communication system known as PROFS. The admiral's projects were completed by late 1983, when Judge Clark left the NSC to become secretary of the interior. Before leaving, he ensured that McFarlane succeeded him as Reagan's third national security advisor. McFarlane, a retired Marine Corps lieutenant colonel who graduated from the Naval Academy a year after Poindexter, selected the rear admiral as his top deputy. "John did not impress you with his in-depth knowledge of international relations," recalled an NSC staffer, "but he was a quick study."[53] The elevation of both McFarlane and Poindexter ultimately imperiled the Reagan presidency.

Meanwhile, Brigadier General Powell continued to ascend the upper ranks of the Army. He benefited greatly from the active influence of powerful mentors such as Lieutenant General Julius W. Becton Jr., a trailblazing African American soldier, and Army Vice Chief of Staff General John A. Wickham Jr. In the summer of 1983, Wickham was promoted to Army chief and Powell, his protégé, was promoted to major general. Powell returned to Washington, DC, as the senior military assistant to Reagan's secretary of defense, Caspar Weinberger. He held the position for three years and became Weinberger's "closest advisor and confidant" at the Pentagon.[54]

Weinberger and McFarlane, like their respective deputies Powell and Poindexter, were staunch Cold Warriors who supported the president's commitment to roll back communist influence in Latin America. Ousting the Soviet-backed Sandinistas in Nicaragua became a near-obsession for the president. However, in December 1982, Congress passed the Boland Amendment to limit American aid to anti-communist "Contra" forces in Nicaragua. The legislation barred the Reagan administration from supporting military operations to overthrow the government in Managua.

Without congressional support for armed interventionism, the Reagan administration relied increasingly on covert operations to destabilize the Sandinista regime. The CIA provided lethal and nonlethal aid to the Contra insurgents. Skirting congressional oversight, the Defense Department also bolstered the CIA program in various ways. For example, in May 1983 U.S. Air Force Major General Richard Secord, who had extensive experience in special operations, oversaw the purchase of arms and ammunition for the Contras from the Israeli government. The weapons had been seized from the Palestine Liberation Organization.

By December 1983, Congress opposed any American involvement in the Nicaraguan civil war and issued further restrictions on aid. The bicameral legislature capped Contra funding at $24 million and explicitly prohibited the CIA from accessing the appropriations. When news broke in April 1984 that the CIA — with Reagan's approval — had planted mines in Nicaraguan harbors, congressional outrage was pronounced. Reagan rightly feared that Congress would eliminate all support for the Contras, but he remained undaunted.

In late May 1984, McFarlane informed Rear Admiral Poindexter and Marine Lieutenant Colonel Oliver North (an eager NSC staff officer) that the president had issued a mandate regarding the Contras: "I want you to do whatever you have to do to help these people keep body and soul together. Do everything you can."[55] McFarlane proceeded to secretly petition funds from the Saudi Arabian government and received $6 million. The next month, Secretary of State George Shultz, who was oblivious to the Saudi initiative, warned Reagan, Weinberger, Casey, and other senior officials that circumventing Congress and soliciting foreign governments for the Contras was "an impeachable offense."[56]

Nevertheless, the president was pleased with the Saudi arrangement. On the advice of CIA Director Casey, North recruited the recently retired Major General Secord to purchase equipment and weapons for the Contras with the Saudi money. North became McFarlane and Poindexter's senior action officer on Nicaragua. With extensive help from Secord, he oversaw the NSC's clandestine operations to support the Contra insurgents. Poindexter later described the exuberant North as "the kingpin to the Central America opposition" and the "switching point that made the whole system work."[57]

In October 1984, Congress finally responded to the Nicaraguan harbor-mining controversy. Passage of a second Boland Amendment strictly forbade the CIA, the Defense Department, and "any other agency or entity" to fund or support military or paramilitary operations in Nicaragua.[58] McFarlane knew that the law pertained to the NSC, but that realization failed to curtail his and the CIA's efforts to fortify the Contras.

Reagan's landslide reelection in November 1984 emboldened McFarlane, Poindexter, and North's attempts to overthrow the Nicaraguan government. North's active participation in coordinating Contra military operations — approved by McFarlane, Poindexter, and Casey — blatantly violated the Boland Amendment. A senior CIA field officer warned that if the Reagan administration's covert activities ever became public the ensuing scandal would be "worse than Watergate."[59]

By February 1985 the Contras were again running low on cash, arms, and equipment. There was scant chance that Congress would come to their aid. Fortunately for Reagan, King Fahd of Saudi Arabia continued to bankroll the anti-communist insurgents, eventually spending more than $30 million on those efforts. Defense Secretary Weinberger, like McFarlane and Poindexter, was happy to learn about the secret Saudi contributions. Weinberger and his senior military assistant, Powell, believed in the "justice of the contra cause" and fully supported the rebel's "serious bid to throw off the Marxist yoke in Managua."[60] Fearing a news leak about the illegal Saudi financing, McFarlane reminded his Pentagon colleagues, including General Jack W. Vessey Jr., the chairman of the Joint Chiefs of Staff, to keep knowledge of Riyadh's involvement "under our hats."[61]

By summer 1985, news reports surfaced alleging accurately that North was providing vigorous support to the Contras. The Reagan administration was forced to respond to congressional inquiries, including those from Michael Barnes, the chair of the House Subcommittee on Western Hemisphere Affairs. The congressman wanted all documents related to North's contacts with Contra leaders since the passing of the second Boland Amendment. Poindexter, who viewed Congress with disdain, considered Barnes "a trouble maker." He had no intention of being forthcoming with Congress. The admiral, who had been recently promoted to three stars, directed the NSC staff, including North, to prepare a superficial response that ostensibly provided "good answers to all of this."[62] He also approved the release of a limited number of documents that contained "no substance."[63]

When McFarlane read the select documents, he concluded that even those materials suggested that North may have broken the law in support of the Contras. As a result, the national security advisor refused to share any records with Congress. In September 1985, he wrote letters instead to Barnes and Lee Hamilton, chair of the House Permanent Select Committee on Intelligence. McFarlane assured both congressmen that he had reviewed all of the pertinent Contra documents and found nothing amiss. In a gross lie he wrote, "At no time did I or any member of the National Security staff violate the letter or spirit of the law," and "We did not solicit funds or other support for military or paramilitary activities either from Americans or third parties."[64]

By this time, McFarlane and the NSC staff (still with Reagan's approval) were entrenched in another controversial covert foreign operation: one designed to improve U.S. relations with Iran and gain the release of seven Americans held hostage by Hezbollah terrorists in Lebanon. As senior deputies to McFarlane and Weinberger, respectively, Poindexter and Powell played material roles in the illicit Middle East initiative and in the cover-up that ensued once the Iran project and the military support of the Contras became public.

On June 17, 1985, National Security Adviser McFarlane provided Defense Secretary Weinberger, Secretary of State Shultz, and CIA Director Casey with an eight-page, top-secret memorandum. It was a bold Cold War initiative recommending that the United States develop closer political relations with Iran — a declared terrorist state — in order to promote American interests in the region. In the draft national security directive, McFarlane reasoned that if Washington did not seize the initiative with Tehran, Moscow would. He promised that the sale of U.S.-made military equipment and arms would draw the Iranian government into the American camp, and he wanted support from Weinberger, Shultz, and Casey before he presented the radical policy shift to the president.[65]

Powell, who read all of Weinberger's mail, including the most highly classified, thought the idea of aiding Iran was disturbing, "a stunner," so he rushed the memorandum to the defense secretary.[66] Like Powell, Weinberger considered the proposal unfathomable, writing across McFarlane's document, "This is almost too absurd to comment on."[67] In mid-July, Weinberger sent his formal and unambiguous response: "Under no circumstances . . . should we now ease our restrictions on arms sales to Iran."[68] In a rare moment of policy solidarity, Shultz concurred with the defense secretary. Casey, on the other hand, was "enthusiastic" about the initiative.[69]

McFarlane was undeterred by Weinberger and Shultz's objections. After communicating with a senior ranking Israeli official, he decided that moderate Iranians, if properly motivated, would use their influence to secure the release of American hostages held in Lebanon. In early July 1985 he informed Weinberger by telephone and Shultz by secret cable that the Israeli government, which was already selling weapons to Iran, had offered to play an intermediary role between Washington and Tehran.[70] The defense secretary, who considered Iran a "barbaric, 13th century empire," dismissed the proposal in conversations with Powell. He opposed any negotiations with Iranian officials because "the only moderates in Iran are in the cemetery."[71] Shultz, on the other hand, had warmed to "the prospect of gaining the release of . . . seven hostages" and the establishment of ties with political moderates in Iran, especially with Israel's support.[72] Despite Weinberger's objection, McFarlane's commitment to a new Iranian policy persisted. On July 13 he informed the president about the Cold War initiative, which he said was aimed, in part, to rescue the hostages in Lebanon. The latter resonated with Reagan.[73]

McFarlane's proposal, including Israel's offer of support, was debated on August 6 at a White House meeting of the president's senior national security team, including Vice Admiral Poindexter. According to McFarlane, the wide-ranging discussion included "the legal ramifications, the political risks, [and] the matter of Congressional oversight."[74] Shultz and even Weinberger expressed a willingness to open back-channel communications with Tehran but objected to "the very bad idea" of Israel shipping batches of its U.S.-made missiles to Iran in return for hostages.[75] Weinberger repeated his belief "that any shipment of arms was probably illegal" and that even a third-party transfer had to be reported to Congress.[76] The meeting ended without resolution. A rueful Powell later admitted that "this scheme looked, at the time, as if it would die of its own foolishness anyway. But we underestimated the President's support for the plan or the determination of the NSC staff to pull it off."[77]

Despite Weinberger and Shultz's objections, Reagan approved McFarlane's plan to negotiate with Tehran through Israel. The national security advisor appointed Poindexter and North as primary contacts for the Israelis. In his memoirs, the president wrote, "The truth is, once we had information from Israel that we could trust the people in Iran, I didn't have to think thirty seconds about saying yes to their proposal. . . . I said there was one thing we wanted: The moderate Iranians had to use their influence with Hizballah [sic] and try to get our hostages freed."[78] According to McFarlane, he informed Shultz, Weinberger, and others of the president's decision.[79] Meanwhile, the Israeli government launched the operation.[80]

On August 22 Israeli officials notified McFarlane that they had successfully delivered ninety-six TOW anti-tank missiles to Iran. The Reagan administration, which had a policy of *never* making deals with terrorists or state sponsors of terrorism such as Iran, had now sanctioned an illegal shipment of U.S.-made weapons to Tehran.[81] The 1976 Arms Export Control Act prohibited the delivery of arms to any nation that supported terrorism, and further required the president to notify Congress if there was suspicion that the law had been violated.[82] Reagan accepted the CIA's recommendation to keep congressional leaders in the dark. Nor did he provide the required written authorization (known as a presidential finding) for the operation, in part because it, too, would require congressional notification.[83]

McFarlane understood the political and legal significance of the arms shipment, and after hearing from the Israelis, he arranged an impromptu nighttime meeting at the Pentagon to debrief Weinberger, Powell, and the acting chairman of the Joint Chiefs of Staff. There, Mc-Farlane recounted the recent course of events, including Reagan's sanctioning of the arms transaction.[84] Afterward, Weinberger appeared more willing to negotiate with Iran for the hostages. He wrote in his diary, "I argued that we tell them we wanted *all* hostages back."[85]

The following day, McFarlane telephoned Reagan and Weinberger. The defense secretary subsequently noted, "Iranian proposal to let us have our Kidnappees — agreed we should deal directly with Iranians & not thru Israelis & that we should get guarantees that we'll get them all & take them off w helos fm [with helicopters from] Tripoli Beach."[86] Anticipating the release of hostages, Reagan wrote in his diary, "They will be delivered to a point on the beach north of Tripoli & we'll take them off to our 6th fleet. . . . Now we wait."[87]

On August 29 McFarland communicated to Weinberger, "Iranians will offer to give us back our hostages. Want meeting in Vienna Tuesday/Wednesday. Asked for Defense representative."[88] The secretary agreed to send an emissary. Shortly thereafter a "senior military officer" traveled to Austria under a false passport along with Lieutenant Colonel Oliver North.[89] Their mission, according to Weinberger's diary, was to "see if Iranians will release our hostages."[90] Two years later, when Powell was shown a number of the defense secretary's diary entries, he admitted to knowing "by this time that there was a serious deal going on with the Iranians."[91] In his memoirs, Powell wrote how during the summer and autumn of 1985, it was becoming all too evident that the president "wanted the hostages freed, and was willing to take political risks to do it."[92]

The arms shipment of August 22, however, did not lead to the release of American hostages. Iran demanded an additional four hundred TOW missiles in return for freeing a single captive. Israel indicated a willingness to continue its intermediary role. Without legal authorization or congressional notification, Reagan approved a second shipment of American-made arms from Israeli stockpiles.[93]

It is evident from Weinberger's diary that he and Powell were again anticipating a release of hostages, including William Buckley, the captured CIA station chief. On September 11, the defense secretary wrote, "Bud McFarlane — says Iranians told Israelis our 7 hostages would be released in 3 groups . . . [and] we will extract them by helicopter."[94] The second batch of missiles was delivered to Iran on September 15, and Weinberger wrote, "A delivery I have for our prisoners."[95] To the president's delight, this shipment led to the immediate release of Reverend Benjamin Weir. His freedom, according to journalist Bob Woodward, was "treated almost as high mass at the White House."[96] The next day, however, a disappointed Weinberger noted, "Saw Colin Powell — no news of release of Buckley — he was not delivered to Cyprus on time."[97] Weinberger also learned from Powell that his office had not been receiving all of the National Security Agency intelligence intercepts pertaining to the Iran initiative. The defense secretary demanded, through Powell, that he be kept fully informed. "We straightened that matter out in a hurry," Powell recalled.[98]

In the weeks following Israel's September 15 shipment of missiles to Tehran, the Iranians requested still more weaponry in exchange for the release of additional hostages. Reagan, delighted by the release of Reverend Weir, sanctioned further negotiations to be coordinated by McFarlane, Poindexter, and the NSC staff. For its part, the Israeli government agreed to ship more missiles to Tehran, but wanted the United States to replenish its diminished stockpiles. McFarlane assured the Israelis of replenishment and informed Weinberger and Shultz about the continuing operation.[99]

By this time, North, as a member of McFarlane's staff, began playing an even larger role in the arms-for-hostages operation. The marine lieutenant colonel later testified, "If I recall properly what happened in '85 — my original point of contact was [Major] General Colin Powell, who was going directly to his immediate superior, Secretary Weinberger. . . . The Israelis expected . . . to have gratis given to them, 508 TOWs in replenishment for what they had shipped in August and September."[100]

In November 1985, McFarlane contacted Weinberger and Shultz to provide updates on the Iran initiative, including the possibility of shipping U.S. HAWK antiaircraft and Phoenix air-to-air missiles to

Iran. Both secretaries questioned the prudence of the arms-for-hostages program. On November 9 McFarlane telephoned an increasingly wary Weinberger on a secure line. After the conversation, the defense secretary wrote in his diary, "Bud McFarlane . . . wants to start 'negot' exploration with Iranians (& Israelis) to give Iranians weapons for our hostages. I objected."[101] The following day, after talking to McFarlane again, Weinberger expressed some flexibility: "We'll demand the release of all hostages. Then we might give them through Israelis Hawks but not Phoenix [missiles]."[102] For his part, Shultz concluded that a shipment of U.S. HAWK and Phoenix missiles to Iran would be "highly illegal" and doubted that Weinberger would condone it.[103]

Nevertheless, on the morning of November 19, McFarlane received Reagan's approval to sell U.S.-stocked missiles to Iran through Israel.[104] The national security advisor first informed Shultz, who registered his objection to the mission but declined to take his opposition directly to the president. McFarlane then telephoned Weinberger. The defense secretary wrote in his diary, "[McFarlane] wants us [the Defense Department] to try to get 500 Hawks for sale to Israel to pass on to Iran for release of 5 hostages Thurs."[105] Weinberger seized the opportunity to express his disapproval. He immediately tasked Powell with drafting a memorandum, one that painted the proposed shipment of HAWK missiles "as negatively as possible."[106]

Powell's "Point Paper" emphasized that such a transaction required Congress to be notified immediately.[107] Weinberger wrote in his diary, "Colin Powell in office re data on Hawks — can't be given to Israel or Iran w/o Cong. notification."[108] According to Powell, the defense secretary then telephoned McFarlane to say the proposed arms transaction "is illegal, it's a bad idea."[109] Undeterred, McFarlane trumped Weinberger the following day. He told the secretary that Reagan decided to bypass the Defense Department and "do it thru Israelis."[110] Like Shultz, Weinberger did not take his protest to the president. Robert M. Gates, then the deputy director of the CIA, later wrote of the Iran initiative, "[N]o one was willing to put his job on the line to stop it. . . . The arms deal could have been stopped at any time if Shultz or Weinberger had thought it important enough."[111] Instead, Weinberger and Powell renewed their vigil, hoping for the release of hostages. On November 23 the defense secretary wrote, "Colin Powell—. . . no hostage release last night."[112] In fact, due to logistical complications, the Israeli arms had not yet reached their destination.

Eventually, eighteen HAWK missiles from Israel's arsenal arrived in Iran. This third shipment of arms had been illegally facilitated by the CIA with assistance by retired Air Force Major General Secord.[113] Weinberger and Powell received confirmation of the delivery the next day. Under the subject line "Lebanese Kidnappings," an intelligence report read, "Delivery Made on 24 November 1985."[114] But Poindexter informed McFarlane that the Iranians were dissatisfied with the arms shipment and not a single hostage was released.[115]

Two weeks later, on December 7, Reagan convened his senior foreign policy team at the White House. The president wanted to discuss "continuing and possibly even expanding the covert operation begun the previous summer."[116] In his diary, the president referred to the Iran initiative as "a complex undertaking with only a few of us in on it."[117] Poindexter, fully informed on the matter, attended the meeting with McFarlane, who had announced that he would resign for personal reasons and that the admiral would replace him as national security advisor. Just before the White House meeting, Weinberger huddled with Powell and Richard Armitage, the assistant secretary of defense for international security affairs, for an update on a new "NSC Plan to let Israelis give Iranians 50 Hawks & 3300 TOWs in return for 5 hostages."[118] Armitage presciently and ominously concluded that there "is no good way to keep this project from ultimately being made public."[119]

At the White House, McFarlane recounted the history of the Iran initiative, including all previous arms shipments.[120] An intense debate ensued. Weinberger and Shultz renewed their opposition to the program on both policy and legal grounds.[121] The defense secretary reiterated the need to notify Congress given the embargo on weapons sales to Iran, and he asserted that "washing" arms shipments through Israel did not make such transactions legal.[122] Poindexter remained silent. Reagan, however, was adamant about rescuing the hostages.[123]

Undeterred by Weinberger and Shultz's warnings, the president expressed his willingness to break the law and risk impeachment to secure the freedom of the hostages. "They can impeach me if they want," Reagan told his advisers. He even joked that "visiting days are Wednesday" at the Leavenworth federal penitentiary. Weinberger snapped, "You will not be alone."[124] The secretary summarized the meeting in his diary entry of December 7: "I argued strongly that we have an embargo that makes arms sales to Iran illegal & the President couldn't violate it — & that 'washing' transaction thru Israel wouldn't make it legal. Shultz, [and Chief of Staff] Don Regan agreed. President sd. [said] he could answer charges of illegality but he couldn't answer charge that 'big strong President Reagan passed up a chance to free hostages.'"[125]

Separate from the president's plans for another arms shipment to Iran was the lingering issue of replenishing Israel's depleted stockpiles. On December 10 McFarlane and Poindexter briefed Reagan, Weinberger, and others in the Oval Office.[126] After this meeting, Weinberger met with Powell and then wrote on his daily notepad, "We still must replace 500 TOWs to Israel."[127]

A NSC memorandum dated January 15, 1986, signaled Weinberger's ongoing, if futile, opposition to additional arms deals with Iran. In the document, Lieutenant Colonel North complained about the defense secretary's obstructionism to his boss Poindexter. North wrote, "Casey believes Cap [Weinberger] will continue to create roadblocks until he is told by you that the President wants to move NOW and that Cap will have to make it work. Casey points out that we have now gone through three different methodologies in an effort to satisfy Cap's concerns and that no matter what we do there is always a new objection.... [Casey] is concerned that Cap will find some new objection unless he is told to proceed."[128]

On January 17 Weinberger met with Powell to discuss U.S. laws "prohibiting" arms sales to Iran.[129] Later that same day, the defense secretary reminded Shultz, Casey, and Poindexter of the "statutes forbidding sales to Iran."[130] Nevertheless, Weinberger relented to White House and CIA pressure, accepting Reagan's determination to secure the return of more hostages. Casey was informed that Weinberger's staff, led by Powell, "had signed off" on the new plan. It called for the Defense Department to transfer missiles to the CIA, which, working with NSC staff and through intermediaries, would sell and deliver the arms to Iran.[131] One of Weinberger's deputy assistant secretaries asked half-jokingly, "Do we have a legal problem with this, is somebody going to jail?" The defense secretary answered, "Yes, we could go to jail, or someone could."[132]

Weinberger had acquiesced to the sale of U.S. arms because Reagan had signed a top-secret presidential finding of necessity drafted by NSC staff and the CIA. It authorized the direct sale of U.S. missiles to Iran without Israel as an intermediary. Poindexter was assuming control and he wanted legal cover for the Iran initiative. He later said, "It sounds self-serving, but until I took over, it was a very poorly run operation."[133] Acting on the president's order, Weinberger told Powell to personally facilitate the transfer of four thousand TOW missiles to the CIA. The perturbed defense secretary informed his senior military assistant, "I want nothing to do with the Iranians. I want the task carried out with the department removed as much as possible."[134] Apparently, Weinberger even kept the shipment secret from the chairman of the Joint Chiefs of Staff, Admiral William J. Crowe Jr.[135]

With these instructions, Powell contacted an old friend, acting army chief of staff General Maxwell "Mad Max" Thurman, and had the weapons transferred from the Defense Department to the CIA. Powell did not tell Thurman or anyone else in the military where the missiles were going. He and Weinberger "treated the TOW transfer like garbage to be gotten out of the house quickly" and "with as few fingerprints as possible on it."[136] The defense secretary had instructed Powell to ship the weapons "in a way that does not contaminate us any more than we are."[137] Powell worked assiduously to minimize intradepartmental knowledge of the arms-for-hostages operation and, utilizing the power of Reagan's executive order, adeptly orchestrated the arms transfer without informing his senior military colleagues of the weapons' ultimate destination, a designated terrorist state.[138] Powell later boldly told federal investigators that his army superiors "had no need to know" about Iran and thus they had no reason or responsibility to notify Congress.[139]

By February 13, 1986, the Defense Department had received a wire transfer of $3.7 million from Iran through various intermediaries, including Secord and the CIA. Four days later, the first five hundred U.S. TOW missiles under the new Poindexter arrangement were delivered to Iran via Israel. A second batch of five hundred was successfully transferred on February 20.[140] Still, no hostages were released.

The hyper-secretive nature of the Pentagon-CIA transaction and Powell's bypassing of normal arms-transfer protocols raised serious concerns at the highest levels of the army. At one point, the director of the Army staff called Powell with a warning: "If arms in that amount are going to a foreign country, Congress has to be notified."[141] Powell was among only five people (including Weinberger and Armitage) in the entire Defense Department who knew that the U.S. weapons were bound for Iran. A crucial question was whether the administration or Defense would provide Congress with timely notification of the arms sales as required by law. Powell understood that "this kind of a transfer requires a notification" and attempted to reassure the army leadership that everything about the arms shipment was aboveboard and congressional notification would be made.[142] Following Weinberger's order to minimize the involvement of the Defense Department, Powell told army leaders that it was the CIA's duty to inform Congress "and that the Army did not have responsibility to do that." He asked the Army's assistant deputy chief of staff, Lieutenant General Vincent Russo, who was himself "very uncomfortable" with the secret operation, to assure Army Secretary John O. Marsh Jr. that "[congressional] notification was being handled . . . that it had been addressed and it was taken care of."[143]

Powell's expressed confidence did not reassure Marsh. He and Army Chief of Staff General Wickham, one of Powell's mentors, insisted that a memorandum be drafted for Powell's review to underscore the need for congressional notification. Wickham later testified, "I felt very uneasy about this process. And I also felt uneasy about the notification dimension to the Congress."[144] The memo was delivered on

March 7. Powell showed it to "an unhappy Weinberger," who foresaw legal and political trouble for the administration. On March 12, just days before Powell completed his three-year assignment as Weinberger's senior assistant, the major general handed the army's communiqué regarding "statutory requirements" to Vice Admiral Poindexter. Powell told him, "Handle it . . . however you plan to do it."[145] Poindexter proceeded to hide the memorandum in a safe.[146] Neither he nor anybody else in the administration ever complied with the law by notifying Congress about the multiple weapons shipments to Iran.

For Powell, the arms-for-hostages operation was unseemly business, and he was happy to leave it and the Pentagon behind. For his years of effective and unflinchingly loyal service to the administration, he received a promotion to lieutenant general and was given a plum assignment as commander of V Corps in West Germany. Weinberger's final evaluation of Powell's performance was effusive: "He was directly involved in every issue I faced as Secretary of Defense. Moreover, he played a pivotal role in the functioning of the entire Department of Defense. In every way, MG Powell's performance was unfailingly superlative. . . . Soldier, scholar, statesman — he does it all. . . . Colin Powell is an emerging national leader with unlimited potential, capable of, indeed deserving of, leadership at the highest levels of the American military."[147]

In April 1986, the month after Powell left Weinberger's side, the illicit Iranian initiative and the illegal Nicaraguan Contra operation became commingled. Poindexter received a secret, six-page memorandum from North recommending a scheme whereby the Iranians would be significantly overcharged for weapons and spare parts and then the NSC, without congressional approval, could divert $14 million in government "profits" to replenish Israeli TOW stockpiles and further fund the Contra insurgency. Poindexter admired North's "neat idea" and told him, "Okay, go do it."[148]

There is no clear evidence that either Powell or Weinberger was aware that the Iranians had been overcharged and that most of the profits would be illegally diverted to Nicaragua to support the anticommunist resistance.[149] Later in 1986, when FBI agents asked Powell if he knew of the diversion, he replied, "No, No, No."[150] In 1995, when Powell finally admitted that laws had been broken during the Iran-Contra affair, he considered the diversion of funds the most flagrant violation. In his autobiography, he wrote, "I knew that Weinberger, as well as the rest of us at Defense, had no knowledge of *the most illegal aspect* of the affair, the diversion of Iranian arms sales profits to the contras."[151]

In May 1986, at Poindexter's urging, Reagan approved a secret mission to Iran led by the recently resigned McFarlane. The primary objective remained an exchange of weaponry and spare parts for hostages. Yet after providing the Iranians with an initial pallet of HAWK spare parts, the mission failed and no hostages were freed. Reagan and Poindexter, who were in regular contact with McFarlane while he was in Tehran, were deeply disappointed with the Iranian "rug merchants."[152] That same month Secretary Shultz warned Poindexter that the ongoing sale of American weapons to Iran was "wrong + illegal + Pres [Reagan] is way overexposed."[153]

Nevertheless, taking his cues directly from the president, Poindexter was determined to save hostages. He even contemplated a military rescue operation. Welcome news arrived in July when the Israelis helped to secure the release of Father Lawrence Jenco, an American Catholic priest. Poindexter, who believed this was a byproduct of McFarlane's secret mission, briefed Reagan, who approved sending more HAWK spare parts to Iran. But bad news arrived two months later when two more Americans were taken hostage. Still, Poindexter directed North, working with Secord in Germany, to continue his arms-for-hostages negotiations with Iran. As a result, in late October Israel secretly delivered 500 TOW missiles to Iran with the expectation that the United States would replenish its stockpile. No hostages were released. Even worse for Reagan, reports of the McFarlane-Iranian negotiations were leaked to a Lebanese magazine, which published the scandalous story on November 3, 1986.

Just four weeks earlier, the Reagan administration's covert Contra operation also became imperiled when a Nicaraguan soldier shot down a CIA airplane carrying weapons for the insurgents. One American, Eugene Hasenfus, survived the plane crash. Captured by the Sandinistas and brought before an international press corps, the ex-marine not only admitted to supplying the Contras but also to working for the U.S. government. CIA director Casey and North agreed that "this whole thing was coming unraveled and that things ought to be 'cleaned up.'"[154] The lieutenant colonel began shredding NSC documents. The final cover-up — the obstruction of justice — had begun.

★ ★ ★ ★

On November 10, 1986, the president and his senior advisors met at the White House to establish a "unified" and fallacious version of events.[155] Poindexter knowingly misstated that the Iranian initiative was less about freeing hostages and more about building ties with Tehran and curbing Iranian-sponsored terrorism. Moreover, he falsely claimed that Israel, without U.S. knowledge, had begun shipping missiles to Iran in the summer of 1985 and that the size of subsequent shipments was negligible. Nobody at the meeting objected to the blatant misrepresentations. Two days later, Poindexter and Reagan repeated those lies to congressional leaders. Weinberger would follow suit. On November 13, Reagan gave a speech on the Iran initiative. He dishonestly asserted, "We did not — repeat — did not trade weapons or anything else for hostages — nor will we."[156]

The FBI leadership knew that the president was lying to the American people.[157] Secretary Shultz, a veteran of the Nixon White House, was disturbed by the emerging cover-up. He confided to a top aide that Vice Admiral Poindexter and others in the administration were "distorting the record," "trying to get me to lie," and "taking the president down the drain. . . . It's Watergate all over."[158]

Poindexter continued to play a lead role in the cover-up and oversaw the concoction of a false chronology of events regarding the Iranian missile sales. The document claimed that Reagan had not approved the initial arms sales to Iran via Israel. Moreover, it failed even to acknowledge the November 1985 HAWK shipment, which the president had approved.[159] These arms transfers had been made without legal authority.

At a press conference on November 19, 1986, Reagan clung to Poindexter's bogus chronology. He claimed that the United States was not involved in arms shipments to Iran until 1986, at which point he had signed a presidential finding that authorized the covert operation. He again dishonestly asserted that there was never an arms-for-hostages program. Two days later, Poindexter, utilizing the chronology, misled Congress by denying that the administration had involvement in 1985 missile shipments to Iran.[160] Soon afterward, the vice admiral destroyed the only copy of the December 1985 *retroactive* presidential finding which factually stated that the purpose of the arms sales was to obtain the release of American hostages. Poindexter later told Congress, "I decided that it would be politically embarrassing to the President at this point because it would substantiate what was being alleged."[161] On November 22, Vice President George H. W. Bush wrote in his diary, "The president has asked us to shut up, and that is exactly what's happening."[162] The next evening, North followed Poindexter's lead: he organized a five-hour "shredding party" to destroy stacks of incriminating government documents pertaining to the Iranian and Nicaraguan operations.[163]

By this time, Attorney General Edwin Meese had assumed control of the cover-up to protect the president. Meese knew that the 1985 arms sales to Iran were "not legal because [of] no finding," so he insisted on the fictitious storyline that Reagan did not know of the 1985 sales or the subsequent diversion of funds to replenish Israel's stockpile and provide support to the Contras.[164] Neither Poindexter, Weinberger, nor Shultz objected to Meese's deceitful plan to insulate the president.

For the cover-up to succeed the attorney general needed somebody to take responsibility for the illicit operations. Poindexter and North were the obvious targets. Meese wrote in a memorandum, "Tough as it seems, blame must be put at NSC's door — rogue operation, going on without President's knowledge or sanction."[165] Richard Secord, however, was the only principal participant in the scandal who wanted Reagan to assume personal responsibility for Iran-Contra. The retired general urged Poindexter not to resign as national security advisor. "You don't understand," the vice admiral informed his collaborator. "It's too late. They're building a wall around him [Reagan]."[166] On the morning of November 25, after more than five years of service at the White House, Poindexter submitted his resignation. Reagan accepted it, while commending the admiral for going down with the NSC ship.[167]

While John Poindexter's military career was coming to a sudden and dishonorable end, Colin Powell's was flourishing. After four months as the three-star commander of V Corps in West Germany, he was recalled to Washington to serve as the deputy national security advisor under Frank Carlucci, the same position that Poindexter had held under McFarlane. Like the admiral, Powell would later be elevated as national security advisor. The lieutenant general had initially resisted his reassignment to Washington. From Germany he warned Carlucci that he had played a major role in orchestrating weapon shipments to Iran, saying, "You know I had a role in this business" and was "up to my ears."[168] But at the behest of the president and Defense Secretary Weinberger, Powell took up his new duties in January 1987. The Carlucci-Powell team was charged with overhauling the NSC structure, processes, and operations.

In February 1987, a special presidential review board known as the Tower Commission published a report assessing the proper functions and procedures of the NSC. Poindexter refused to cooperate with the commission's investigation, which eventually discovered that the admiral had willfully deleted more than a thousand government emails related to Iran-Contra. Much to Poindexter's chagrin, all of those documents were successfully recovered from backup storage tapes. In the end, the Tower Commission concluded that the vice admiral's involvement in the Iranian and Nicaraguan operations had been "amateurish" and that he had "failed grievously" in sanctioning the diversion of U.S. arms sale proceeds to the Israelis and Contras.[169]

Congress began televised hearings on the Iran-Contra affair in May 1987. Poindexter and North agreed to testify after being granted immunity. When North appeared he employed the so-called Nuremberg defense, claiming that he was merely an officer following orders: "I have never carried out a single act, not one, in which I did not have authority from my superiors. . . . I saluted smartly and charged up the hill. That's what lieutenant colonels are supposed to do." He further testified that his sacred duty was fidelity to the president, not honesty to Congress or the American public.[170] Poindexter testified in July. He readily admitted to misleading Congress and withholding critical information. The vice admiral said, "I simply didn't want outside interference." On the critical diversion question, Poindexter adhered to the administration's fabricated script; he claimed that the president had no knowledge of it. "I made a very deliberate decision," the admiral testified, "not to ask the President [for permission] so that I could insulate him from the decision and provide some future deniability for the President if it ever leaked out. . . . the buck stops here with me."[171]

In the end, the majority congressional report, which had the support of all Democrats and three Republican senators, assailed the Reagan administration for its "secrecy, deception, and disdain for the law." Poindexter and the NSC staff were severely criticized for their "pervasive dishonesty" and obstruction of congressional oversight. "Congress," the report read, "cannot legislate good judgment, honesty, or fidelity to law."[172] The report chastised Poindexter for his destruction of the retroactive 1985 arms-for-hostages finding: "In destroying the record of the President's post hoc approval of the November 1985 shipment, Poindexter also sought to destroy the proof of Presidential accountability that the law seeks to achieve."[173] Even the minority Republican report slighted Poindexter for lacking "policy judgment" and "operational experience." The report concluded that the admiral "was not well equipped" to lead complicated covert operations, especially ones that were "bound to raise politically sensitive questions." Poindexter was an able "technician," but not someone experienced enough in foreign affairs to "initiate policy or engage in jurisdictional battles."[174]

Poindexter was also a prime target of a criminal investigation launched in late 1986 by the Office of the Independent Counsel, led by Lawrence Walsh, a retired federal judge. In March 1988, Walsh indicted

Poindexter, North, and Secord collectively on conspiracy, theft, and obstruction charges. However, because of complications related to the congressional immunities granted to Poindexter and North, a U.S. district judge severed the prosecutions. Each would be tried separately.

North was prosecuted first, in early 1989. He testified for two days. As with his congressional testimony, asserted that his activities were fully sanctioned by his superiors, including Poindexter. North claimed that he never operated without "express permission" and readily admitted to giving Congress "factually incorrect" information.[175] When asked about his willful lying to the House intelligence committee at Vice Admiral Poindexter's behest, he said, "I was put in a situation where . . . I knew that it would be wrong, but I didn't think it was unlawful. . . . I felt like a pawn in a chess game being played by giants."[176] He then proceeded to confirm that after the Iran-Contra scandal broke Poindexter destroyed the December 1985 presidential finding that attempted to retroactively authorize the arms-for-hostages program.

In May 1989 North was found guilty on three felony counts, including destroying and falsifying evidence related to the illicit operations in Iran and Nicaragua. The judge stated that North had willfully and even "excessively" participated in a "scheme that reflected the total distrust in some constitutional values" and a "tragic breach of the public trust."[177] Nevertheless, the marine was shown extraordinary leniency: three suspended prison sentences ranging from one to three years, two years of probation, 1,200 hours of community service, and $150,000 in fines.[178]

Secord's trial was scheduled for mid-November 1989. He faced a dozen criminal charges, most stemming from false statements made during the congressional hearings. To avoid a jury trial, the retired general agreed to cooperate with the independent counsel and pleaded guilty to a single felony, that of testifying falsely under oath. He was sentenced to twenty-four months of probation. Upon leaving the courthouse, Secord again justly condemned Reagan for not accepting responsibility for the Contra and Iranian operations: "I think former President Reagan has been hiding out. I think it's cowardly. . . . [H]e was well aware of the general outlines of the so-called Iran-Contra affair."[179]

Meanwhile, Poindexter had retired from the Navy in 1987 after being demoted to the rank of two-star admiral. He was also indicted on obstruction charges for falsifying and destroying documents, for lying to the Senate and House intelligence committees, and for conspiring with North and others in these crimes. His trial began in March 1990. The judge overseeing the case ordered Reagan to submit pertinent portions of his diary to the court and to sit for a videotaped courtroom deposition. While being deposed, the former president sought to help Poindexter. On multiple occasions he openly winked and smiled at the admiral.[180] Under oath, Reagan acknowledged his close working relationship with Poindexter, but repeatedly testified that he could not remember many key facts about the two covert operations.[181] Poindexter did not testify. Like North's attorneys, the admiral's lawyers argued that he was merely a military officer following the directives and wishes of his superior.

The evidence against Poindexter was overwhelming. North testified for several days. He asserted that Poindexter was fully aware of the covert operations and admitted that both he and the admiral had made "absolutely false" and "patently untrue" statements to Congress. More evidence of Poindexter's dishonesty surfaced when an FBI agent who had interviewed him immediately after his resignation testified that the admiral said he had no knowledge of the 1985 Iranian arms shipments, the destruction of NSC documents, or the diversion of funds to the Contras. Thereafter, an NSC staffer testified that the day before Poindexter tendered his resignation the admiral had deleted five thousand emails from his government account.[182]

On April 2, 1990, after closing statements, the judge told the jury that to convict Poindexter they must be certain of his "specific intent," meaning "intending with a bad purpose either to disobey or disregard the law."[183] Five days later, the jurors found Poindexter guilty of all five felony charges. The judge sentenced the vice admiral to six months in federal prison. The judge wrote, "If the court were not to impose such a penalty here, . . . its actions would be tantamount to a statement that a scheme to lie and to obstruct Congress was of no great moment."[184] The jury foreman later told reporters, "All in all, I think he [Poindexter] was very dedicated. But guilty as charged."[185] At the time, the admiral was the highest-ranking government official ever convicted of obstruction of justice.[186]

Despite the vagaries and criminalities of the Iran-Contra affair, Colin Powell continued to prosper from it remarkably. He later candidly acknowledged the bizarre reality that the scandal had benefited his career. "If it hadn't been for Iran-Contra," he quipped, "I'd still be an obscure general somewhere. Retired, never heard of."[187] Indeed, by the time of Poindexter's conviction, Powell had been promoted to four stars and made chairman of the Joint Chiefs of Staff under President George H. W. Bush. The specter of his involvement in the Iran-Contra scandal, however, dogged him. Starting in December 1986 and continuing through November 1992, government investigators questioned Powell nearly a dozen times about his and Weinberger's roles in Iran-Contra. The interviews were variously conducted by the FBI, the White House, Congress, the Army inspector general, the General Accounting Office, and the Office of Independent Counsel.

In a clear obstruction of justice, Weinberger and Powell concealed from federal investigators their knowledge of the defense secretary's voluminous diary, which contained incriminating information related to Iran-Contra. In June 1987, when the defense secretary was asked if he had any personal notes pertaining to national security meetings, his response was purposefully misleading: "[I] occasionally take a few notes, but not really very often."[188] That same month, when investigators asked Powell if Weinberger kept a diary, he said, "The Secretary, to my knowledge, did not keep a diary."[189] Powell also misled investigators about his own note-taking habits.[190] Five years later in April 1992, after the independent counsel discovered Weinberger's large collection of notes — some seven thousand pages — Powell finally came clean. In a sworn affidavit (and then in his autobiography), he confirmed that the "small mountain" of notepads did indeed constitute the defense secretary's "personal diary which reflected a record of his life."[191]

Weinberger's diary contained incontrovertible evidence that he and Powell had lied under oath about their contemporaneous knowledge of the illegal 1985 arms shipments to Iran and the need to resupply Israel.

In November 1986, Weinberger told Congress he did not learn of Israel's 1985 shipments and the need to replenish Israeli stockpiles until 1986. "No," he said. "I heard about that only much later after these things started to come out, and as I say I heard — only heard that statements were being made, not that that [arms shipments] had actually happened."[192] In July 1987, Weinberger was asked again whether he had known, in 1985, of the need to resupply Israel. He answered, "No, I have no memory of that."[193] When asked more specifically if he had had contemporaneous knowledge of the November 1985 HAWK shipment to Iran, Weinberger lied again: "No, I did not."[194]

In the years before Weinberger's notes were discovered, Powell had also repeatedly denied that he and Weinberger knew of Israel's arms shipments in 1985. In April 1987, congressional investigators asked Powell about the Iran operation and Israel's 1985 shipments. Powell told them that he was "aware of the Iran Initiative, but that the transfer of Israeli arms to Iran was *new* to him" and that "he is *now* aware that Israeli shortages existed in certain areas at that time."[195] In June 1987, Powell was questioned again about when he learned of the multiple 1985 Israeli shipments. He said, "It would be in calendar year 1986." When asked specifically about the November 1985 HAWK shipment, Powell said, "It was '86 not '85." He later stated that his recollections of the Iran initiative before mid-January 1986 "*all* have to do with discussions about a *possible* initiative [with Iran]."[196] In July 1987, Powell again told federal investigators that he had no contemporaneous knowledge of "Israel's involvement in the shipping of HAWK missiles to Iran in 1985."[197]

In April 1992, Powell was shown Weinberger's November 22, 1985, diary entry: "Israelis will sell 120 Hawks, older models to Iranians — Friday [hostage] release. Called Colin Powell — re above." In response, Powell said, "I assume this is an accurate statement by Mr. Weinberger." Powell was also shown Weinberger's December 10, 1985, diary entry: "We still must replenish 500 TOWs to Israel." Powell said, "This implies obviously that 500 TOWs have gone somewhere that must be replaced and I assume we were aware of it by this time." Powell was asked if Weinberger debriefed him after the December 10, 1985, White

House meeting about Iran and Israel. Powell told the investigator that "he would be surprised if he was not briefed on the Israeli missile replenishment issue."[198] Seven months later, when a federal attorney asked Powell if the Israelis expected their missile stockpiles to be replenished by the Defense Department, the irritated general barked, "You can't buy them at Kmart."[199]

Faced with the evidence of Weinberger's daily notes, Powell finally admitted the truth in 1992: he and the defense secretary had contemporaneous knowledge of the 1985 arms shipments and of the need to resupply Israel. Powell also confessed that he had regular and concurrent conversations with Weinberger about the Iran initiative as represented in the secretary's notes.[200] The independent counsel later reported that the defense secretary and Powell "were consistently informed of proposed and actual arms shipments to Iran during 1985 and 1986."[201]

Weinberger also made new admissions after his diary was uncovered. In May 1992 he told Lawrence Walsh (the independent counsel investigating Iran-Contra) that his diary notes were accurate, that he had contemporaneous knowledge of the November 1985 arms shipment to Iran, and that he always believed the weapons transfers to Iran through Israel had been illegal. Weinberger offered to testify to those facts, but he refused to plead guilty to any crime, not even a single misdemeanor.[202] The latter was unacceptable to Walsh. A month later, a grand jury indicted Weinberger on five felony charges for lying to Congress about the 1985 arms sales and for obstructing federal investigations. He was arraigned on June 19, 1992.[203]

Powell was fortunate to escape indictment. Walsh had determined that the general's false testimony regarding Weinberger's diary alone was "corrupt enough to meet the . . . test of obstruction."[204] In his final 1993 report to Congress, Walsh concluded that "Weinberger lied to investigators to conceal his knowledge of the Iran arms sales" and that "General Powell was one of the handful of senior DoD [Department of Defense] officials who were privy to detailed information regarding arms shipments to Iran during 1985 and 1986. . . . [I]nvestigators quickly learned that

Powell was a knowledgeable party." The report further concluded that some of Powell's statements to investigators "were questionable and seem generally designed to protect Weinberger."[205] And while Powell was characterized as a frequently "cooperative witness," the report condemned his sworn testimony as being "at least misleading" and "hardly constituted full disclosure."[206] Walsh decided not to indict the four-star general in 1992, concluding that "while Powell's prior inconsistent statements could have been used to impeach his credibility, they did not warrant prosecution."[207] While Powell has admitted that his extensive testimony in the Iran-Contra saga was often oriented toward protecting Weinberger, he has long presented himself as a victim of an unethical independent counsel who recklessly impugned his character and sullied his reputation by characterizing him as "a liar."[208]

Weinberger's trial was scheduled for January 5, 1993. Powell was to be an important witness. James Brosnahan, Walsh's lead prosecutor in the case, knew that the general and others would face "the hard choice of either telling the truth or risking their own prosecution for perjury or obstruction of justice."[209] Powell was saved from testifying when just a week before the trial, President George H. W. Bush (who as vice president wholly supported the Iranian and Nicaraguan initiatives) pardoned Weinberger. Powell and others had encouraged the president to do so, but given Bush's personal involvement in the scandal his action looms as a gross abuse of power. Nevertheless, with the stroke of the presidential pen, the cover-up of Iran-Contra crimes was tightly sealed.

Weinberger's last-minute reprieve outraged Brosnahan and Walsh. The latter immediately issued a statement of condemnation: "President Bush's pardon . . . undermines the principle that no man is above the law. It demonstrates that powerful people with powerful allies can commit serious crimes in high office — deliberately abusing the public trust without consequence."[210] Arthur Liman, the chief counsel for the Senate committee investigating Iran-Contra, later wrote that Bush's pardon set "a terrible precedent, since it said that a cabinet officer could lie to a prosecutor and the Congress with impunity."[211]

★ ★ ★ ★

Iran-Contra — the original crimes and subsequent obstruction of justice — is a complicated saga about the abuse of presidential power *and* the willful complicity of presidential subordinates, including John Poindexter and Colin Powell. Despite repeated attempts by Congress to preclude any American military support for the Nicaraguan rebels, Ronald Reagan explicitly instructed his national security advisor to do "whatever you have to do to help these people keep body and soul together."[212] Regarding his arms-for-hostages operation with the Iranians, Reagan brazenly informed his senior advisors that he was willing to break the law and suffer impeachment and imprisonment to save the hostages in Lebanon. Many subordinates, such as McFarlane, Poindexter, and North, enthusiastically executed the president's illicit operations. Others, like Shultz, Weinberger, and Powell, grudgingly submitted. After the scandal broke and multiple federal investigations began, they *all* knowingly obstructed justice to protect the president and themselves.

Powell and Poindexter's misconduct reveals the potentially disastrous consequences of excessive loyalty to one's superiors. Blind loyalty leads to conformity and complicity. As senior government officials, the flag officers had a duty to report the extralegal operations to either their military superiors or to Congress, or to the Pentagon Inspector General or the Justice Department. By dint of their solemn professional oaths, their ultimate loyalty was to the Constitution and the American people, not to the secretary of defense or even the president. Still, in his best-selling 1995 autobiography, Powell lavished praise on Weinberger for expressing opposition to the Iran initiative and for *not* resigning. (The general omitted from his book Weinberger's backing of the illicit Contra program.) Powell even argued that the secretary was "one of the true heroes of the Iran-Contra matter" and that "senior officials cannot fall on their swords every time they disagree with a President."[213] But as Weinberger, Powell, and Judge Walsh knew, the debate over arms-for-hostages was not a rudimentary policy disagreement; it was about the administration's willful violation of the law and its visceral contempt for congressional oversight.

Unfortunately, obstructionism by American generals and admirals continued in the decades after Iran-Contra. As chronicled in chapter 6 of this volume, a massive cover-up in the Navy and Marine Corps ensued after dozens of sexual assaults at the 1991 Tailhook convention became public. Furthermore, in 1999 Army Major General David R. E. Hale, once the Army deputy inspector general and commander of NATO forces in Southern Europe, was accused of having adulterous affairs with the wives of four subordinates. He denied the charges and was allowed to retire honorably. However, at his subsequent court-martial, Hale pleaded guilty to eight counts of misconduct, including lying about the sexual liaisons; he was demoted to brigadier general.[214] In 2007 four Army general officers, including Lieutenant General Philip Kensinger, were reprimanded for "a perfect storm of mistakes, misjudgments and a failure of leadership" in the aftermath of Army Ranger Pat Tillman's friendly-fire death in Afghanistan.[215] Tillman, a professional football player, had quit the National Football League to join the U.S. Army after 9/11. Kensinger was eventually demoted to major general for making false statements, deceiving investigators and superiors, and failing to accurately inform the Tillman family about the fratricide. As detailed in chapter 7, a long string of Navy admirals has been censured, demoted, or imprisoned for attempting to conceal their improper relationships with a criminal defense contractor who was arrested in 2013. In October 2016, retired Marine General James E. "Hoss" Cartwright, once the vice chairman of the Joint Chiefs of Staff, pleaded guilty to lying to FBI investigators. Years earlier, he had denied being a source for two journalists who were reporting on secret U.S.-Israeli cyberattacks on Iran's nuclear program. Federal prosecutors recommended a two-year prison term. Two weeks before his sentencing, in January 2017, President Barack Obama intervened and pardoned Cartwright.[216]

Dishonesty is frequently at the heart of obstruction cases. Again and again, admirals and generals who have committed crimes or learned of lawbreaking by others have lied to federal investigators.

They are often motivated by self-preservation or a deep desire to loyally protect wayward military and civilian superiors. Regardless of intent, they dishonor themselves and damage the military's reputation by breaching their oath to obey the rule of law and serve the greater public interest. Obstruction of justice, lying included, erodes trust and credibility. It is essential to the health of the American profession of arms that obstructionist flag officers are held publicly accountable. If not, obstruction becomes rationalized and normalized by the uniformed leadership, thus unleashing a cancer that will degrade an institution which, in a democratic society, must be absolutely trustworthy.

CHAPTER SIX

SEX CRIMES

The Tailhook Admirals

SEX CRIME—any unlawful sexual act, including indecent
exposure, harassment, abusive contact, assault, and rape

In November 2020, the Department of Defense's Office of Inspector
General (DoDIG) released its annual *Top DoD Management Challenges* report. This document identifies and assesses the Pentagon's most serious
performance and management problems. A foremost mission of the
DoDIG is to ensure ethical conduct throughout the department as its
personnel "must strive to act above reproach."[1] As with previous reports,
the 2020 assessment indicated that sex crimes, especially sexual assault
against women, remained a persistent problem within the U.S. armed
forces. The inspector general characterized sexual misconduct as "an enduring ethical challenge."[2] In recent years, the office has prioritized investigations into alleged unethical conduct, especially sexual misbehavior by generals, admirals, and civilian executives. "Failing to appropriately
address senior official misconduct," the DoDIG has warned, "can lead to

an erosion of trust in the DoD and can impact the leadership of the DoD." General Mark Milley told the inspector general staff, "If we lose that trust and confidence, we have lost everything."[3]

There is reason for concern. Between fiscal years [FY] 2015 and 2019, the DoDIG *substantiated* 278 allegations of serious misbehavior by senior leaders in the Defense Department. Half of those cases related to "personal misconduct and ethical violations," including sex crimes.[4] During those four years, the total number of complaints against senior military officials increased 26 percent to 896, and the inspector general's substantiation rates in its formal investigations doubled from 26 to 51 percent.[5]

The sexual conduct of military officers is regulated by three articles of the Uniform Code of Military Justice (UCMJ). Article 120 of the UCMJ delineates the crimes of rape, sexual assault, aggravated and abusive sexual contact, and sexual threats. General Article 134 denounces "all conduct of a nature to bring discredit upon the armed forces" and "all disorders and neglects to the prejudice of good order and discipline." Article 134 details the military's prohibitions against bigamy, indecent conduct, child pornography, and pandering and prostitution, and it defines the wrongful nature of extramarital sexual conduct. Finally, Article 133 of the UCMJ condemns any and all "conduct unbecoming an officer," which "connotes failings in an officer's personal character."[6]

★ ★ ★ ★

Beginning in the autumn of 1991 and extending through early 1994, the American people received an unexpected two-part education in sexual harassment and sexual assault that pervaded civilian and military society. The first began on October 6, 1991, when National Public Radio reported that Supreme Court nominee Clarence Thomas stood accused of making unwelcomed sexual advances and comments to Anita Hill, a former subordinate at the Department of Education and the Equal Employment Opportunity Commission (EEOC). The bombshell news compelled the Senate Judiciary Committee to reopen the recently concluded confirmation hearings.

Hill, a law professor at the University of Oklahoma, testified before the Senate Judiciary Committee on October 11, 1991. During the early 1980s, she had worked as an assistant to Thomas at the Education Department and thereafter at the EEOC. Hill claimed that Thomas, despite being her superior, repeatedly asked her for dates, made sexual overtures, and discussed sex while at work. Before a riveted national television audience, Hill testified that Thomas: "[described] acts that he had seen in pornographic films involving such matters as women having sex with animals and films showing group sex or rape scenes. He talked about pornographic materials depicting individuals with large penises or large breasts involved in various sex acts. On several occasions, Thomas told me graphically of his own sexual prowess."[7]

Thomas categorically denied Hill's accusations of harassment. He also criticized the Judiciary Committee — chaired by Delaware Senator Joe Biden — as racist for even considering the belated charges. In his testimony, Thomas disparaged the hearings as "a circus. It's a national disgrace. And from my standpoint, as a black American, it is a high-tech lynching for uppity blacks who in any way deign to think for themselves . . . and it is a message that unless you kowtow to an old order. . . . You will be lynched, destroyed, caricatured by a committee of the U.S. Senate rather than hung from a tree."[8]

The intense and salacious hearings created political drama and a media frenzy. The Thomas-Hill testimony also brought unprecedented attention to the subject of workplace sexual harassment. On October 15, with the support of eleven Democrats, Biden not included, the Senate narrowly confirmed Thomas's appointment by a vote of 52-48. In the months and years that followed, the EEOC received a record number of complaints of workplace sexual harassment.[9]

Two weeks after the Senate voted to confirm Justice Thomas, a second bomb shook the nation's capital. The Associated Press distributed a story by the *San Diego Union* with the headline: "Women Reportedly Abused by Navy Pilots at Seminar: Investigation Is Underway of 5 Separate Reports of Physical and Verbal Assault."[10] The so-called seminar was actually a large convention organized by and for the U.S. Navy's aviation community. The annual gathering had been held in Las Vegas since 1963 and was called "Tailhook," named for the metal hook under a Navy or Marine Corps jet that snags arresting cables across the deck of an aircraft carrier. Although Tailhook conventions featured professional presentations, panel discussions, and defense contractor exhibitions, they had always been disorderly, drunken affairs. By design the 1991 Tailhook, which attracted five thousand people, had been declared "the Mother of all Hooks."[11] As the *San Diego Union* had reported, women had indeed been assaulted at Tailhook '91. In fact, a Pentagon investigation would later determine that at least eighty-three women, including many naval officers, and seven men were physically abused by aviators in the Navy and Marine Corps.

Responsibility for the fast-breaking sex scandal fell to Chief of Naval Operations (CNO) Admiral Frank B. Kelso, Assistant Chief of Naval Aviation Vice Admiral Richard M. Dunleavy, and their civilian superior, Secretary of the Navy H. Lawrence "Larry" Garrett III, a retired naval aviator. The Navy conducted two internal investigations that documented some of the debauchery and criminal activity that occurred at Tailhook '91. Both probes, however, were egregiously flawed and purposefully incomplete. Perhaps above all, the Navy's investigators made no attempt to address leadership accountability for the Tailhook disaster. Thirty-three admirals, including Kelso and Dunleavy, and two Marine Corps generals had attended the convention but they were not even interviewed about the abuses.

Tailhook '91 is a dreadful saga of organized sexual assault and widespread unbecoming conduct by officers in the U.S. military. It is also the story of a cover-up culture that shielded officer misbehavior up and down the chain of command. Secretary Garrett's mismanagement of the Navy's investigations ultimately led to his dismissal in June 1992. Dunleavy was demoted for not preventing or stopping the flagrant misconduct in Las Vegas. Kelso not only witnessed misconduct at Tailhook, but also perjured himself at a related military court hearing. He was eventually humiliated and forced into early retirement. In totality, five admirals were retired prematurely. Another admiral who was already in retirement was demoted, and two more were relieved of their commands and reassigned. Still, not a single officer in the Navy or the Marine Corps was convicted at court-martial or imprisoned for the wanton sex crimes committed at Tailhook.

★ ★ ★ ★

Three years after the Korean War, a group of active-duty Navy and Marine Corps "Tailhooker" aviators organized an informal reunion at a beach community in Baja, California, just south of Tijuana, Mexico. The Tailhook gathering became an annual event and in 1958 was relocated to San Diego, California. The reunions gave birth to the Tailhook Association, a private, nonprofit booster organization whose membership included thousands of active-duty and retired aviators as well as corporate defense contractors and other civilians involved with naval aviation. The annual "symposium," which moved to Las Vegas, Nevada, in 1963, grew over time to include aerospace exhibits and official U.S. Navy briefings and professional development programs. The Navy granted the Tailhook Association rent-free offices at the Miramar, California, Naval Station and allowed the use of military aircraft to transport personnel to and from Las Vegas.[12]

Despite the proliferation of professional events at the Tailhook conventions, socialization and alcohol consumption remained central to the gatherings. In the 1960s, defense contractors rented hotel suites to host hospitality parties. The early Las Vegas symposiums took place at the Sands Hotel and Casino, and the festivities and antics got out of control. In 1967, a group of pilots broke down the door of a defense contractor's suite, consumed all available alcohol, and threw furniture out of the fifteenth-floor window. In a nearby room, other aviators tossed out a piano. As a result, the Sands management banned the Tailhook convention from returning, but the rowdy aviators were soon welcomed by the Las Vegas Hilton.[13]

The drinking and raucous behavior at Tailhook was not limited to junior officers. Flag officers encouraged both mischief and extraordinary informality. Admiral John K. "Jack" Ready was famous for demonstrating his ability to drink beers while standing on his head. Another admiral landed a jet at nearby Nellis Air Force Base, folded up its wings, and drove the aircraft with a police escort to the Hilton property. Another character, Rear Admiral Jeremy D. "Bear" Taylor, who flew two hundred combat missions in Vietnam, dressed in a Civil War costume and rode a white horse into the Hilton's lobby.[14]

Changes came to Tailhook during the 1970s when the Department of Defense issued new regulations prohibiting defense contractors from hosting parties for the aviators. As a result, individual Navy and Marine Corps squadrons began renting their own suites. The rambunctious parties continued, and the squadrons competed for crowd popularity.[15]

The Tailhook conventions of the 1980s were notorious affairs. Their "spiritual leader" was none other than John F. Lehman Jr., Ronald Reagan's influential and controversial Secretary of the Navy.[16] Lehman, who served as secretary from 1981 to 1987, was a regular participant at official Tailhook functions and at informal social events. The latter featured loud music, chanting, X-rated videos, drunkenness, go-go dancers, strippers, sex workers, and consensual sex. At one squadron suite party, Navy and Marine Corps officers witnessed Lehman push dollar bills into a dancer's G-string and then pick her up and carry her out the door. That same year Tailhook debauchery reached a new low with male officers queuing up "for oral sex performed by women who would blow the semen out of their mouths and over the gathered crowd."[17]

Some senior Navy leaders believed the vulgar behavior of the aviators had gone beyond the pale. After the 1985 convention, Commander Randall H. "Duke" Cunningham, the Navy's only fighter ace of the Vietnam War, complained to the Tailhook Association. Cunningham, himself a board member, observed "with disdain" the misconduct of junior officers and the failure of senior officers to control them. He wrote that the Tailhookers' heavy drinking had "produced walking zombies that were viewed by the general public and detracted from the Association/USN [U.S. Navy] integrity." Cunningham stated that reforms needed to be made before the next convention as "dancing girls performing lurid sexual acts on Naval aviators in public would make prime conversation for the media."[18]

Cunningham was not alone in his criticism. Vice Admiral Edward H. Martin, Deputy Chief of Naval Operations (Air Warfare), sent a blistering letter to Rear Admiral James E. Service, a former president of the Naval War College and the newly appointed commander of Naval Air Forces, Pacific Fleet. Martin, who had been tortured as a prisoner of war in North Vietnam, learned about the "grossly appalling" behavior and "drunken melee" in the Hilton hallways and hospitality suites. He complained, "Heavy drinking and other excesses were not only condoned, they were encouraged. . . . We can ill afford this type of behavior and indeed must not tolerate it. . . . We will not condone institutionalized indiscretions."[19] In turn, Admiral Service warned the Tailhook board of directors that if they did not take corrective action, then the Navy would withdraw its support, including the gratis transportation to and from Las Vegas.[20]

On September 26, 1985, the Tailhook Association convened a special board meeting to address the problems of excessive drinking, lewd conduct, and inadequate "adult supervision."[21] This resulted in the association's president, Navy Captain Jack W. Snyder, writing a six-page apology to Vice Admiral Martin. Snyder, the commander of the West Coast training squadron, promised significant reforms, including perhaps banning hospitality suites altogether. In short, Snyder pledged that the association would put "the word 'professionalism' back into the centerpoint of 'Hook '86."[22] With this commitment in hand Martin was placated, but unbeknownst to the admiral, the Tailhook board later voted not to take any meaningful corrective action other than issuing convention "rules" to squadron commanders ahead of each gathering.[23] William McMichael, who wrote a vivid history of the Tailhook scandal, characterized these written instructions as "a Band-Aid on a sucking chest wound."[24]

Boosted by the blockbuster film *Top Gun*, starring Tom Cruise as cocky Navy pilot Pete "Maverick" Mitchell, naval aviation was flying high by the time of the 1986 Tailhook convention. Secretary of the Navy Lehman was excited to celebrate with his fellow aviators in Las Vegas. On a Friday night, he entered the hospitality suite of Attack Squadron VFA-127, where a sex worker was stripping. Lehman joined her, dropping to the floor between her legs. A crowd of officers cheered him on. Lying on his back, the secretary placed a rolled dollar bill in his mouth. The naked woman gyrated her hips over his face. She then positioned herself on his mouth and "snatched the bill with her labia."[25] So much for enhanced adult supervision.

The debauchery only got worse by Tailhook 1990, when one of Lehman's successors, Navy Secretary H. Lawrence Garrett III, was in attendance. After reports of women being assaulted, the Tailhook Association board began to worry that it did not have adequate liability insurance. Beyond covering the misadventures of its own members, the board sought "maximum protection" to cover the large number of underage women ("Vegas Locals") who regularly attended the wild parties.[26]

Garrett, a former Navy aviator and Vietnam veteran, had previously served as the Navy undersecretary and as the Defense Department's chief legal officer. President George H. W. Bush appointed him as secretary. At Tailhook 1990, Garrett socialized freely with drunken aviators on the infamous third floor of the Hilton Hotel. (The expansive third floor boasts twenty-six suites connected by long hallways, a swimming pool, and a large common area.) He visited several hospitality suites, including one that offered free leg shavings to women. Garrett saw a woman on a bed with her skirt raised up, having her legs shaved by a junior officer while "an admiral rubbed her stomach." According to one witness, the conduct "neither startled him nor appalled him."[27]

The nature of the annual Navy event in Las Vegas remained common knowledge. After the 1990 convention, a military base newspaper in Texas proudly reported that its hungover squadron had returned home safely with no aviator "convicted of any crimes, felonies, that is," even after three nights of "celebration, joviality, and debauchery." The paper reported that this Texas squadron had dispensed forty kegs of beer, three hundred fifteen liters of tequila, and fifteen cases of other liquor.[28]

In the summer of 1991, Secretary Garrett's office received his invitation to attend the upcoming Tailhook. Several senior subordinates advised him not to join the "annual bacchanalia" because his attendance would suggest that he condoned its excesses, many of which violated the Uniform Code of Military Justice. Marybel Batjer, Garrett's special assistant and political advisor, was adamant that he not go, writing across the invitation letter, "Yuk! Yuk! NO! NO! You can't go to Tailhook." The Judge Advocate General of the Navy, John E. "Ted" Gordon, agreed with Batjer. Nevertheless, Garrett and CNO Frank Kelso, felt obligated to attend, partly to show support for the aviators returning from the Persian Gulf War and partly to boost morale at a time when the Bush administration was cutting budgets and canceling popular military aircraft programs such as the F-14D Tomcat and A-12 Avenger.[29]

Tailhook '91 opened on the morning of Thursday, September 5, and closed with a Sunday buffet brunch on September 8. The convention, which ultimately attracted five thousand people, featured presentations and panels on naval aviation with a special focus on Gulf War operations. The serious partying began early on Friday, September 6. That night Vice Admirals Richard M. Dunleavy and Jack H. Fetterman Jr. escorted Kelso, the Navy's senior ranking officer, through several of the hospitality suites on the Hilton's third floor. The CNO had occasion to look into a suite where once again women were receiving free leg shaves.[30]

Dunleavy, the assistant chief of naval aviation, was most responsible for planning the aviator convention in coordination with the Tailhook Association. At one point, he took Kelso to the crowded third floor pool deck and left him talking with Captain Robert L. Beck, a Navy reservist. A commotion arose nearby. A group of raucous junior officers surrounded a young, bikini-clad woman and began chanting, "Tits! Tits! Tits!" They wanted her to take off her top and expose her breasts. Kelso asked Beck, "Am I hearing what I think I'm hearing?" The captain responded, "Admiral if you think you are hearing 'tits,' you're absolutely right." Before long a very loud cheer erupted and the bikini top was hoisted up into the air. Kelso remarked, "Well, I guess that's the end of that." But the growing crowd began a new chant, "Bush! Bush! Bush!" as the officers called for the woman's bikini bottom. Hotel security intervened and dispersed the men. Kelso too walked away.[31]

The aviators' crass and overt sexism was again on display during Tailhook's crowded "Flag Panel" on Saturday afternoon. The panel included eight admirals, including Dunleavy and Fetterman, and one Marine Corps lieutenant general. Admiral Kelso watched from the audience. The purpose of this packed event was to allow junior officers to ask starkly candid questions to senior leadership. (Dunleavy even wore a shirt with a target on it.) At one point a female aviator asked when women would get the chance to fly in combat. Male officers in the crowd jeered. The question caught Dunleavy off guard. "Hoo, boy," he replied with a smile. The admiral stated that such a decision would be made by Congress, which led to more booing and laughing from men in the audience.[32] The flag officers were subsequently criticized by the Navy IG for failing to "strongly counter" the crowd's "very negative reaction" to female officers.[33]

Later that evening, after Secretary Garrett "rallied the troops" at the keynote banquet, he visited multiple hospitality suites on the Hilton's disorderly third floor. At approximately 10 p.m., he entered the notorious Rhino Room, which featured a large dildo attached to a rhinoceros mural. A plastic tube connected the dildo to a drink dispenser behind the mural. When a woman "pleased the rhino" by putting her hand or mouth around the dildo, alcohol squirted out.[34] Garrett would later claim that he saw nothing untoward in the suites. In his reliable chronicle of the Tailhook scandal (based on extensive interviews with direct witnesses), Gregory L. Vistica writes, "He [Garrett] would have to have been blind not to see the rhino and its drink-dispensing dildo."[35]

Even more appalling than the boorish behavior inside the Rhino Room and other suites, organized criminal assault was occurring just outside their doors. By 1991, "The Gauntlet" of the third floor had become a terrifying and abusive tradition, a ritual of sexual violence against women, including female officers. Starting about 9 p.m., a drunken but organized mob of officers filled the poorly lit hallway and lined up against the walls. Some of the men wore t-shirts that read "Women are property" and "He-Man Woman Haters Club." When unsuspecting women came out of the hotel elevator and entered the corridor, several men rapidly closed in behind them. They pushed the women down the line, with dozens of screaming and chanting Navy and Marine Corps officers grabbing their breasts and crotches, pinching and biting their butts, and pulling and ripping their clothing. At a minimum, five women were assaulted on the first night of Tailhook '91; eleven more on Friday; and no fewer than fifty-three on Saturday night.[36]

Some of the Tailhook '91 victims were teenagers; they were students from the University of Nevada, Las Vegas. A group of A-6 Intruder pilots printed and distributed party invitations across the college campus. The invitation read, "A-6 Tailhookers All-Weather Attack. . . . Please join the Intruders for an evening of imbibing, chicanery, & debauchery. Las Vegas Hilton Suite 307." One of the victims at Tailhook '91 was eighteen years old. Helicopter pilots in suite 315 knowingly plied this legally underage woman with alcohol. She became "severely intoxicated" and nearly passed out. The naval officers began to worry about their moral and legal predicament. So, to avoid "embarrassing the squadron" and escape "responsibility for her intoxication," two of the pilots carried her out of the suite, grabbing her by her ankles and wrists. They dropped her on the hallway floor at the end of the raging gauntlet. The pilots returned to their suite and shut the door. Meanwhile, several other naval officers in the hall picked up the teenager, not to help her, but to carry her through the gauntlet. The mob assaulted her, yanking off her pants and underwear.[37]

The most infamous and consequential assault occurred on Saturday night around 11:30 p.m. Lieutenant Paula Coughlin, a Navy CH-53E helicopter pilot, was at the convention as the aide to Rear Admiral John W. Snyder. He had been president of the Tailhook Association six years earlier when Vice Admiral Martin complained about the "grossly appalling" behavior on the Hilton's third floor. Coughlin exited the elevator on the Hilton's third floor searching for friends whom she had agreed to meet. A man near the elevator recognized her. As she walked down the hallway, he led the drunken crowd to chant, "Admiral's Aide! Admiral's Aide!" Another officer approached Coughlin and bumped her hip with force, knocking her off balance. Yet another grabbed her buttocks with both hands and lifted her forward. The chanting men swarmed around Coughlin and grabbed her breasts. Frantic and furious, she twice shouted, "What the fuck do you think you're doing?!" A man bear-hugged her from behind and they fell onto the beer-soaked carpet. She bit her attacker's left forearm and right hand, and broke free. Someone else grabbed at her underwear. She tried to escape into one of the hospitality suites but two officers blocked her entry. Coughlin pleaded for another officer to help her, but instead he gripped her breasts. She finally broke free and entered an open suite. A fellow officer remarked, "I guess you've just been through the gauntlet."[38]

The next morning, Coughlin called her superior, Rear Admiral Jack Snyder. She told him that she had been attacked. "I was almost gangbanged last night," she said, "by a bunch of fucking F-18 pilots." Snyder, a Tailhook veteran and former board president, told his aide, "It's so wild down there. That's why I went, had one margarita, said hello to a few friends, and left."[39] When the two met for breakfast, Coughlin again brought up the assault, telling Snyder, "It was really bad. These guys started grabbing at me and grabbing my rear, they were so out of line, I can't tell you how out of control." The admiral shook his head and said, "I know. That's what you've got to expect on the third deck with a bunch of drunk aviators."[40] Later, Vice Admiral Dunleavy, who had overseen the Navy's planning for Tailhook '91, would admit to condoning the gauntlet. "It was my impression from what I saw," he said, "that no one was upset, and I felt that they [women] wouldn't have gone down the hall if they didn't like it."[41]

After Coughlin returned to her duty station, Naval Air Aviation Pax River, she began to tell others about the sexual assault. By September 18, Snyder had finally come to understand the seriousness of the problem and discussed it with Coughlin the next day. At that September 19 meeting, Snyder said that he and Coughlin should write separate letters to Vice Admiral Dunleavy requesting a formal investigation. More than a week passed without Snyder writing to Dunleavy. Worried about the delay, Coughlin took the initiative and provided a copy of her letter to the Navy's Bureau of Personnel. Her letter summarizing the terrifying assault ultimately reached Vice Chief of Naval Operations Admiral Jerome "Jerry" Johnson, who worked for Admiral Kelso. Johnson immediately ordered Rear Admiral Duvall M. "Mac" Williams, Commander of the Naval Investigative Service (NIS), to open a criminal investigation.[42]

Meanwhile, a full month after the 1991 convention, Captain Frederic G. Ludwig, the Tailhook Association's president, sent out a remarkable letter applauding "the biggest and most successful Tailhook we have ever had. We said it would be the 'Mother of all Hooks,' and it was." Vice Admiral Dunleavy had helped craft the letter. Ludwig was especially happy that the convention had the sanction of the Navy's most senior leaders. "Our very senior leadership, including the Secretary and the CNO," he wrote, "were thoroughly impressed and immensely enjoyed their time at Tailhook '91." Ludwig also fully admitted that crimes had occurred at Tailhook and that they must be prevented in the future. He reported that property damage at the hotel totaled $23,000 and "most serious," he wrote, "was 'the Gauntlet' on the third floor. I have five separate reports of young ladies . . . who were verbally abused, had drinks thrown on them, were physically abused and were sexually molested. Most distressing was the fact an underage young lady was severely intoxicated and had her clothing removed by members of the Gauntlet." Ludwig promised the aviators that he would conduct "damage control work."[43] The captain's disturbingly candid communique would become known as "the ho-ly shit" letter.[44]

A reporter at the *San Diego Union* obtained a copy of Ludwig's incriminating letter and published an article on October 29, 1991.[45] The Associated Press picked up the story and it landed like a Mark 83 bomb in the nation's capital. The *Washington Post*'s headline read: "Navy 'Gauntlet' Probed; Sex Harassment Alleged at Fliers' Convention."[46] Arizona Senator John McCain, a former naval aviator and Vietnam

POW, lambasted the Navy and entered Ludwig's damning letter into the *Congressional Record*. McCain described the sexual assaults at Tailhook as "very despicable behavior" and said that people in the military should be "ashamed and embarrassed" because "there is no excuse for it." He demanded an investigation and accountability for those responsible.[47]

Navy Secretary Garrett had learned of Coughlin's accusations but only saw Ludwig's letter the day before the news broke. He immediately terminated the Navy's relationship with the Tailhook Association. In a letter to Ludwig, Garrett expressed his "absolute outrage" over the acknowledged sexual assaults and declared, "No man who holds a commission in the Navy will ever subject a woman to the kind of abuse in evidence at Tailhook '91 with impunity."[48] Garrett then established a task force, led by Navy Undersecretary Dan Howard, to oversee two separate investigations. The first was an expansion of the NIS's existing inquiry into the attack on Lieutenant Coughlin. A second investigation, assigned to Navy Inspector General (NIG) George W. Davis VI, was to report on personal misconduct in Las Vegas and on the Navy's relationship with the thirty-five-year-old Tailhook Association.

Operating in a crisis climate, CNO Kelso could not simply wait for the investigations to play out. He needed to demonstrate accountability within the Navy. On November 4, 1992, Kelso temporarily suspended Rear Admiral Snyder from his prestigious aviation command at Pax River. The stated reason was Snyder's "failure to take timely and appropriate action" to investigate Coughlin's allegation of felonious assault.[49] An unnamed Navy flier told the *Washington Post* that this type of public rebuke was "the kind of thing where they leave a pistol on the table and everybody leaves the room. . . . It's a real signal."[50] In December, Kelso made Snyder's removal permanent.[51] Kelso and Undersecretary Howard also wanted to fire Vice Admiral Dunleavy, but the admiral escaped the chopping block. He was a close friend of Secretary Garrett and already near retirement.[52]

In February 1992, Rear Admiral Williams of the NIS learned that his old friend Garrett had spent time in the infamous Rhino Room during Tailhook '91. An NIS investigator quipped, "I hope to God he was drinking beer and not making the Rhino happy."[53] The information about Garrett stemmed from a witness statement by Marine Corps Captain Raymond Allen. Williams chose *not* to disclose this embarrassment to Admirals Kelso and Johnson. Instead, he locked a copy of Allen's statement in his safe and later excluded it from the NIS's report. It was a decision that would come back to haunt him.[54]

On April 28, Garrett and Kelso received a briefing on the two Tailhook investigations; both were coming to a close. By then, 1,500 officers had been interviewed. Howard's task force overseeing the investigations had convened more than twenty times, and the NIS and NIG inquiries consumed more than twelve thousand work hours, which had cost the Navy a million dollars. Investigators had documented rampant misbehavior, including two dozen criminal assaults by Navy and Marine Corps officers. Despite these findings, Garrett and Kelso learned that the net results of the probes were meager — only two suspects had been identified. This is because the Tailhookers were "closing ranks." The mass obstruction of justice was causing investigators to run "into a stone wall of silence and lies."[55]

Barbara Pope, a member of the Tailhook task force and the assistant secretary of the Navy for manpower and reserve affairs, appropriately cried foul. "People are lying," she exclaimed, "and we're doing nothing about it." She wanted the squadron commanders involved with Tailhook hospitality suites to compel their subordinate officers to cooperate with investigators. "I don't know about you," she said to Garrett and Kelso, "but I don't have confidence in these people's leadership abilities."[56]

To blunt the expected criticism of the reports' lack of individual accountability, Garrett attempted preemptive action. He leaked to the press a memorandum stating that he was "appalled by the unacceptable behavior and attitudes" of officers attending Tailhook. The secretary added that the NIS and NIG investigations revealed "a lack of responsibility, absences of moral judgment, and inadequate standards of integrity on the part of Navy and Marine Corps officers who could have asserted positive leadership but failed to do so. It is simply not good enough to abstain from unacceptable conduct, we must demand much more from our officers; society expects no less."[57]

The long-awaited NIS and NIG reports were released on April 30, 1992. The NIS's two-thousand-page, fifteen-pound report was an unwieldy compilation of victim complaints, witness statements, interview reports, and prosecutive summaries. No title page, no table of contents, no executive summary, and no index made the voluminous report more difficult to digest. Spread throughout, however, were stories of gross misconduct and a detailed analysis of the infamous gauntlet.[58]

By comparison, the concise sixteen-page NIG report was accessible and easily comprehended. The report described Tailhook's chauvinistic "gang mentality" atmosphere and how it led to rampant misbehavior, including the sexual assaults. The inspector general scolded the Tailhookers for not taking personal responsibility for their actions. He noted that in their interviews with his office, Navy and Marine Corps officers demonstrated "a marked absence of moral courage and personal integrity" and a belief that they could "get away with 'manhandling' selected women in the gauntlet to the point of assault." The inspector general also criticized senior military leaders for not stopping the misconduct. Rear Admiral Davis wrote, "The activities . . . in the corridor and suites, if not tacitly approved, were allowed to continue by the leadership of aviation community and the Tailhook Association."[59] Still, the inspector general did not identify any criminal suspects nor did he assign individual responsibility for the misconduct.

The two Navy reports received widespread press coverage. The lack of accountability generated outrage in Congress. Senators Sam Nunn (Democrat, Georgia) and John Warner (Republican, Virginia) informed Defense Secretary Richard "Dick" Cheney that the Senate Armed Services Committee would immediately freeze *all* Navy and Marine Corps officer promotion recommendations until they were notified which officers had attended Tailhook '91. This was drastic: it affected nearly five thousand officers, most of whom were not even at Tailhook. But Nunn and Warner were determined to hold the Navy accountable for the depravity and crimes committed in Las Vegas.[60]

In mid-May, Barbara Pope, the first female assistant secretary in the Navy's 217-year history, arranged a meeting with her boss's boss, Secretary Garrett. He had just returned from a two-week trip to Australia. She told Garrett that the NIS and NIG reports were embarrassingly inadequate and "not up to Navy standards." First, countless Navy and Marine Corps officers had lied to investigators. Second, the "issue of leadership and accountability" went unaddressed. Pope said she would not stand behind the two reports and threatened to resign if Garrett did not take further action.[61] Senator McCain later characterized the Navy's two investigations as "a manifestation of the old 'circle the wagons' syndrome. It was terribly mishandled. It was — it was bungled to an alarming degree. There was — it was a disaster."[62]

Fearful of having the Navy's senior female official resign in protest, Garrett acted swiftly. He tasked Admiral Gordon with identifying more sailors and marines who had violated the Uniform Code of Military Justice, and the higher they ranked the better. Gordon quickly identified seventy officers who had committed various infractions; none of them, however, were squadron commanders. Garrett, in turn, referred the seventy cases to the chain of command for appropriate discipline.[63]

Seven months after Tailhook and only one month away from retirement, Vice Admiral Dunleavy fielded questions from military affairs reporters. He finally accepted responsibility for the gross misconduct. Dunleavy admitted, "We in naval aviation leadership . . . failed," and he accurately characterized what happened to women in Las Vegas as "despicable." And while he rightly concluded, "I should be fired," he also misled reporters with false claims: "We [admirals] weren't there to step in and stop it" and "It's not until afterwards that we hear about these goddamn stories."[64]

Dunleavy's attempt to assume some leadership responsibility and to shield his superiors from blame failed. In June, a serious question arose as to whether Secretary Garrett himself had visited the infamous third floor of the Las Vegas Hilton. Admiral Kelso contacted Rear Admiral

Williams and inquired whether his NIS investigation had turned up any information that would "implicate the secretary with regard to Tailhook." Williams, who did in fact possess evidence that Garrett had been in the Rhino Room, lied to Kelso, telling him, "No, there is nothing out there."[65]

As a result, on June 8, Garrett released a statement declaring that he had not seen any misconduct and had not visited any of the party suites. Soon afterward, however, Vice CNO Johnson learned that Williams had lied to Kelso. A credible witness statement placed Garrett in Tailhook's "bawdiest suite." Williams not only verbally withheld this from his superiors, he also omitted it from the NIS's massive report released to the public.[66] Johnson and Kelso were furious. They wanted Williams fired. Garrett, however, protected his friend and instead offered his own resignation to Defense Secretary Cheney. It was refused.[67]

All of this forced Garrett to issue a carefully guarded second public statement. On June 16, the secretary declared that he had just learned from a new supplemental NIS report that he had indeed visited a party suite at Tailhook. "The closest he came to any of the suites," the statement read, "to the best of his recollection, was on one occasion" when he and others walked over to a suite's patio entrance "to get something to drink."[68] The press ran with the breaking story. Under public pressure, Garrett asked the Defense Department inspector general to conduct a brand new, comprehensive investigation of Tailhook '91.

The Bush White House was facing criticism from congressional Republicans and Democrats who perceived a Navy cover-up, and consequently was losing patience with Garrett. National Security Advisor Brent Scowcroft, a retired three-star general, described the Tailhook debacle as "a disgrace." He said, "There ought to be some high-level people held responsible."[69] The pressure reached a breaking point for the president in late June when Paula Coughlin went public. She appeared on the front page of the *Washington Post* with the headline: "A Gauntlet of Terror, Frustration — Navy Pilot Recounts Tailhook Incident." She was also interviewed on ABC's *World News Tonight* with Peter Jennings.[70] Wearing her uniform, Coughlin told Jennings, "I love the Navy. . . . I was attacked by naval officers and Marine Corps officers who knew who I was. And it was sport for them."[71]

Moved by Coughlin's account of the assault, George and Barbara Bush invited Coughlin to the White House. Moreover, the president wanted Garrett fired; it was an election year. The secretary submitted his letter of resignation the next day. Garrett accepted responsibility for Tailhook but was stubbornly adamant that he had not seen any misconduct in Las Vegas. "I want you to know," he wrote to the president, "I neither saw nor engaged in any offensive conduct. I further accept responsibility, and hold myself accountable to you and all of the innocent men and women in the Department of the Navy for the leadership failure which allowed the egregious conduct at Tailhook to occur in the first place."[72] Chief of Naval Operations Kelso also offered to resign, but Defense Secretary Cheney rejected it.[73]

President Bush selected Sean O'Keefe, a young Cheney protégé, to replace Garrett. His mission was to reform the Navy's sexist culture, even though Cheney had stated publicly that Tailhook '91 was an "isolated incident that should not reflect on the Navy as a whole."[74] On September 21, 1992, O'Keefe received the first of two Tailhook reports from the DoDIG. *Tailhook 91 — Part 1: Review of the Navy Investigations* assessed the Navy's two previous probes into the notorious Las Vegas convention. For context, the DoDIG report provided a brief history of the Tailhook Association and stated that unbecoming conduct had become ritualized long before 1991. Moreover, the misconduct was not a secret within the Navy, and the participation of *senior* naval leaders gave sanction to the improprieties. The misbehavior of officers at Tailhook, the inspector general reported, was "known within the Navy to be incompatible with Navy policies dealing with sexual harassment and abuse of alcohol" and "the presence of the Secretary [of the Navy] and flag officers gave tacit approval to the event, including those aspects of the convention that were contrary to established Navy policies."[75]

While the DoDIG's second report would later detail the crimes and gross improprieties at Tailhook, the first report, which focused on the

Navy's internal investigations, confirmed that miscreant behavior had been rampant at the 1991 convention with "men exposing themselves, women baring their breasts, shaving of women's legs and pubic areas, and women drinking from dildos that dispensed alcoholic beverages." The inspector general also confirmed the presence of a hallway "gauntlet" that had led to "violent grabbing, groping and other clearly assaultive behavior."[76]

On the whole, the first DoDIG report was a scathing indictment of the Navy's "overall management" of its two investigations into Tailhook. The inspector general stated that Under Secretary Dan Howard and Judge Advocate General (JAG) Admiral Ted Gordon were both "uncertain as to their roles and responsibilities" in overseeing the Navy investigations.[77] The inspector general further chastised the Navy's entire management team for not ensuring effective cooperation and coordination between the two Navy inquiries and for not developing a joint comprehensive investigative plan, especially once Navy leadership became aware of the wide scope of misconduct at Tailhook.[78]

In short, the DoDIG concluded that the Navy's investigations into Tailhook were egregiously flawed and *purposefully* inadequate. The Navy had chosen not to investigate many apparent violations of law and service regulations and had not addressed "individual accountability for leadership failure that created an atmosphere in which the assaults and other misconduct took place."[79] Of central concern to the inspector general was the Navy's decision not to interview more than thirty admirals and Marine Corps generals who had attended the Tailhook '91. The DoDIG did not shy away from assigning blame and responsibility: "The inadequacies of the investigations were due to the collective management failures and personal failures on the part of the Under Secretary, the Navy IG, the Navy JAG and the Commander of the NIS."[80]

Moreover, the DoDIG identified the Navy's motivation for conducting inadequate and misleading investigations. "In our view," the inspector general concluded, "the deficiencies in the investigations were the result of an attempt to limit the exposure of the Navy and senior Navy officials to criticism regarding Tailhook 91." The Tailhook task force members knew that "the Navy as an institution could be vulnerable to considerable criticism" and they "erred when they allowed their concern for the Navy as an institution to obscure the need to determine account-ability for the misconduct and the failure of leadership that occurred."[81]

The DoDIG report assailed Under Secretary Howard, who had led the task force overseeing the two internal investigations. He was criti-cized for not exercising more authority and control over the probes. The inspector general rejected Howard's position that he was merely "an information gatherer."[82] The report determined that "his failure to provide effective leadership and direction to the Naval IG, and the Commander, NIS, as an abrogation of responsibility."[83] Howard was sharply criticized for not expanding the investigation to encompass the wide array of misconduct contrary to the NIG's recommendation that he conduct a comprehensive "all-up investigation."[84] The DoDIG concluded that Under Secretary Howard's "failure to exercise leader-ship to ensure the overall adequacy of the Navy investigations into Tailhook was a key failure in the matter."[85]

Similarly, the DoDIG criticized the performance of Rear Admiral Gordon, the Navy JAG who was advising Howard. The inspector gen-eral faulted the Navy's top lawyer for not reviewing the NIG and NIS investigative reports for "legal sufficiency" and for not assessing their adequacy "in addressing all relevant issues including individual ac-countability for misconduct."[86] The DoDIG also upbraided Gordon for failing to remedy a serious conflict of interest that arose during the investigations, writing that the JAG demonstrated remarkably poor "professional judgment" in his refusal to act on a "serious" problem.[87]

The two admirals who led the NIS and the NIG investigations were also subjected to withering criticism. The DoDIG did credit Admiral Da-vis's NIG for recommending a more comprehensive investigation, for identifying the misuse of Navy transport aircraft for Tailhook, and for recognizing that a harrowing convention climate had created a "gang mentality which eventually led to the sexual assaults."[88] Nevertheless, the DoDIG condemned Davis for not assigning adequate staff to con-duct a major investigation. According to the Defense Department's report, "By only assigning six of his staff members on a part-time basis, the NIG limited his ability to obtain required information and performed only superficial work on issues that required depth and breadth."[89] The inspector general also criticized Davis's decision to not interview Navy and Marine Corps flag officers who had attended Tailhook even though his NIG report stated that the atmosphere of misconduct at the convention had been condoned and encouraged by senior naval officials. The DoDIG concluded further that Davis's decision to limit the NIG investigation to lower-ranking officers was not just uneven, but also unethical. The DoDIG wrote, "To refer those individuals, serving in the grade of captain and below while ignoring the need to determine the accountability of more senior officers who attended Tailhook 91, is unfair and inconsistent."[90]

The DoDIG report saved its harshest criticism for Rear Admiral Williams, the Commander of the NIS. As with Davis, the inspector general assailed Williams for not expanding his probe to include all possible crimes and the many serious violations of military regulations. "Given the significance of the investigation and its potential impact on the Navy," the inspector general asserted that "the Commander, NIS, should have designated a larger full-time team of agents to the case to ensure that all aspects of Tailhook 91 were thoroughly and aggressively pursued."[91] Williams was also criticized for his desire to terminate the NIG investigation as quickly as possible and for his refusal to interview flag officers who attended Tailhook. "The Commander's overriding goal, and the motivation for his actions was to keep the investigation within narrow limits and to dissuade the investigators from pursuing issues that might lead them to question the conduct of senior officials at Tailhook 91," wrote the DoDIG.[92]

The inspector general even questioned Williams's suitability to lead a sex crimes investigation and also suggested that the admiral was not above lying to his superiors or federal investigators. Of concern was Williams's long-standing opposition to women serving in the Navy. The admiral had made clear his "strong personal preference for working with men" and his belief that "women do not belong in military service."[93] The DoDIG reported on Williams's heated argument with Assistant Secretary Pope, during which the admiral disparaged "a lot of female Navy pilots" as "go-go dancers, topless dancers or hookers."[94] Worse still was his characterization of Lieutenant Paula Coughlin, who famously had shouted to her Las Vegas attackers, "What the fuck do you think you're doing?" Admiral Williams told one of his female NIS agents, "Any woman that would use the F word on a regular basis would welcome this type of activity."[95]

The inspector general further criticized Williams for withholding evidence that proved Secretary Garrett had visited the Rhino Room. Both Williams and JAG Gordon had falsely told CNO Kelso, Vice Chief Johnson, and federal investigators that they did not learn of this evidence until well after the Navy had released the NIS and NIG reports. But the DoDIG report cast considerable doubt on those denials: "We find it remarkable that the Commander would not be aware of sensitive information in a case he personally became deeply involved with when the information was widely known among his subordinate managers and field personnel. Further, given the close relationship between the Commander [Williams] and JAG [Gordon], we believe that the Commander would have informed the JAG immediately on learning that a Marine Corps officer had placed the Secretary of the Navy in the Rhino Suite."[96]

In its conclusion, the DoDIG's report made three recommendations to Navy Secretary O'Keefe, one regarding process and two on personnel. First, the secretary should consider organizational and procedural reforms that would help the Navy "improve the investigative process." Second, O'Keefe should also strongly consider whether Under Secretary Howard and Admirals Williams, Davis, and Gordon "should continue in their current leadership roles." Finally, the inspector general recommended that the Secretary consider "appropriate disciplinary action" against Gordon and Williams for "their failure to fulfill their professional responsibilities in the Navy's Tailhook investigation."[97]

O'Keefe embraced the report and the need for the Navy to transform its sexist and obstructionist culture. At a televised press conference on September 24, he exclaimed, "We get it. We know that the larger issue is a cultural problem which has allowed demeaning behavior and attitudes towards women to exist within the Navy Department. . . . [S]exual harassment will not be tolerated. Those who don't get the message will be driven from our ranks."[98] The secretary proceeded to announce that Williams and Gordon would be retiring and that Rear Admiral Davis, like Rear Admiral Snyder earlier, would be relieved of his command and assigned elsewhere. Surprisingly, O'Keefe spared Howard, who was retained as under secretary. O'Keefe did announce that going forward the Navy's Office of Inspector General would be commanded by a three-star admiral, not a rear admiral, and that the Navy's Investigative Service would be reorganized and led by a senior civilian executive.

By the time the DoDIG's second Tailhook report was released in April 1993 (*Tailhook 91 — Part 2: Events at the 35th Annual Tailhook Symposium*), both O'Keefe and Howard had left government service. Democrat Bill Clinton had defeated President George H. W. Bush in the 1992 presidential election. As result of O'Keefe's departure, CNO Admiral Kelso began serving as the acting secretary of the Navy.

On April 23, 1993, Kelso and Marine Corps Commandant Carl Mundy convened a press conference at the Pentagon to remark upon the DoDIG's second report, which focused specifically on the misconduct at Tailhook '91. The two leaders sought to assure the public that the Navy recognized its cultural problem of chauvinism and sexual misconduct and was taking administrative and legal action against known suspects and implementing necessary reforms. But Kelso used contradictory language. On the one hand, he insisted that the problem was "not an epidemic." On the other hand, he described the crisis as a "watershed event" in Navy history and promised to change "the institutional mindset" that had allowed for the "egregious conduct." Mundy made clear that he was *not* an aviator and that he only recently learned of Tailhook. He described the aviators' behavior in Las Vegas as reflecting a complete disregard "for the most basic fundamentals of professional conduct, human dignity, and respect for others." When a reporter asked Kelso, if he would resign over the scandal (considering he had attended Tailhook), the admiral said that while he took responsibility for the misbehavior, he had no intention of resigning.[99]

In *Report of Investigation: Tailhook 91—Part 2: Events at the 35th Annual Tailhook Symposium*, the DoDIG described in graphic detail the convention's widespread disreputable and criminal misconduct. Beyond chronicling what happened, the inspector general explained why Tailhook "degenerated to a point where indecent assaults, indecent exposure, and excessive alcohol consumption became commonplace."[100] From the outset, the inspector general assigned blame to the Navy's senior military and civilian leadership for knowing about serious misconduct at previous Tailhook conventions and choosing not to prevent their recurrence in 1991. Moreover, the vast majority of the thirty-two active-duty flag officers and three Navy reserve admirals who had attended Tailhook '91 had admitted to visiting the scandalous third floor of the Las Vegas Hilton. "Tailhook '91 did not occur in a historical vacuum," the report asserted, and "some of the Navy's most senior officers were knowledgeable as to the excesses practiced at Tailhook '91 and, by their inaction, those officers served to condone and even encourage the type of behavior that occurred there."[101]

After interviewing nearly three thousand people and investing sixty thousand hours of labor, DoDIG investigators discovered that at least eighty-three women and seven men had been assaulted at Tailhook '91. Furthermore, they determined that twenty-three officers warranted disciplinary referral to the Navy for their roles in the assaults. Each assault was detailed in the report. A total of 117 officers— but no flag officers—were either connected to these assaults or to instances of indecent exposure, unbecoming conduct, or "failure to act in a proper leadership capacity."[102] The inspector general also reported countless attempts to cover up the Tailhook scandal. Hundreds of officers lied to investigators, refused to provide pertinent information, or purposely misled them "in an effort to protect themselves or their fellow officers."[103] As a result, the DoDIG concluded that "the number of individuals involved in all types of misconduct or other inappropriate behavior was more widespread than these figures would suggest. Furthermore, several hundred other officers were aware of the misconduct and chose to ignore it."[104]

The inspector general determined that multiple factors contributed to the extensive malfeasance at Tailhook '91. To begin, some Navy and Marine Corps officers saw themselves as "returning heroes" from the Persian Gulf War and viewed the convention as a "free-fire zone" where they could celebrate "without regard to rank or ordinary decorum." Many officers also perceived naval aviation as having a unique warrior culture "separate from the main stream of the Armed Forces." The popular Tom Cruise movie *Top Gun* had further glorified naval aviators and "fueled misconceptions on the part of junior officers as to what was expected of them." The DoDIG further concluded that the most common explanation for the gross misbehavior in Las Vegas was that such conduct was "expected" and that Tailhook was "comprised of 'traditions' built on [the] lore" of previous conventions.[105]

The inspector general also concluded that the Tailhook disaster had resulted from an abject failure of senior leadership. Flag officers in naval aviation were the most culpable. Again and again the DoDIG asserted that the outrageous behavior at the Tailhook conventions was common knowledge and that admirals and Marine Corps generals in the aviation community had allowed it to continue:

> In our view, by September 1991, both individually and collectively, the senior leaders of naval aviation were unwilling to take the kinds of measures necessary to effectively end the types of misconduct that they had every reason to expect would occur at Tailhook '91. . . . The Tailhook traditions (the gauntlet, hallwalking, leg shaving, mooning, streaking, and lewd sexual conduct) so deviated from the standards of behavior the nation expects of its military officer that the repetition of this behavior year after year raises serious questions about the senior leadership of the Navy.[106]

The inspector general's report specifically targeted Vice Admiral Dunleavy, the former assistant chief of naval aviation, for his "failure of leadership." According to the report, Dunleavy, who had quietly retired in July, initially lied to investigators and told them that he had not witnessed the gauntlet or any female leg shavings. Later, however, Dunleavy admitted that he had actually "encouraged" the leg shavings and had indeed "observed the activity that occurred during the gauntlet," including officers yelling, "Show us your tits!"[107] The three-star admiral told investigators that he did not intervene to break up the gauntlet for two reasons. First, the noise in the crowded hallway was so loud that he "would not be heard above the commotion." Second, from his perspective, the gauntlet "appeared to be in fun, rather than molestation" and that "they [women] would not have gone down the hall if they did not like it." In the end, the DoDIG determined that Dunleavy's horrendous judgment "represents a serious, individual failure to recognize the impropriety of these activities and to take action to stop them."[108]

The DoDIG also questioned the honesty of other flag officers who had attended Tailhook '91. Thirty-three of the thirty-five senior officers had attended prior conventions; indeed, two of the admirals were past presidents of the Tailhook Association. The inspector general expressed "reservations about the categorical denials of some flag officers that they were completely unaware of any specific misconduct, especially when viewed in light of their past experiences at prior Tailhook conventions." In fact, the preponderance of the evidence led the DoDIG to conclude that "there was general knowledge among the Navy's senior aviation leadership of the inappropriate behavior that had become commonplace on the third floor during annual Tailhook conventions."[109]

In the report, the inspector general noted that he would forward to Les Aspin, President Clinton's secretary of defense, the investigative files on the thirty-three admirals and two Marine Corps generals who attended Tailhook '91. Aspin and the incoming secretary of the Navy, John Dalton, would have to determine "whether action is warranted with respect to the responsibility of each flag officer for the overall leadership failure that culminated in the events of Tailhook '91." The DoDIG made no punitive recommendations.[110]

John Dalton, a Naval Academy graduate, was sworn into office as secretary of the Navy on July 21, 1993. He immediately made ethical conduct the foundation of his leadership. Secretary Dalton declared,

"I place the highest value on honesty, moral integrity, and the consideration of others."[111] With that guiding mindset, he began reviewing the flag officer files and conducted more than a dozen interviews with senior leaders. By October 1, the secretary had concluded that several admirals must be punished for the debauchery and crimes committed at Tailhook. Secretary Dalton informed Secretary Aspin, "I believe the damage done to the Navy's reputation by incidents at Tailhook could have been prevented or minimized by aggressive leadership and foresight by senior Navy officials."[112] Dalton's list of culprits included the CNO and senior leaders in naval aviation. He recommended that President Clinton fire Admirals Kelso and Dunleavy's two deputies, Rear Admiral Riley Mixson and Reserve Rear Admiral Wilson Flagg, both of whom had attended Tailhook '91.

Clinton left the decisions to Aspin. The defense secretary met with Kelso and then the president. Aspin ultimately decided that Kelso would be spared, but several senior aviators would be punished. On October 15, Dalton announced the penalties. Dunleavy, already in retirement, would be demoted from three stars to two. "More than any other individual," the secretary said, "Admiral Dunleavy was responsible for the failures at Tailhook," and his "performance of duties after Tailhook were similarly flawed."[113] Mixson and Flagg, who were approaching retirement, were forced out of the Navy. Mixson was specifically faulted for observing a crowd of chanting officers standing around "a woman drinking from a 'Rhino penis dispenser,' and [for] witnessing incidents of leg shaving," but not stopping the misbehavior.[114]

The three admirals received formal letters of censure for failed leadership. Dalton explained that "Admiral Dunleavy and these two other officers had an obligation to make themselves aware of the behavior of their juniors in general and persons within their administrative chains of command in particular. They were expected to ensure that such conduct was not unbecoming of naval officers, discreditable to the naval service or otherwise unacceptable."[115] Secretary Dalton continued, "There were ample signs that trouble could arise" at Tailhook '91.[116]

Of the thirty-two other flag officers who attended Tailhook, only two were exonerated. Most, including Admiral Kelso, received nonpunitive reprimands known as letters of caution. The performance of these senior officers, Dalton concluded, "was not all that could have been."[117]

By the time of Dalton's announcements, forty lower-ranking Navy and Marine Corps officers had been disciplined, receiving a mixture of monetary fines and punitive and nonpunitive letters of reprimand. In addition, several courts-martial were about to commence wherein some officers, including Navy Commander Thomas R. Miller, were accused of observing misconduct at Tailhook on Saturday night, September 7, 1991, and not stopping it.

In November, Miller's lawyer entered a pretrial motion with Judge William T. Vest Jr., a Navy captain, to dismiss all charges against his client on the grounds that Admiral Kelso had been present on the controversial third floor of the Hilton Hotel. He argued that the CNO should have recused himself and not assigned other officers, who were junior to him, to oversee the criminal investigations involving Tailhook. The attorney maintained that Kelso's attendance at the convention legally precluded him from acting as an "accuser" and from referring charges against his client (or anybody else) because the admiral had a "personal interest" in the outcome of the investigation. Moreover, if Commander Miller was guilty of not stopping officer misconduct, so was the admiral. For his part, Kelso had previously sworn under oath that he had *not* been on the third floor on Saturday night, he had not visited any of the hospitality suites, and that he never witnessed any misconduct at Tailhook.[118]

Before ruling on the motion, Judge Vest heard weeks of testimony about Kelso's activities at Tailhook, and the admiral himself was called to the stand. Many of the prosecution's witnesses — including active-duty admirals — gave testimony that either confused or contradicted their earlier sworn statements, which had squarely placed Kelso on the third floor on that infamous Saturday night. Rear Admiral James H. Finney had previously said, "I saw him [Kelso] Saturday night out there. . . . I'd say around 11:00 [p.m.]." On the stand in front of Vest, however, Finney testified, "I can't tell for sure whether I saw him Saturday night or not."[119] Similarly, Rear Admiral Paul W. Parcells testified, "I still feel that I saw him there. But my degree of confidence in those feelings is very, very low," and Vice Admiral William C. Bowes told the court, "I can't remember precisely seeing him there. I thought I had seen him."[120]

Kelso's executive assistant, Captain Phillip G. Howard, who had originally told investigators that he "went to the third floor . . . with the CNO [Kelso]" on Saturday night, testified in court that Kelso did not visit the third deck at all on Saturday.[121] Retired Captain Daniel P. Whalen, who knew and liked Kelso, also contradicted his previous sworn statement that he had witnessed the admiral on the deck. In court, Whalen said that he was no longer "positive" that he observed Kelso on Saturday night. Judge Vest intervened several times to remind a visibly anguished Whalen that he was under oath.[122]

The most incredible obfuscation came with the testimony of Lieutenant Ellen E. Moore, who had previously sworn that Kelso was on the pool deck on Saturday night. In court she stated in a shaking voice, "Currently, I do not have a specific recollection of seeing Admiral Kelso on the pool patio that Saturday." Moore said she could not even remember ever discussing Kelso's whereabouts with DoDIG investigators. Frustrated with her testimony, Judge Vest questioned her directly. Her answers remained painfully muddled and abstruse: "I have an ambiguous recollection" and "I would feel more comfortable if I had clearer recollections." When Vest reminded her that she was under oath, Moore testified, "I have a problem with my potentially getting caught up in misrepresenting my ambiguity."[123]

At one point in the hearing, Judge Vest expressed mounting concern. He was deeply unsettled by so many witnesses changing their testimony, all in favor of Kelso's claim that he had not been on the deck Saturday night. It was clear to Vest that "institutional pressures . . . have been demonstrated at least several times in this court."[124]

When Kelso appeared at the hearing on November 29, he was unequivocal as to what he remembered. He testified that he was not on the third floor Hilton pool deck on Saturday night. Furthermore, he said, "I was not in any suites at Tailhook" and had "no personal interest in the case."[125] But the certainty of Kelso's testimony differed significantly from his interview with DoDIG investigators earlier in the year. In an April interview, Kelso was informed that many witnesses had observed him on the deck Saturday night, and as a result, the admiral was read his legal rights. He was suspected of "false swearing and giving a false statement." According to the federal investigator, Kelso became noticeably distressed and asked, "Could I have possibly found my way to the third floor and crossed the patio?" In the end, the admiral told the investigator that "to the best of [his] recollection," he had not gone to the third floor on the Saturday of Tailhook '91.[126]

The recently retired Vice Admiral Dunleavy testified in Vest's courtroom the day after Kelso. He took full responsibility for the Tailhook debacle. "It's like [being] the captain of a ship," he said. "You run it aground, you've got to take the hit. I was the responsible guy." The admiral swore that he did not see Kelso on the third floor on Saturday night, but conceded Kelso could have been there. Dunleavy accidentally damaged the CNO's believability when he said that he accompanied Kelso through the controversial hospitality suites on Friday night. "Yes, in fact, I escorted him, and we walked around. From the patio, finally made a swing through the suites down the passageway, up to another suite and back out on the patio."[127]

Kelso's credibility plummeted further when Navy Reserve Captain Robert L. Beck and other defense witnesses took the stand. Beck testified that he and Kelso had been on the third floor Friday night and that they had witnessed a crowd of chanting officers encircle a young woman and demand that she take off her bikini top, which she ultimately did. The aviators also demanded that she remove her bikini bottom, chanting, "Bush! Bush! Bush!" When a defense attorney asked Beck if his candid testimony might endanger his chances of being promoted to admiral because it contradicted Kelso's testimony, he answered plainly, "Yes."[128]

In their closing statements, the defense attorneys stated with confidence that they had not only proven Kelso abused his command influence as an accuser, but he had also covered up his own misconduct at Tailhook and had not stopped the unbecoming conduct of military officers. "The court," asserted one lawyer, "already had enough evidence for a pre-trial investigating officer to recommend court-martial for Kelso on charges of making a false official statement." The attorney also underscored how many defense witnesses had risked their careers by giving testimony that contradicted the Navy's most senior military leader.[129]

During the next six weeks, Judge Vest analyzed fifteen hundred pages of hearing records and hundreds of related documents. He delivered his 111-page finding on February 8, 1994. His ruling sided with the defense and against the Tailhook admirals and the government prosecutors who had sought to defend them. The judge believed that many senior officers had witnessed unbecoming and even criminal misconduct and deliberately chose not to intercede. "It is clear from the record," Vest wrote damningly, "that no one attempted to intervene to end the lewd and improper sexually oriented behavior. Conduct which began as being merely in bad taste quickly escalated and finally ended in physical assaults. If proper leadership had been shown, the subsequent assaults and other inappropriate conduct might have been prevented."[130] Vest viewed Tailhook '91 as "a personal embarrassment for all senior naval officers" because they failed to intervene, and thus the "opportunity to spare the Navy and the Marine Corps the chagrin and humiliation that has been heaped on it was lost."[131]

Judge Vest was certain that CNO Kelso had witnessed misconduct in Las Vegas and ignored it. "This court," Vest wrote, "has found that Admiral Kelso was present on the third-floor patio on both Friday and Saturday evenings, near the location where the alleged assaults on female attendees occurred. This court has also found that Admiral Kelso witnessed improper conduct being committed by junior officers."[132] As a result of Kelso's personal interest in the outcome of the Tailhook courts-martial, Vest dismissed those cases without prejudice. He also disqualified Kelso's handpicked convening authorities who were adjudicating all cases related to Tailhook.

Equally disturbing to Vest was the behavior of Navy flag officers *after* the scandal broke. The judge concluded that Kelso and others sought to cover up their failed leadership by both limiting the Tailhook investigations and by giving false testimony. Vest wrote, "This court finds that Admiral Kelso manipulated the initial investigative process in a manner designed to shield his own personal involvement in Tailhook '91. This manipulation of the process by Admiral Kelso and others was for their own personal ends."[133] Vest was unambiguous in stating that there had been an "improper exercise of command position" and that "there has been both actual and apparent unlawful command influence."[134] The judge characterized the testimony of the government's pro-Kelso witnesses as "highly contradictory, and often implausible." In marked contrast, he described defense witnesses as "convincing" and supported by "many corroborating facts and circumstances."[135]

Vest's ruling, most especially his censure of Kelso, reverberated throughout the Navy. Secretary Dalton, who had already tried to fire Kelso once before, announced to the press that he would "carefully review the facts" before deciding the admiral's fate.[136] Kelso was furious with Vest's finding. He continued to claim, defiantly and falsely, that he had not witnessed misconduct at Tailhook and that he had not exercised unlawful command influence on the subsequent investigations. "I said from the beginning," he told *ABC News*, "I didn't see anything untoward at Tailhook and I stick by that. I did nothing to influence the process. I'm going to continue to serve in my job."[137]

But the jig was up. The nation's most senior admiral could no longer outrun the truth. The Clinton administration knew that the discredited Kelso could not remain at the helm of the shell-shocked Navy. In a press statement announcing the CNO's early retirement, the president's new defense secretary, William Perry, tried to soften the blow to Kelso's ego and reputation. While Perry said that he did not "question the correctness" of Vest's ruling, he cited the original DoDIG report on Tailhook, which had not revealed incriminating evidence against Kelso. According to Secretary Perry and in stark contrast to Vest's judicial findings, the admiral was "a man of the highest honor and integrity."[138] Kelso played the role of a martyr. He told reporters: "I clearly have become the lightning rod for Tailhook and I think it's in the best interest of the Navy if I proceed on and retire."[139] "This," the admiral declared, "is the end of Tailhook."[140]

★ ★ ★ ★

Tailhook was a colossal failure in military leadership. Years before the disastrous 1991 convention, dozens of flag officers and civilian executives knew that Navy and Marine Corps aviation officers were making a mockery of the Uniform Code of Military Justice. In 1985, Vice Admiral Edward Martin was appropriately appalled by the public drunkenness and other excesses occurring in Las Vegas, and he formally criticized Navy leadership for condoning and encouraging the officer misconduct: "We can ill afford this type of behavior and indeed must not tolerate it."[141] Martin's outrage over the breach in military law and ethics fell upon deaf ears. No meaningful reforms were attempted; nobody was held accountable. As Judge Vest later wrote, "The failure by those responsible to take strong corrective action regarding inappropriate behavior that obviously occurred at past Tailhook symposiums is incomprehensible."[142] As a result of leadership's dereliction of duty, officer behavior at the aviator conventions continued to degrade materially.

At Tailhook '91, the secretary of the Navy, the chief of naval operations, the assistant chief of naval operations for air warfare, and two dozen other flag officers visited parties on the raucous and bawdy third floor of the Hilton Hotel. Most, if not all, witnessed conduct unbecoming of officers. Not one senior leader intervened. Why? Captain Robert Stumpf, commander of the Navy's Blue Angels flying team, answered this way: "[Intervening] would have been bad form and certainly not in the spirit of the Tailhook that had been established by tradition over the decades preceding. . . . It [intervening] just didn't even occur to me or any of the other senior officers who were there."[143] Such bald negligence only encouraged the reckless attitude of drunken subordinates, many of whom committed criminal assaults against ninety women and men. "The greatest responsibility," Judge Vest concluded, "must lie with the most senior officers, and Adm. Kelso was the most senior officer present."[144] Dozens of flag officers were, in varying degrees, complicit in the unethical and criminal circus that was Tailhook '91.

Unfortunately, more than twenty-five years later, sexual misconduct remains pervasive in the U.S. military. In 2021, the Department of Defense announced publicly that reports of sexual assault against service personnel — mostly women — continued to rise. The number increased from 2,828 in fiscal year 2012 to 4,794 in fiscal year 2016, and to 6,290 in fiscal year 2020.[145] In 2022, the Department of Defense stated further that reports of sexual assaults increased 13 percent in fiscal year 2021.[146] Disturbingly, more than a few admirals and generals have been perpetrators of sexual crimes.

Within three years of CNO Kelso's retirement, three admirals were found guilty of sexual misbehavior. In 1995, two-star Admiral Ralph L. Tindal, the deputy commander of NATO forces in Portugal and Spain, was found guilty of adultery, sexual harassment, fraternization, and conduct unbecoming an officer. He had engaged in a year-long relationship with a female enlisted aide. Tindal was demoted to one star, placed under house arrest for thirty days, fined $7,686, and forced into retirement.[147] In 1996, the Navy censured retired two-star admiral Richard C. Macke, who while married and on active duty, had a long and "unduly familiar relationship" with a female Marine Corps lieutenant colonel.[148] Macke had been a four-star admiral in command of U.S. Forces in the Pacific, but was fired and retired at the lower rank after admittedly making "insensitive and offensive" comments about the kidnapping and rape of a twelve year-old girl by U.S. service personnel in Okinawa, Japan.[149] In 1997, Rear Admiral R. M. Mitchell Jr. was found guilty of conduct unbecoming an officer. He stood accused of creating a toxic command climate and sexually harassing a female subordinate. The admiral was reprimanded, fired as commander of Naval Supply Systems, and forced to retire.[150]

Sexual misconduct continues to haunt the Navy. In 2016, Rear Admiral Rick Williams was reprimanded and relieved as commander of

Carrier Strike Group Fifteen after admitting to watching hours of pornography on his shipboard computer.[151] In 2019, Rear Admiral Stephen Williamson was fired as director of industrial operations at Naval Sea Systems Command for having an adulterous relationship with a female civilian subordinate.[152] Williamson confessed to the affair and retired shortly afterward. That same year, four-star admiral William Moran, who was slated to become CNO, was instead forced into early retirement. He admitted to exercising poor judgment by not taking deliberate action after a favorite subordinate was accused of sexually harassing three female Navy officers.[153] In May 2021, the Navy Inspector General substantiated allegations that Rear Admiral Trent DeMoss had sexually harassed women through "unwelcomed and unwanted" touching and kissing while commander of Fleet Readiness Centers in Patuxent River, Maryland. DeMoss was demoted to captain and forced to retire.[154]

Flag officer sexual misconduct has not been limited to the Navy. In 1990, the U.S. Air Force abruptly fired and retired Lieutenant General Peter Kempf, the commander of the Twelfth Air Force and U.S. Southern Command Air Forces. Although kept from the public at the time, government investigators had discovered Kempf's inappropriate sexual relationship with "at least" one female subordinate.[155] Just five years later, one of Kempf's successors with the Twelfth Air Force and Southern Command, Lieutenant General Thomas R. Griffith, was also relieved and subsequently retired as a two-star general after admitting to an adulterous affair and failing to lead by example.[156] In 1996, the Air Force concluded that Brigadier General Robert Newell was guilty of "inappropriate conduct" with a female subordinate. The former commander of Airborne Warning and Control Systems planes was demoted to colonel and retired.[157]

Perhaps the most egregious case of sexual misconduct in the Air Force came to a close in 2005 when the service's Judge Advocate General, Major General Thomas Fiscus, was forced into retirement at the lower rank of colonel. The Air Force inspector general (AFIG) substantiated allegations that Fiscus — over a course of ten years — had repeatedly made unprofessional public displays of affection and unwanted sexual advances, and had wrongfully engaged in inappropriate relationships with a dozen female subordinates, including military lawyers, enlisted paralegals, and Pentagon civilians. In light of Fiscus's key leadership role as "the Air Force provider of guidance for the prevention of sexual harassment," the AFIG underscored the "stunning hypocrisy" and the "tremendous disgrace" of the general's own sexual harassment of JAG Corps subordinates.[158] Ultimately Fiscus, a married man, received a nonjudicial reprimand for fraternization, unbecoming conduct, engaging in unprofessional relationships, and obstructing justice.

The Air Force's problems did not stop with Fiscus. In 2006, Brigadier General Richard S. Hassan, the director of the service's senior leader management office, was demoted to colonel and forced to retire for sexually harassing female subordinates and creating a hostile work environment.[159] In 2013, the AFIG substantiated allegations that Brigadier General David C. Uhrich, a commander with Air Combat Command, Joint Base Langley-Eustis, had engaged in a "romantic relationship" with a woman not his wife and had abused alcohol by "repeatedly drinking while on duty."[160] In 2014, Lieutenant General Craig Franklin of the Third Air Force in Europe, resigned his command and retired early as a two-star general after being severely criticized for overturning the sexual assault conviction of a decorated fighter pilot.[161] That same year, Brigadier General Jon Weeks was permanently relieved of command of the Air Force Special Operations Air Warfare Center at Hurlburt Field, Florida. The decision was based on a preliminary investigation of "an alleged inappropriate personal relationship." Weeks retired in 2015 at the reduced rank of colonel.[162] In 2017, the Air Force served Brigadier General Jose Monteagudo a letter of counseling for a years-long inappropriate relationship with a married subordinate officer while in command of the 944th Fighter Wing at Luke Air Force Base in Arizona. He was forced into retirement the next year.[163]

Like senior airmen, Army generals have continued to commit sexual offenses. In 1997, Brigadier General Stephen N. Xenakis, was relieved of command of the Eisenhower Army Medical Center and other responsibilities. He was reprimanded for the "perception an adulterous relationship" with the nurse attending to his critically ill wife.[164] That same year, the commander of the Army's Aberdeen Proving Ground, Major General John Longhouser, retired after admitting to investigators his sexual affair with a Department of Defense civilian employee not his wife. He retired as a one-star.[165] In 1999, Major General David R. E. Hale, whose last assignment was Deputy Inspector General of the Army, pled guilty to eight counts of unbecoming conduct, including his adulterous affairs with the wives of *four* subordinate officers.[166] He had previously retired honorably while under investigation. After his court-martial, Hale escaped prison time, but was demoted to one star and ordered to pay $22,000 in penalties. Also in 1999, Major General John J. Maher was found guilty at a nonjudicial administrative hearing of having adulterous affairs with the wives of two fellow officers and of having "an inappropriate personal relationship" with an enlisted soldier.[167] Maher, the former vice director of the Joint Chiefs of Staff, was demoted to colonel and forced to retire.

One of the most incredible and shameful cases of sexual misconduct became public in 2000. The Army inspector general (AIG) substantiated the allegation that Major General Larry Smith had sexually harassed and assaulted Lieutenant General Claudia Kennedy in her Pentagon office when she was a two-star and the assistant deputy chief of staff for Intelligence. Smith, formerly the commander of U.S. Army Security Assistance Command, had been slated to become the Army's deputy inspector general, but instead was officially reprimanded and retired.[168]

The problem of senior leader sexual misconduct in the Army has not abated. In 2007, the AIG substantiated allegations that Brigadier General Anthony Tata had "at least two" adulterous affairs. He filed for retirement the next year.[169] Since 2010, at least a *dozen* generals have been retired, fired, or otherwise punished for committing sexual offenses. Major General John Custer retired in 2010 shortly after an AIG investigation substantiated several allegations against him. The AIG concluded that Custer had maintained a long-term inappropriate relationship with a woman not his wife. Moreover, he had "failed to demonstrate exemplary conduct" when sending subordinates sex-related emails and also allowing a woman to lick his medals while he attended a wedding in full dress uniform.[170] In 2011, Army Major General Glenn Rieth resigned in disgrace as the commander of the New Jersey National Guard after admitting to an adulterous affair with a married civilian aide.[171] In March 2013, Major General Ralph Baker was fired as the commander of Combined Joint Task Force-Horn of Africa (CJTF-HOA) after coming under a criminal investigation for the sexual assault of a senior civilian policy advisor. Six months later, he was demoted to one star, fined, and retired.[172] In August 2013, the Army admonished Brigadier General Martin Schweitzer after an AIG investigation substantiated allegations that he had sent vulgar and sexually explicit emails about a female member of Congress. Schweitzer had been selected for promotion to two stars, but was retired the next year.[173] In August 2014, Major General Michael Harrison, the former commander of U.S. Army forces in Japan, was demoted and retired for failing to pursue a woman's sexual assault claim against a colonel under his command. The colonel was eventually suspended and subjected to an administrative discipline.[174] In a rare court-martial of a flag officer, the Army also brought charges against Brigadier General Jeffrey Sinclair, a highly decorated deputy commander of the Eighty-Second Airborne. He was accused of wrongful sexual conduct, improper relationships with four female junior officers, and forcible sodomy. In a 2014 plea arrangement, the general pled guilty to inappropriate relationships with three women, possession of pornography, and "the maltreatment" of his mistress, a female captain. Like Hale and Maher, Sinclair skirted prison. He was demoted to lieutenant colonel, fined $20,000, and forced to retire.[175] The Army also forced Brigadier General Bryan Roberts to retire in 2014. At a nonjudicial Article 15 proceeding the prior year, the former commander of the U.S. Army Training Center in Fort Jackson, South Carolina, was found guilty of adultery, assault, and conduct unbecoming an officer. He was demoted to colonel.[176]

In 2016, two Army National Guard brigadier generals, Michael White and Michael Bobeck, were admonished for inappropriate sexual relationships. White was formally reprimanded and Bobeck was fired from his position with the Joint Chiefs of Staff.[177] That same year, the Army retired Major General David Haight, operations director at U.S. European Command, for conducting an eleven-year affair and living a "swinger lifestyle" that included the swapping of sexual partners. Like Sinclair, he was demoted to lieutenant colonel.[178] In May 2019, Army Brigadier General Mike Canzoneri resigned abruptly as the assistant adjutant general of the Florida National Guard after the *Tampa Bay Times* reported that he was under investigation for multiple acts of sexual misconduct.[179] In August 2019, the Army fired Lieutenant General Bradley Becker, the commander of its Installation Management Command, for failing to "show himself a good example of virtue and honor and . . . to guard against and suppress all dissolute and immoral practices." Army investigators determined that Becker, while married, had maintained an inappropriate relationship with a woman not his wife and that his testimony about the matter was neither "forthcoming" nor "credible." He retired in early 2020, demoted to major general.[180]

Similar to the Army, the Air Force continues to punish generals for sexual misconduct. In 2016, Lieutenant General John Hesterman was fired as assistant vice chief of staff after an AFIG investigation found him guilty of wrongfully engaging in an "unprofessional relationship" with a married female lieutenant colonel.[181] For his unbecoming conduct, the married Hesterman was reprimanded and forced to retire. The following year, retired four-star general Arthur Lichte, who had once led Air Mobility Command, was demoted to major general and fined $60,000. While still on active duty, he had coerced a female subordinate officer into having sex on multiple occasions.[182] Then, in June 2019, Major General Peter Gersten (a pilot with four hundred combat flight hours) was relieved of command of the Air Force Warfare Center at Nellis Air Force Base in Nevada. He was suspected of having an unprofessional relationship. An AFIG report released in 2021 concluded that Gersten had at least three inappropriate sexual relationships, including one with a junior officer (all occurred while he was married). According to the AFIG, the general had gained "notoriety" for sleeping with his subordinates. The major general was demoted to colonel and retired.[183]

In February 2021, Defense Secretary Lloyd Austin acknowledged the U.S. military's systemic sex crimes problem and called for a ninety-day Independent Review Commission (IRC) on sexual assault in the military. He received the commission's final report on June 21, 2021. The next day, Austin issued a press release stating his broad support for the IRC's recommendations in an attempt to "finally end the scourge of sexual assault and sexual harassment in the military." Most significantly, the secretary announced that the Pentagon would work with Congress to revise the Uniform Code of Military Justice and remove the chain of command from the prosecution of sex crime cases. Secretary Austin concluded his statement with the following: "As I made clear on my first full day in office, this is a leadership issue. And we will lead. Our people depend on it. They deserve nothing less."[184] In December 2021, President Joe Biden signed the National Defense Authorization Act, which included the transformational criminal justice reforms advocated by Austin and the IRC.[185]

CHAPTER SEVEN

PUBLIC CORRUPTION

Fat Leonard's Dirty Dozen Admirals

PUBLIC CORRUPTION—the breach of public trust
and abuse of position by self-serving government
officials and their private-sector accomplices

The U.S. Department of Defense will always be susceptible to corruption. The most shocking case in the twentieth century was a public bribery and procurement fraud perpetuated during the Reagan administration's massive upsurge in military spending. In brief, the scandal involved Defense Department employees accepting cash bribes from American and foreign-owned businesses in exchange for proprietary information on contract bids. This information enabled select defense contractors to outmaneuver competitors and win profitable weapon systems contracts. The FBI-led investigation, codenamed Operation Illwind, led to the arrest and indictment of sixty people, including government officials, military consultants, and defense contractors. Their prosecution led not only to prison time for many of the criminals, including an assistant secretary of the Navy and a deputy assistant secretary of the Air Force, but also resulted in $622 million worth of recoveries, fines, forfeitures, and restitutions.[1]

Military contract fraud remains a serious problem. The Department of Defense inspector general (DoDIG), whose mission includes detecting and deterring fraud, waste, and abuse, announced in a fiscal year 2020 report that fraud, corruption, and contract mismanagement persisted as one of the Pentagon's "most serious management and performance challenges."[2] Among the many "longstanding problems" was not securing fair and reasonable prices for contracted supplies and services and not ensuring adequate contract oversight.[3] As a result, the inspector general reported that the Defense Department continues to overpay "millions of dollars each year," creates "life and safety concerns for the warfighter," and impedes the military's ability "to prepare for and execute its missions."[4]

The DoDIG further warned that the Pentagon remained at "high risk" for fraud.[5] In fiscal year 2019 alone, the inspector general's Defense Criminal Investigative Service (DCIS) initiated *one hundred* formal investigations into allegations that contractors engaged in "defective pricing, cost and labor mischarging, and false claims."[6] For example, the DoDIG cited a long-term probe of Virginia-based Northrop Grumman Corporation. Between 2010 and 2013, the defense contractor had allegedly inflated the number of billable work hours on two U.S. Air Force communications contracts in the Middle East. In November 2018, after the DCIS investigation substantiated the allegations, Northrop Grumman settled the case. The contractor paid the government $25.8 million and forfeited $4.2 million.[7]

The inspector general has underscored that while every fraud and corruption investigation uncovers unique elements, the findings usually involve private contractors exploiting "a vulnerability" in the procurement process.[8] One glaring vulnerability is the potential to personally corrupt military and civilian officials.

The American wars in Afghanistan and Iraq were rife with theft, fraud, and public corruption. Between 2005 and 2015, more than one hundred U.S. service members (officers and enlisted personnel) were convicted of crimes valued at more than $50 million.[9] One of the most elaborate corruption schemes occurred at the Army Contracting Command at Camp Arifjan in Kuwait. In the summer of 2004, Major John Cockerham began awarding Army supply contracts across the Middle East in exchange for bribes. Soon thereafter Cockerham recruited his roommate, Major Eddie Pressley, into the conspiracy, and in 2005 together they enticed Major James Momon (a West Point graduate) to join them. Federal investigators would later document that the trio collected at least $14 million in bribes from defense contractors.[10] In 2006 multiple government agencies, including the FBI, began probing complaints of corruption at Camp Arifjan. Another contracting official, Major Gloria Davis, soon admitted to an Army investigator that she had accepted at least $225,000 in bribes from Lee Dynamics International, an American supply company owned by George Lee Jr., a Vietnam War veteran. Major Davis, 47, committed suicide soon after her confession.[11]

In 2008 Major Cockerham pleaded guilty to conspiracy, bribery, and money laundering and was sentenced to seventeen years in prison and $9.6 million in restitution.[12] The following year, Major Momon pleaded guilty to conspiracy and receiving $1.6 million in bribes and agreed to pay $5.7 million in restitution. After cooperating with investigators, Momon was sentenced to an eighteen-month prison term.[13] In 2011 Major Pressley was convicted at trial of bribery, conspiracy, money laundering, and honest services fraud and was sentenced to twelve years of imprisonment and the forfeiture of $21 million.[14] Two additional army majors associated with Cockerham, Charles Bowie Jr. and Christopher Murray, also pleaded guilty to participating in the bribery ring and were sentenced to four and a half, and two years' imprisonment, respectively.[15] After pleading guilty to bribery, contractor George Lee was sentenced to four and a half years in federal prison in 2015.[16]

Public corruption in the U.S. Department of Defense has continued. Robert Porter, a retired colonel in the Army National Guard, was sentenced to 366 days in prison in 2017 after pleading guilty to conspiracy to commit bribery and bribery of a public official. While on active duty and serving as the director of the National Guard Bureau's Strength Directorate, Porter steered $5.5 million in federal contracts to Military Personnel Services Corporation, founded by John L. Jones, a retired Army National Guard brigadier general. Porter also directed $4.5 million in contracts to Financial Solutions, a company owned by Charles Sines, a retired Army National Guard colonel. In return, Porter received a percentage of the contract revenue. Like Porter, the elderly Jones cooperated with federal investigators and pleaded guilty. He paid a $12,500 fine and served two years' probation. Sines, 57, committed suicide the night before his trial was to begin.[17]

In 2019, U.S. Army colonels Anthony Roper and Anthony Williams were sentenced to five years in prison for accepting bribes from Calvin Lawyer and Joseph Young, both retired Army colonels. In addition to their prison terms, Roper was fined $200,000 and Williams agreed to forfeit $1.2 million derived from the scheme. While stationed at Fort Gordon, Georgia, Roper and Williams had steered $20 million in federal procurement contracts to Lawyer's company, the CREC group, and to Young's JY & Associates. Lawyer was sentenced to five years' imprisonment and paid a $3 million personal money judgment and a $2 million civil penalty. Young received a five-year sentence and was ordered to pay a $50,000 fine and $1.13 million in restitution.[18]

In 2020 Erik Martin, a civilian employee of the U.S. Marine Corps Reserves, pleaded guilty to conspiracy to commit bribery. He accepted at least $100,000 in kickbacks for awarding $2 million in transportation contracts to companies associated with Darrel Fitzpatrick, an Atlanta businessman. Martin was sentenced to forty-five months in prison, while his co-conspirator was given five years.[19]

In 2021 Ephraim Garcia, a civilian employee of the U.S. Army's Directorate of Public Works, and John Winslett, a government contractor, were sentenced to prison for separate acts of bribery and kickbacks. Garcia admitted to conspiring with Kuwait-based contracting company Gulf Link Venture Co. to gain through bribery subcontracts from the prime base contractor at Camp Arifjan in Kuwait. He was sentenced to two years' confinement. Winslett, on the other hand, confessed to paying over $100,000 in bribes to two U.S. Army contracting officials at Schofield Barracks, Hawaii. In return he obtained $19 million in federal contracts for his employer, REK Associates. Winslett also admitted to receiving more than $700,000 in kickbacks from a subcontractor who benefitted from REK's ill-gotten contracts. Winslett was sentenced to nearly six years in prison.[20]

In 2022, a federal judge sentenced Florida businessman William S. Wilson to fifteen years in prison for operating a bribery and kickback conspiracy that defrauded the federal government. Among his crimes, he bribed Matthew Kekoa LumHo, an employee in the Department of Defense's Office of Inspector General — the very agency responsible for fighting fraud and corruption in the Defense Department. LumHo had steered $1.5 million in telecommunications contracts to Wilson's companies; he received approximately $41,000 in kickbacks. LumHo was convicted at trial and sentenced to seven and a half years' incarceration.[21]

As demonstrated in Operation Illwind and in the more recent cases above, federal employees at all levels can be tempted to accept bribes and kickbacks in exchange for their influence on defense contracts. The U.S. military has regulatory and procedural safeguards to mitigate the corruption of its personnel, and punitive Article 132 of the Uniform Code of Military Justice (UCMJ) explicitly forbids "frauds against the United States." Still, members of the armed forces are human beings, and their conduct is dependent on the strengths or weaknesses of their personal and professional moral codes.

★ ★ ★ ★

If Operation Illwind was the Defense Department's most significant corruption controversy of the twentieth century, the Navy's "Fat Leonard scandal" is the most notorious of the twenty-first century to date. This extraordinary contracting and national security scandal is especially disturbing because it involved widespread and long-lived corruption within the Navy officer corps. It is not a case of "a few bad apples," but rather like Tailhook, a demonstration of an appalling subculture within the U.S. military.

Leonard Glenn "Fat Leonard" Francis, a Singapore-based defense contractor, gained his unflattering sobriquet because of his enormous size, standing six foot three inches and weighing more than three hundred pounds. Born into a prosperous Malaysian family in 1964, the gregarious Francis attended private schools in Singapore. At the age of twenty he opened a bar and associated with gangsters. Before long, Francis was arrested for driving the getaway car in an armed robbery. The police raided his home and discovered illegal handguns, ammunition, foreign currency, and a bulletproof jacket. Francis was arrested, tried, and convicted in the Penang High Court. The judge sentenced the upstart entrepreneur to thirty-six months in prison and six cane strokes to his bare buttocks.[22]

Out of prison in the early 1990s, Francis assumed control of his family's business and renamed it Glenn Defense Marine Asia (GDMA). The company provided wide-ranging husbanding services to ships and crews at various ports in Asia (supplying fuel, tugboats, and waste removal to barges, dock security, and port authority and customs management). Ever ambitious, Francis sought to expand his business and targeted contracts with the U.S. Navy's Seventh Fleet, which operated sixty to seventy vessels in the Western Pacific Ocean. The contractor's timing was near perfect. In 1992, the Philippine government terminated a military bases agreement with the United States that had included the Navy's Subic Bay port facility. Moreover, the American military began outsourcing more and more services in pursuit of cost-cutting and thus became increasingly dependent on defense contractors.

Francis developed a comprehensive criminal scheme to win Navy port of call contracts. He planned to defraud the U.S. government of tens of millions of dollars by overbilling GDMA's husbanding services. To realize his ambitions, Francis required the support of Navy officials who would use their influence to steer ships and submarines to ports where GDMA provided services. He also needed Navy personnel to overlook and approve the company's fraudulent invoices. Moreover, Francis sought connections with well-placed co-conspirators who could provide classified information on planned ship movements and proprietary data on GDMA's competitors.

It is deeply unsettling that Francis had little difficulty recruiting officers of the Seventh Fleet to join his corrupt scheme. From the 1990s until 2013, Fat Leonard attracted dozens and dozens of co-conspirators by providing the sailors individually and collectively with a steady stream of opulent banquets, top-shelf alcohol, luxurious hotel suites, international travel, sex workers, and envelopes of cash. In 2018, one retired Navy captain admitted to *Rolling Stone* magazine that the Seventh Fleet "has always been the wild, wild west for the Navy. It's like the prime liberty. Anything you want to do, anything you want to get, you can get at 7th Fleet. The Navy doesn't want to project that image, but sailors want to go to Thailand and the Philippines because of what's offered there. Francis understood that."[23]

Naval Criminal Investigative Service (NCIS) officials began receiving complaints of Francis's fraudulent activities in 2006. They opened a series of investigations, but these early probes failed to uncover the frauds because senior navy officers friendly to Francis used their influence to have the cases closed. Moreover, the defense contractor had corrupted an NCIS agent who regularly supplied confidential information about the investigations. In a 2011 email Francis bragged, "I have inside Intel from NCIS and read all the reports. I will show you a copy of a Classified Command File on me from NCIS ha ha."[24] But by then, NCIS agents had launched a new, closely held investigation into Francis's operations and had cultivated confidential sources within GDMA.[25]

After three years of investigation, federal agents finally arrested Francis on September 16, 2013. The U.S. government immediately cancelled $205 million in active contracts with GDMA. In January 2015, Francis entered into a plea agreement with the Department of Justice. He pleaded guilty to bribery, conspiracy to commit bribery, and conspiracy to defraud the United States. He admitted to defrauding the government out of $20-plus million and agreed to cooperate in the ongoing federal investigation. Government officials estimated that Francis had cheated the Navy out of at least $35 million.

As of autumn 2022, the Justice Department had charged thirty-four people, mostly Navy personnel, with crimes related to Francis's corruption scheme. More than three-quarters have pleaded guilty, including one rear admiral. Earlier in 2017, another rear admiral and eight other officers were collectively indicted on conspiracy charges; initially all pleaded not guilty. By early February 2022, however, four of the nine — a Marine Corps colonel, a Navy chief warrant officer, a Navy commander, and a Navy captain — had pleaded guilty to bribery. Four months later, another four of the nine (three captains and a commander) were convicted of conspiracy. Their jury deadlocked on the charges against the rear admiral.[26] In addition to these cases, the Justice Department transferred to the Navy for review some four hundred investigative files on government personnel, including sixty admirals. The Navy established a consolidated disposition authority to adjudicate these cases and has thus far disciplined fifty officers, including ten admirals.[27]

* * * *

In early May 2016, Admiral John M. Richardson wrote an impassioned letter to two hundred admirals before they convened their annual leadership symposium on Navy priorities and strategies. The chief of naval operations (CNO) implored his fellow admirals to engage in deep ethical reflection and to hold each other accountable for upright conduct. "We share a professional and moral obligation," he wrote, "to continuously examine our motivations and personal conduct, and, where required, adjust our behaviors back in line with our values."[28]

Richardson was under pressure to restore the reputation of the Navy's senior leadership, which had suffered serious and various blows in recent years. In November 2013, two admirals — both senior intelligence officers — had been stripped of their access to classified information because they were suspected of accepting improper gifts from Leonard Francis.[29] In December 2014, Richardson admonished a third admiral for his indecorous relationship with Francis.[30] The next year and on Richardson's recommendation, Navy Secretary Richard V. Spencer issued Secretarial Letters of Censure to three other admirals for their illicit partnerships with Francis.[31] In 2015 the Navy also fired a two-star admiral for being falling-down drunk and wandering a Florida resort buck naked.[32]

Quoting John Paul Jones, Admiral Richardson's message asserted that the Navy needed not just competent leaders with "strong operational skills," but also ethical leaders who are "perfectly esteemed." He wrote, "When we misstep, it is a shocking disappointment that brings into question trust and confidence."[33] Three weeks after the admirals convened at the 2016 symposium, federal agents arrested one from their ranks. The Justice Department indicted Rear Admiral Robert "Bob" Gilbeau for accepting improper gifts from Francis, for destroying evidence of their relationship, and for lying to investigators. He was but one of Fat Leonard's dirty dozen admirals.

Bob Gilbeau served three tours with the Seventh Fleet beginning in the late 1990s. He first met Francis in 1997 while serving aboard the USS *Boxer*. During a port visit to Bali, Indonesia, the defense contractor plied Gilbeau and another officer with complimentary dinners, alcohol, hotels rooms, and sex workers.[34] He and Francis maintained a close relationship for the next twenty years.

Commander Gilbeau returned to the Western Pacific in January 2003. As the supply officer on the USS *Nimitz*, he was responsible for procuring goods and services for the ship's operation. During numerous port visits he again accepted Francis's offers of lavish dinners, expensive hotel rooms, and sex workers. In one email to Francis, Gilbeau announced that he was returning to Singapore and requested a "particularly memorable" sex worker nicknamed the "handball player." Francis responded, "The Kahuna above has heard our prayers" and "The handball player is waiting eagerly to play." In return, Gilbeau approved inflated invoices from Francis's GDMA. At a Singapore port in October, Gilbeau authorized an especially egregious payment — triple the usual amount — for the removal of sewage and wastewater. Gilbeau received a $40,000 cash kickback for the illegal transaction.[35]

In 2005 and by then at the rank of captain, Gilbeau was stationed in Singapore. He helped to lead Navy logistics for the Tsunami Relief Crisis Action Team, which was responding to the Southeast Asia Tsunami of December 2004. On multiple occasions, Francis supplied "Tsunami Bob" with pricey dinners, expensive hotel rooms, and alcohol-fueled parties at the Brix Nightclub and the Tiananmen Karaoke Bar.[36]

By the summer of 2010, Gilbeau had been promoted to rear admiral. He had served a year-long assignment in Baghdad, Iraq, where he was awarded a Purple Heart for injuries sustained during a mortar attack. In August, Gilbeau assumed command of the Defense Contract Management Agency International, which led to a December rendezvous with Francis in Singapore. One evening, living on Francis's largesse, the so-called Casanova admiral dined at the Mezz9 Restaurant in the Hyatt hotel, partied at the Brix and Tiananmen clubs, and capped the night by having sex with two Vietnamese sex workers. The following day Francis emailed Gilbeau asking, "How was the after action from the 1st night? Require AAR (After Action Report) Sir." The admiral replied, "Very nice. . . . BZ." (BZ stands for "Bravo Zulu," a naval term meaning "well done.")[37]

Gilbeau learned that the Navy was investigating Francis for fraud and public corruption in September 2012. The admiral grew increasingly nervous about his own ties to Francis. On November 27, he answered a Foreign Contract Questionnaire truthfully, informing his command that he had been in contact with Francis during the month prior. But he also lied on the document, claiming that he never accepted gifts from the defense contractor. On February 20, 2013, Gilbeau agreed to an interview with NCIS agents. The admiral admitted that he and Francis dined together regularly, but Gilbeau falsely stated that he always paid for "his half of the dinner."[38]

When Francis was arrested seven months later in September 2013, Gilbeau was stationed in Afghanistan as the director of the Operational Contract Support Drawdown Cell, which was responsible for reducing and reorganizing the military's contracted personnel. With news of Fat Leonard's arrest, the admiral began to panic and his behavior became paranoid and erratic. He destroyed documents and deleted computer files that connected him to the contractor. Gilbeau also halted his aide's access to his government email accounts and refused to meet with people unless they removed their cell phone batteries.[39]

Federal agents arrested Gilbeau on June 9, 2016. He was charged with destroying evidence, lying to investigators about his relationship with Francis, and receiving "things of value over the course of years."[40] Laura E. Duffy, the U.S. Attorney for the Southern District of California, emphasized that her office would not grant any favors to flag officers. "Of those who wear our nation's uniform in the service of our country, only a select few have been honored to hold the rank of Admiral—and not a single one is above the law. . . . Whether the evidence leads us to a civilian, to an enlisted service member or to an admiral . . . we will continue to hold responsible all those who lied or who corruptly betrayed their public duties for personal gain."[41] Chief of Naval Operations John Richardson issued a public condemnation. He characterized Gilbeau's conduct as "inconsistent with our standards and the expectations the nation has for us as military professionals. It damages the trust that nation places in us, and is an embarrassment to the Navy."[42]

When Gilbeau appeared in a San Diego federal courtroom, he carried a small white therapy dog, Bella, who sported a tiny Navy vest. The admiral pleaded guilty to making a false official statement and confessed to "concealing the duration and extent of his relationship" with Francis. He also admitted that he had lied about receiving gifts and about paying for his own dinners when the two socialized. Gilbeau further acknowledged that he had deleted computer files and destroyed documents after learning that Francis had been arrested.[43]

At the time, Gilbeau was the highest-ranking officer charged in the Fat Leonard scandal and the first active-duty admiral convicted of a felony. He faced up to five years in prison. Navy Secretary Ray E. Mabus Jr. considered "dropping Gilbeau from the rolls," which meant a termination of rank, privileges, retirement compensation, and medical care.[44] Gilbeau's sentencing was postponed for nearly a year while he was free on bond. In September 2016, the Navy demoted him to captain and forced him into retirement. Gilbeau was given an "other than honorable" discharge, which made him ineligible to claim disability benefits from the Department of Veterans Affairs. Still, as a captain, he received an annual pension worth more than $100,000 per year.[45]

Before his court sentencing, Gilbeau penned a letter to the judge apologizing for his criminal conduct and expressing his professional embarrassment. "To the Navy," he wrote, "I want to say I am sorry . . . I have no one to blame but myself." "I am devastated," he continued, "by the situation I currently find myself in." The former admiral begged for the court's mercy because of faltering mental health. Gilbeau wrote, "I do not desire a defense of my charges based on mental illness, but I do ask that this horrible condition that I suffer is taken into account as a potential mitigating factor."[46] Admiral William F. Moran, the vice chief of naval operations, wrote a countervailing letter to the court. Moran chastised Gilbeau for inflicting "immeasurable damage" on the Navy and underscored to the judge that the former admiral had "grossly dishonored his uniform and betrayed his fellow shipmates, the United States Navy and his country."[47]

Judgment day arrived on May 17, 2017. Gilbeau reentered the courtroom with his therapy dog. At the hearing, Gilbeau's lawyer argued that prison time was unjust and that the former admiral would suffer severely without Bella to calm his anxiety and high blood pressure. The prosecutor, on the other hand, recommended an eighteen-month sentence. She asserted that Gilbeau was exaggerating the extent of his health failings, which had only emerged after Francis's arrest in 2013.[48]

In the end, Judge Janis L. Sammartino agreed with the government's lawyers and sentenced Gilbeau to eighteen months in prison at the Federal Correctional Institution in Englewood, Colorado. He was fined $100,000 and ordered to pay $50,000 in restitution. After incarceration, Gilbeau was subject to three years of probation and three hundred hours of community service. Sammartino scolded the disgraced admiral: "You did everything possible to hide and conceal your relationship with Leonard Francis and in the process you tried to thwart the investigation. . . . You violated the law. You dishonored your shipmates, the Navy and the United States of America."[49]

Acting U.S. Attorney Alana W. Robinson emphasized the historic conviction of an active-duty admiral and condemned Gilbeau's extraordinary misconduct. "This is the first time our nation will incarcerate a Navy admiral for a federal crime committed during the course of his official duty, and it is truly a somber day," she said. "When tempted by parties and prostitutes, one of our most respected leaders chose karaoke over character, and cover-up over confession, and in doing so he forever tarnished the reputation of a revered institution."[50]

Assistant U.S. Attorney Mark W. Pletcher further underscored the importance of holding senior public officials accountable. He told the court, "Beyond the tragedy, today is also a day of great importance, as one of finality for Mr. Gilbeau; one of healing for the U.S. Navy; and more broadly, it is one of great importance for our constitutional democracy. We the People consent to be governed. We live by the Rule of Law, applicable to all regardless of rank, stature or privilege. In our country, no one is above the law."[51]

★ ★ ★ ★

By the time the Navy had demoted and retired Gilbeau, the service had already disciplined four other admirals who were tangled up in the Fat Leonard scandal. Three of them, Rear Admirals Terry B. Kraft and David R. Pimpo and Vice Admiral Michael H. Miller, received Secretarial Letters of Censure on the same day. The trio had served together as part of Carrier Strike Group Seven in the Western Pacific, and each had accepted valuable gifts from Leonard Francis. The fourth flag officer, Vice Admiral Timothy M. Giardina, received a relatively mild reprimand for his improper relationship with Francis while serving as the chief of staff for the Seventh Fleet and as the deputy commander of the U.S. Pacific Fleet.

Terry Kraft befriended Leonard Francis in early 2006 while serving as the commanding officer of the aircraft carrier USS *Ronald Reagan*. During the ship's Asian deployment, Kraft was treated to multiple extravagant, alcohol-drenched meals at world-class restaurants in Hong Kong and other ports of call (for example, one meal cost more than $700 per person). Kraft attempted to skirt government ethics rules by reimbursing Francis with personal checks of less than $75. Kraft consumed gratis alcohol, cigars, and lavish dinners valued in excess of $5,000. He later justified his misconduct by claiming that his superior had "directed" him to attend the opulent banquets.[52]

In 2006, the NCIS received information that Francis was overcharging the *Ronald Reagan* for wastewater and sewage removal and that some officers aboard the carrier knew of the fraud. After investigators substantiated the allegations, they referred the case to Kraft as the ship's commander. The skipper took no action and later denied knowing anything about the sewage and wastewater removal controversy.[53] Kraft's misconduct continued into 2007.[54] Kraft received additional gifts from Francis in exchange for issuing official endorsements that proclaimed the Glenn Defense Marine Asia company as "the best in the world" and "unrivaled in the delivery of customer service."[55] He was promoted to rear admiral the next year.

By 2015, Kraft had risen to commander of the U.S. Naval Forces in Japan, and his relationship with Francis was under investigation. In February, the Navy determined that Kraft had violated government regulations by accepting expensive gifts from a prohibited source and by issuing improper endorsements of Francis's company. Admiral John M. Richardson, the Navy's consolidated disposition authority for Fat Leonard–related cases, condemned Kraft's conduct while in command of the *Ronald Reagan*. Richardson wrote that the admiral had exercised "very poor judgment" and that his "repeated acceptance of improper gifts" failed to provide proper leadership and instead created "throughout the deployment of USS RONALD REAGAN (CVN-76), a weak ethical tone which permeated his command."[56]

Navy Secretary Mabus rebuked Kraft with a letter of censure, which was released to the press in February 2015. Mabus wrote that admirals hold "positions of unique trust and responsibility" and therefore "must uphold and be held to the highest standards of personal and professional behavior." After reviewing Kraft's conduct as skipper of the *Ronald Reagan*, the secretary concluded that censure was "both necessary and appropriate." He determined that Kraft had violated Navy standards by cultivating an "inappropriately familiar relationship" with Francis. Kraft's "poor judgment and a failure of leadership," Mabus wrote, had created an "unacceptable ethical climate" on the aircraft carrier.[57] In addition to the reprimand, Kraft was fined $7,500, relieved of command, and forced into retirement.[58]

David Pimpo, who had served under Kraft as the supply officer on the USS *Ronald Reagan*, was no stranger to Navy misconduct investigations. Shortly after being selected for flag rank, Pimpo's international travel expenses were scrutinized by the Navy Inspector General (NIG) in 2012. A whistleblower accused him and two other senior officers of taking "a taxpayer financed vacation to London." Investigators eventually concluded that there were legitimate reasons for their trip, but that Pimpo and the others had violated government travel regulations by booking "unnecessarily expensive" flights to England and by staying at luxury hotels priced at more than $400 per room, per night. The NIG report stated that the officers had "failed to use available contract air fare and improperly claimed and accepted per diem exceeding what was permitted."[59] Pimpo was given an administrative warning, but was still promoted to rear admiral.[60]

Like Kraft, Pimpo was soon under investigation for his illicit involvement with Leonard Francis. During the *Ronald Reagan*'s 2006–2007 deployment, Pimpo's supply department won multiple awards, including the Blue "E" Supply Excellence commendation, yet he was also accepting improper dinners from Francis at expensive restaurants. He would later confess to accepting many free or discounted offerings from Francis, including "luxury travel," lodging, gifts, and a prepaid tour of Hong Kong. At one point, Fat Leonard provided Pimpo two weeks of free hotel rooms for the entire "senior carrier Strike Group Seven leadership."[61]

In early 2015, Admiral Richardson admonished Pimpo for "the frequency in which he accepted numerous gifts from Mr. Francis" and "for being influenced in the performance of his official acts." Richardson wrote that Pimpo had "failed to display the requisite leadership by personal example that is required . . . of all commanding officers and their subordinates."[62] Rear Admiral Pimpo also received a Secretarial Letter of Censure, was relieved of command, demoted to captain, and forced into retirement.[63]

Pimpo's colleague Vice Admiral Mike Miller had hoped to retire in summer 2014 after completing a four-year term as the superintendent of the Naval Academy. He had graduated from the academy four decades prior. But the Navy stalled Miller's retirement because he, like Pimpo and Kraft, was under investigation for his protracted relationship with Leonard Francis. Indeed, in 2011, when Francis visited the Naval Academy to witness a change of command ceremony, Miller gave him a private tour of Buchanan House, his official residence.[64]

The precise origins of the Miller-Francis friendship are not clear, but in early 2006 then-Rear Admiral Miller emailed the defense contractor to say that he was looking forward to "renewing" their relationship.[65] At the time, the admiral was commander of Carrier Strike Group Seven, which was deploying to the Western Pacific with the USS *Ronald Reagan* as its flagship.

In June 2006, the *Ronald Reagan* made port calls in Singapore, Malaysia, and Hong Kong. At each layover, Francis treated Miller and other senior officers to extravagant dinners and provided gifts at discounted prices. The first expensive meal occurred in Singapore at JAAN, which was rated one of the best restaurants in Asia; the second transpired at the award-winning Chalet Suisse restaurant in Kuala Lumpur. The third dinner, on June 11, included a French banquet at Restaurant Petrus in the Island Shangri-La which offered stunning views of Victoria Harbor. Pimpo attended another posh dinner with Francis at Spoon, a gourmet French eatery at The InterContinental hotel in Hong Kong. The cost of the meals averaged $750 per person. To appear in compliance with ethics regulations, Miller and others wrote token personal checks to Francis, ranging from $50 to $70 per dinner. Likewise, the admiral underpaid for an assortment of gifts, including a camera, three chairs, and a model ship, all worth some $5,000.[66]

In return for his munificence, Francis was allowed to overcharge the Navy for his husbanding services, and GDMA received formal endorsements from Miller and other senior officers. He also parlayed the testimonials into more contracts with the U.S. government. Two days after the dinner in Hong Kong, for example, Admiral Miller wrote to Francis: "Words cannot adequately express my appreciation for the service you have provided in all our ports of call. You are as much a member of the U.S. Navy team as any of us, and we are all proud to call you 'Shipmate.'"[67] Miller later praised GDMA as a "superior" contractor relative to its competitors.[68] The inflated invoices were obviously illegal and the official endorsements violated Navy ethics regulations.

In early 2015, the Navy completed its review of Miller's relationship with Francis. It found that the admiral had improperly solicited and accepted numerous gifts from a prohibited source, and in return he issued inappropriate official endorsements for the benefit of the contractor's business. Admiral Richardson, the consolidated disposition authority, concluded that Miller had "exercised very poor judgment" and "through his repeated and increasingly familiar contacts with Mr. Francis, RADM [Rear Admiral] Miller failed to display the requisite leadership by personal example." Moreover, as a result of his frequent misconduct, Miller had established "a weak ethical tone which permeated the senior leadership of the Strike Group."[69]

As with Admirals Kraft and Pimpo, Miller received a formal censure from Navy Secretary Mabus, who wrote, "This display of poor judgment was aggravated by the fact that you issued these endorsements within days after the extravagant GDMA-hosted dinners."[70] Miller accepted responsibility for "isolated incidents," but contended that "refusing these gifts" would have been "logistically difficult."[71] He was allowed to retire with three stars.

Two months before Miller, Kraft, and Pimpo's censures, Admiral Richards reprimanded Vice Admiral Tim Giardina. After nearly four decades of military service, 2014 was an especially bad year for Giardina. The highly decorated officer was the subject of two unrelated criminal investigations; both had unhappy endings. Federal investigators determined that during two tours of duty in the Western Pacific, Giardina established a long-lived and inappropriate relationship with Leonard Francis. As a captain serving as chief of staff for the Seventh Fleet between 2003 and 2005, Giardina knowingly received multiple prohibited gifts from Francis that included expensive dinners in Singapore and Malaysia. Years later, after being promoted to rear admiral and assuming duties as the deputy commander of the U.S. Pacific Fleet, Giardina renewed his ties with Francis by meeting him in private and providing Francis with his personal email address.[72]

In December 2014, Admiral Richardson informed the secretary of the Navy that he had reprimanded Giardina for his misconduct as a captain and again as a rear admiral.[73] He also informed the NIG that Giardina had "displayed poor judgment when, despite his knowledge that Francis had previously attempted to influence him with improper gifts, he continued to interact with Mr. Francis, such as, while serving as a flag officer in the position of Deputy Commander U.S. Pacific Fleet."[74] The reprimand was not made public.

This illicit relationship with Fat Leonard was the least of Giardina's concerns. On July 16, 2013, the vice admiral's immediate superior, Air Force General C. Robert Kehler, Commander of U.S. Strategic Command (STRATCOM), learned that Giardina, who was his deputy commander, was being investigated by Iowa state authorities for manufacturing and passing counterfeit casino chips. A month earlier on June 15, Giardina had played poker late into the night at the Horseshoe Casino in Council Bluffs, Iowa, not far from his residence at Offutt Air Force Base. That night the admiral gambled and lost three $500 doctored chips. He went home around 2 a.m. The counterfeits went undetected until another card player, who was holding one of the phony chips, attempted to cash out.[75]

Casino surveillance video established that Giardina had introduced each of the bogus chips during the game. Moreover, an analysis of security footage revealed that the vice admiral was a habitual poker player who was known inside the casino as "Navy Tim." Giardina had gambled on average fifteen hours per week for more than a year, and it was noted that he exhibited some "odd behaviors" such as "taking cigarette butts out of public ash trays and smoking them" and almost always wearing the same civilian clothes when he gambled.[76]

On June 18, 2013, a special agent of Iowa's Division of Criminal Investigation interviewed Giardina. The admiral claimed that he was unaware that the chips were counterfeit. He claimed that while he was in a casino bathroom, he had simply purchased the chips from another gambler who wanted to avoid paying taxes on his winnings. Giardina said that he received a mere $2,025 in chips in exchange for $2,000 cash. The admiral admitted that the private purchase of valid chips was illegal, but he denied knowing that he was buying fake chips. In self-defense, Giardina asserted that as someone who earned $200,000 a year, he could never be tempted into a low-stakes counterfeiting operation. In addition, he said, he was an experienced polygraph taker because of his security clearance renewals. Giardina told the special agent, "[What] they're really trying to do is find out if you got, you know, if you're having sex with animals or somethin' really crazy or you've got this wild life that you could be blackmailed into givin' . . . military secrets out." Still, he refused to provide the investigator with a description of the man from the bathroom. He did, however, offer to "do some checking" to find out who he is, and he guaranteed the agent that he was innocent saying, "I did . . . did not . . . not do anything wrong."[77]

When General Kehler became aware of the Iowa state criminal investigation, he restricted Giardina's duties and asked the NCIS to open an independent inquiry. Giardina refused to cooperate with NCIS investigators and, most remarkably, he continued to gamble for three months until four local casinos banned him from entry. In early September 2013, Kehler suspended Giardina from his position as STRATCOM deputy commander and blocked his access to classified material. News of the suspension and the counterfeit chip investigation broke that month. On October 2, the Pottawattamie County attorney, content to have the Navy discipline Giardina, decided not to press charges after the admiral agreed to sign an affidavit admitting that he had lied to the state investigator about how he "came into possession of the chips in question."[78]

In early 2014, while the NCIS investigation continued, a disgraced and desperate Giardina was transferred to the staff of the vice chief of naval operations at the Pentagon. On April 26, he wrote a statement to Admiral William Gortney, who would adjudicate his case. Giardina expressed regret for lying about the origins of the chips and for not immediately surrendering them to casino security. He now claimed, however, that he found the chips in a bathroom toilet stall and that he was merely "a patsy for someone who wanted the chips to be found." "This lapse in judgment," he wrote to Gortney, "does not make me a thief and a criminal."[79]

In the end, federal prosecutors did not believe there was sufficient evidence to prove Giardina had manufactured the fake chips, even though an Army criminal laboratory had found some of his DNA under a counterfeit chip's adhesive sticker. Nevertheless on May 6, 2014, the Navy announced that Giardina had violated Article 133 of the UCMJ and was found guilty on two counts of conduct unbecoming an officer. First, he had failed to turn in the "found" chips and indeed proceeded to gamble with them. Second, he had lied to the Iowa state investigator about having purchased the chips in the bathroom. For these offenses, Admiral Gortney issued an official letter of reprimand, demoted Giardina to rear admiral, and fined him $4,000.[80] Giardina immediately requested retirement. Because he was still under investigation for his illicit relationship with Leonard Francis, his application was tabled. After being further admonished by Admiral Richardson for his dealings with Fat Leonard, Giardina was permitted to retire in July 2015, exactly forty years after graduating from the Naval Academy.

★ ★ ★ ★

The Navy also reprimanded three *retired* rear admirals, Richard B. Wren, Kenneth J. "K. J." Norton, and Mark C. Montgomery, for their prior improper relationships with Leonard Francis. Before retiring in 2011, Admiral Wren's final assignment was as commander of the U.S. Naval Forces in Japan. Four years into his retirement, he was interviewed by federal investigators about his past interactions with Malaysian defense contractor Leonard Francis. By the time of that meeting, Francis and several others had already been arrested and pleaded guilty to corruption and conspiracy charges. During the interview, Wren attempted to mislead the federal agents and distance himself from the criminal contractor. Three years after the interview, in June 2018, Navy Secretary Richard Spencer issued Wren a scathing letter of censure for conduct unbecoming an officer.[81]

The Navy investigation determined that Admiral Wren was guilty of various ethical and criminal violations while serving as commander of Carrier Group Five/USS *Kitty Hawk* and as commander, Naval Forces, Japan. Spencer chastised the retired admiral for having "demonstrated exceedingly poor judgment and leadership by repeatedly and improperly accepting gifts from Mr. Leonard Francis."[82] In 2008 Wren and other naval officers enjoyed a gratis dinner in Japan that cost $8,827. Another complimentary dinner came a few months later in Hong Kong when the aging *Kitty Hawk* made its last port visit to a foreign country. Wren and eight officers, including members of his staff, consumed food and alcohol worth $32,422. Also in 2008, Francis delivered to Wren "two boxes of steaks, a bag full of wine and cigars, and three bottles of Dom Perignon." The next year, after taking command of Naval Forces, Japan, Wren received from Francis a "$2,000 box of steaks."[83]

In his letter of censure, Secretary Spencer excoriated the retired admiral for not only accepting gifts but also for lying to investigators. "As a senior officer, you had a duty to represent the United States and the United States Navy in a way that upheld the values of our great nation and Navy. Rather, you intentionally disregarded the ethical standards long established for the naval service and brought ill-repute and disgrace upon our honored institution." He added that Wren had "engaged in conduct that reflected unethical and improper personal behavior and set poor standards of leadership." Furthermore, his conduct was "an embarrassment" to all honorable officers, sailors, and civilians.[84]

On December 1, 2014, Rear Admiral Kenneth Norton, a helicopter pilot and ship commander, retired after thirty-three years of service.

His record appeared impeccable. Norton's first sea tour was in 1983 in the Western Pacific with a helicopter anti-submarine squadron attached to the USS *Kitty Hawk* carrier. From October 2004 to October 2005 he commanded the USS *Camden*, a *Sacramento*-class fast combat support ship, and from May 2008 to August 2010 he commanded the aircraft carrier USS *Ronald Reagan*. Norton's final assignment was as commander of the Naval Safety Center in Virginia. Upon retirement, he told his Minnesota hometown newspaper that he had never anticipated a lengthy stay in the Navy. "But every time I thought I was going to take the exit ramp," he said, "I was having too much fun or felt compelled to continue in my Navy career."[85]

Norton's pleasant retirement was disrupted in November 2017 when the Navy announced that he had been censured for having an illicit relationship with Leonard Francis. Beyond the written condemnation, the Navy stripped Norton of his Legion of Merit medal, which is awarded for exceptionally meritorious conduct. While on active duty, Norton indeed was having too much fun. A Navy investigation determined that as commander of the *Ronald Reagan*, he had "repeatedly and improperly" accepted gifts from Francis, including expensive dinners, cigars, alcohol, and a stay at a beach villa that cost $1,500 per night. Investigators also found that Norton attended three parties with sex workers.[86] The Navy's internal review concluded that he had demonstrated not just bad judgment and leadership but "*exceedingly poor judgment and leadership*" and that he "intentionally disregarded the ethical standards long established for the naval service and brought ill-repute and disgrace upon the U.S. Navy."[87]

Navy Secretary Spencer was equally unsparing in his public condemnation of Norton's willful misbehavior, which he "found to have constituted conduct unbecoming an officer." He emphasized the necessity of holding senior officers responsible for unethical behavior. "The Navy," Spencer said, "has a long tradition of holding leaders accountable and commanding officers are placed in unique positions of trust and responsibility. It is incumbent that they be held to the highest standards of both personal and professional behavior." Spencer continued, "I decided that Rear Adm. (ret.) Norton's conduct reflected improper personal behavior and set a wholly unethical tone of leadership. Censure was both necessary and appropriate."[88] At that point in time, Norton was the fourth admiral to be censured by the Navy Secretary in the Fat Leonard scandal.

At Rear Admiral Mark Montgomery's retirement ceremony in October 2017, the commander of U.S. Pacific Command, Admiral Harry B. Harris Jr. presented him with the Defense Distinguished Service Medal, the highest joint service decoration and the highest noncombat military award. In tribute to Montgomery, Harris said, "It's no exaggeration to say that his knowledge and understanding of the Indo-Asia-Pacific are unmatched. In fact, one could go so far to say, he's a national treasure."[89]

Within a few months, Montgomery, who had been a White House fellow, was working in Washington, DC, as a civilian policy director for the Senate Armed Services Committee. Committee chair Senator John McCain, a veteran Navy aviator, had recruited him. In June 2018 the Trump administration nominated Montgomery for a leadership position at the U.S. Agency for International Development. On November 15, 2018, however, the White House abruptly withdrew the nomination. The Navy was about to reprimand the retired two-star for his criminal relationship with Leonard Francis.

News of the official censure broke on November 26. The Navy determined that while he was commander of Destroyer Squadron Fifteen from 2007 to 2009, Montgomery had "committed graft and taken illicit gifts" from Francis and then "took action to financially benefit" the defense contractor's business.[90] During those years, an estimated seventy-five out of Montgomery's one hundred port calls were at facilities controlled by Francis's company.[91] The Navy also concluded that Montgomery attempted to cover up his misconduct by lying to federal investigators in a January 2018 interview (while in retirement). Although he had committed egregious crimes under the UCMJ, formal prosecution was problematic because the statute of limitations had expired.[92]

On December 14, 2018, the Navy released the details of Montgomery's misconduct and the secretary of the Navy's condemnation of his behavior. Montgomery had "repeatedly and improperly solicited and accepted gifts" and "repeatedly and improperly endorsed, provided information to, and took action to financially benefit GDMA." According to the Navy's findings, on August 23, 2007, Montgomery had successfully intervened on Francis's behalf when officials had not selected his company to refuel two ships. For GDMA, Montgomery represented a "top shelf friendship!" Then in September 2007, Montgomery endorsed Francis's enterprise in a Navy communiqué. In October Montgomery provided Francis with advance notice that a Navy ship would be visiting Kota Kinabalu, Malaysia, where GDMA controlled the port. Soon thereafter at Montgomery's request, Francis paid $2,609 toward his family's upgraded hotel stay in Hong Kong.[93]

The graft continued throughout 2008. In January Montgomery enjoyed a gratis feast on the forty-fifth floor of the Ritz-Carlton in Tokyo. In April he gave Francis advance notice that Navy ships would be visiting ports in Vietnam and Cambodia. A few days later, Francis paid most of Montgomery's $2,000 tab at the Grand Hyatt in Hong Kong. In late April, Montgomery helped Francis plan a $32,000 banquet for Navy officers at the Pierre II French restaurant on the twenty-fifth floor of the Mandarin Oriental Hong Kong hotel. After this epicurean dinner, Montgomery slipped Francis advance information about the logistical requirements for a guided-missile destroyer's upcoming port visit. Later that year, Francis provided Montgomery free transportation and a deeply discounted hotel room in Singapore. When Francis asked if the American wanted an upgraded suite worth $1,600, Montgomery replied that he would be "thrilled" to have it. Afterward, Montgomery again endorsed Francis's company on Destroyer Squadron Fifteen letterhead.[94]

In a November 2018 letter of censure, Secretary Spencer wrote that Montgomery's criminal conduct had "cast a shadow over the reputation of all the outstanding men and women who served during your tenure in command." He continued, "Your willingness to accept those gifts provided the worst type of example for subordinate officers within your chain of command and other officers who observed your interaction with Mr. Francis."[95] In a public statement issued in December 2018, Spencer further deplored Montgomery's misconduct. "Ethical behavior," he stated, "is a foundation of the Navy's ability to function, and any officer placed in a position of command must treat our ethical standards with the utmost seriousness. Instead, RADM (Ret.) Montgomery disregarded them and abused his position to benefit himself."[96] Montgomery was the sixth flag officer to receive a Secretarial Letter of Censure in the Fat Leonard scandal.

Despite the Navy's categorical condemnations, Montgomery remained unapologetic. In a 2019 interview with *USNI News*, the disgraced admiral professed absolute innocence and criticized the Navy's internal investigation. Montgomery even offered effusive praise for Francis, who years earlier had pleaded guilty to bribing "scores" of senior naval officers and bilking the U.S. government out of tens of millions of dollars. Montgomery characterized Francis as a "savvy" and "aggressive" operator, who "supported our ships, made sure they got what they wanted." Francis, he continued, possessed "a knack for solving tough problems for the Navy that made him essential to service in the Pacific."[97]

★ ★ ★ ★

One of Leonard Francis's business objectives was to secure U.S. diplomatic protections that enabled his company's ships to travel in and out of Asian ports without being subjected to local taxes, customs duties, and onboard inspections. He secured this political immunity by bribing American embassy personnel — especially Navy attachés — with meals, alcohol, and sex workers. It appears that Francis was most successful in corrupting Captain Michael G. Brooks, the naval attaché at the U.S. embassy in Manila. From 2006 to 2008, Brooks worked tirelessly to help Francis, whom he called "boss." Brooks's efforts included giving GDMA ships free rein at Philippine ports. In 2017, the captain pleaded guilty to conspiracy to commit bribery and admitted to soliciting bribes and accepting sex with sex workers. He was sentenced to forty-one months' imprisonment and $71,000 in fines and restitution.[98]

Similarly, Francis successfully corrupted Adrian Jansen, a naval attaché in Indonesia. Over the course of three years from 2010 to 2013, Jansen socialized with Fat Leonard, who provided gifts, including gratis luxurious meals. Jansen's services to Francis remains unclear but the two grew so close that by 2013 Francis underwrote a private "farewell luncheon" for the departing attaché who had been selected for rear admiral. At that gratis celebration, Jansen embraced Fat Leonard's gift of expensive wines.[99]

Jansen's subsequent assignments included two years at the Defense Intelligence Agency in Washington, DC, and a year as the defense attaché at the U.S. Embassy in Beijing, China. By 2017, the rear admiral had returned to Washington as commander of Naval Installations Command, and that is when Judge Advocate General (JAG) investigators reported his misconduct with Francis in Indonesia. Jansen's case was reviewed by Admiral Philip S. Davidson, who had succeeded Admiral Richardson as the Navy's Consolidated Disposition Authority for GDMA investigations. On February 10, Davidson convened a meeting wherein Jansen pleaded guilty to accepting gifts and not reporting them. Davidson found Jansen's misbehavior in violation of UCMJ Article 92, "Failure to Obey an Order." Jansen requested retirement three days later.[100]

In a February 17, 2017, finding letter sent to the NIG, Admiral Davidson reproached Jansen for his reckless conduct in Indonesia. Jansen had violated Navy ethics regulations and was negligently and willfully derelict in the performance of his duties. Davidson substantiated the JAG's allegations that Jansen, as a senior officer with security clearance, had failed to report his relationship with Francis (a foreign national), and had knowingly accepted expensive gifts and then failed to properly report them to federal authorities. Davidson found that Jansen was "in contact with, and socialized directly, with, Mr. Francis on numerous occasions" and documented Jansen's receipt of gifts worth more than $5,000 in 2011, 2012, and 2013. Davidson further concluded that Jansen's access to classified material presented a national security risk.[101]

As punishment, Davidson issued the admiral a punitive letter of reprimand and ordered a forfeiture of $7,500 from his $156,072 annual salary. He also recommended that the Navy secretary revoke Jansen's service award for his tour as naval attaché in Indonesia. Davidson further proposed that Jansen's access to classified information be suspended immediately and that the Defense Department consider rescinding his security clearance. "Overall, RDML Jansen failed to live up the standards expected of an officer of his rank and experience during his interactions with Mr. Francis and GDMA," wrote Davidson.[102] On February 24, Davidson wrote to the Commander of Navy Personnel Command to recommend that Jansen be "allowed to retire at the earliest opportunity" and at the lower rank of captain.[103] Nevertheless, the Navy Secretary allowed the disgraced admiral to retire at full rank.

By comparison, Admiral Davidson's treatment of Rear Admiral Babette "Bette" Bolivar was lenient. On March 1, 2017, less than a month after Jansen's reprimand, Bolivar assumed command of U.S. Navy Region Southeast, which is responsible for eighteen Navy installations in the southeastern United States and the Caribbean. The new posting featured a historic transfer of command between two female admirals.[104] Bolivar was a trailblazing Filipino-American officer. Previously, she had been the first woman admiral to command both Navy Region Northwest and also Joint Region Marianas in the Pacific.[105] Bolivar's stellar career, however, was imperiled when federal investigators determined that years earlier she had engaged in misconduct with Leonard Francis. Her case was referred to Admiral Davidson.

In summer 1998, Bolivar was in command of the USS *Salvor*, a diving and salvage ship deployed to the Western Pacific. One of her primary missions was recovering and clearing vessels stranded in and around Apra Harbor, Guam, following Typhoon Paka. In August, the *Salvor* docked in Kota Kinabalu, Malaysia, where Bolivar came into contact with Francis. Two decades later, Admiral Davidson substantiated the allegations that she and members of her crew had "wrongly accepted improper gifts of a free hotel room, dinner, drinks, entertainment and a golf excursion" from Francis.[106] Davidson "lightly wrapped"

Bolivar with a nonpunitive reprimand.[107] He did not believe harsher punishment was warranted given that she was not aware of Francis's criminal activity, nor did she solicit any gifts or act to benefit his company. Moreover, Davidson wrote, Bolivar had proven a "significant contributor and valued leader in the Navy," someone with an "exemplary career."[108] News of Bolivar's involvement with Fat Leonard did not become public until August 2019, five months after she assumed command of U.S. Navy Region Southwest, which consists of three major Navy installations near San Diego and two naval air stations in Nevada.

★ ★ ★ ★

Like Admiral Bolivar, Vice Admiral Ted N. "Twig" Branch escaped significant punishment for his improper relationship with Leonard Francis. But the federal investigation into Branch's misbehavior was a long, drawn-out, bizarre affair. On November 7, 2013, seven weeks after Francis was arrested, the Navy announced that it had stripped Vice Admiral Branch of his access to classified information and placed him on leave. The decision came after the Justice Department told Navy officials about "very strong" evidence of Branch's improper relationship with Francis.[109] The three-star admiral had recently been promoted and made the director of Navy Intelligence (DNI) and the deputy chief of naval operations (DCNO) for information warfare. The notion that the Navy's chief intelligence officer might have accepted bribes from Francis raised "serious questions about whether national security may have been compromised."[110] The Navy said it was only "prudent" to halt Branch's access to classified data given the sensitive nature of the admiral's duties and the need to protect the integrity of the Department of Justice's (DOJ) investigation.[111]

Branch first met Francis in 2000 when he was the executive officer on the aircraft carrier USS *John C. Stennis*. During the ship's layover at the port in Kuala Lumpur, Malaysia, Francis treated Branch to dinner and gave him "a ceremonial dagger" as a gift. Branch was also alleged to have attended a private after-dinner party where Francis gave him a

Malaysian pewter tea set and provided "the services of a prostitute."[112] Francis and Branch remained in "regular contact" over the years. They were happily reunited in 2005 when the naval officer became commander of the USS *Nimitz*, which deployed to Southeast Asia. On May 17 of that year, Francis emailed Branch. He offered to arrange dinners, drinks, and "a few rounds of great golf at the most scenic courses" in Kuala Lumpur and Hong Kong. Francis bragged about losing a significant amount of weight over the years, but assured Branch that "I'm still the same old fun loving Leonard you all know." Branch responded, "We are looking forward to HK and KL. It will be good to see you."[113]

A few weeks later in Hong Kong, Branch brought Francis aboard the *Nimitz* for a private lunch. Francis reciprocated by hosting Branch and approximately twenty officers for an expensive meal at an acclaimed restaurant with views overlooking the harbor. The banquet — which featured Remy Martin cognac, Chateau Lynch-Bages wine, and Cohiba cigars — cost nearly $700 per person. When the *Nimitz* departed Hong Kong, Branch sent Francis a formal communiqué and copied multiple Navy headquarters. The *Nimitz* commander lauded Francis's company for "outstanding" and "over the top customer service."[114]

Branch met with Francis again in July 2005 when the *Nimitz* docked at Kuala Lumpur. Branch was alleged to have attended a party that included sex workers. The latter was never substantiated, but the commander did accept various illicit gifts, including expensive cigars and a coffee-table book from Singapore. After the *Nimitz* left port, Branch sent Francis another glowing tribute. "True to form Leonard, you provided absolutely the highest quality service to my ship and crew. Your commitment to the Navy and the professionalism you and your staff displayed is unmatched."[115]

In late 2015, nearly two years after being stripped of his access to classified security information, Branch was still under investigation. Shockingly, he remained in his critical position as the Navy's senior intelligence, cyber, and information officer. The Navy's chief spokesperson explained that Branch was performing "managerial duties" while his deputies "handle the classified aspects" of his job.[116] On September 19,

2015, a widely respected Navy analyst and historian, Norman Polmar, penned an op-ed in the *Navy Times*. Polmar argued that it defied logic to think that Branch could perform his duties satisfactorily without having access to classified materials.[117] Four months later, the vice admiral was still atop naval intelligence without having security clearance. Polmar told the *Washington Post*, "I have never heard of anything as asinine, bizarre or stupid in all my years."[118]

With the investigation ongoing, Branch spoke publicly in February 2016 by granting an interview to Military.com. The vice admiral described his surreal situation as "less than optimal" and "frustrating in the extreme." He declared that he had no intention of retiring. "I will lead in this capacity," the admiral said, "until somebody tells me to go home." While Branch did not deny he had an inappropriate relationship with Francis, he insisted that he was not a threat to national security. "Probably the most important point is," he said, "I am not a danger to national security, nor have I ever been, nor will I ever be, and the idea that I would be is insulting."[119] At the behest of Defense Secretary Ashton B. Carter, Branch retired in October 2016.

In September 2017 the Navy announced that the DOJ had previously elected not to prosecute Branch and had referred his case to the Navy for an internal examination. A Navy spokesperson also stated that Admiral Davidson, the current disposition authority for Fat Leonard cases, had completed a comprehensive review of Branch's case. Davidson determined that the evidence "substantiated misconduct" by Branch for his unethical relationship with Francis.[120] As a result, Davidson took "appropriate administrative action" against the retired admiral and then closed the case.[121] The exact nature of the reprimand was not disclosed. The *Washington Post* later reported that Branch had "accepted meals and gifts" from Francis, and while the Navy cited him for four counts of misconduct, it could not "verify allegations" that he also consorted with sex workers.[122]

Vice Admiral Branch was not the only senior intelligence officer swept up in the Fat Leonard whirlwind. On November 5, 2013, the NCIS conducted an interview with Rear Admiral Bruce F. Loveless, the director of Intelligence Operations in Washington, DC. The two-star admiral reported directly to Branch. The NCIS agent wanted to learn about Loveless's own relationship with Leonard Francis, who had been arrested seven weeks earlier on corruption charges. Loveless was asked if, while in the Navy, he had ever stayed in a hotel room that he did not pay for. The admiral responded, "No. I don't think so." When asked if he had ever received "anything" of value from Francis, Loveless snapped, "Never."[123] Two days later, the Navy temporarily suspended both Loveless and Branch from their Pentagon duties and denied them access to classified materials. Though not formally charged with crimes, both admirals stood accused of improperly accepting gifts and services from Francis.[124]

It remains unclear when Francis first initiated his relationship with Loveless, who before his promotion to rear admiral had served seven years in the Western Pacific (from 2005 to 2012). The two men likely met after 2005, when then-Captain Loveless joined Carrier Strike Group Five, Battle Force Seventh Fleet (CTF 70). He served aboard the carrier USS *Kitty Hawk* for two years as the assistant chief of staff for intelligence. Records indicate that by early 2006 Loveless's friend and shipmate Commander Donald "Bubbles" Hornbeck had already established a corrupt partnership with Fat Leonard.

Hornbeck, the deputy assistant chief of staff for operations for CTF 70, helped Francis by persuading Navy officials to divert ships to ports controlled by GDMA in April 2006. Francis rewarded his efforts. When Hornbeck was promoted to captain in July 2006, Francis agreed to cover all expenses for his "wetting down" party at Raffles, a five-star hotel in Singapore. Seventy-five people attended the celebratory event.[125] Such blatantly unethical conduct transpired even though the Seventh Fleet JAG had circulated an ethics memorandum to all senior officers reminding them about strict regulations in their dealings with defense contractors in foreign ports.[126]

Loveless's involvement with Fat Leonard intensified after July 2007 when he transferred to the USS *Blue Ridge*, the command and control ship of the Seventh Fleet. Hornbeck joined that carrier in January and, soon afterward, during the ship's port visit to Hong Kong, Francis hosted "a lavish party and [engaged] the services of prostitutes" for some of the senior officers. The officers had assisted the defense contractor in securing a rich husbanding agreement for Navy vessels in the Philippines. Francis's raucous sex party was held in the General Douglas MacArthur Suite of the Manila Hotel. The unabashed partygoers incorporated some of the suite's historic memorabilia, including a replica of the general's famous corncob pipe, into their "sex acts."[127]

In mid-September 2007 Francis traveled to Yokosuka, Japan, the forward deployed base of the USS *Blue Ridge*. There he organized a gratis dinner for Loveless, Hornbeck, and other officers, including Captain James "JD" Dolan, the assistant chief of staff for logistics for the Seventh Fleet, and Captain David "Too Tall" Lausman, the commanding officer of the *Blue Ridge*. According to court records, the purpose of the meeting was "vetting and incorporating certain additional members of the Seventh Fleet staff . . . into the conspiracy," which was organized to financially benefit GDMA.[128] The conspirators referred to themselves by various names including "the Band of Brothers," "the Wolfpack," and the "familia." The tripartite clique of Loveless, Hornbeck, and Dolan, all 0-6s (the rank of captain), were jokingly referred to as "the 0-6 Ensigns."[129]

For two months after the vetting dinner, senior officers on the *Blue Ridge* supplied Francis with computer disks containing the classified movement schedules for ships belonging to the Seventh Fleet. With Navy officers "in his pocket," Fat Leonard later boasted that he could easily "move [U.S. Navy] carriers like paper ships in the water."[130] The officers also began exerting influence on Navy officials to pay GDMA a "cancellation settlement" fee after the USS *Kitty Hawk* canceled a port visit to Hong Kong.[131]

On December 1, 2007, with the USS *Blue Ridge* docked in Singapore, Francis hosted Loveless, Lieutenant Commander Stephen Shedd (the Seventh Fleet's South Asia Policy and Planning Officer), and others at an extravagant dinner costing $5,000. Moreover, he bribed Shedd by giving him and his wife Ulysse Nardin watches valued at

$25,000. The next month, the lieutenant commander provided Francis with additional classified information related to Seventh Fleet ship schedules. In turn, Francis sent "cigars and fine wine" to Captains Hornbeck and Lausman and wines to Captains Loveless and Dolan.[132]

For several days in late January and early February 2008, the USS *Blue Ridge* paid a port visit to Hong Kong. Francis arranged hotel rooms for Loveless, Hornbeck, Dolan, and Shedd on the Harbor View Club Floor at the JW Marriot. The luxurious rooms cost $626 per night, per room. Francis paid for the accommodations and provided the officers with "fictitious receipts" reflecting a rate of $126 per night, tax included. On January 29, Francis hosted another gratis dinner with live entertainment for Loveless and the others in the Alsace Room of the opulent Restaurant Petrus. The party enjoyed an eight-course meal that featured "black truffle soup, rock lobster salad, osetra caviar, pan-seared duck liver with pear and sunchoke, Dover sole, grilled Wagyu beef tenderloin Rossini, a selection of fine cheeses, and baked Alaska for dessert." Each course was paired with an expensive wine or champagne and the total cost of the feast was $18,371.[133]

The following day Hornbeck emailed Francis: "Just wanted to send a quick note to say thank you for including me in the get-together last night. Really enjoyed talking to you — and the food, music, and wine were wonderful." Hornbeck also had the audacity to ask Francis for a job with GDMA after he retired from the Navy.[134] Two weeks later, Francis "humbly" requested a favor from Captain Lausman to write an official letter of commendation for GDMA's Hong Kong services "to ensure everyone knows of your satisfaction with my company's support." Lausman happily obliged.[135]

During the subsequent three months, officers of the *Blue Ridge* routinely passed along classified information pertaining to the movement of Navy ships and submarines, including port visit schedules for aircraft carriers transiting through the Seventh Fleet's area of operation. In addition, they provided Francis with "proprietary invoice information" on his competitors and wrote "Bravo Zulu" letters commending Francis's husbanding services. Francis used the testimonials to gain new contracts from the U.S. government. *Blue Ridge* officers also pressed Navy officials to pay GDMA's inflated invoices.[136]

Francis's bribery of the Seventh Fleet's officer corps continued during spring 2008. On May 2, the USS *Blue Ridge* made a port visit to Laem Chabang, Thailand. Loveless, Hornbeck, Dolan, and Shedd solicited hotel rooms from Francis. The defense contractor not only paid for their stay at the Conrad Hotel in Bangkok but also supplied "numerous prostitutes." Two days later, Shedd emailed Francis noting that his three compatriots "were all smiles on the drive home over their 'one night in Bangkok.'"[137]

On May 6, the *Blue Ridge* docked in Singapore for several days. The four smiling officers as well as Captain Lausman, the aircraft carrier's skipper, were given rooms at the luxurious Shangri-La Hotel. Francis also hosted sailors at an expensive dinner at Mezza 9 at the Grand Hyatt hotel. Afterward, the defense contractor arranged for "several prostitutes to entertain Dolan, Hornbeck, and Loveless." The next day, Hornbeck emailed Francis to thank him for "a fantastic dinner" and for arranging a sex worker, whom he called "My new Mongolian Friend."[138]

The corruption continued on the night of May 8. Francis hosted another dinner for officers of the *Blue Ridge* at the Japanese restaurant Nadaman, located inside the Shangri-La Hotel. The collective bill exceeded $8,000. On May 10, Lieutenant Commander Shedd emailed Francis: "The 3 ensigns [Loveless, Hornbeck, and Dolan] were all grins this morning as we got underway! Hornbeck said he couldn't have survived another night in Singapore with you!"[139]

A few days before the USS *Blue Ridge* made a port visit in Indonesia, Shedd emailed Francis more classified schedules of Navy vessel movements in the Western Pacific. The carrier arrived in Jakarta on May 12. At his expense, Francis arranged rooms for Loveless, Hornbeck, Dolan, and others at the Shangri-La Hotel and at the Magellan Sutera Harbor. As before, the defense contractor supplied the officers with the services of sex workers. His bribery continued days later when the *Blue Ridge* docked in Malaysia. Loveless, Hornbeck, and Dolan roomed at the Shangri-La Hotel in Kota Kinabalu. Francis's company, which provided husbanding services at the Indonesian port, billed the Navy $2,218,037.[140]

It appears that Loveless's final engagement with Francis came at the end of May 2008, when the *Blue Ridge* made another port call in the Philippines. Francis traveled to Manila to make hotel arrangements for Loveless, Hornbeck, Dolan, and others at the luxurious Makati Shangri-La. During that layover, the contractor booked the hotel's Presidential Suite for the purpose of hosting a "raging multi-day party." The party included "a rotating carousel of prostitutes" and the swapping of sex partners. By the end of the debauchery, the naval officers had exhausted the hotel's entire stock of Dom Perignon. The bill for the stay exceeded $50,000. Five days later, Shedd emailed Francis, "I finally detoxed myself from Manila. That was a crazy couple of days. It's been a while since I've done 36 hours of straight drinking!!!"[141] In July Francis emailed Shedd and Hornbeck a picture of a naked sex worker who had been present at the party in the Presidential Suite in Manila. Francis wrote, "I thought this photo will bring memories of the Ens[igns] in Manila."[142] That was Loveless's last month on the *Blue Ridge*; he went ashore at Pearl Harbor to assume command of the Joint Intelligence Operations Center, U.S. Pacific Command.

Five years later in November 2013, Rear Admiral Loveless told an NCIS special agent that he had never received anything of value from Leonard Francis. That denial caused the Navy to suspend him from duty and terminate his access to classified information. In 2014 Loveless began a new assignment as the corporate director for information warfare, but the Navy refused to grant the career intelligence officer access to classified materials as long as he remained under federal investigation.[143]

In October 2016, while the Fat Leonard investigation progressed, Loveless was allowed to retire, but at the lower rank of one-star admiral.[144] A stunning turning point came thirteen months into his retirement. Loveless was arrested by federal agents at his home in Coronado, California. On March 14, 2017, the retired admiral and eight others, including Hornbeck, Dolan, Lausman, and Shedd, were indicted for public corruption by Alana W. Robinson, Acting U.S. Attorney of the Southern

District of California. "This is a fleecing and betrayal of the United States Navy in epic proportions," Robinson said in a statement, "and it was allegedly carried out by the Navy's highest-ranking officers. The alleged conduct amounts to a staggering degree of corruption by the most prominent leaders of the Seventh Fleet . . . actively working together as a team to trade secrets for sex, serving the interests of a greedy foreign defense contractor, and not those of their own country."[145]

Loveless was indicted on three counts. All nine defendants were indicted for conspiracy to commit bribery, intentionally colluding to "commit an offense against the United States." Loveless was specifically accused of obstructing justice by making false statements to federal investigators. According to the indictment, the admiral's motive was "to conceal the nature and extent of his corrupt relationship with Francis."[146] The nine defendants were also collectively indicted for "conspiracy to commit honest service fraud" whereby they conspired "to devise a material scheme and artifice to defraud" the United States and Navy "of their rights to the honest, loyal, and faithful services, decisions, actions, and performance, through bribery and kickbacks and concealment of information." Moreover, the nine had "transmitted and caused to be transmitted writing, signs, and signals by means of wire communication in interstate and foreign commerce, including many emails among the conspirators."[147]

In a third criminal count, Loveless, like the other eight conspirators, was charged with bribery. The retired admiral's indictment stated that beginning in July 2007 and continuing through September 2013, he had engaged in grievous misconduct and had "corruptly demanded, sought, received, accepted, and agreed to receive and accept things of value, personally and for other persons, including entertainment, hotel stays, and the services of prostitutes, in return for being induced to do and omit to do acts in violation of his official duties, as opportunities arose."[148]

Within hours of his arrest, Loveless appeared before a federal judge. He pleaded not guilty. The judge released him without bond.[149] At the time, Loveless, a former two-star, was the highest-ranking officer indicted in the Fat Leonard scandal and his arrest made international news.

Even late-night talk show host Stephen Colbert weighed in. The comedian explained to his audience that he had been so preoccupied with President Donald Trump jokes that he nearly missed commenting on a salacious military corruption scandal. "Why in God's name," he quipped, "did I only hear about it now? I mean, what has happened to us as a nation when we let ourselves be distracted by Trump's phony wiretap claims and two pages of his twelve-year-old tax returns when I could have been making jokes about rear admirals and their seamen in Manila, Philipenis. That's why I got into this game!"[150]

In 2021 two of Loveless's accused co-conspirators, a Marine Corps colonel and a Navy chief warrant officer, pleaded guilty to bribery.[151] In January 2022 Commander Shedd also pleaded guilty to bribery, and the following month, Captain Hornbeck followed suit.[152] In June 2022, a jury convicted four other conspirators (former Navy captains David Newland, James Dolan, and David Lausman, and former Navy commander Mario Herrera), but deadlocked on the charges against Loveless.[153]

★ ★ ★ ★

The scope and longevity of the Fat Leonard corruption case is staggering. Sustained over two decades and ensnaring dozens upon dozens of officers, the conspiracy bilked an estimated $35 million from American taxpayers. Moreover, the ease with which Leonard Francis, a gregarious foreign national, seduced and bribed so many military officers is astounding. Through his ambition and effectiveness, Francis exposed a critical vulnerability in the U.S. government's systems of procurement and contract management and in national security more broadly. According to one retired naval officer, "The Soviets couldn't have penetrated us better than Leonard Francis. . . . At one time he had infiltrated the entire leadership line."[154]

In December 2019, with the scandal entering its seventh year, a new chief of naval operations, Admiral Michael Gilday, dispatched a message to all Navy personnel. To mitigate the Navy's susceptibility to corruption, he implored everyone to reflect upon personal and institutional ethics and their oaths to the Constitution. "That oath," Gilday wrote, "is what binds us together. It is the foundation of our profession. It is our north star. It defines us." Sailors and Marines, he emphasized, must have integrity and act as standard-bearers: "We must be above reproach. And we must not give anyone cause to question our fundamental values. That is what sets us apart as a fighting force." The CNO also alerted all commanders: "Leaders, I am counting on you [because] there is much work to be done."[155]

While not as torrid or widespread as the Navy's Fat Leonard corruption scandal, Army and Air Force flag officers have also breached the public trust by abusing their positions of power regarding defense contracts. In January 2008, for example, the Defense Department's inspector general concluded that Air Force Major General Stephen Goldfein, while in command of the Air Warfare Center, Nellis Air Force Base, Nevada, had misused his rank by improperly influencing the federal procurement process. According to the DoDIG, the general displayed "a pattern" of misconduct that constituted "preferential treatment" in the awarding of an inflated $49.9 million contract to Strategic Message Solutions (SMS), a newly created and under-resourced marketing company. The 2005 contract was to provide multimedia entertainment during performances by the Thunderbirds Air Demonstration Squadron. The inspector general, however, characterized SMS as "a skeleton operation without the resources to undertake a contract effort of this magnitude." One of the contractor's silent partners, Air Force General Hal Hornburg (retired in 2004), had recently been Goldfein's immediate superior. Hornburg was also a personal friend of then–Air Force Vice Chief of Staff General Michael Moseley, who had intimate knowledge of the contract. Goldfein was reprimanded for his misconduct and retired. Moseley himself ultimately received a letter of admonishment for his involvement.[156]

Similarly, in February 2015, Army Major General Dana Pittard, a former commander of Fort Bliss, Texas, received a letter of reprimand from General Daniel Allyn for his "excessive involvement" and a "gross lack of good judgment" regarding a government contract.[157] Pittard, a fast-rising officer and a former military assistant to President Bill Clinton, had wittingly and improperly involved himself in the procurement process for a renewable energy program at Fort Bliss. Subordinate officers accused their commander of going to "unusual lengths to push a no-bid contract" for a company managed by two of his former West Point classmates. Pittard met with the duo in private and provided "non-public" information related to the proposed project.[158] The two-star retired seven months after his admonishment.

Public corruption occurs on many levels, ranging from small, seemingly inconsequential favors among a select group of people — so-called petty corruption — to corruption on a broad, far-reaching scale — grand corruption. No breach of the public trust can be tolerated, especially within the Department of Defense where enormous sums of money and national security are at stake. There must be accountability and transparency, particularly when senior military officers commit corrupt acts such as bribery and fraud. They are, after all, entrusted to set the highest examples of integrity and impartiality.

CONCLUSION

The most important factor of all is character,
which involves integrity, unselfishness and devoted purpose,
a sturdiness of bearing when everything goes wrong
and all are critical, and a willingness to sacrifice self
in the interest of the common good.

— George C. Marshall

On the evening of June 1, 2020, a chaotic scene emerged in the nation's capital. It was unnervingly similar to the Hoover administration's thrashing of the B.E.F. nine decades prior. At 6:30 p.m. federal police officers dressed in riot gear (many mounted on horseback) used exploding munitions, flash-bang shells, and gas canisters to forcibly remove Black Lives Matters supporters and journalists from Lafayette Square. At that very moment, President Donald Trump gave a brief speech in the Rose Garden. He declared: "I am the president of law and order" and "as we speak I am dispatching thousands and thousands of heavily armed soldiers, military personnel, and law enforcement officers to stop the rioting, looting, vandalism, and assaults, and the wanton destruction of property."[1] Only five months before his reelection bid, Trump was determined to show his political base and the international community that he was in control and not hiding in the White House emergency bunker where he had taken refuge two days earlier.

After his remarks, the president returned to the White House. He told his aides and several senior advisors, including Attorney General Bill Barr, Defense Secretary Mark Esper, and chairman of the Joint Chiefs of Staff Mark Milley, "We're going to the church [in Lafayette Square]."[2] Before a throng of reporters and television news crews, Trump led a procession to the recently cleared square where traces of tear gas and pepper spray lingered in the air. The president stopped outside St. John's Church for a peculiar photo op: his daughter Ivanka gave him a Bible to hold up in the air. The presence of Secretary Esper and especially of General Milley, who was wearing combat fatigues, suggested that the Pentagon condoned the president's hardnosed treatment of the largely peaceful civil rights demonstrators. The optics conveyed the politicization of the U.S. military.

After the staged event, Milley and Esper suffered swift and sharp criticism. Perhaps the most pointed came from retired Marine Corps General James Mattis, who had served and then resigned in protest as Trump's first secretary of defense. In *The Atlantic*, Mattis defended the constitutional rights of the Black Lives Matters movement and derided the actions of the president and Pentagon leadership. Mattis was livid that military officers who had sworn allegiance to the Constitution might have been ordered to violate the rights of fellow citizens. Moreover, he wrote, there was that "bizarre photo op for the elected commander-in-chief, with military leadership standing alongside." Esper and Milley's presence at Lafayette Square, Mattis asserted, had tarnished "the moral ground that ensures a trusted bond between men and women in uniform and the society they are sworn to protect, and of which they themselves are a part."[3] Was General Milley yet another bad general?

A careful examination of Milley's relationship with Trump reveals not a dishonorable leader, but an effective and ethical flag officer who had made an honest if serious mistake by joining the president at Lafayette Square. He had not been told in advance about Trump's plans. Milley immediately recognized the severity of his transgression. He told his aides, "He [Trump] burned me. Fuck these guys. I'm not playing political games."[4] On June 2, Milley sent a memorandum to the military's senior leadership underscoring their oath to support and defend the Constitution. At the bottom he scrawled, "We all committed our lives to the idea that is America — we will stay true to that oath and the American people."[5]

Accepting that he had blundered at Lafayette Square, Milley considered resigning. He called a former chairman of the Joint Chiefs of Staff, General Colin Powell, and asked whether he should step down. Powell shouted, "Fuck no! I told you never to take the job. You never should have taken the job. Trump's a fucking maniac."[6] Instead of resigning, Milley issued a public apology. In a prerecorded video address, he underscored the sanctity of the Constitution, the persistence of racism and discrimination in the United States, and the patriotic role of peaceful protesters. Milley did not criticize the president. As for his participation at Lafayette Square, the general admitted: "I should not have been there. My presence . . . created a perception of the military involved in domestic politics. . . . It was a mistake I have learned from, and I sincerely hope we all can learn from it. . . . We must hold dear the principle of an apolitical military."[7]

Milley knew that Trump and Mark Meadows, the White House chief of staff, would dislike the public apology. The general understood that he might be fired for appearing disloyal. The day after Milley's address, an angry president asked him why he had apologized, asserting that it made the Army general appear weak. The chairman explained that he could not allow the military to be politicized. "I can't do it. It's wrong," he said. "And that's why I apologized."[8] Milley, a former Catholic altar boy, told Meadows, "This was about me going to confession, Chief." Lafayette Square was "way fucking wrong" and had a "dramatic" negative effect on the armed forces.[9]

Unlike so many flag officers during the Iraq War, Milley prided himself on giving the president and his senior advisors unvarnished professional advice, even when he knew that his views differed from the administration. Before Lafayette Square, Trump had wanted to deploy *active-duty* troops to American cities to overpower civil rights protesters and arrest those committing vandalism. The irate president told aides that he wanted the military to "beat the fuck" out of the demonstrators and vandals.[10] Trump asked Milley directly, "Can't you just shoot them? Just shoot them in the legs or something."[11] General Milley insisted that law enforcement and the National Guard, not the regular army, should handle such domestic problems. This advice only further enraged the president, who shouted at Milley and others advisors, "You are losers! You are all fucking losers!"[12] Milley further maintained that there was no national insurrection and no need for regular troops. Referring to Abraham Lincoln, the general told Trump, "That guy had an insurrection. What we have, Mr. President, is a protest."[13] On another occasion Meadows proposed a massive Fourth of July military parade with combat vehicles positioned on the White House lawn and more than one hundred aircraft flying overhead. Milley objected. Flabbergasted by the proposal, he declared, "This is what North Korea does. This is what Stalin does."[14] The general was blunt again when Trump asked him about military installations bearing the names of Confederate army generals. Milley answered unequivocally that they all should be renamed. "These guys were traitors," he bellowed. "They betrayed the country."[15]

Already unsettled by the Lafayette Square fiasco and Trump's inclination to deploy active-duty soldiers into U.S. cities, Milley began to worry about the coming presidential election. At the risk of being fired and forced into retirement, he told some confidants that his new primary mission as chairman was to prevent Trump's politicization of the military, especially troop deployments that could lead to the killing of fellow citizens. Milley was determined to safeguard not only the "integrity of the U.S. military" but also his "personal integrity."[16] The general informed Secretary of State Mike Pompeo, a West Point graduate, that "this military's not going to be used" by the president. Moreover, he said, "We've got to make sure it's a free and fair election."[17]

The November 3, 2020, election transpired with Joseph R. Biden Jr. defeating Trump. The incumbent, however, refused to concede. Angry and defiant, Trump provoked his supporters by making wild and unsubstantiated claims of massive election fraud. The volatile president also began firing people he thought disloyal. General Milley and Defense Secretary Esper, another West Point graduate, were on the short list. Like Milley, Esper had apologized publicly for Lafayette Square, and he had made clear his opposition to deploying active-duty troops against protestors; he got the axe on November 9. Chief of Staff Meadows told the outgoing secretary, "[W]e don't think you're sufficiently loyal." To which Esper retorted, "That's the president's prerogative. My oath is to the Constitution, not to him."[18]

That night, a dejected Pompeo visited Milley at the chairman's official residence, Quarters Six on Grant Avenue, Fort Myer. He told the general, "The crazies are taking over," and as a result, the duo had to "stand together shoulder to shoulder."[19] The next day, Milley received a telephone call from distressed CIA director Gina Haspel. She was equally disturbed by Esper's firing. Haspel warned the chairman, "We are on the way to a right-wing coup. The whole thing is insanity. He [Trump] is acting out like a six-year-old with a tantrum."[20]

Milley was upset, but not surprised by Esper's firing. On November 11, Veterans Day, speaking at the opening of the new National Army Museum, the general chose his words carefully. He wanted to underscore the ultimate duty of America's armed forces. Milley reminded his audience: "We do not take an oath to a king or a queen, a tyrant or a dictator. We do not take an oath to an individual." Instead, the Constitution was the military's "moral north star."[21] In the end, Milley was not fired — saved apparently by Meadows, Ivanka Trump, and Ivanka's husband, Jared Kushner.[22]

Esper's firing and Trump's ongoing refusal to concede the 2020 election worried Milley. Also concerned were Nancy Pelosi, Speaker of the U.S. House of Representatives, and Representative Adam Smith, the chairman of the House Armed Services Committee. Pelosi telephoned

Milley: "We are all trusting you. Remember your oath." Smith called too: "Risk just went up."[23] Milley feared the president would coopt the military and invoke the Insurrection Act of 1807 to remain in office. The chairman called Trump's former national security advisor, retired Army Lieutenant General H. R. McMaster, to ask, "What the fuck am I dealing with?" McMaster replied, "[T]he weirdest shit ever." He warned Milley about the violent and racist factions among Trump's legion of acolytes.[24]

Trump was refusing to concede, and he was also staging political rallies and employing inflammatory rhetoric. Milley thought the propaganda smacked of Nazism and called it "the gospel of the Fuhrer."[25] The chairman contemplated the surreal idea of a presidential coup with "[American-Nazi] brown shirts in the streets." Not on my watch, the general told his senior deputies: "They may try, but they're not going to fucking succeed."[26]

On January 6, 2021, two weeks before Biden's inauguration, Milley was in his Pentagon office watching television news. Trump and a slate of his devotees were provoking a large crowd of diehard supporters who had gathered at his request in the nation's capital. They were there to protest the pending congressional certification of the election results. Milley was disgusted by the display. At approximately 2:00 p.m., hundreds of rally-goers began to attack police officers guarding the Capitol Complex. Milley advised Chris Miller, the acting defense secretary, to have the attorney general deploy "every cop in D.C." to the Capitol.[27] He further recommended the mobilization of the D.C. National Guard as well as Guard units from surrounding states. At 3:04 p.m., Miller granted Army Secretary Ryan McCarthy, one of Trump's most loyal political appointees at the Pentagon, the authority to mobilize the D.C. National Guard to support the U.S. Capitol Police. At 3:15 p.m., Republican Senator Dan Sullivan of Alaska called Chairman Milley: "This is really fucked up down here." Seven minutes later Democratic Congressman Adam Smith telephoned, "Bring overwhelming force. The mob has overwhelmed us." Vice President Mike Pence called the Pentagon at 4:00 p.m., "Get troops here; get them here now."[28] At either 4:35 p.m. or 5:08 p.m. (the time is disputed), Army Secretary McCarthy *finally* ordered the

D.C. National Guard to deploy. The troops did not reach the Capitol until 5:20 p.m.[29] After hours of intense hand-to-hand combat, the insurrection was put down. Throughout the chaotic ordeal Trump never called the Defense Department, Homeland Security, nor the Justice Department. Later that night, Congress reconvened, certified the presidential election, and declared Joe Biden the next president of the United States.

Still, Trump and millions of his fiercest supporters refused to concede the election. Milley, who believed that the president had suffered a "serious mental decline," anticipated more treasonous trouble before the inauguration on January 20.[30] He maintained regular contact with Meadows and Pompeo to "keep tabs" on the obstinate and bombastic Trump.[31] In a telephone conversation with Speaker Pelosi, Milley assured her that "checks and balances in the system" would prevent Trump from taking rash military action such as instigating a war or launching a nuclear weapon.[32] "I can assure you," Milley stated categorically, "that the United States military is steady as a rock and we're not going to do anything illegal, immoral or unethical with the use of force. We will not do it."[33]

In coordination with other government leaders, Milley made preparations to ensure the peaceful transfer of presidential power. He imagined that Trump's diehard followers might attempt some sort of rearguard action to prevent Biden's inauguration. As a result, the nation's capitol was fortified with barricades, fences, and more than twenty thousand National Guard troops and law enforcement officers. In mid-January, Milley participated in contingency drills at Fort Myer. "Here's the deal," he told a group of interagency leaders. "These guys are Nazis, they're boogaloo boys, they're Proud Boys. These are the same people we fought in World War II. Everyone in this room, whether you're a cop, whether you're a soldier, we're going to stop these guys to make sure we have peaceful transfer of power. We're going to put a ring of steel around this city and the Nazis aren't getting in."[34] Six days later, under peaceful conditions, Biden was sworn into office. Milley was elated. And despite Milley's having been appointed by Trump, and in spite of his participation in the Lafayette Square spectacle, the new president chose to retain him as the chairman of the Joint Chiefs of Staff.

In this historic episode, General Milley stands as an exemplar of good leadership: effective, ethical, and lawful. One can easily imagine that different flag officers — for example, Trump loyalists akin to Army Lieutenant General Mike Flynn or Air Force Lieutenant General Thomas McInerney — might have acted very differently.[35] Individuals do indeed effect change. Serving in remarkably challenging political circumstances, Milley adhered strictly to his oath to the Constitution. As a military officer, he understood that his ultimate allegiance was to the rule of law and the nation itself, not to the commander in chief. After his misstep at Lafayette Square, Milley did the honorable thing. He took personal responsibility and apologized publicly, a morally courageous act that jeopardized his career. Furthermore, he learned from the blunder. Thereafter, Milley dedicated himself to shielding the armed forces from further politicization. Central to his effective generalship was his blunt candor, which he acknowledged might cause him to be fired and retired prematurely. In a display of Kantian ethics, Milley embraced his obligation to be honest and forthcoming, regardless of the consequences. It is significant that he recognized his personal integrity — not just the military's — was at stake. General Milley's actions embodied the concept of *moral maturity* whereby "a moral leader assesses his own beliefs, how those beliefs are manifest in his actions and the actions of his unit, and how closely aligned those actions are with the expectations of his nation, service and mission."[36]

★ ★ ★ ★

Since the Revolutionary War, the large majority of American admirals and generals have served honorably, and yet so many continue to disgrace themselves and the profession of arms. Why is it that a conspicuous minority of flag officers fail to live up to the military's high standards of integrity? Are not these senior leaders, lauded as paragons of virtue, among the nation's best and brightest in uniform, ever schooled in and teachers of duty, honor, country?

Wayward admirals and generals are most certainly deficient in moral development and personal responsibility. It is astonishing how many are outright criminals. Too often flag officers consciously or unconsciously cross the ethical bridge from a place of moral clarity, healthy self-confidence, and proper ambition to a point of hubris, self-deception, greed, and toxicity. For many, the crossing is gradual; for others, the trip is swift. Many senior leaders, while well-intended and of good character, are corrupted gradually by power, seduced by their status and the magnitude of their influence and span of control. This negative transformation is sometimes characterized as the "Bathsheba or King David Syndrome," wherein the biblical king David, once a model of honorable, visionary leadership, becomes corrupted by the accumulation of power and the trappings of success.[37] Meanwhile, other dishonorable admirals and generals possess dubious traits and ethics from the outset, only to be fully exposed after acquiring and exercising newfound authority. Regardless of how they are corrupted, too many flag officers become, in the immortal words of John Stuart Mill, "absolute princes" (and princesses), who, "accustomed to unlimited deference," develop attitudes of self-righteousness, certitude, and infallibility. This moral devolution causes them to lose "practical judgment."[38]

Perhaps it is not surprising that superciliousness is a bright red thread binding this book's chapters. What does surprise and even shock is the remarkable lack of discipline and self-control exhibited by so many accomplished senior leaders. Whether General Jacob Smith on the battlefields of the Philippines, Admiral Hyman Rickover in the bureaucracy of Washington, DC, or Vice Admiral Richard Dunleavy in a Las Vegas hotel, bad leaders fail to restrain themselves and others from ugly impulses. They become intoxicated by the power entrusted to them. "The effect of power and publicity on all men," Henry Adams wrote, "is the aggravation of self, a sort of tumor that ends by killing the victim's sympathies; a diseased appetite, like passion for drink and perverted tastes; one can scarcely use expression too strong to describe the violence of egotism it stimulates."[39] Furthermore, the recent

CONCLUSION   303

Fat Leonard scandal has made painfully clear that seemingly good but intemperate military officers are readily corruptible — entirely susceptible to the temptations of sex, alcohol, cash, and luxury. We can never lose sight of the fact that self-entitlement, illusory control, and moral indifference can have dangerous national security implications.

Beyond towering hubris and waning willpower, rogue generals and admirals frequently lose sight of two core elements of honorable leadership. The first is the absolute necessity of honesty and moral courage. Good leaders demonstrate a moral willingness to risk their careers, reputations, and relationships by doing what is ethically and legally correct. They understand and accept that exercising the best and most admirable leadership has its hazards. As novelist James Branch Cabell penned, "One has to pay at all times, and sometimes one has to pay rather dearly, for being honest."[40] By contrast, timidity, self-protecting silence, obedience, and conformity in the face of wrongdoing amounts to ignoble complicity, which is itself worthy of punishment. None other than General George Patton wrote: "I find that moral courage is the most valuable and most usually absent [leadership] characteristic. Much of our trouble is directly attributable to 'the fear of they.'"[41] Senior leaders, more than anybody in the armed services, must be willing to speak out against unethical and illegal behavior, and must act decisively when illicit activity is afoot.

Even more worrisome than moral cowardice is the blurring of a flag officer's sense of *ultimate duty*. There is a uniformed chain of command that leads from the enlisted ranks directly to the secretary of defense and the president, but admirals and generals do not swear fealty oaths to any superior or to any branch of service. Rather, by legal and moral design, they pledge themselves to serve and protect the Constitution and the American people — not the military leadership or the Executive Branch. Key to that oath of honor is being wholly and boldly honest with one's superiors (those in uniform and Executive Branch civilians) *and* with Congress. As demonstrated by the examples of John Poindexter, Colin Powell, Johnny Johnson, and many generals in the lead-up to the Iraq War, the dire mistake of misplaced loyalty can arise either deliberately or from an abject failure of moral courage. America's flag officers must be fully cognizant of their competing loyalties, and when hard pressed in difficult situations they, like General Milley, must take career risks and choose candor and the higher loyalty.

In addition to personal failures, the misconduct of admirals and generals is also the byproduct of faulty institutional systems and flawed organizational cultures. Even good people can be corrupted by bad situations. The problems stem in part from the military's worship of utilitarian ethics and the corresponding prioritization of mission success over professed values of ethical and legal conduct. Too often, hard-driving *effective* admirals and generals are rewarded for placing mission achievement—and career interests—above honorable behavior. Perhaps most notably, toxic leaders lack compassion and empathy and abuse subordinates whom they treat as mere cogs in the military machine, the means to the commander's ends. There is, in other words, systemic enabling of bad leadership within the Defense Department. And faulty promotion systems rely upon the complicity of superiors, peers, and subordinates who prize outcomes over people and process and *choose* silence and inaction after witnessing or becoming aware of bad behavior. Worse still—as seen in the Iran-Contra, Tailhook '91, Abu Ghraib, and Fat Leonard scandals—there remains an impulse to defend and protect transgressors and mitigate their punishment. This cronyism and attendant circle-the-wagons mentality only further pollutes a culture that allows bad leadership to take hold. As in American civilian society, culpability for bad leadership in the armed forces is widespread.

While the purpose of this book is to alert and inform, not prescribe, one must begin to ask, what might be done to curtail future misconduct of generals and admirals?[42] On the individual level, flag officers must be earnestly committed to a continuation of personal moral development, ever clinging to a healthy degree of humility. As they rise in rank, they must be constantly self-aware and remain sharply attuned to the ethical and legal dangers that accompany positions of authority: hubris, greed, intemperance, callousness, self-deception, selfishness, moral cowardice, and misdirected loyalty. With better awareness of the hazards accompanying the accumulation of power, admirals and generals will, one hopes, develop the capacity and fortitude to bypass that bridge to leadership's dark side.

Moreover, flag officers must not limit their ethical reasoning to utilitarianism, but rather contemplate operational means as much as the mission's ends. They must demand that core moral principles be protected regardless of the consequences. In addition, admirals and generals must be made to understand — over and over again — that one's moral development is in need of regular, concerted attention. "The knowledge needed by a senior commander," Carl von Clausewitz wrote, "is distinguished by the fact that it can only be attained by a special talent, through the medium of reflection, study, and thought."[43] This returns us to John Stuart Mill, who espoused, "[While] everyone well knows himself to be fallible, few think it necessary to take any precautions against their own fallibility."[44]

The American people need and deserve thoughtful and *morally ambitious* military leaders — people of competence *and* character — who not only communicate high standards and set the example, but also demand virtuous behavior from every person within their sphere of influence. Moreover, cases of senior leader misconduct can provide learning opportunities for the military with the goal of preventing future failures. "When we fail to hold the standard," writes Marine Corps Commandant David Berger, "we establish new lower standards . . . [and] elite organizations do not accept mediocrity and they do not look the other way when teammates come up short of expectations. We must hold each other accountable."[45]

The curbing of flag officer misconduct requires unswerving institutional commitment, robust congressional oversight, and public accountability. While certainly appearing regal, America's admirals and generals are not royalty, and any demonstration of impunity at the senior ranks of the military is intolerable. It is vital that admirals and generals be reminded — regularly — of their own fallibility and of the unique ethical responsibilities of command in a democratic country. Flag officers are not above the law and in fact must be held to the highest standards.

As leaders, they must be the exemplars. Those who do falter must be held publicly accountable, not only for the sake of proper justice but also for deterrent effect. For deterrence to serve as a mitigating force, errant senior leaders must suffer consequential penalties, not merely be fired and retired and thus allowed to enjoy princely pensions, healthcare benefits, and other lifetime privileges. Voltaire emphasized this very point in his satirical novel *Candide*. "In this country, it is thought wise," he wrote, to severely punish flag officer malfeasance in order "to encourage the others."[46] Without strict and visible accountability — the disinfectant of public sunlight — confidence, trust, and mission effectiveness erode, and such erosion endangers our society, the very society these generals and admirals are sworn to protect.

NOTES

Note to the Author's Note

1. Letter from Jackie Speier to James Mattis, March 13, 2017, https://speier.house.gov/_cache/files/2/7/27fae8fb-a312-45ba-b9b3-7869bc15ff25/1949681B8AC9D2CE288B0749E0ACBC1C.20170309-dod-on-custer-updated.pdf.

Introduction

1. T. Mueller, *Crisis of Conscience*, 10.

2. Malcolm, *Tragedy of Benedict Arnold*, xi.

3. Tom Vanden Brook, "Senior Military Officials Sanctioned for More Than 500 Cases of Serious Misconduct," *USA Today*, October 24, 2017.

4. U.S. Department of Defense, Office of the Inspector General, *Top DoD Management Challenges: Fiscal Year 2018*.

5. U.S. Department of Defense, Office of the Inspector General, *Top DoD Management Challenges: Fiscal Year 2018*.

6. Tom Vanden Brook, "Air Force Busts Retired Four-Star General Down Two Ranks for Coerced Sex," *USA Today*, February 1, 2017; Michelle Tan, "Army Demotes Former Defense Secretary's 3-Star Aide after Scathing IG Investigation, *Army Times*, February 9, 2017; Tom Vanden Brook, "Army General Loses Star, Must Retire: Wayne Grigsby Was Warned about Inappropriate Relationship with

Female Captain," *USA Today*, June 24, 2017; Tom Vanden Brook, "Army Sacks General for Sexy Texts to Wife of a Sergeant," *USA Today*, October 15, 2017; Ken Chamberlain, "2-Star to Lose One Star over Texts to Wife of Enlisted Soldier," *Army Times*, February 17, 2018; Craig Whitlock, "Admiral, Seven Others Charged with Corruption in New 'Fat Leonard' Indictment," *Washington Post*, March 14, 2017; Julie Watson, "'Fat Leonard' Bribery Trail to Expose Pervasive Problem, Analysts Say," *Navy Times*, March 2, 2022; Eric Lichtblau, "Admiral and 8 Other Navy Officers Indicted on Bribery Charges," *New York Times*, March 14, 2017.

7. Todd South, "Marine One-Star Cited for Misusing Aide, Taking Gifts from Subordinates," *Marine Corps Times*, July 5, 2018; U.S. Department of Defense, Office of the Inspector General, *Report of Investigation: Rick A. Uribe, Brigadier General, U.S. Marine Corps*.

8. Tom Vanden Brook, "Army Strips Star from Robbie Asher, Ex-General of Oklahoma National Guard, over Relationship," *USA Today*, April 11, 2019.

9. Meghann Myers, "Two-Star Army General Relieved Amid Investigation," *Army Times*, August 22, 2018; "Update: On Major General Hurley and His Alleged Philandering Ways — The Mystery Deepens as to What Is Really Going On in the U.S. Army," MilitaryCorruption.com, October 19, 2018, https://militarycorruption.com/hurley-update1/; "Update: Major General Paul Hurley Is Allowed to Slither out of the Army — Retiring to Avoid Prosecution Is Right out of the 'Military Play Book,' Designed to Protect Flag-Ranking Officers from Any Accountability," MilitaryCorruption.com, March 7, 2019, https://militarycorruption.com/paul-hurley/. On June 7, 2022, the Office of the Chief of Staff of the Army emailed the author Hurley's official resume, indicating his demotion and retirement.

10. U.S. Navy, "SECNAV Censured Three Naval Officers," press release, June 20, 2018; Dan Lamothe, "Navy Officers Censured for Bringing 'Embarrassment' on the Service in 'Fat Leonard' Scandal," *Washington Post*, June 20, 2018; Geoff Ziezulewicz, "SECNAV Censures Three More Navy Officers in 'Fat Leonard' Scandal," *Navy Times*, June 25, 2018; Gidget Fuentes, "Retired Flag Officer Who 'Abused His Position to Benefit Himself' Censured in Fat Leonard Scandal," *USNI News*, December 14, 2018; Geoff Ziezulewicz, "Navy Releases New Details on Retired Admiral and Former Trump Nominee's 'Fat Leonard' Censure," *Navy Times*, December 14, 2018; Manu Raju, "Rep. Ronny Jackson Made Sexual Comments, Drank Alcohol and Took Ambien While Working as White House Physician, Pentagon Watchdog Finds," CNN.com, March 3, 2021; Catie Edmondson, "Watchdog Finds G.O.P. Congressman Harassed Staff and Recklessly Drank While Serving as White House Physician," *New York Times*,

March 3, 2021; U.S. Department of Defense, Office of Inspector General, *Report of Investigation: Rear Admiral (Lower Half) Ronny Lynn Jackson, M.D., U.S. Navy, Retired*.

11. Geoff Ziezulewicz, "Why SOUTHCOM Says It Fired Admiral Who Ran the Guantanamo Bay Detention Center," *Navy Times*, September 12, 2019.

12. Alene Tchekmedyian and Paul Pringle, "Head of California Air National Guard Removed Amid Allegations of Cover-up and Retaliation," *Los Angeles Times*, April 5, 2019.

13. Tom Vanden Brook, "Army Reprimands Retired Four-Star General in Alleged Groping Incident from 25 Years Ago," *USA Today*, June 13, 2019.

14. Jennifer McDermott, "Navy's Top Admiral Discusses War College Probe," *Newport Daily News*, June 12, 2019; U.S. Department of the Navy, Office of Naval Inspector General, *Report of Investigation: Misconduct by RADM Jeffrey A. Harley, Former President, Naval War College*.

15. Gina Harkins, "Navy Rear Admiral Removed from Job over Inappropriate Relationship," *Task & Purpose*, August 3, 2019, https://taskand purpose.com/news/navy-rear-admiral-removed-from-job-over-inappropriate -relationship/; Geoff Ziezulewicz, "The One-Star, His NAVSEA Employee, Rumors of a Romance and the Scandal That Finally Got Him Fired," *Navy Times*, February 11, 2020.

16. David Roza, "'If He Was on the Battlefield, He Probably Would've Been Shot in the Back' — Inside the Toxic Command of Air Force Lt. Gen. Lee Levy," *Task & Purpose*, December 3, 2019, https://taskandpurpose.com/news/ air-force-general-lee-levy/.

17. Katelyn Ferral, Molly Beck, and Patrick Marley, "Wisconsin National Guard Chief Resigns after Report Shows Sexual Assault Investigations Violated State and Federal Law," *Milwaukee Journal Sentinel*, December 11, 2019.

18. Rachel S. Cohen, "Air Force Delays Court-Martial of Two-Star General Charged with Sex Assault," *Air Force Times*, January 7, 2022; Eileen McClory, "Court-Martial of Air Force General Scheduled for January at Wright-Patterson," *Stars and Stripes*, July 28, 2021; Chad Garland, "Air Force to Court-Martial a General on Sexual Assault Charge for First Time," *Stars and Stripes*, April 22, 2021; Jesus Jimenez and Vimal Patel, "General Convicted of Sex Abuse Forfeits Pay but Avoids Prison," *New York Times*, April 26, 2022.

19. Davis Winkle, "Two-Star General among Group of Soldiers Punished after Sexual Misconduct Probe," *Army Times*, May 25, 2021.

20. Kyle Rempfer, "Army General Loses Star, Retires over Sexual Misconduct Complaint He Disputes," *Army Times*, August 18, 2020.

21. Alex Horton, "Two-Star Marine General Fired after Allegations He Used a Racial Slur Around Subordinates," *Washington Post*, October 20, 2020; Luis Martinez, "Top Marine General Removed after Being Investigated over Use of a Racial Slur," ABCNews.com, October 20, 2020; Patricia McKnight, "Ousted Marine General Defends Using 'N-Word' as 'Teaching Moment,'" *Newsweek*, April 25, 2022.

22. Paul Pringle and Alene Tchekmedyian, "Turmoil Shakes California National Guard with Firing, Suspension of Top Generals," *Los Angeles Times*, May 1, 2021.

23. David Winkie and Meghann Myers, "Top Army Spokesman Suspended after Abysmal Climate Survey," *Army Times*, September 22, 2021; Haley Britzky, "Inside the Office of a One-Star Army General That 100% of Soldiers Rated 'Hostile,'" *Task & Purpose*, October 4, 2021, https://taskandpurpose.com/news/army-amy-johnston-public-affairs-office/; David Winkie, "Top Army Public Affairs Officer Retiring after Command Climate Inquiry," *Army Times*, February 22, 2022; Haley Britzky, "Army General Clear to Retire after Soldiers Reported Hostile Workplace in Climate Survey," *Task & Purpose*, February 22, 2022, https://taskandpurpose.com/news/army-general-amy-johnston-retiring-toxic-leadership/.

24. U.S. Department of Defense, Office of Inspector General, *Semiannual Report to the Congress, October 1, 2021, through March 31, 2022*, p. 46.

25. John Adams, "'A Dissertation on the Canon and the Feudal Law,' No. 3," Papers of John Adams, vol. 1, https://www.masshist.org/publications/adams-papers/index.php/view/ADMS-06-01-02-0052-0006.

26. Kellerman, *Bad Leadership*, 11.

27. Janosi, "Correspondence between Lord Acton and Bishop Creighton," 307–21.

28. "Abuse of Iraqi POWs by GIs Probed," *CBS News*, April 27, 2004, https://www.cbsnews.com/news/abuse-of-iraqi-pows-by-gis-probed/; "Col. Janis Karpinski, the Former Head of Abu Ghraib Admits She Broke the Geneva Conventions but Says the Blame 'Goes All the Way to the Top,'" *Democracy Now!*, October 26, 2005, https://www.democracynow.org/2005/10/26/col_janis_karpinski_the_former_head; Mayer, *Dark Side*, 241; Karpinski, *One Woman's Army*, 5, 207–37.

29. This and the subsequent definitions of the seven types of criminal or unethical leadership are my own.

30. S. C. Miller, *"Benevolent Assimilation,"* 220.

31. Austin Scott, "President Fires Gen. Singlaub as Korea Staff Chief," *Washington Post*, May 22, 1977.

32. Singlaub, *Hazardous Duty*, 404.

33. George C. Wilson, "Gen. Singlaub Agrees to Retire after 2nd Attack on Carter Policy," *Washington Post*, April 29, 1978.

34. Perret, *Old Soldiers Never Die*, 568.

35. Myers, *Eye on the Horizon*, 223.

36. Perry, *Pentagon Wars*, 158.

37. Packer, *Assassins' Gate*, 244–46.

38. Sorely, *Honorable Warrior*, 300, 304.

39. Jeff Schogol, "The Air Force Said This Colonel Was an Incredibly Toxic Leader. Then She Was Promoted to One-Star General," *Task & Purpose*, August 19, 2020, https://taskandpurpose.com/news/air-force-toxic-commander-promoted/.

40. Wortman, *Admiral Hyman Rickover*.

41. Duncan, *Rickover*, 25.

42. Blair, "Man in Tempo 3."

43. Duncan, *Rickover*, 125.

44. Stephen Losey, "Fired Air Force One-Star Made Inappropriate Comments About Women, Failed to Report Suicide Attempts," *Air Force Times*, October 29, 2018.

45. Todd South, "Retired Army Major General Reduced to Second Lieutenant for Sex Crime Conviction," *Army Times*, June 7, 2021.

46. Vistica, *Fall from Glory*, 308.

47. Zimmerman, *Tailspin*, 23, 27.

48. Lisa Rein, "Army Recruiting Scandal Nets New Indictments as Long Probe of Kickbacks Continues," *Washington Post*, October 23, 2015; Rowan Scarborough, "Army Top Brass Skirt Punishment in Fraud Probe as Lower Ranks Take Blame," *Washington Times*, March 13, 2016; U.S. Army Inspector General Agency, *Report of Investigation (Recruiting Assistance Programs)*, http://www.defendourprotectors.com/wp-content/uploads/2018/08/IG_Review2.pdf.

49. Tom Wright, interview with Leonard Francis, *Fat Leonard*, podcast audio, October 5, 2021, https://fatleonardpodcast.com/episodes/.

50. Greg Moran, "Jury Convicts Four Former Navy Officers in 'Fat Leonard' Bribery Trial," *San Diego Union-Tribune*, June 29, 2022.

51. Sam LaGrone, "Paying the Price: The Hidden Cost of the 'Fat Leonard' Investigation," *USNI News*, January 24, 2019; U.S. Department of Justice, U.S. Attorney's Office, Southern District of California, "Former U.S. Navy Captain

Pleads Guilty as the Seventh Fleet Navy Bribery Trial Approaches," press release, February 2, 2022.

52. Perret, *Old Soldiers Never Die*, 558.

ONE   War Crimes: Jacob H. "Hell Roaring Jake" Smith

1. Conti and Oden, *1–2 Kings, 1–2 Chronicles, Ezra, Nehemiah, Esther*, 173.
2. Haque, *Law and Morality at War*, 1.
3. *Journals of the Continental Congress*, June 30, 1775, http://memory.loc.gov/cgi-bin/query/r?ammem/hlaw:@field(DOCID+@lit(jc00249)).
4. Ford, *Writings of George Washington*, 3:122–23.
5. Adjutant General's Office, "Instructions for the Government of Armies of the United States in the Field, General Order No. 100," April 1863, https://avalon.law.yale.edu/19th_century/lieber.asp.
6. Witt, *Lincoln's Code*, 231–49; Tooley, "All the People," 355–79.
7. Adjutant General's Office, "Instructions for the Government of Armies."
8. Adjutant General's Office, "Instructions for the Government of Armies."
9. United Nations, "War Crimes," https://www.un.org/en/genocideprevention/war-crimes.shtml.
10. Huggins, *America's Use of Terror*, 148.
11. Kramer, *Blood of Government*, 87–158.
12. Grunder and Livezey, *Philippines and the United States*, 65.
13. A. MacArthur, *Annual Report of Major General Arthur MacArthur* (1901), vol. 1, 10.
14. A. MacArthur, *Annual Report of Major General Arthur MacArthur* (1901), vol. 1, 19, 23.
15. S. C. Miller, *"Benevolent Assimilation,"* 205.
16. Linn, *Philippine War, 1899–1902*, 312.
17. "Major Wallers Testifies," *New York Times*, April 9, 1902; Schott, *Ordeal of Samar*, 265–66; G. Jones, *Honor in the Dust*, 292–93.
18. Bruno, "Violent End of Insurgency," 43.
19. Feight, "General Jacob H. Smith"; G. Jones, *Honor in the Dust*, 237.
20. "Jacob Hurd Smith," Arlington Cemetery, http://www.arlingtoncemetery.net/jhsmith.htm; "'Hell Roaring' Jake Smith, Butcher of Samar, Wounded at Shiloh," Shiloh National Military Park, https://www.facebook.com/ShilohNMP/posts/hell-roaring-jake-smith-butcher-of-samar-wounded-at-shilohjacob-hurd-smith-born-/649036331853023/.

21. Smith, *Personal Reminiscences*, 3.

22. Smith, *Personal Reminiscences*, 12.

23. Smith, *Personal Reminiscences*, 14.

24. Fritz, "Before the 'Howling Wilderness,'" 187.

25. Fritz, "Before the 'Howling Wilderness,'" 187.

26. Schott, *Ordeal of Samar*, 70; Fritz, "Before the 'Howling Wilderness,'" 188.

27. Fritz, "Before the 'Howling Wilderness,'" 188.

28. Fritz, "Before the 'Howling Wilderness,'" 189–90.

29. G. Jones, *Honor in the Dust*, 237; Fritz, "Before the 'Howling Wilderness,'" 189.

30. J. H. Smith to General, September 16, 1898, *Annual Report of [Nelson A. Miles] the Major-General Commanding the Army to the Secretary of War* (November 5, 1898), 319. Special Collections, University of Washington.

31. J. H. Smith to General, September 16, 1898, and J. H. Smith to Adjutant Second Infantry, July 5, 1898, and Wm. M. Wherry to Adjutant-General, July 5, 1898, *Annual Report of [Nelson A. Miles] the Major-General Commanding the Army to the Secretary of War* (November 5, 1898), 319, 394, 396.

32. Wm. M. Wherry to Adjutant-General, July 5, 1898, and J. H. Smith to Adjutant Second Infantry, July 5, 1898, *Annual Report of [Nelson A. Miles] the Major-General Commanding the Army to the Secretary of War* (November 5, 1898), 395–96.

33. J. H. Smith to Adjutant Second Infantry, July 5, 1898, and J. Ford Kent to Adjutant-General, September 16, 1898, *Annual Report of [Nelson A. Miles] the Major-General Commanding the Army to the Secretary of War* (November 5, 1898), 319, 397.

34. Wm. M. Wherry to the Adjutant-General, August 27, 1898, *Annual Report of [Nelson A. Miles] the Major-General Commanding the Army to the Secretary of War* (November 5, 1898), 399.

35. John S. Mallory to Adjutant-General Second Division, Eighth Army, August 8, 1899, *Annual Report of [Nelson A. Miles] the Lieutenant-General Commanding the Army to the Secretary of War* (1900), 136.

36. Smith to Adjutant-General, August 28, 1899, *Annual Report of the War Department* (1899), vol. 1, part 5, 588–89.

37. J. H. Smith to Acting Assistant Adjutant-General, September 1, 1899, *Annual Report of the War Department* (1900), vol. 1, part 8, 189–94.

38. March, Assistant Adjutant-General to General Wheaton, August 16, 1899, *Annual Report of the War Department* (1900), vol. 1, part 8, 26.

39. A. MacArthur to Adjutant-General, August 17, 1899, *Annual Report of the War Department* (1900), vol. 1, part 8, 27.

40. A. MacArthur to Adjutant-General, August 19, 1899, *Annual Report of the War Department* (1900), vol. 1, part 8, 27.

41. "Continuing the Policy of Conciliation: Otis Still Lenient in Dealing with Natives of Luzon; Smith More Severe," *San Francisco Call*, August 28, 1899.

42. Dyer, *From Shiloh to San Juan*, 256.

43. Silbey, *War of Frontier and Empire*, 116.

44. Battle Summary, November 5, 1899, *Annual Report of [Nelson A. Miles] the Lieutenant-General Commanding the Army to the Secretary of War* (1900), 12.

45. A. MacArthur to Adjutant General, November 5, 1899, *Report of Maj. Gen. E. S. Otis* (May 14, 1900), 48. Special Collections, University of Washington.

46. Smith to Adjutant-General, November 10, 1899, *Annual Report of the War Department* (1900), vol. 1, part 8, 197.

47. A. MacArthur to Adjutant-General, November 5, 1899, *Report of Maj. Gen. E. S. Otis* (May 14, 1900), 52–53.

48. Smith to Adjutant-General Second Division, November 11, 1899, *Annual Report of the War Department* (1900), vol. 1, part 8, 197.

49. A. MacArthur to Adjutant-General, November 5, 1899, *Report of Maj. Gen. E. S. Otis* (May 14, 1900), 48.

50. Linn, *Philippine War, 1899–1902*, 153.

51. Wolf, *Little Brown Brother*, 279.

52. Linn, *Philippine War, 1899–1902*, 159.

53. "Death for Luzon Bandits," *New York Times*, December 13, 1899.

54. "Death for Luzon Bandits."

55. Kramer, *Blood of Government*, 87–159; Huggins, *American Use of Terror*, 145–73.

56. Kramer, *Blood of Government*, 154.

57. Huggins, *American Use of Terror*, 158.

58. Huggins, *American Use of Terror*, 159.

59. Linn, *Philippine War, 1899–1902*, 269.

60. A. MacArthur to Adjutant-General, February, 15, 1900, *Report of Maj. Gen. E. S. Otis* (May 14, 1900), 228.

61. Carpenter, "Uncle Sam's Pirates," 168–69.

62. Brown, *History of the Ninth Infantry, 1799–1909*, 372; Loyd Wheaton to Adjutant-General, *Annual Report of Major General Arthur MacArthur* (1900), vol. 1, Exhibit A, 4; A. MacArthur to Adjutant-General, April 7–8, 1900, *Report of Maj. Gen. E. S. Otis* (May 14, 1900), 234.

63. G. Jones, *Honor in the Dust*, 239.

64. Linn, *Philippine War, 1899–1902*, 271–72.

65. Fritz, "Before the 'Howling Wilderness,'" 189.

66. Report of Brig. Gen. J. H. Smith, April 30, 1901, *Annual Report of Lieutenant-General [Nelson A. Miles] Commanding the Army to the Secretary of War* (1901), part 3, appendix C, 109–17.

67. Fritz, "Before the 'Howling Wilderness,'" 189.

68. A. W. Prautch, "The Religious Situation in the Philippines," *The Christian Advocate*, December 13, 1900.

69. LeRoy, *Americans in the Philippines*, 300–303; A. MacArthur to Adjutant-General, December 29, 1900, U.S. Army, Adjutant General, *Correspondence Relating to the War with Spain*, 1:1239–40.

70. Linn, *Philippine War, 1899–1902*, 210; Kramer, *Blood of Government*, 133–34.

71. Linn, *Philippine War, 1899–1902*, 212–13.

72. Report of Brig. Gen. J. H. Smith, April 30, 1901, *Annual Report of Lieutenant-General [Nelson A. Miles] Commanding the Army to the Secretary of War* (1901), part 3, appendix C, 109–17.

73. Linn, *Philippine War, 1899–1902*, 273.

74. Linn, *Philippines War, 1899–1902*, 212.

75. Silbey, *War of Frontier and Empire*, 156.

76. Linn, *Philippine War, 1899–1902*, 273.

77. Report of Brig. Gen. J. H. Smith, April 30, 1901, *Annual Report of Lieutenant-General [Nelson A. Miles] Commanding the Army to the Secretary of War* (1901), part 3, appendix C, 109–17.

78. Linn, *Philippine War, 1899–1902*, 213.

79. Linn, *Philippine War, 1899–1902*, 212.

80. Huggins, *America's Use of Terror*, 161.

81. Linn, *U.S. Army Counterinsurgency*, 60.

82. G. Jones, *Honor in the Dust*, 218.

83. Report of Brig. Gen. J. H. Smith, April 30, 1901, *Annual Report of Lieutenant-General [Nelson A. Miles] Commanding the Army to the Secretary of War* (1901), part 3, appendix C, 109–17.

84. A. MacArthur, *Annual Report of Major General Arthur MacArthur* (1901), vol. 1, 30.

85. Report of Brig. Gen. J. H. Smith, April 30, 1901, *Annual Report of Lieutenant-General [Nelson A. Miles] Commanding the Army to the Secretary of War* (1901), part 3, appendix C, 109–17.

86. A. MacArthur, *Annual Report of Major General Arthur MacArthur* (1901), vol. 1, 19; Sexton, *Soldiers in the Sun*, 267.

87. Linn, *Philippine War, 1899–1902*, 306.

88. S. C. Miller, *"Benevolent Assimilation,"* 201.

89. S. C. Miller, *"Benevolent Assimilation,"* 206.

90. S. C. Miller, *"Benevolent Assimilation,"* 205.

91. S. C. Miller, *"Benevolent Assimilation,"* 205.

92. Bruno, "Violent End of Insurgency," 37.

93. Bruno, "Violent End of Insurgency," 37.

94. G. Jones, *Honor in the Dust*, 341.

95. G. Jones, *Honor in the Dust*, 240, 243.

96. G. Jones, *Honor in the Dust*, 242.

97. Jacob H. Smith, "Campaign in Samar and Leyte from 10th of October to 31st of December, 1901," *Manila Critic*, February 1, 1901.

98. Schott, *Ordeal of Samar*, 70–72; G. Jones, *Honor in the Dust*, 242, 409. S. C. Miller, *"Benevolent Assimilation,"* 220.

99. Schott, *The Ordeal of Samar*, 75–76; G. Jones, *Honor in the Dust*, 243; S. C. Miller, *"Benevolent Assimilation,"* 220. The marines confiscated three church bells fearing they would be melted down to make weapons. For a century after the war, the bells were kept as trophies and as memorials to the slain American soldiers. The bells remained in U.S. possession until late 2018 when Defense Secretary James N. Mattis, a retired Marine Corps general, authorized the bells' return to the citizens of Balangiga. See Kent Miller and Colin Woodward, "Mattis Visits F. E. Warren AFB to Help Send Historic Bells, an Army War Trophy, Back to the Philippines," *Air Force Times*, November 14, 2018.

100. S. C. Miller, *"Benevolent Assimilation,"* 220.

101. S. C. Miller, *"Benevolent Assimilation,"* 220; G. Jones, *Honor in the Dust*, 243–46.

102. Brian McAllister Linn, "'We Will Go Heavily Armed': The Marines' Small War on Samar, 1901–1902," in Evans, *U.S. Marines and Irregular Warfare, 1898–2007*, 41–53; S. C. Miller, *"Benevolent Assimilation,"* 212.

103. Feight, "General Jacob H. Smith," 4.

104. G. Jones, *Honor in the Dust*, 251.

105. G. Jones, *Honor in the Dust*, 251–52.

106. G. Jones, *Honor in the Dust*, 254.

107. Linn, *Philippine War, 1899–1902*, 315.

108. Linn, *Philippine War, 1899–1902*, 315.

109. Linn, *Philippine War, 1899–1902*, 320.

110. Linn, *Philippine War, 1899–1902*, 320.

111. S. C. Miller, *"Benevolent Assimilation,"* 222.

112. Stanley Karnow, "Two Nations," https://www.pbs.org/wgbh/american experience/features/bataan-two-nations/.

113. Kramer, *Blood of Government*, 145; G. Jones, *Honor in the Dust*, 253.

114. G. Jones, *Honor in the Dust*, 253.

115. Linn, *Philippine War, 1899–1902*, 313–14.

116. Bruno, "Violent End of Insurgency," 41.

117. Schott, *Ordeal of Samar*, 285–89.

118. G. Jones, *Honor in the Dust*, 254–66.

119. G. Jones, *Honor in the Dust*, 266.

120. G. Jones, *Honor in the Dust*, 266.

121. S. C. Miller, *"Benevolent Assimilation,"* 227.

122. Linn, *Philippine War, 1899–1902*, 318–19.

123. Mettraux, "US Courts-Martial," 137.

124. G. Jones, *Honor in the Dust*, 290.

125. Schott, *Ordeal of Samar*, 215.

126. Schott, *Ordeal of Samar*, 220–21.

127. Schott, *Ordeal of Samar*, 245.

128. Schott, *Ordeal of Samar*, 258–59.

129. Schott, *Ordeal of Samar*, 258–62; Sexton, *Soldiers in the Sun*, 258.

130. Schott, *Ordeal of Samar*, 259–62.

131. Schott, *Ordeal of Samar*, 265–66; G. Jones, *Honor in the Dust*, 293.

132. Schott, *Ordeal of Samar*, 274–75.

133. Schott, *Ordeal of Samar*, 272.

134. G. Jones, *Honor in the Dust*, 295.

135. Bruno, "Violent End of Insurgency," 44.

136. Corbin (by direction of the Secretary of War) to Chaffee, April 16, 1902, U.S. Army, Adjutant General, *Correspondence Relating to the War with Spain*, 2:1327–28; G. Jones, *Honor in the Dust*, 306–9.

137. Linn, "'We Will Go Heavily Armed,'" 41–53.

138. Corbin (by direction of the Secretary of War) to Chaffee, April 16, 1902, U.S. Army, Adjutant General, *Correspondence Relating to the War with Spain*, 2:1327–28; G. Jones, *Honor in the Dust*, 309; S. C. Miller, *"Benevolent Assimilation,"* 236.

139. Friedman, *Law of War*, 800; Mettraux, "US Courts-Martial," 139.

140. Friedman, *Law of War*, 801; Chaffee to Adjutant-General, May 5, 1902, U.S. Army, Adjutant General, *Correspondence Relating to the War with Spain*, 2:1336.

141. "Gen. Smith's Orders," *New York Times*, April 27, 1902.

142. G. Jones, *Honor in the Dust*, 314–15.

143. Friedman, *Law of War*, 812; Mettraux, "US Courts-Martial," 139–40.

144. Friedman, *Law of War*, 813; "President Retires Gen. Jacob H. Smith," *New York Times*, July 17, 1902.

145. Bruno, "Violent End of Insurgency," 43; G. Jones, *Honor in the Dust*, 333.

146. "Gen. J. H. Smith Severely Criticized," *New York Times*, April 29, 1902.

147. "Smith Likened to King Herod," *Chicago Daily Tribune*, April 29, 1902.

148. "Philippine Question Up in the Senate," *New York Times*, May 7, 1902.

149. "Smith's Cruel Order," *Washington Post*, April 30, 1902.

150. Friedman, *Law of War*, 810–13.

151. Bruno, "Violent End of Insurgency," 43.

152. Bruno, "Violent End of Insurgency," 43.

153. Bruno, "Violent End of Insurgency," 43.

154. Friedman, *Law of War*, 799–800; "President Retires Gen. Jacob H. Smith," *New York Times*, July 17, 1902.

155. Fritz, "Before the 'Howling Wilderness,'" 189.

156. "Gen. Smith Says He Was Not Severe," *New York Times*, August 4, 1902.

157. "Gen. Smith Says He Was Not Severe."

158. Feight, "General Jacob H. Smith," 6–7.

159. Feight, "General Jacob H. Smith," 6.

160. "Smith Exalted by Fellow-Townsmen. Not a Picture of Roosevelt Was Seen at Banquet Given Soldier," *Akron Times-Democrat*, August 21, 1902.

161. "Gen. Jacob H. Smith Honored," *New York Times*, August 20, 1902.

162. "Smith Exalted by Fellow-Townsmen."

163. "Gen. Jacob H. Smith," *New York Times*, August 21, 1902.

164. "Gen. Jacob H. Smith Dead," *New York Times*, March 3, 1918.

165. S. C. Miller, *"Benevolent Assimilation,"* 206; Linn, *Philippine War, 1899–1902*, 313.

166. G. Jones, *Honor in the Dust*, 341.

167. S. C. Miller, *"Benevolent Assimilation,"* 205.

168. Linn, *Philippine War, 1899–1902*, 313.

169. H. Jones, *My Lai*, 245–49.

170. Fred P. Graham, "General Cleared of MyLai Charges, *New York Times*, January 30, 1971.

171. H. Jones, *My Lai*, 267–68; Peers, *My Lai Inquiry*, 221.

172. Turse, *Kill Anything That Moves*, 200.

173. Turse, *Kill Anything That Moves*, 200–204.

174. William Beecher, "General, Ex-Aide Accused of Murdering Vietnamese," *New York Times*, June 3, 1971.

175. Turse, *Kill Anything That Moves*, 204.

176. "Abuse of Iraqi POWs by GIs Probed," *CBS News*, April 27, 2004, https://www.cbsnews.com/news/abuse-of-iraqi-pows-by-gis-probed/.

177. "Col. Janis Karpinski, the Former Head of Abu Ghraib Admits She Broke the Geneva Conventions but Says the Blame 'Goes All the Way to the Top,'" *Democracy Now!*, October 26, 2005, https://www.democracynow.org/2005/10/26/col_janis_karpinski_the_former_head.

178. "Blame 'Goes All the Way to The Top.'"

179. Mayer, *Dark Side*, 241.

180. Karpinski, *One Woman's Army*, 198; Mayer, *Dark Side*, 241.

181. Karpinski, *One Woman's Army*, 197–98.

182. Mayer, *Dark Side*, 241.

183. Peters, "Adjudication Deferred," 944.

184. Peters, "Adjudication Deferred," 927.

TWO Insubordination: Douglas MacArthur

1. *The Articles of War*, 1920, articles 62 and 90; *Uniform Code of Military Justice*, 2018, articles 88 and 117.

2. U.S. Constitution, art. II, § 2.

3. Chaffin, *Pathfinder*, 465; Inskeep, *Imperfect Union*, 172–81.

4. Kearns Goodwin, *Team of Rivals*, 395.

5. McPherson, *Tried by War*, 46.

6. Kearns Goodwin, *Team of Rivals*, 378–79; emphasis original.

7. Kearns Goodwin, *Team of Rivals*, 379; Johnson, *Winfield Scott*, 232–33; J. S. D. Eisenhower, *Agent of Destiny*, 395–96.

8. Johnson, *Winfield Scott*, 17, 98–102; J. S. D. Eisenhower, *Agent of Destiny*, 19, 122–23; Peskin, *Winfield Scott*, 78–80.

9. McPherson, *Tried by War*, 48; Kearns Goodwin, *Team of Rivals*, 383.

10. Kearns Goodwin, *Team of Rivals*, 447–48.

11. McPherson, *Tried by War*, 121; Kearns Goodwin, *Team of Rivals*, 476–78.

12. Wildenberg, *Billy Mitchell's War*, 121.

13. Wildenberg, *Billy Mitchell's War*, 126.

14. Wildenberg, *Billy Mitchell's War*, 137–38.

15. Wildenberg, *Billy Mitchell's War*, 137.

16. Gallery, "If This Be Treason," 15–16, 45.

17. Gilliland and Shenk, *Admiral Dan Gallery*, 205.

18. "Internal Scandals Led to Firing of Air National Guard Commander," *Mohave Valley Daily News*, September 16, 2012.

19. Dennis Wagner, "State Air National Guard Leaders Dismissed," *Arizona Republic*, August 25, 2012.

20. The Soviet Union would surely have vetoed the resolution as a member of the U.N. Security Council, but at the time, it was boycotting the council on the grounds that Communist China did not have a seat on that body.

21. James Reston, "As a U.N. General, M'Arthur Faces New Tasks: Besides Running a War, He Must Please Washington, Other Capitals," *New York Times*, July 9, 1950.

22. Moten, *Presidents and Their Generals*, 236.

23. Truman, *Memoirs*, 2:447.

24. *Articles of War*, articles 62, 64, 90, and 95.

25. Perret, *Old Soldiers Never Die*, 43.

26. Moten, *Presidents and Their Generals*, 229.

27. Herman, *Douglas MacArthur*, 53.

28. Kenney, *MacArthur I Know*, 229–30.

29. Herman, *Douglas MacArthur*, 88.

30. D. MacArthur, *Reminiscences*, 45.

31. D. MacArthur, *Reminiscences*, 45.

32. D. MacArthur, *Reminiscences*, 46.

33. Perret, *Old Soldiers Never Die*, 84.

34. Herman, *Douglas MacArthur*, 108–12.

35. Herman, *Douglas MacArthur*, 117–18.

36. Herman, *Douglas MacArthur*, 130.

37. Herman, *Douglas MacArthur*, 151.

38. Herman, *Douglas MacArthur*, 151.

39. D. MacArthur, *Reminiscences*, 85.

40. Hoover, *Memoirs*, 2:339.

41. MacArthur, *Reminiscences*, 89.

42. MacArthur, *Reminiscences*, 89.

43. Schaller, *Douglas MacArthur*, 14.

44. Herman, *Douglas MacArthur*, 219.

45. James, *Years of MacArthur*, 1:399.

46. As chief of staff, MacArthur reformed the Army's medals policy and made certain that he was the first soldier awarded the reconstituted Silver

Star and Purple Heart. Each was engraved "No. 1." See, Perret, *Old Soldiers Never Die*, 154.

47. Miles, *Fallen Leaves*, 309.

48. D. MacArthur, *Reminiscences*, 95.

49. D'Este, *Eisenhower*, 222.

50. James, *Years of MacArthur*, 1:404.

51. James, *Years of MacArthur*, 1:404.

52. James, *Years of MacArthur*, 1:404.

53. Hoover, *Memoirs*, 3:226–27; Herman, *Douglas MacArthur*, 223–25.

54. Ambrose, *Eisenhower*, 98.

55. Schaller, *Douglas MacArthur*, 16.

56. MacArthur's distasteful behavior extended to his personal life. While still in the Philippines in 1929, he kindled a romantic relationship with a sixteen-year-old Filipino actress and dancer, Isabel Rosario Cooper. He was thirty-four years her senior and he signed his love letters to her as "Daddy." When MacArthur became chief of staff, he quietly shipped his adolescent mistress to Washington, DC, and sequestered her in an apartment. The relationship lasted five years, but at its bitter and complicated conclusion in 1934, MacArthur paid her $15,000 (equivalent to $328,000 in 2022) to return his racy letters, which if made public would unleash a humiliating and career-threatening sex scandal. See Herman, *Douglas MacArthur*, 237–42; Perret, *Old Soldiers Never Die*, 147–48, 167–70.

57. D. MacArthur, *Reminiscences*, 101.

58. D. MacArthur, *Reminiscences*, 101.

59. Perret, *Old Soldiers Never Die*, 202.

60. D'Este, *Eisenhower*, 227.

61. D'Este, *Eisenhower*, 226; Herman, *Douglas MacArthur*, 279.

62. Herman, *Douglas MacArthur*, 285.

63. White, *In Search of History*, 18.

64. Roll, *George Marshall*, 182.

65. John J. Abbatiello, "Lewis Brereton," in Jennings and Steele, *Worst Military Leaders in History*, 151–65; Limneos, "Death from Within," 6–29; Bartsch, *December 8, 1941*.

66. Herman, *Douglas MacArthur*, 382–84. For this and all monetary inflation comparisons, please refer to https://www.minneapolisfed.org/about-us/monetary-policy/inflation-calculator.

67. Vader, *New Guinea*, 90.

68. Schaller, *Douglas MacArthur*, 79.

69. McManus, "Man Who Would Be President," 34–43.

70. Schaller, *Douglas MacArthur*, 79–81.

71. Manchester, *American Caesar*, 418; Schaller, *Douglas MacArthur*, 83.

72. Manchester, *American Caesar*, 363.

73. McManus, "Man Who Would Be President," 42.

74. Persico, *Roosevelt's Centurions*, 390–91.

75. D. MacArthur, *Reminiscences*, 197.

76. Perry, *Most Dangerous Man in America*, 270.

77. D. MacArthur, *Reminiscences*, 197–98.

78. Perret, *Old Soldiers Never Die*, 406.

79. Manchester, *American Caesar*, 369.

80. D. MacArthur, *Reminiscences*, 248.

81. Perret, *Old Soldiers Never Die*, 501.

82. Manchester, *American Caesar*, 153.

83. Perry, *Most Dangerous Man in America*, 328.

84. Faubion Bowers, "The Late General MacArthur, Warts and All," in Leary, *MacArthur and the American Century*, 254.

85. Perret, *Old Soldiers Never Die*, 472.

86. Perret, *Old Soldiers Never Die*, 529.

87. "Would Meet 'Duty': General Says He Would Be 'Recreant' to Balk Call of the People," *New York Times*, March 9, 1948.

88. Allison, *Ambassador from the Prairie*, 129.

89. Brands, *General vs. the President*, 107.

90. Herman, *Douglas MacArthur*, 720.

91. Moten, *Presidents and Their Generals*, 235–36.

92. "Chiang Is Jubilant on M'Arthur Pact; M'Arthur Conferring with Chinese Nationalists," *New York Times*, August 2, 1950; Brands, *General vs. the President*, 121.

93. James, *Years of MacArthur*, 454.

94. Manchester, *American Caesar*, 566; Brands, *General vs. the President*, 124.

95. James, *Years of MacArthur*, 457–58.

96. Herman, *Douglas MacArthur*, 726.

97. Bradley, *General's Life*, 551.

98. Acheson, *Present at the Creation*, 423–24.

99. Manchester, *American Caesar*, 570.

100. Walters, *Silent Missions*, 197.

101. Harry S. Truman to Douglas MacArthur, September 29, 1950, Public Papers of the Presidents, https://www.presidency.ucsb.edu/documents/message -congratulating-general-macarthur-the-liberation-seoul.

102. Herman, *Douglas MacArthur*, 747.

103. Bradley, *General's Life*, 556–57.

104. James, *Years of MacArthur*, 3:485.

105. Pearlman, *Truman and MacArthur*, 104.

106. Acting Secretary of State to the United States Mission at the United Nations, September 26, 1950, https://history.state.gov/historicaldocuments /frus1950v07/d543.

107. Acheson, *Present at the Creation*, 456.

108. Truman to Nellie Noland, October 13, 1950, in Ferrell, *Off the Record*, 195–96.

109. "Substance of Statements Made at Wake Island Conference, Compiled by General of the Army Omar Bradly," October 15, 1950, Truman Library, https:// www.trumanlibrary.gov/library/oral-histories/andvimage1; Brands, *General vs. the President*, 181–82.

110. Bradley, *General's Life*, 576–78.

111. Herman, *Douglas MacArthur*, 765.

112. Herman, *Douglas MacArthur*, 765.

113. Herman, *Douglas MacArthur*, 768–69.

114. Manchester, *American Caesar*, 602–3; Bradley, *General's Life*, 585.

115. Bradley, *General's Life*, 587.

116. Brands, *General vs. the President*, 212.

117. Manchester, *American Caesar*, 614; emphasis original.

118. Ridgway, *Korean War*, 62.

119. Frank, *Trials of Harry S. Truman*, 288.

120. Brands, *General vs. the President*, 266.

121. Acheson, *Present at the Creation*, 515; Bradley, *General's Life*, 620; emphasis original.

122. Collins, *War in Peacetime*, 255; Bradley, *General's Life*, 623–27.

123. Manchester, *American Caesar*, 634.

124. Acheson, *Present at the Creation*, 518–19.

125. Acheson, *Present at the Creation*, 518–19; Truman, *Memoirs*, 2:442.

126. Manchester, *American Caesar*, 638–39.

127. Ferrell, *Off the Record*, 210–11.

128. Bradley, *General's Life*, 633; Roll, *George Marshall*, 582.

129. Moten, *Presidents and Their Generals*, 254.

130. Perret, *Old Soldiers Never Die*, 568.

131. Truman, *Memoirs*, 2:449.

132. MacArthur address to joint session of Congress, April 19, 1951, transcript in *New York Times*, April 20, 1951.

133. James, *Years of MacArthur*, 3:630.

134. James, *Years of MacArthur*, 3:630–31; emphasis original.

135. Brands, *General vs. the President*, 353–55.

136. Brands, *General vs. the President*, 355.

137. Brands, *General vs. the President*, 362.

138. Manchester, *American Caesar*, 684; James, *Years of MacArthur*, 3:646.

139. James, *Years of MacArthur*, 3:644.

140. Pearlman, *Truman and MacArthur*, 2.

141. Perret, *Old Soldiers Never Die*, 558.

142. Truman, *Memoirs*, 2:444.

143. D. D. Eisenhower, *At Ease*, 213.

144. Pearlman, *Truman and MacArthur*, 246.

145. Eric Schmitt, "General to Be Disciplined for Disparaging President," *New York Times*, June 16, 1993; Art Pine, "General to Retire over Clinton Flap," *Los Angeles Times*, June 19, 1993.

146. Pine, "General to Retire over Clinton Flap."

147. Michael R. Gordon, "General Ousted for Derisive Remarks about President," *New York Times*, June 19, 1993.

148. Tom Bowman, "3-Star General Says Army Is Too Small to Do Its Job," *Baltimore Sun*, January 20, 2004.

149. Tom Bowman, "Unceremonious End to Army Career," *Baltimore Sun*, May 29, 2005; Margolick, "Night of the Generals," 46–80.

150. Thom Shanker, "Mideast Commander Retires after Irking Bosses," *New York Times*, March 12, 2008.

151. Barnett, "Man between War and Peace," 144–53.

152. Ulrich, "General Stanley McChrystal Affair," 89.

153. Bacevich, *Breach of Trust*, 121.

154. Hastings, "Runaway General."

155. Peter Spiegel, "McChrystal on Defensive for Remarks," *Wall Street Journal*, June 21, 2010.

156. R. M. Gates, *Duty*, 487.

157. Obama, *Promised Land*, 578–79.

158. Obama, *Promised Land*, 578.

159. Rod Nordland, "General Fired over Karzai Remarks," *New York Times*, November 5, 2011; Tim Mak, "General Ousted for POLITICO Quotes," Politico.com, November 4, 2011; Tim Mak, "General: Afghan Leaders out of Touch," Politico.com, November 3, 2011.

160. Barton Gellman, "What Happened to Michael Flynn?," *The Atlantic*, July 8, 2022; Robert Draper, "Michael Flynn Is Still at War," *New York Times Magazine*, February 4, 2022; Glenn Thrush and Michael Crowley, "Flynn Decision Imperils 'Rule of Law' Obama Says in Call with Backers," *New York Times*, May 10, 2020; Clapper, *Facts and Fears*, 331; Greg Miller and Adam Goldman, "Head of Pentagon Intelligence Agency Forced Out, Officials Say," *Washington Post*, April 30, 2014.

161. Sharon LaFraniere and Julian E. Barnes, "For Flynn, Dropped Charges Are the Latest in a Life of Reversals," *New York Times*, May 9, 2020.

162. Simon Montlake, "Disgraced General to Far-Right Hero: Michael Flynn Rides the Next Wave," *Christian Science Monitor*, April 28, 2022; Murray Waas, "Michael Flynn Ignored Official Warnings About Receiving Foreign Payments," *The Guardian*, April 8, 2021; Marty Lederman, "Understanding the Michael Flynn Case," www.JustSecurity.org, May 29, 2020, https://www.justsecurity.org/70431/understanding-the-michael-flynn-case-separating-the-wheat-from-the-chaff-and-the-proper-from-the-improper/.

163. Dan Lamothe and Craig Whitlock, "Michael Flynn Cited for Unauthorized Foreign Payments," *Washington Post*, July 8, 2022.

THREE Moral Cowardice: Harold K. "Johnny" Johnson

1. W. I. Miller, *Mystery of Courage*, 254–55; emphasis original.
2. Felice, *How to Save My Honor*, 183.
3. For more on the Powell Doctrine, see Walter LaFeber, "The Rise and Fall of Colin Powell and the Powell Doctrine," *Political Science Quarterly* 124, no. 1 (Spring 2009): 71–93.
4. Recchia, *Reassuring the Reluctant Warriors*, 189.
5. Myers, *Eyes on the Horizon*, 223.
6. Perry, *Pentagon's Wars*, 147.
7. Perry, *Pentagon's Wars*, 158.
8. Perry, *Pentagon's Wars*, 145.
9. Recchia, *Reassuring the Reluctant Warriors*, 213.
10. Dubik, "Taking a 'Pro' Position," 18.

11. Stoler and Holt, *Papers of George Catlett Marshall*, 7:509–10.

12. Roll, *George Marshall*, 203.

13. McNamara, *In Retrospect*, 176.

14. Sorley, *Honorable Warrior*, 174.

15. Sorley, *Honorable Warrior*, 245–46.

16. *[Hearing on] Air War against North Vietnam before the Senate Prepared-ness Investigating Subcommittee of the Committee on Armed Services*, 90th Cong. 405 (August 28, 1967) (testimony of Gen. Harold K. Johnson, Chief of Staff, United States Army).

17. Sorley, *Honorable Warrior*, 268–69.

18. Sorley, *Honorable Warrior*, 304.

19. Sorley, *Honorable Warrior*, 7.

20. Sorley, *Honorable Warrior*, 10–11.

21. Sorley, *Honorable Warrior*, 11.

22. Sorley, *Honorable Warrior*, 15.

23. Sorley, *Honorable Warrior*, 21–22.

24. Sorley, *Honorable Warrior*, 35.

25. Sorley, *Honorable Warrior*, 55.

26. Sorley, *Honorable Warrior*, 67.

27. Sorley, *Honorable Warrior*, 60–61.

28. Sorley, *Honorable Warrior*, 80.

29. Sorley, *Honorable Warrior*, 79.

30. Sorley, *Honorable Warrior*, 96.

31. Sorley, *Honorable Warrior*, 101.

32. Sorley, *Honorable Warrior*, 98.

33. Sorley, *Honorable Warrior*, 102.

34. Sorley, *Honorable Warrior*, 110.

35. Sorley, *Honorable Warrior*, 114; emphasis original.

36. Sorley, *Honorable Warrior*, 126.

37. Sorley, *Honorable Warrior*, 133.

38. Sorley, *Honorable Warrior*, 141.

39. Sorley, *Honorable Warrior*, 141.

40. Singlaub, *Hazardous Duty*, 265.

41. Sorley, *Honorable Warrior*, 145.

42. Logevall, *Choosing War*, 52.

43. Herring, *From Colony to Superpower*, 729.

44. Sorley, *Honorable Warrior*, 149.

45. Logevall, *Choosing War*, 91.

46. McMaster, *Dereliction of Duty*, 64–65.
47. Sorley, *Honorable Warrior*, 189.
48. Sorley, *Honorable Warrior*, 189.
49. Sorley, *Honorable Warrior*, 152.
50. Logevall, *Choosing War*, 145.
51. Logevall, *Choosing War*, 145.
52. McMaster, *Dereliction of Duty*, 93.
53. McMaster, *Dereliction of Duty*, 93; emphasis original.
54. McMaster, *Dereliction of Duty*, 94.
55. McMaster, *Dereliction of Duty*, 109–10.
56. Sorley, *Honorable Warrior*, 175.
57. Sorley, *Honorable Warrior*, 175–76.
58. Sorley, *Honorable Warrior*, 246.
59. Sorley, *Honorable Warrior*, 181.
60. Sorley, *Honorable Warrior*, 295.
61. Sorley, *Honorable Warrior*, 181.
62. Sorley, *Honorable Warrior*, 182.
63. Sorley, *Honorable Warrior*, 182.
64. Palmer, *25-Year War*, 27.
65. McMaster, *Dereliction of Duty*, 132–33.
66. McMaster, *Dereliction of Duty*, 121–33.
67. Matthews, "To Defeat a Maverick," 671.
68. McMaster, *Dereliction of Duty*, 149.
69. McMaster, *Dereliction of Duty*, 153.
70. Matthews, "To Defeat a Maverick," 671.
71. Matthews, "To Defeat a Maverick," 671.
72. McMaster, *Dereliction of Duty*, 168.
73. Perry, *Four Stars*, 148.
74. Perry, *Four Stars*, 146.
75. Fry, *Debating Vietnam*, 90; Perry, *Four Stars*, 146.
76. Fry, *Debating Vietnam*, 87.
77. Gelb, *Irony of Vietnam*, 121.
78. Logevall, *Choosing War*, 369.
79. Sorley, *Honorable Warrior*, 335n1.
80. Halberstam, *Best and the Brightest*, 564.
81. Perry, *Four Stars*, 148.
82. McMaster, *Dereliction of Duty*, 245.
83. Sorley, *Honorable Warrior*, 197.

84. Sorley, *Honorable Warrior*, 195.

85. Sorley, *Honorable Warrior*, 198.

86. Sorley, *Honorable Warrior*, 196.

87. Sorley, *Honorable Warrior*, 196.

88. McMaster, *Dereliction of Duty*, 246; Palmer, *25-Year War*, 38–40.

89. Sorley, *Honorable Warrior*, 198.

90. Sorley, *Honorable Warrior*, 198.

91. Logevall, *Choosing War*, 370.

92. McNamara, *In Retrospect*, 177.

93. VanDeMark, *Into the Quagmire*, 111.

94. VanDeMark, *Into the Quagmire*, 100.

95. VanDeMark, *Into the Quagmire*, 107.

96. Karnow, *Vietnam*, 418.

97. E. Thomas, *Very Best Men*, 307.

98. Robarge, *John McCone*, 410.

99. Robarge, *John McCone*, 410.

100. "Letter from the Director of Central Intelligence McCone to President Johnson," in *Foreign Relations of the United States, 1964–1968*, vol. 2, *Vietnam, January–June 1965*, 234.

101. McMaster, *Dereliction of Duty*, 265.

102. McMaster, *Dereliction of Duty*, 271.

103. Perry, *Four Stars*, 152.

104. Perry, *Four Stars*, 152.

105. McMaster, *Dereliction of Duty*, 304.

106. Sorley, *Honorable Warrior*, 209.

107. McMaster, *Dereliction of Duty*, 304.

108. McMaster, *Dereliction of Duty*, 310–11.

109. McMaster, *Dereliction of Duty*, 311.

110. Ellsberg, *Secrets*, 91.

111. Perry, *Four Stars*, 153.

112. Perry, *Four Stars*, 153.

113. McMaster, *Dereliction of Duty*, 314.

114. McMaster, *Dereliction of Duty*, 314.

115. Perry, *Four Stars*, 153.

116. Perry, *Four Stars*, 153.

117. Perry, *Four Stars*, 153; Singlaub, *Hazardous Duty*, 277.

118. Sorley, *Honorable Warrior*, 212.

119. Sorley, *Westmoreland*, 212; emphasis original.

120. Sorley, *Westmoreland*, 269.

121. Sorley, *Honorable Warrior*, 270.

122. McMaster, *Dereliction of Duty*, 330.

123. Singlaub, *Hazardous Duty*, 279; McMaster, *Dereliction of Duty*, 330.

124. Ellsberg, *Secrets*, 96.

125. Ellsberg, *Secrets*, 96; McMaster, *Dereliction of Duty*, 319.

126. Ellsberg, *Secrets*, 94–95.

127. Sorley, "To Change a War," 107.

128. Sorley, *Honorable Warrior*, 270.

129. Sorley, "To Change a War," 107. Other versions of this include: "I should have gone to see the president. I should have taken off my stars. I should have resigned. It was the worst, the most immoral decision I've ever made." See Perry, *Four Stars*, 156. General Johnson told Harry Summers that he had rationalized the moment, convincing himself he could do more by staying with the Army's system than by resigning. "And now, I will go to my death with that lapse in moral courage." See Summers in Mathews and Brown, *Parameters of Military Ethics*, xvii; and Singlaub, *Hazardous Duty*, 283. Singlaub tells of meeting Johnson circa 1975, "I told the General frankly I had been disappointed that he did not object more strenuously to the execution of that terribly flawed Buildup Plan. The General smiled thinly and nodded, allowing how he had mistakenly hoped to accomplish more by staying within the system than by acting on his principles and resigning." Singlaub, *Hazardous Duty*, 542n37.

130. Moore and Galloway, *We Were Soldiers Once . . . and Young*, 28.

131. Moore and Galloway, *We Were Soldiers Once . . . and Young*, 17.

132. Sorley, *Honorable Warrior*, 222.

133. Ricks, *Generals*, 257; Cooper, "Longest War," 77–80.

134. Cooper, "Longest War," 77–80.

135. Ricks, *Generals*, 258.

136. Perry, *Four Stars*, 156.

137. Perry, *Four Stars*, 157.

138. Sorley, *Honorable Warrior*, 228, 231.

139. Sorley, *Honorable Warrior*, 227.

140. Sorley, *Honorable Warrior*, 228.

141. Sorley, *Honorable Warrior*, 232.

142. Sorley, *Honorable Warrior*, 229; emphasis added.

143. Sorley, "To Change a War," 97.

144. Birtle, "PROVN, Westmoreland, and the Historians," 1218.

145. Birtle, "PROVN, Westmoreland, and the Historians," 1218.

146. Birtle, "PROVN, Westmoreland, and the Historians," 1244; emphasis original.

147. Davidson, *Vietnam at War*, 410.

148. Sorley, *Honorable Warrior*, 255.

149. Perry, *Four Stars*, 158.

150. Gelb, *Irony of Vietnam*, 271.

151. Sorley, *Honorable Warrior*, 224.

152. Sorley, *Honorable Warrior*, 259.

153. Sorley, *Honorable Warrior*, 259.

154. Sorley, *Honorable Warrior*, 263.

155. Sorley, *Honorable Warrior*, 264.

156. Sorley, *Honorable Warrior*, 268.

157. Fry, *Debating Vietnam*, 101.

158. McNamara, *In Retrospect*, 284; Fry, *Debating Vietnam*, 103.

159. McNamara, *In Retrospect*, 284–85.

160. Fry, *Debating Vietnam*, 108.

161. Fry, *Debating Vietnam*, 105–6.

162. Sorley, *Honorable Warrior*, 285.

163. Sorley, *Honorable Warrior*, 285; McNamara, *In Retrospect*, 284.

164. McNamara, *In Retrospect*, 286.

165. McNamara, *In Retrospect*, 290.

166. Sorley, *Honorable Warrior*, 284.

167. McNamara, *In Retrospect*, 290.

168. McNamara, *In Retrospect*, 290.

169. Fry, *Debating Vietnam*, 129. In his memoir, McNamara admits that "strong differences of judgment did divide us. And the frictions they caused created stress, which took its toll." See McNamara, *In Retrospect*, 291.

170. Perry, *Four Stars*, 164.

171. Perry, *Four Stars*, 164; Sorley, *Honorable Warrior*, 286.

172. Perry, *Four Stars*, 165.

173. Perry, *Four Stars*, 165.

174. Perry, *Four Stars*, 165.

175. Perry, *Four Stars*, 165–66; Sorley, *Honorable Warrior*, 286–87.

176. Sorley, *Honorable Warrior*, 286.

177. Sorley, *Honorable Warrior*, 286.

178. Perry, *Four Stars*, 165.

179. *[Hearing on] Air War against North Vietnam*, 90th Cong. 411 (testimony of Gen. Harold K. Johnson, Chief of Staff, United States Army).

180. *[Hearing on] Air War against North Vietnam*, 90th Cong. 405 (testimony of Gen. Harold K. Johnson, Chief of Staff, United States Army).

181. *[Hearing on] Air War against North Vietnam*, 90th Cong. 406 (testimony of Gen. Harold K. Johnson, Chief of Staff, United States Army).

182. *[Hearing on] Air War against North Vietnam*, 90th Cong. 389 (testimony of Gen. Harold K. Johnson, Chief of Staff, United States Army).

183. *[Hearing on] Air War against North Vietnam*, 90th Cong. 397, 407 (testimony of Gen. Harold K. Johnson, Chief of Staff, United States Army).

184. *[Hearing on] Air War against North Vietnam*, 90th Cong. 385 (testimony of Gen. Harold K. Johnson, Chief of Staff, United States Army).

185. *[Hearing on] Air War against North Vietnam*, 90th Cong. 386 (testimony of Gen. Harold K. Johnson, Chief of Staff, United States Army).

186. *[Hearing on] Air War against North Vietnam*, 90th Cong. 390 (testimony of Gen. Harold K. Johnson, Chief of Staff, United States Army).

187. *[Hearing on] Air War against North Vietnam*, 90th Cong. 402 (testimony of Gen. Harold K. Johnson, Chief of Staff, United States Army).

188. *[Hearing on] Air War against North Vietnam*, 90th Cong. 413 (testimony of Gen. Harold K. Johnson, Chief of Staff, United States Army).

189. *[Hearing on] Air War against North Vietnam*, 90th Cong. 394 (testimony of Gen. Harold K. Johnson, Chief of Staff, United States Army).

190. *[Hearing on] Air War against North Vietnam*, 90th Cong. 421, 433 (testimony of Gen. Harold K. Johnson, Chief of Staff, United States Army).

191. McNamara, *In Retrospect*, 284.

192. McNamara, *In Retrospect*, 286.

193. "Generals Out of Control," *New York Times*, September 1, 1967; Fry, *Debating Vietnam*, 136.

194. Herring, *America's Longest War*, 179.

195. Sorley, *Honorable Warrior*, 298.

196. Sorley, *Honorable Warrior*, 301.

197. Robarge, *John McCone*, 410.

198. Felice, *How Do I Save My Honor?*, 183.

199. Sorley, "To Change a War," 107.

200. Perry, *Four Stars*, 156.

201. Greg Jaffe, "The Two-Star Rebel," *Wall Street Journal*, May 13, 2006; Margolick, "Night of the Generals," 46–80.

202. Margolick, "Night of the Generals."

203. Jaffe, "Two-Star Rebel;" Thom Shanker, "Army Career Behind Him, General Speaks Out on Iraq," *New York Times*, May 13, 2007.

204. Jaffe, "Two-Star Rebel;" Margolick, "Night of the Generals."

205. Jaffe, "Two-Star Rebel."

206. *Hearing on the Planning and Conduct of the War in Iraq before the U.S. Senate Democratic Policy Committee* (September 25, 2006), https://www.dpc .senate.gov/hearings/hearing38/transcript.pdf.

FOUR   Toxic Leadership: Hyman G. Rickover

1. Reed, *Tarnished*, 26.

2. Aspin, "Joint Ethics Regulation (JER)," DoD Directive 5500.7-R. August 30, 1993. (Aspin was Secretary of Defense at the time of issue.)

3. Bullis and Reed, *Report to the Secretary of the Army: Assessing Leaders to Establish and Maintain Positive Command Climates*, 1; Reed, "Toxic Leadership," 67–71.

4. Reed and Bullis, "Impact of Destructive Leadership," 5–18.

5. Reed and Olsen, "Toxic Leadership," 58–64.

6. U.S. Department of Defense, Office of Inspector General, *Report of Investigation: Lieutenant General Patrick J. O'Reilly, U.S. Army, Director, Missile Defense Agency*, 11.

7. U.S. Department of the Army, Office of Inspector General, *Report of Investigation: Brigadier General Eugene L. Mascolo, U.S. Army, Director, Joint Staff, Joint Force Headquarters, Connecticut National Guard*, 1, 11.

8. U.S. Department of the Army, Office of Inspector General, *Report of Investigation: Brigadier General Scott "Rock" Donahue, Former Commanding General, U.S. Army Engineer Division, South Pacific, U.S. Army Corps of Engineers, San Francisco, California*, 1.

9. Adam Ashton, "JBLM General's 'Caustic' Leadership Put Medical Staff under Stress, Report Shows," *News Tribune*, April 16, 2015.

10. Davis Winkie, "Army 3-Star Suspended amid Investigation into Alleged Toxic, Racist Work Environment," *Army Times*, February 16, 2022; Corey Dickstein, "Army 3-Star Suspended amid Toxic Climate Investigation, Allegations of Racism," *Stars and Stripes*, February 16, 2022; Haley Britzky, "Army 3-Star General Suspended amid Investigation into Toxic Climate and Racist Comments," *Task & Purpose*, February 16, 2022, https://taskandpurpose.com /news/army-general-duane-gamble-suspended-toxic-climate/; Max Hauptman, "Army 3-Star General Demoted after Investigation into 'Racist and Toxic' Command Climate," *Task & Purpose*, April 6, 2022, https://taskandpurpose .com/news/duane-gamble-gomor/.

11. Ariel Sabar, "Admiral's Rigor Drove Rise and Fall," *Baltimore Sun*, June 5, 2003; Matthew Dodd, "Leadership Failure at Naval Academy," Leatherneck .com, June 28, 2003, https://www.leatherneck.com/forums/showthread.php ?8080-Leadership-Failure-at-Naval-Academy; Nelson Hernandez, "Turmoil at Naval Academy Began at the Top This Time," *Washington Post*, June 6, 2003.

12. "Document: Gauoette [*sic*] Inspector General Report," *USNI News*, April 16, 2013; C. J. Chivers and Thom Shanker, "Admiral at Center of Inquiry Is Censured by Navy," *New York Times*, March 26, 2013.

13. Craig Whitlock, "Pentagon Investigations Point to Military System That Promotes Abusive Leaders," *Washington Post*, January 28, 2014; Jeff Schogol, "Hits Continue for Air Force Top Brass," *Air Force Times*, February 10, 2014; "Excerpts from Military Investigations into Allegations of Toxic Leadership," *Washington Post*, January 28, 2014.

14. Milley, "Army Profession and Leadership Policy."

15. Wilkie, "Harassment Prevention and Response in the Armed Forces."

16. Reed and Olsen, "Toxic Leadership: Part Deux," 64.

17. Blair, "Man in Tempo 3."

18. Blair, "Man in Tempo 3."

19. Blair, "Man in Tempo 3."

20. Stavridis, *Sailing True North*, 173.

21. Oliver, *Against the Tide*, 136.

22. Oliver, *Against the Tide*, 122.

23. Stavridis, *Sailing True North*, 179.

24. Polmar and Allen, *Rickover*, 479.

25. Polmar and Allen, *Rickover*, 161.

26. Degler, "Southern Eccentric," 339.

27. Blair, "Man in Tempo 3"; Wortman, *Admiral Hyman Rickover*, 15–16.

28. "Admiral Hyman Rickover," CBS's *60 Minutes*, December 9, 1984, http://www.people.vcu.edu/~rsleeth/Rickover.html (transcript); Duncan, *Rickover*, 14.

29. "Admiral Hyman Rickover," CBS's *60 Minutes*.

30. Schratz, "Admiral Rickover," 96–101.

31. Stavridis, *Sailing True North*, 172.

32. Duncan, *Rickover*, 21.

33. Duncan, *Rickover*, 25–26.

34. Duncan, *Rickover*, 23.

35. Duncan, *Rickover*, 31.

36. Rickover, "Doing a Job," Speech at Columbia University, November 5, 1981, in Cantonwine, *Never-Ending Challenge of Engineering*, 175.

37. Duncan, *Rickover*, 29.

38. Duncan, *Rickover*, 46.

39. Beach, *Salt and Steel*, 179–80.

40. Duncan, *Rickover*, 50.

41. Duncan, *Rickover*, 56.

42. Duncan, *Rickover*, 62; emphasis added.

43. Blair, "Man in Tempo 3."

44. Duncan, *Rickover,* 63.

45. Duncan, *Rickover*, 64.

46. Duncan, *Rickover*, 65.

47. Blair, "Man in Tempo 3."

48. Duncan, *Rickover*, 73, 75.

49. Rockwell, *Rickover Effect*, 29.

50. Wallace, "Deluge of Honors," 108.

51. Duncan, *Rickover*, 83.

52. Duncan, *Rickover*, 83.

53. Duncan, *Rickover*, 88.

54. Duncan, *Rickover*, 92.

55. Rockwell, *Rickover Effect*, 42.

56. Rockwell, *Rickover Effect*, 54.

57. Rockwell, *Rickover Effect*, 56–57.

58. Polmar and Allen, *Rickover*, 125.

59. Wallace, "Deluge of Honors," 118.

60. Duncan, *Rickover*, 110–11. Despite Rickover's haranguing of defense contractors, he readily accepted illegal gifts from them, including diamond and jade jewelry for his wife. He also directly asked for personal gifts and services. Late in his career, a Navy investigation determined that the admiral had accumulated gifts worth $67,628 (approximately $250,000 in 2022). The Secretary of the Navy issued Rickover a letter of censure. Always self-righteous, an unrepentant Rickover declared, "My conscience is clear on this subject." See, Wortman, *Admiral Hyman Rickover*, 257–58.

61. Wallace, "Deluge of Honors," 118.

62. Wallace, "Deluge of Honors," 114, 116.

63. Duncan, *Rickover*, 117–18.

64. Duncan, *Rickover*, 120.

65. Duncan, *Rickover*, 102.

66. Wortman, *Admiral Hyman Rickover*, 119.

67. Duncan, *Rickover*, 125.

68. Wortman, *Admiral Hyman Rickover*, 134.

69. Polmar and Allen, *Rickover*, 335.

70. Nixon, "Remarks at a Promotion Ceremony."

71. Duncan, *Rickover and the Nuclear Navy*, 305–7.

72. Oliver, *Against the Tide*, 126.

73. "Adm. Rickover Dies — Father of Nuke Fleet," *Los Angeles Times*, July 9, 1986.

74. Polmar and Allen, *Rickover*, 327.

75. Zumwalt, *On Watch*, 85.

76. Stavridis, *Sailing True North*, 189, 191.

77. Wortman, *Admiral Hyman Rickover*, 198.

78. Wallace, "Deluge of Honors," 113.

79. Polmar and Allen, *Rickover*, 456.

80. Rockwell, *Rickover Effect*, 84.

81. Wallace, "Deluge of Honors," 105.

82. Oliver, *Against the Tide*, 63.

83. Blair, "Man in Tempo 3."

84. "Admiral Hyman Rickover," CBS's *60 Minutes*.

85. Oliver, *Against the Tide*, 119.

86. Polmar and Allen, *Rickover*, 327.

87. Wortman, *Admiral Hyman Rickover*, 198.

88. "Admiral Hyman Rickover," CBS's *60 Minutes*.

89. "Admiral Hyman Rickover," CBS's *60 Minutes*.

90. "Admiral Hyman Rickover," CBS's *60 Minutes*.

91. Zumwalt, *On Watch*, 88.

92. Zumwalt, *On Watch*, 89–91.

93. Polmar and Allen, *Rickover*, 281–82.

94. Polmar and Allen, *Rickover*, 284–85.

95. Oliver, *Against the Tide*, 98.

96. Oliver, *Against the Tide*, 98.

97. Oliver, *Against the Tide*, 98–99.

98. Oliver, *Against the Tide*, 99.

99. Polmar and Allen, *Rickover*, 289.

100. Polmar and Allen, *Rickover*, 289–90.

101. Carter, *Why Not the Best?*, 59; emphasis original.

102. Carter, *Why Not the Best?*, 57.

103. Polmar and Allen, *Rickover*, 462.

104. "Admiral Hyman Rickover," CBS's *60 Minutes*.

105. Thomas L. Foster, "Technology and Leadership," in Laver and Matthews, *Art of Command*, 201–2.

106. Foster, "Technology and Leadership," 201.

107. Rockwell, *Rickover Effect*, 81; emphasis original.

108. Duncan, *Rickover and the Nuclear Navy*, 243.

109. George C. Wilson, "Rickover Is Forced to Retire," *Washington Post*, November 14, 1981.

110. Lehman, *Command of the Seas*, 2–3.

111. Lehman, *Command of the Seas*, 3.

112. Lehman, *Command of the Seas*, 1.

113. Lehman, *Command of the Seas*, 4.

114. Lehman, *Command of the Seas*, 5.

115. Lehman, *Command of the Seas*, 6.

116. Rockwell, *Rickover Effect*, 363.

117. Wortman, *Admiral Hyman Rickover*, 90.

118. Neil Henry, "Rickover's Nuclear Navy: Making Men into Machines," *Washington Post*, June 16, 1981.

119. Laing, "Leadership in Command."

120. Henry, "Rickover's Nuclear Navy."

121. Lehman, *Command of the Seas*, 23.

122. Laing, "Leadership in Command."

123. Sam LaGrone, "Interview: U.S. Navy Personnel Chief Worries over Potential Service Retention Problems," *USNI News*, December 2, 2014; Snodgrass, "Keep a Weather Eye on the Horizon," 1–29; Mark D. Faram, "Why Big Navy Wants to Do More to Retain Sailors," *Navy Times*, March 4, 2019.

124. Stavridis, *Sailing True North*, 190.

125. Heather Stephenson, "How to Be an Ethical Leader," *TuftsNow*, November 18, 2019, https://now.tufts.edu/articles/how-be-ethical-leader; Stavridis, *Sailing True North*, 191.

126. U.S. Department of Defense, Office of Inspector General, *Report of Investigation: Brigadier General Norman Cooling, USMC*, 17–23.

127. U.S. Department of Defense, Office of Inspector General *Report of Investigation: Brigadier General Norman Cooling, USMC*, 24–29.

128. U.S. Department of Defense, Office of Inspector General, *Report of Investigation: Brigadier General Norman Cooling, USMC*, 36–38.

129. U.S. Department of Defense, Office of Inspector General, *Report of Investigation: Brigadier General Norman Cooling, USMC*, 35, 38.

130. Stephen Losey, "AFSOC One-Star Falsely Claimed Flight Hours, Disrespected Subordinates, IG Found," *Air Force Times*, May 31, 2019.

131. Tom Roeder, "Methodical Rise Preceded Spectacular Fall for Air Force Academy Commandant Kristin Goodwin," *Colorado Springs Gazette*, May 6, 2019; Stephen Losey, "IG Found Former Academy Commandant Misused Travel, Had Poor Command Climate; She Will Seek Redress for Firing," *Air Force Times*, November 21, 2019.

132. Stephen Losey, "Two-Star Fired from Top Secret Program Office; Under Multiple IG Investigations," *Air Force Times*, June 10, 2019; Stephen Losey, "Maj. Gen. Dunlop Created Toxic Environment in Top Secret Program Office, IG Finds," *Air Force Times*, August 17, 2020.

133. Lipman-Blumen, *Allure of Toxic Leaders*, 219; emphasis original.

FIVE   Obstruction of Justice: John M. Poindexter and Colin L. Powell

1. Meacham et al., *Impeachment*, 83–153.

2. Meacham et al., *Impeachment*, 155–204.

3. Neil A. Lewis, "Libby Guilty of Lying in C.I.A. Leak Case," *New York Times*, March 7, 2007.

4. Barbara Starr, "Admiral's Affair Included Sex at White House," CNN.com, May 9, 2008; U.S. Department of Defense, Office of Inspector General, *Alleged Misconduct: Vice Admiral John D. Stufflebeem, U.S. Navy, Director, Navy Staff*.

5. Spencer S. Hsu, "Flynn Committed Perjury and His Guilty Plea of Lying to FBI Should Not Be Dismissed as DOJ Requests, Court-Appointed Expert Finds," *Washington Post*, June 10, 2020.

6. Philip Bump, "Paul Manafort Becomes the Fifth Trump Campaign Team Member to Plead Guilty to Criminal Charges," *Washington Post*, September 14, 2018.

7. R. S. Mueller, *Report on the Investigation into Russian Interference in the 2016 Presidential Election*; Quinta Jurecic, "Obstruction of Justice in the Mueller Report: A Heat Map, April 21, 2019, https://www.lawfareblog.com/obstruction-justice-mueller-report-heat-map; George T. Conway III, "Donald Trump's New Reality," *Washington Post*, January 22, 2021.

8. Darren Samuelsohn and Josh Gerstein, "Roger Stone Sentenced to over 3 Years in Prison," Politico.com, February 20, 2020.

9. 18 U.S. Code 1503, "Obstruction of Justice," https://www.law.cornell
.edu/wex/obstruction_of_justice#:~:text=18%20U.S.C.,the%20due%20
administration%20of%20justice.%22.

10. Article 131b, "Obstructing Justice," Uniform Code of Military Justice,
https://jsc.defense.gov/Portals/99/Documents/UCMJ%20-%2020December
2019.pdf?ver=2020-01-28-083235-930.

11. William R. Peers, "Summary of Peers Report," University of Missouri,
Kansas City, March 1970, http://law2.umkc.edu/faculty/projects/ftrials
/mylai/summary_rpt.html.

12. William Yardley, "Soldier Is Convicted of Killing Afghan Civilians for
Sport," *New York Times*, November 10, 2011; Rob Hotakainen, "Convicted U.S.
Leader of Afghan 'Kill Team' Wins a New Hearing," *McClatchyDC.com*, June 28,
2016, www.mcclatchydc.com/news/nation-world/national/article86382867
.html#storylink=cpy.

13. Carl Prine and Jim Wilhelm, "American Soldier Charged in Iraq Killings of Deaf, Unarmed Teens," *Pittsburgh Tribune-Review*, November 15, 2013.

14. Adam Ashton, "Soldier Demoted after Pleading Guilty to Threatening
Reporter's Family," *News Tribune*, November 20, 2014.

15. Greg Jaffe, "Soldiers Who Served Under Clint Lorance in Afghanistan
See Trump's Pardon as Betrayal," *Washington Post*, July 2, 2020.

16. Reagan, "Evil Empire Speech."

17. Caspar Weinberger to Colin Powell, June 18, 1985, Records of the Independent Counsel Lawrence Walsh, National Archives.

18. Byrne, *Iran-Contra*, 189.

19. Byrne, *Iran-Contra*, 276–77.

20. Timberg, *Nightingale's Song*, 35.

21. Timberg, *Nightingale's Song*, 36.

22. Timberg, *Nightingale's Song*, 35; Maura Dolan, "Opaque Figure in Iran
Drama: Clues to Poindexter Found in Early Life," *Los Angeles Times*, May 3, 1987.

23. Timberg, *Nightingale's Song*, 35.

24. Matthews, *Colin Powell*, 16.

25. Matthews, *Colin Powell*, 16.

26. Timberg, *Nightingale's Song*, 38.

27. Timberg, *Nightingale's Song*, 38–39, 47.

28. Timberg, *Nightingale's Song*, 48.

29. United Press International, "Poindexter: A Land-Based Sailor," *Chicago Tribune*, July 16, 1987.

30. Timberg, *Nightingale's Song*, 48.
31. Matthews, *Colin Powell*, 17.
32. Matthews, *Colin Powell*, 19.
33. Matthews, *Colin Powell*, 24.
34. Timberg, *Nightingale's Song*, 105.
35. Dolan, "Opaque Figure in Iran Drama."
36. Timberg, *Nightingale's Song*, 163.
37. Timberg, *Nightingale's Song*, 167.
38. Timberg, *Nightingale's Song*, 167.
39. Dolan, "Opaque Figure in Iran Drama."
40. Timberg, *Nightingale's Song*, 167; Peter Grier, "In the Spotlight: Did Power Change the Admiral?," *Christian Science Monitor*, July 16, 1987.
41. Timberg, *Nightingale's Song*, 243.
42. Timberg, *Nightingale's Song*, 242.
43. Timberg, *Nightingale's Song*, 243.
44. Matthews, *Colin Powell*, 28.
45. Matthews, *Colin Powell*, 29.
46. Matthews, *Colin Powell*, 35.
47. Matthews, *Colin Powell*, 37.
48. Matthews, *Colin Powell*, 39.
49. Matthews, *Colin Powell*, 39, 50.
50. Matthews, *Colin Powell*, 59.
51. Matthews, *Colin Powell*, 69.
52. Grier, "Did Power Change the Admiral?"
53. Dolan, "Opaque Figure in Iran Drama."
54. Matthews, *Colin Powell*, 83.
55. McFarlane, *Special Trust*, 68.
56. Byrne, *Iran-Contra*, 78.
57. Byrne, *Iran-Contra*, 4.
58. Byrne, *Iran-Contra*, 42.
59. Byrne, *Iran-Contra*, 42.
60. Powell, *My American Journey*, 338–39; Byrne, *Iran-Contra*, 81–82.
61. McFarlane, *Special Trust*, 75.
62. Byrne, *Iran-Contra*, 141.
63. Byrne, *Iran-Contra*, 141.
64. Byrne, *Iran-Contra*, 142–43.
65. Byrne, *Iran-Contra*, 60–61.

66. Powell, *My American Journey*, 304.

67. Weinberger to Powell, June 18, 1985, Records of the Independent Counsel Lawrence Walsh, National Archives.

68. Caspar Weinberger to Robert McFarlane, "U.S. Policy toward Iran," July 16, 1985, Records of the Independent Counsel Lawrence Walsh, National Archives.

69. Byrne, *Iran-Contra*, 61.

70. "Deposition of General Colin L. Powell," Records of the Independent Counsel Lawrence Walsh, National Archives; Byrne, *Iran-Contra*, 68.

71. "Interview with Major General Colin Powell," April 17, 1987, Records of the Independent Counsel Lawrence Walsh, National Archives; Powell, *My American Journey*, 305.

72. Byrne, *Iran-Contra*, 69.

73. Byrne, *Iran-Contra*, 70–71.

74. Byrne, *Iran-Contra*, 71.

75. Byrne, *Iran-Contra*, 70–71.

76. McFarlane, *Special Trust*, 28, 32.

77. Powell, *My American Journey*, 308.

78. Reagan, *An American Life*, 506.

79. McFarlane, *Special Trust*, 35.

80. Byrne, *Iran-Contra*, 72.

81. Reagan, "Remarks Announcing the Release of the Hostages"; Bryne, *Iran-Contra*, 75–76, 154–56.

82. Byrne, *Iran-Contra*, 75–76, 104–5.

83. Byrne, *Iran-Contra*, 75–76, 104–5, 154–56.

84. "Deposition of General Colin L. Powell," June 19, 1987, Records of the Independent Counsel Lawrence Walsh, National Archives.

85. Walsh, *Final Report*, vol. 1, part 8, August 4, 1993.

86. Matthews, *Colin Powell*, 87.

87. Brinkley, *Reagan Diaries*, 350.

88. "The Testimony of Colin Powell," April 22, 1992, Records of the Independent Counsel Lawrence Walsh, National Archives.

89. Walsh, *Final Report*, vol. 1, part 8, August 4, 1993.

90. Walsh, *Final Report*, vol. 1, part 8, August 4, 1993.

91. Powell, "Record of Interview," July 18, 1987, Records of the Independent Counsel Lawrence Walsh, National Archives.

92. Powell, *My American Journey*, 308.

93. Byrne, *Iran-Contra*, 73–74.

94. Byrne, *Iran-Contra*, 75.

95. Walsh, *Final Report*, vol. 1, part 8, August 4, 1993.

96. Woodward, *Veil*, 414.

97. Walsh, *Final Report*, vol. 1, part 8, August 4, 1993; Byrne, *Iran-Contra*, 75.

98. Powell, *My American Journey*, 308.

99. Byrne, *Iran-Contra*, 94.

100. Oliver North, Congressional Testimony, July 7, 1987, Records of the Independent Counsel Lawrence Walsh, National Archives.

101. "The Testimony of Colin Powell," April 22, 1992, Records of the Independent Counsel Lawrence Walsh, National Archives; Byrne, *Iran-Contra*, 94.

102. "The Testimony of Colin Powell," April 22, 1992, Records of the Independent Counsel Lawrence Walsh, National Archives; Byrne, *Iran-Contra*, 94.

103. Byrne, *Iran-Contra*, 95.

104. Byrne, *Iran-Contra*, 95.

105. Walsh, *Final Report*, vol. 1, part 8, August 4, 1993; Byrne, *Iran-Contra*, 95.

106. Byrne, *Iran-Contra*, 96; Powell, *My American Journey*, 310.

107. "Interview with Major General Colin Powell," April 17, 1987, and "Powell Outline: Weinberger's Notes," Records of the Independent Counsel Lawrence Walsh, National Archives.

108. Walsh, *Final Report*, vol. 1, part 8, August 4, 1993.

109. Walsh, *Final Report*, vol. 1, part 8, August 4, 1993.

110. Byrne, *Iran-Contra*, 96.

111. R. M. Gates, *From the Shadows*, 399–400; emphasis original.

112. Walsh, *Final Report*, vol. 1, part 8, August 4, 1993.

113. Byrne, *Iran-Contra*, 101–5.

114. Walsh, *Final Report*, vol. 1, part 8, August 4, 1993.

115. McFarlane, *Special Trust*, 46.

116. Reagan, *An American Life*, 512.

117. Brinkley, *Reagan Diaries*, 374.

118. Walsh, *Final Report*, vol. 1, part 8, August 4, 1993.

119. Walsh, *Final Report*, vol. 1, part 8, August 4, 1993.

120. McFarlane, *Special Trust*, 46.

121. Byrne, *Iran-Contra*, 106.

122. Walsh, *Final Report*, vol. 1, part 8, August 4, 1993.

123. Reagan, *An American Life*, 510.

124. Byrne, *Iran-Contra*, 107, 325.

125. Walsh, *Final Report*, vol. 1, part 8, August 4, 1993.

126. Walsh, *Firewall*, 347.

127. "The Testimony of Colin Powell," April 22, 1992, Records of the Independent Counsel Lawrence Walsh, National Archives.

128. Hamilton and Inouye, *Report of the Congressional Committees Investigating the Iran-Contra Affair*, 206.

129. Walsh, *Final Report*, vol. 1, part 8, August 4, 1993.

130. Walsh, *Final Report*, vol. 1, part 8, August 4, 1993.

131. Byrne, *Iran-Contra*, 158.

132. Byrne, *Iran-Contra*, 372; T. Draper, *Very Thin Line*, 250–51; Walsh, *Final Report*, vol. 1, part 8, August 4, 1993.

133. Byrne, *Iran-Contra*, 154.

134. Powell, *My American Journey*, 311.

135. Crowe, *Line of Fire*, 300.

136. Powell, *My American Journey*, 311; Means, *Colin Powell*, 218.

137. Means, *Colin Powell*, 219.

138. Parry, *America's Stolen Narrative*, 176–79; Parry, Parry, and Parry, *Neck Deep*, 102–6.

139. "Powell FBI Interview Transcript," December 4–5, 1986, and "Testimony of Colin L. Powell," December 22, 1986, Records of the Independent Counsel Lawrence Walsh, National Archives.

140. Byrne, *Iran-Contra*, 165–67.

141. Powell, *My American Journey*, 311.

142. "Powell FBI Interview Transcript," December 4–5, 1986, Records of the Independent Counsel Lawrence Walsh, National Archives.

143. Parry, *America's Stolen Narrative*, 178; Parry, Parry, and Parry, *Neck Deep*, 104.

144. Parry, *America's Stolen Narrative*, 178; Parry, Parry, and Parry, *Neck Deep*, 104.

145. "Deposition of General Colin L. Powell," June 19, 1987, and "Memorandum for Vice Admiral Poindexter," March 12, 1986, Records of the Independent Counsel Lawrence Walsh, National Archives.

146. Parry, *America's Stolen Narrative*, 178.

147. "Officer Efficiency Report," May 1986, Powell Papers, Special Collections, National Defense University Library, Fort Lesley J. McNair, Washington, DC.

148. Byrne, *Iran-Contra*, 189; Timberg, *Nightingale's Song*, 372.

149. Byrne, *Iran-Contra*, 163, 277.

150. "Powell FBI Interview Transcript," December 4–5, 1986, Records of the Independent Counsel Lawrence Walsh, National Archives.

151. Powell, *My American Journey*, 336; emphasis added.

152. Byrne, *Iran-Contra*, 206.

153. Byrne, *Iran-Contra*, 190.

154. "Iran-Contra Hearings: 'I Came Here to Tell You the Truth'; Country and Orders Above All," *New York Times*, July 8, 1987.

155. Byrne, *Iran-Contra*, 257.

156. Byrne, *Iran-Contra*, 262.

157. Weiner, *Enemies*, 363.

158. Byrne, *Iran-Contra*, 258.

159. Byrne, *Iran-Contra*, 256.

160. Byrne, *Iran-Contra*, 265.

161. Byrne, *Iran-Contra*, 269.

162. Weiner, *Enemies*, 363.

163. Byrne, *Iran-Contra*, 274–75.

164. Byrne, *Iran-Contra*, 276.

165. Byrne, *Iran-Contra*, 276–77.

166. Byrne, *Iran-Contra*, 278.

167. Timberg, *Nightingale's Song*, 441–42.

168. Matthews, *Colin Powell*, 98.

169. Byrne, *Iran-Contra*, 285.

170. Byrne, *Iran-Contra*, 297.

171. Byrne, *Iran-Contra*, 299.

172. Byrne, *Iran-Contra*, 303.

173. Hamilton and Inouye, *Report of the Congressional Committees Investigating the Iran-Contra Affair*, 380.

174. Hamilton and Inouye, *Report of the Congressional Committees Investigating the Iran-Contra Affair*, 533–34.

175. Walsh, *Firewall*, 199.

176. Walsh, *Firewall*, 200.

177. Byrne, *Iran-Contra*, 315; Walsh, *Firewall*, 208.

178. North's verdict was later overturned by an appeals court in a two to one vote, not because of his innocence but rather because his trial "may have been tainted" by the lieutenant colonel's immunized testimony before Congress. See Byrne, *Iran-Contra*, 316.

179. Walsh, *Firewall*, 223.

180. Walsh, *Firewall*, 228.

181. Byrne, *Iran-Contra*, 317.

182. Walsh, *Firewall*, 236–38.

183. Walsh, *Firewall*, 245.

184. Byrne, *Iran-Contra*, 318.

185. Walsh, *Firewall*, 246.

186. Poindexter's verdict was later overturned by an appeals court in a two to one vote, not because of his innocence but rather because his trial had been "tainted" by the admiral's immunized testimony before Congress. See Byrne, *Iran-Contra*, 318.

187. H. L. Gates, *Thirteen Ways of Looking at a Black Man*, 78.

188. Walsh, *Firewall*, 395.

189. "Deposition of General Colin L. Powell," June 19, 1987, and "Interview with Major General Colin Powell," April 17, 1987, Records of the Independent Counsel Lawrence Walsh, National Archives.

190. In 1987, when investigators asked Powell if he had taken notes in meetings with Weinberger, he replied, "I would occasionally take notes, sometimes not." To the contrary, Powell had a reputation as a habitual note taker. His closest friend at the Pentagon, Richard Armitage, testified that Powell "took extensive notes in spiral notebooks while he was Caspar Weinberger's military assistant," going through as many as five books a week. Powell informed investigators that he purposely destroyed all of his meeting notes. "Deposition of General Colin L. Powell," June 19, 1987, "Colin Powell's Notes," February 3, 1992, and "The Testimony of Colin Powell," April 22, 1992, Records of the Independent Counsel Lawrence Walsh, National Archives.

191. Powell, *My American Journey*, 306; Colin Powell, "Affidavit," April 21, 1992, and "The Testimony of Colin Powell," April 22, 1992, Records of the Independent Counsel Lawrence Walsh, National Archives.

192. Walsh, *Firewall*, 388.

193. Walsh, *Firewall*, 389.

194. Walsh, *Firewall*, 387.

195. "Interview with Major General Colin Powell," April 17, 1987, Records of the Independent Counsel Lawrence Walsh, National Archives; emphasis added.

196. "Deposition of General Colin L. Powell," June 19, 1987, Records of the Independent Counsel Lawrence Walsh, National Archives; emphasis added.

197. "Record of Interview with General Colin L. Powell," July 6 and 9, 1987, Records of the Independent Counsel Lawrence Walsh, National Archives.

198. "The Testimony of Colin Powell," April 22, 1992, Records of the Independent Counsel Lawrence Walsh, National Archives.

199. "OIC Interview of General Colin Powell," November 5, 1992, Records of the Independent Counsel Lawrence Walsh, National Archives.

200. Colin Powell, "Affidavit," April 21, 1992, Records of the Independent Counsel Lawrence Walsh, National Archives.

201. Walsh, *Final Report*, vol. 1, part 8, August 4, 1993.

202. Walsh, *Firewall*, 406.

203. David Johnston, "Weinberger Faces 5 Counts in Iran Contra Indictment," *New York Times*, June 16, 1992; Walsh, *Final Report*, vol. 1, part 8, August 4, 1993.

204. Walsh, *Firewall*, 403.

205. Walsh, *Final Report*, vol. 1, part 8, August 4, 1993.

206. Walsh, *Final Report*, vol. 1, part 8, August 4, 1993.

207. Walsh, *Final Report*, vol. 1, part 8, August 4, 1993.

208. Colin Powell, interview with the author, June 22, 2017; Walsh, *Final Report*, vol. 3, Responses, August 4, 1993; Powell, *My American Journey*, 341–43.

209. Parry, *America's Stolen Narrative*, 148.

210. David Johnston, "Bush Pardons 6 in Iran Affair, Aborting a Weinberger Trial; Prosecutor Assails 'Cover-Up,'" *New York Times*, December 25, 1992.

211. Liman, *Lawyer*, 348.

212. McFarlane, *Special Trust*, 68.

213. David Johnston, "Powell Backs Weinberger Testimony," *New York Times*, June 7, 1992; Powell, *My American Journey*, 308.

214. Elizabeth Becker, "Army Demotes Retired NATO Commander Who Admitted Affairs with Wives of Subordinates," *New York Times*, September 3, 1999.

215. David Morgan, "Army Censures General over Tillman Case," *Reuters*, July 31, 2007.

216. Carlie Savage, "Obama Pardons James Cartwright, General Who Lied to F.B.I. in Leak Case," *New York Times*, January 17, 2017.

SIX   Sex Crimes: The Tailhook Admirals

1. U.S. Department of Defense, Office of Inspector General, *Fiscal Year 2020 Top DoD Management Challenges*, 95.

2. U.S. Department of Defense, Office of Inspector General, *Fiscal Year 2020 Top DoD Management Challenges*, 97.

3. U.S. Department of Defense, Office of Inspector General, *Fiscal Year 2019 Top DoD Management Challenges*, 47, 51.

4. U.S. Department of Defense, Office of Inspector General, *Fiscal Year 2019 Top DoD Management Challenges*, 48–53.

5. U.S. Department of Defense, Office of Inspector General, *Fiscal Year 2019 Top DoD Management Challenges*, 51–52.

6. Joint Service Committee on Military Justice, "Manual of Courts-Martial, United States, 2019," IV-83-97, IV-134–50, https://jsc.defense.gov/Portals

/99/Documents/2019%20MCM%20(Final)%20(20190108).pdf?ver=2019
-01-11-115724-610.

7. Anita Hill, "Opening Statement: Sexual Harassment Hearings Concerning Judge Clarence Thomas," October 11, 1991, https://cpb-us-e1.wp mucdn.com/blogs.uoregon.edu/dist/7/11428/files/2015/06/Hill-Opening -Statement-1991-1zxyhrw.pdf.

8. CNSNews.com Staff, "Flashback—Clarence Thomas: 'It's a High-Tech Lynching for Uppity Blacks,'" September 17, 2018, https://www.cnsnews.com /news/article/cnsnewscom-staff/flashback-clarence-thomas-denies-anita-hill -allegations-calls-senate.

9. Christina Cauterucci, "Sexual Harassment Claims Spiked after the Clarence Thomas Hearings. They're Spiking Again Now," https://slate.com /news-and-politics/2018/10/eeoc-2018-sexual-harassment-metoo-clarence -thomas-anita-hill.html.

10. McMichael, *Mother of All Hooks*, 50.

11. U.S. Department of Defense, Office of Inspector General, *Report of Investigation: Tailhook 91*, part 1, 2–3, Enclosure 3.

12. Vistica, *Fall from Glory*, 232–33; McMichael, *Mother of All Hooks*, 21; "The Navy Blues," PBS's *Frontline*, October 15, 1996, https://www.pbs.org /wgbh/pages/frontline/shows/navy/tailhook/assoc.html; U.S. Department of Defense, Office of Inspector General, *Report of Investigation: Tailhook 91*, part 2, 105–6.

13. Vistica, *Fall from Glory*, 233; McMichael, *Mother of All Hooks*, 18.

14. Vistica, *Fall from Glory*, 234.

15. Department of Defense, Office of Inspector General, *Report of Investigation: Tailhook 91*, part 2, 25–26; "Navy Blues," PBS's *Frontline*.

16. Vistica, *Fall from Glory*, 238.

17. McMichael, *Mother of All Hooks*, 17–18, Vistica, *Fall from Glory*, 234.

18. U.S. Department of Defense, Office of Inspector General, *Report of Investigation: Tailhook 91*, part 2, 26–27.

19. U.S. Department of Defense, Office of Inspector General, *Report of Investigation: Tailhook 91*, part 1, 2–3.

20. U.S. Department of Defense, Office of Inspector General, *Report of Investigation: Tailhook 91*, part 2, 27.

21. U.S. Department of Defense, Office of Inspector General, *Report of Investigation: Tailhook 91*, part 2, 28.

22. Vistica, *Fall from Glory*, 237.

23. U.S. Department of Defense, Office of Inspector General, *Report of Investigation: Tailhook 91*, part 2, 27–28.

24. McMichael, *Mother of All Hooks*, 21.

25. Vistica, *Fall from Glory*, 14, 246.

26. U.S. Department of Defense, Office of Inspector General, *Report of Investigation: Tailhook 91*, part 2, 28.

27. Vistica, *Fall from Glory*, 312.

28. Vistica, *Fall from Glory*, 313.

29. Vistica, *Fall from Glory*, 308–12.

30. Vistica, *Fall from Glory*, 327.

31. Beck, *Inside the Tailhook Scandal*, 129–31, 139, 143–44; Vistica, *Fall from Glory*, 327.

32. McMichael, *Mother of All Hooks*, 35–36.

33. U.S. Department of Defense, Office of Naval Inspector General, *Report of Investigation: Department of the Navy/Tailhook Association Relationship and Personal Conduct Surrounding Tailhook '91 Symposium*, Enclosure 2, 4.

34. McMichael, *Mother of All Hooks*, 9.

35. Vistica, *Fall from Glory*, 328; McMichael, *Mother of All Hooks*, 67, 72, 75.

36. U.S. Department of Defense, Office of Inspector General, *Report of Investigation: Tailhook 91*, part 2, 37–43.

37. U.S. Department of Defense, Office of Inspector General, *Report of Investigation: Tailhook 91*, part 2, 142; McMichael, *Mother of All Hooks*, 40–41.

38. Zimmerman, *Tailspin*, 24–26.

39. Zimmerman, *Tailspin*, 23.

40. Zimmerman, *Tailspin*, 27.

41. Vistica, *Fall from Glory*, 335.

42. McMichael, *Mother of All Hooks*, 48–49; Vistica, *Fall from Glory*, 340.

43. U.S. Department of Defense, Office of Inspector General, *Report of Investigation: Tailhook 91*, part 1, 2–3, Enclosure 3.

44. McMichael, *Mother of All Hooks*, 49–50; Vistica, *Fall from Glory*, 333–34.

45. McMichael, *Mother of All Hooks*, 50–51; Vistica, *Fall from Glory*, 332–35.

46. "Navy 'Gauntlet' Probed; Sex Harassment Alleged at Fliers' Convention," *Washington Post*, October 30, 1991.

47. McMichael, *Mother of All Hooks*, 51, 73; Vistica, *Fall from Glory*, 336.

48. McMichael, *Mother of All Hooks*, 51; Vistica, *Fall from Glory*, 338.

49. John Lancaster, "Admiral Punished in Abuse Probe," *Washington Post*, November 6, 1991.

50. Lancaster, "Admiral Punished."

51. "Admiral Is Permanently Removed for Response in Sex Abuse Case," *New York Times*, December 21, 1991.

52. Vistica, *Fall from Glory*, 351.

53. McMichael, *Mother of All Hooks*, 68.

54. McMichael, *Mother of All Hooks*, 78–79; Vistica, *Fall from Glory*, 351.

55. Vistica, *Fall from Glory*, 344–46, Zimmerman, *Tailspin*, 75; McMichael, *Mother of All Hooks*, 69–70.

56. Vistica, *Fall from Glory*, 345.

57. Vistica, *Fall from Glory*, 345–46.

58. Zimmerman, *Tailspin*, 73–74; John Lancaster, "Navy Harassment Probe Stymied," *Washington Post*, May 1, 1992.

59. U.S. Department of Defense, Office of Naval Inspector General, *Report of Investigation: Department of the Navy/Tailhook Association Relationship and Personal Conduct Surrounding Tailhook '91 Symposium*, 3–4.

60. McMichael, *Mother of All Hooks*, 73–74; Vistica, *Fall from Glory*, 348.

61. McMichael, *Mother of All Hooks*, 70, 272–73; Vistica, *Fall from Glory*, 348–49.

62. "Navy Blues," PBS's *Frontline*.

63. Vistica, *Fall from Glory*, 349; Zimmerman, *Tailspin*, 83–84.

64. "Vice Admiral Takes the Blame in Tailhook Scandal," *Los Angeles Times*, May 6, 1992; John Lancaster, "The Sex Life of the Navy," *Washington Post*, May 17, 1992.

65. McMichael, *Mother of All Hooks*, 77; Vistica, *Fall from Glory*, 351.

66. McMichael, *Mother of All Hooks*, 76.

67. McMichael, *Mother of All Hooks*, 76–80; Vistica, *Fall from Glory*, 351.

68. McMichael, *Mother of All Hooks*, 80; Vistica, *Fall from Glory*, 351–52.

69. Vistica, *Fall from Glory*, 352.

70. John Lancaster, "A Gauntlet of Terror, Frustration — Navy Pilot Recounts Tailhook Incident," *Washington Post*, June 24, 1992.

71. Zimmerman, *Tailspin*, 91; McMichael, *Mother of All Hooks*, 80–81; Vistica, *Fall from Glory*, 352–54.

72. Vistica, *Fall from Glory*, 354–55.

73. McMichael, *Mother of All Hooks*, 223–24.

74. Zimmerman, *Tailspin*, 99.

75. U.S. Department of Defense, Office of Inspector General, *Report of Investigation: Tailhook 91 – Part 1*, 29.

76. U.S. Department of Defense, Office of Inspector General, *Report of Investigation: Tailhook 91 – Part 1*, 4.

77. U.S. Department of Defense, Office of Inspector General, *Report of Investigation: Tailhook 91 – Part 1*, 11.

78. U.S. Department of Defense, Office of Inspector General, *Report of Investigation: Tailhook 91 – Part 1*, 12–14.

79. U.S. Department of Defense, Office of Inspector General, *Report of Investigation: Tailhook 91 – Part 1*, 31.

80. U.S. Department of Defense, Office of Inspector General, *Report of Investigation: Tailhook 91 – Part 1*, 1, 31.

81. U.S. Department of Defense, Office of Inspector General, *Report of Investigation: Tailhook 91 – Part 1*, 31.

82. U.S. Department of Defense, Office of Inspector General, *Report of Investigation: Tailhook 91 – Part 1*, 11, 14.

83. U.S. Department of Defense, Office of Inspector General, *Report of Investigation: Tailhook 91 – Part 1*, 14.

84. U.S. Department of Defense, Office of Inspector General, *Report of Investigation: Tailhook 91 – Part 1*, 14.

85. U.S. Department of Defense, Office of Inspector General, *Report of Investigation: Tailhook 91 – Part 1*, 15.

86. U.S. Department of Defense, Office of Inspector General, *Report of Investigation: Tailhook 91 – Part 1*, 19–20.

87. U.S. Department of Defense, Office of Inspector General, *Report of Investigation: Tailhook 91 – Part 1*, 23.

88. U.S. Department of Defense, Office of Inspector General, *Report of Investigation: Tailhook 91 – Part 1*, 10.

89. U.S. Department of Defense, Office of Inspector General, *Report of Investigation: Tailhook 91 – Part 1*, 24.

90. U.S. Department of Defense, Office of Inspector General, *Report of Investigation: Tailhook 91 – Part 1*, 24–25.

91. U.S. Department of Defense, Office of Inspector General, *Report of Investigation: Tailhook 91 – Part 1*, 8.

92. U.S. Department of Defense, Office of Inspector General, *Report of Investigation: Tailhook 91 – Part 1*, 19.

93. U.S. Department of Defense, Office of Inspector General, *Report of Investigation: Tailhook 91 – Part 1*, 15–16.

94. U.S. Department of Defense, Office of Inspector General, *Report of Investigation: Tailhook 91 – Part 1*, 15.

95. U.S. Department of Defense, Office of Inspector General, *Report of Investigation: Tailhook 91 – Part 1*, 16.

96. U.S. Department of Defense, Office of Inspector General, *Report of Investigation: Tailhook 91 – Part 1*, 28.

97. U.S. Department of Defense, Office of Inspector General, *Report of Investigation: Tailhook 91 – Part 1*, 32.

98. Melissa Healy, "Pentagon Blasts Tailhook Probe, Two Admirals Resign," *Los Angeles Times*, September 25, 1992.

99. "Tailhook Investigation Report," https://www.c-span.org/video/?40032 -1/tailhook-investigation-report.

100. U.S. Department of Defense, Office of Inspector General, *Report of Investigation: Tailhook 91 – Part 2*, 81.

101. U.S. Department of Defense, Office of Inspector General, *Report of Investigation: Tailhook 91 – Part 2*, xi, 2.

102. U.S. Department of Defense, Office of Inspector General, *Report of Investigation: Tailhook 91 – Part 2*, 2.

103. U.S. Department of Defense, Office of Inspector General, *Report of Investigation: Tailhook 91 – Part 2*, 81.

104. U.S. Department of Defense, Office of Inspector General, *Report of Investigation: Tailhook 91 – Part 2*, 2.

105. U.S. Department of Defense, Office of Inspector General, *Report of Investigation: Tailhook 91 – Part 2*, 81–83.

106. U.S. Department of Defense, Office of Inspector General, *Report of Investigation: Tailhook 91 – Part 2*, 87.

107. U.S. Department of Defense, Office of Inspector General, *Report of Investigation: Tailhook 91 – Part 2*, 91–92.

108. U.S. Department of Defense, Office of Inspector General, *Report of Investigation: Tailhook 91 – Part 2*, 92.

109. U.S. Department of Defense, Office of Inspector General, *Report of Investigation: Tailhook 91 – Part 2*, 92.

110. U.S. Department of Defense, Office of Inspector General, *Report of Investigation: Tailhook 91 – Part 2*, xii, 96.

111. Vistica, *Fall from Glory*, 374.

112. Vistica, *Fall from Glory*, 377.

113. "Admirals Punished for Tailhook Censures a Blot on Navy Careers," *Baltimore Sun*, October 16, 1993.

114. "Admirals Punished for Tailhook Censures."

115. "Tailhook Scandal Costs Retired Admiral a Star," *Washington Post*, October, 16, 1993.

116. Neil A. Lewis, "Tailhook Affair Brings Censure of 3 Admirals," *New York Times*, October 16, 1993.

117. McMichael, *Mother of All Hooks*, 225.

118. McMichael, *Mother of All Hooks*, 244, 249.

119. McMichael, *Mother of All Hooks*, 245–46.

120. McMichael, *Mother of All Hooks*, 268–69.

121. McMichael, *Mother of All Hooks*, 254–55.

122. McMichael, *Mother of All Hooks*, 262.

123. McMichael, *Mother of All Hooks*, 263–64.

124. McMichael, *Mother of All Hooks*, 264.

125. McMichael, *Mother of All Hooks*, 251–52.

126. McMichael, *Mother of All Hooks*, 248–49.

127. McMichael, *Mother of All Hooks*, 259.

128. McMichael, *Mother of All Hooks*, 268.

129. McMichael, *Mother of All Hooks*, 276.

130. Vistica, *Fall from Glory*, 379–80.

131. Vistica, *Fall from Glory*, 380.

132. Vistica, *Fall from Glory*, 379–80; McMichael, *Mother of All Hooks*, 286.

133. Vistica, *Fall from Glory*, 379–80.

134. McMichael, *Mother of All Hooks*, 285–86, 293.

135. McMichael, *Mother of All Hooks*, 286–87.

136. McMichael, *Mother of All Hooks*, 293.

137. McMichael, *Mother of All Hooks*, 297.

138. McMichael, *Mother of All Hooks*, 297–98; John Lancaster, "Top Navy Admiral Kelso to Retire Early in Aftermath of Tailhook Scandal," *Washington Post*, February 16, 1994.

139. McMichael, *Mother of All Hooks*, 297–98.

140. Lancaster, "Kelso to Retire Early"; Gilbert A. Lewthwaite, "Kelso Retiring to End Tailhook Uproar," *Baltimore Sun*, February 16, 1994.

141. U.S. Department of Defense, Officer of Inspector General, *Report of Investigation: Tailhook 91 – Part 1*, 2–3.

142. Zimmerman, *Tailspin*, 272.

143. "Navy Blues," PBS's *Frontline*.

144. Zimmerman, *Tailspin*, 272.

145. U.S. Department of Defense, *Annual Report on Sexual Assault in the Military*, May 2021, p. 5.

146. U.S. Department of Defense, *Annual Report on Sexual Assault in the Military*, September 2022, p. 3.

147. Eric Schmitt, "New Navy Scandal: An Admiral Guilty of Sex Harassment," *New York Times*, December 9, 1995; Dana Priest, "Navy Admiral Punished in Adultery Case," *Washington Post*, December 9. 1995.

148. John Diamond, "Navy Censures Ex-Admiral for Relationship with Female Officer," *AP News*, October 15, 1996, https://apnews.com/article/71a 5323671b77e28c4ba84559a203fe3; Dale Eisman, "Retired Pacific Admiral Is Censured 'Unduly Familiar' Relationship with Marine Corps Officer Is Cited," *The Virginia-Pilot*, October 16, 1996.

149. "Fired Admiral Gives Public Apology," CNN.com, November 20, 1995, http://www.cnn.com/WORLD/9511/macke_speaks/.

150. Dana Priest, "Admiral, Army Counsel Probed for Harassment," *Washington Post*, May 31, 1997; "Admiral, Rebuked for Harassment, Seeks to Retire," *Los Angeles Times*, June 7, 1997.

151. Meghann Myers, "Strike Group Boss Watched Porn for Hours on His Navy Computer: Report," DefenseNews.com, March 8, 2016; Jeanette Steele, "Admiral Ousted over Porn Allegation," *San Diego Union-Tribune*, January 11, 2016.

152. Geoff Ziezulewicz, "The One-Star, His NAVSEA Employee, Rumors of a Romance and the Scandal That Finally Got Him," *Navy Times*, February, 11, 2020.

153. Geoff Ziezulewicz, "Adm. Bill Moran Out as Navy's Next CNO," *Navy Times*, July 8, 2019.

154. Diana Stancy Correll, "Rare Firing of Flag Officer for Sexual Harassment Came after Unwanted Kissing," *Navy Times*, March 17, 2022.

155. Steve McGonigle and Ed Timms, "Military Justice May Have Some 'General' Flaws," *Dallas Morning News*, January 3, 1993; Tamara Jones, "Air Force Adultery Trial On Hold," *Washington Post*, May 21, 1997.

156. Dana Priest, "Air Force Removes General, Citing Affair with Civilian," *Washington Post*, June 27, 1995; Jones, "Air Force Adultery Trial."

157. "Air Force General Is Demoted," *Washington Post*, December 27, 1996.

158. Nicole Gaudiano, "Busted to Colonel: Fallen Star; How the Air Force's Judge Advocate General Lost His Two-Star Career over His Own Misconduct," *Air Force Times*, January 24, 2005; U.S. Air Force, Inspector General of the Air Force, *Report of Investigation, Maj Gen Thomas J. Fiscus*.

159. Josh White, "General Accused of Harassment Is Demoted: Air Force Report Says Hassan Made Overtures to Female Subordinates," *Washington Post*, February 9, 2006.

160. U.S. Air Force, Inspector General of the Air Force, *Report of Investigation: Brigadier General David C. Uhrich*; Craig Whitlock, "Military Brass, Behaving Badly: Files Detail a Spate of Misconduct Dogging Armed Forces," *Washington Post*, January 26, 2014.

161. Craig Whitlock, "Air Force General to Retire after Criticism for Handling of Sexual Assault Case," *Washington Post*, January 8, 2014; Chris Wilson,

"Following McCaskill Request, Lieutenant General Craig Franklin Resigns Command, Will Retire from Air Force," KoamNewsNow.com, January 8, 2014, https://www.koamnewsnow.com/following-mccaskill-request-lieutenant-general-craig-franklin-resigns-command-will-retire-from-air-force/.

162. "Air Warfare Center Commander Fired," *Air Force Magazine*, January 13, 2014. On June 16, 2022, the Air Force's Senior Leader Management Office sent an email to the author Week's retirement date and rank.

163. Stephen Losey, "'Dishonored and Disgraced': IG Slams AFCENT One-Star for 'Inappropriate Relationship,'" *Air Force Times*, June 28, 2018.

164. Eric Schmitt, "General Removed over Relationship," *New York Times*, May 30, 1997; Tom Bowman, "General Sues the Army over Taped Phone Call: Alleged Affair Sparked Loss of His Command, Letters of Reprimand," *Baltimore Sun*, February 26, 1998.

165. Phillip Shenon, "Commander at Aberdeen to Retire over an Affair," *New York Times*, June 3, 1997.

166. Elizabeth Becker, "Army Demotes Retired NATO Commander Who Admitted Affairs with Wives of Subordinates," *New York Times*, September 3, 1999.

167. Elizabeth Becker, "General Is Demoted 2 Ranks and Made to Retire in Sex Case," *New York Times*, November 17, 1999.

168. Martin Kettle, "Sexual Harassment Claim Sticks against US General," *The Guardian*, May 11, 2000; Steven Lee Meyers, "Army Rescinds Job of General Accused of Sexual Advance," *New York Times*, May 23, 2000; Christopher Marquis, "General Seeks to Retire as Charges Are Supported," *New York Times*, July 8, 2000; Kennedy, *Generally Speaking*, 165–67, 200–201.

169. Bruce Siceloff, "Tony Tata's Army Career Included Phony Court Order, at Least 2 Affairs," *Raleigh News & Observer*, September 19, 2015; "Army Inspectors: Tata Had Adulterous Affairs During Service," MilitaryTimes.com, September 20, 2015.

170. Tom Vanden Brook, "Army Brass, Led by Future Joint Chiefs Head Martin Dempsey, Gave Amorous General a Pass," *USA Today*, March 10, 2017.

171. Jeane MacIntosh, "Guard Big Resigns over Affair," *New York Post*, December 2, 2011; Craig Whitlock, "Inside Chris Christie's Militia, Flab and Cronyism Trigger Mutiny in the Ranks," *Washington Post*, September 21, 2015.

172. Dan Lamothe, "Army General, Accused of Sexual Assault by Senior Adviser, Retired Quietly with Demotion," *Washington Post*, October 1, 2014.

173. U.S. Department of the Army, Office of Inspector General, *Report of Investigation 13-024, BG Martin P. Schweitzer*; Craig Whitlock, "Military Brass,

Behaving Badly: Files Detail a Spate of Misconduct Dogging Armed Forces,"
Washington Post, January 26, 2014.

174. "Two-Star Demoted for Lack of Attention to Sex Assault Case, Army
Says," *Army Times*, August 27, 2014; Craig Whitlock, "Army General Disciplined over
Mishandling of Sexual-Assault Case in Japan," *Washington Post*, April 22, 2014.

175. Gregg Zoroya, "General Avoids Jail Time in Case Involving Affair
with Subordinate," *USA Today*, March 20, 2014; Alan Blinder, "General in Sex
Case to Retire with a 2-Rank Demotion," *New York Times*, June 20, 2014.

176. U.S. Department of the Army, Office of Inspector General, *Report of
Investigation: Brigadier General Bryan T. Roberts*; Whitlock, "Military Brass, Behaving Badly." Roberts's demotion was confirmed by the Army in an email to
the author on July 17, 2022.

177. Tom Vanden Brook, "Joint Staff General's Girlfriend Problem
Grounds Career," *USA Today*, September 23, 2016; Craig Whitlock, "Army General Demoted as Sex Scandals Continue," *Washington Post*, June 22, 2017.

178. Lolita C. Baldor, "Two-Star General Demoted after Affair," *Army Times*,
December 16, 2016; Tom Vanden Brook, "New Details Show How 'Swinger' Army
General's Double Life Cost Him His Career," *USA Today*, August 24, 2016.

179. Howard Altman, "Investigations Underway into Sexual Misconduct
Allegation at Florida National Guard," *Tampa Bay Times*, March 29, 2019; Zach-
ary T. Sampson, "Under Investigation by the Army, Florida National Guard's
No. 2 Leaders Steps Down," *Tampa Bay Times*, May 7, 2019.

180. Jeff Schogol, "We Finally Know Why the Army Fired Its Three-Star General in Charge of Housing," *Task & Purpose*, October 27, 2021, https://taskand
purpose.com/news/army-lt-gen-bradley-becker-firing/. Becker's retirement and
demotion were confirmed by the Army in an email to the author on July 20, 2022.

181. U.S. Air Force, Office of Inspector General, *Report of Investigation Lt Gen
John W. Hesterman III*; Dan Lamothe, "'Sexually Suggestive' Relationship Ends Career of Air Force General Who Ran Air War," *Washington Post*, March 17, 2016.

182. Tom Vanden Brook, "Air Force Busts Retired Four-Star General
Down Two Ranks for Coerced Sex," *USA Today*, February 1, 2018.

183. Stephen Losey, "Sex with Subordinate, Inappropriate Relationships Cost
Fired Warfare Center Commander Two Stars," *Air Forces Times*, January 8, 2021.

184. Secretary of Defense Lloyd J. Austin III, "Statement on the Conclusion of Independent Review Commission," press release, June 22, 2021.

185. Glenn Thrush, "Biden Signs $770 Billion Defense Bill," *New York
Times*, December 27, 2021; "Lawmakers Reach Deal to Overhaul How Military
Handles Sexual Assault Cases," *New York Times*, December 7, 2021.

1. "Operation Illwind," Federal Bureau of Investigation, https://www
.fbi.gov/history/famous-cases/operation-illwind.

2. U.S. Department of Defense, Office of Inspector General, *Fiscal
Year 2020 Top DoD Management Challenges*, i.

3. U.S. Department of Defense, Office of Inspector General, *Fiscal Year
2020 Top DoD Management Challenges*, 117–19.

4. U.S. Department of Defense, Office of Inspector General, *Fiscal Year
2020 Top DoD Management Challenges*, I, 117–19.

5. U.S. Department of Defense, Office of Inspector General, *Fiscal
Year 2020 Top DoD Management Challenges*, 120.

6. U.S. Department of Defense, Office of Inspector General, *Fiscal Year
2020 Top DoD Management Challenges*, 120.

7. U.S. Department of Defense, Office of Inspector General, *Fiscal Year
2020 Top DoD Management Challenges*, 121.

8. U.S. Department of Defense, Office of Inspector General, *Fiscal
Year 2020, Top DoD Management Challenges*, 120.

9. Julia Harte, "U.S. Military Personnel Have Been Convicted of $50
Million Worth of Crimes in Iraq and Afghanistan," The Center for Public Integrity, May 5, 2015, https://publicintegrity.org/national-security/u-s-military
-personnel-have-been-convicted-of-50-million-worth-of-crimes-in-iraq-and
-afghanistan/.

10. Harte, "U.S. Military Personnel."

11. Eric Schmitt and James Glanz, "U.S. Says Company Bribed Officers
for Work in Iraq," *New York Times*, August 31, 2007; Ginger Thompson and Eric
Schmitt, "Graft in Military Contracts Spread from Base," *New York Times*, September 24, 2007; Jeremy Roebuck, "Iraq War Bribes of $1 Million-Plus Land
Military Contractor in Federal Prison," *Philadelphia Inquirer*, July 8, 2015.

12. U.S. Department of Justice, "Army Officer, Wife and Relatives Sentenced in Bribery and Money Laundering Scheme Related to DOD Contracts in
Support of Iraq War," press release, December 2, 2009.

13. U.S. Department of Justice, "Former U.S. Army Major Sentenced to
18 Months in Prison for Bribery Scheme Related to Depart of Defense Contracts in Kuwait," press release, November 13, 2012.

14. U.S. Department of Justice, "Former Major Sentenced to Prison in
Bribery and Money Laundering Scheme Related to DOD Contracts in Support
of Iraq War," press release, January 6, 2012.

15. U.S. Department of Justice, "Retired Army Major Sentenced to 24 Months in Prison for Engaging in Money Laundering Related to Contracting in Support of Iraq War," press release, December 13, 2011; U.S. Department of Justice, "Retired Army Major Sentenced to 57 Months in Prison for Role in Bribery Scheme Involving DOD Contracts in Kuwait," press release, December 16, 2009.

16. Roebuck, "Iraq War Bribes"; U.S. Department of Justice, "Former Military Contractor Sentenced to 54 Months in Prison for Paying Bribe to Army Officer during Iraq War," press release, July 8, 2015.

17. Rachel Weiner, "Former National Guard Colonel Sentenced to a Year in Prison in Bribery Scheme," *Washington Post*, May 26, 2017; "Former Guard One-Star Pleads Guilty in Bribery Scheme," *Army Times*, February 19, 2015; U.S. Department of Justice, Eastern District of Virginia, "Three Owners and CEO of Falls Church Based Contracting Company Indicted on National Guard Bribery Case," press release, July 15, 2015; U.S. Department of Justice, "Five National Guard Officials and One Civilian Charged with Bribery," press release, October 1, 2014.

18. U.S. Department of Justice, U.S. Attorney's Office, Southern District of Georgia, "Former Army Colonel, Wife Sentenced to Prison for Roles in Fort Gordon Fraud, Kickback Scheme," press release, February 5, 2019; U.S. Department of Justice, U.S. Attorney's Office, Southern District of Georgia, "Former Army Colonel Sentenced to Federal Prison for Fort Gordon Fraud, Kickback Scheme," press release, August 30, 2019; Sandy Hodson, "Fourth Colonel to Serve Prison Time for Fort Gordon Bribery and Bid-Rigging Scheme," *Augusta Chronicle*, August 6, 2020.

19. U.S. Department of Justice, U.S. Attorney's Office, Eastern District of Louisiana, "Marine Corps Official Sentenced to Prison for Taking $100,000 in Bribes in Exchange for Directing over $2,000,000 Worth of Transportation Contracts to Associate," press release, July 1, 2021; U.S. Department of Justice, U.S. Attorney's Office, Eastern District of Louisiana, "Atlanta Man Sentenced to Jail for Bribing U.S. Marine Corps Official in Exchange for $2,000,000 in Transportation Contracts," press release, October 1, 2021.

20. U.S. Department of Justice, "Former U.S. Army Employee Sentenced for Kickback Scheme to Steer U.S. Government Contracts," press release, November 10, 2021; U.S. Department of Justice, U.S. Attorney's Office, District of Hawaii, "Former Government Contractor Sentenced for Role in Bribery and Kickback Scheme, press release, January 15, 2021; Harm Venhuizen and Kyle Rempfer, "Contractor Sentenced for Schofield Barracks Bribery Scheme," *Army Times*, January 16, 2021.

21. U.S. Department of Justice, U.S. Attorney's Office, Eastern District of Virginia, "Florida Man Sentenced for Paying Bribes and Kickback and Defrauding the United States," February 4, 2022; Rachel Weiner, "Former Defense, Justice Employee Sentenced to More Than 7 Years for Fraud," *Washington Post*, January 14, 2022.

22. Matthew Gault, "How a Malaysian Playboy Controlled the Most Powerful Naval Force on the Planet," Medium.com, April 13, 2015, https://medium .com/war-is-boring/how-a-malaysian-playboy-controlled-the-most-powerful -naval-force-on-the-planet-eddb7d7fbf48; Tom Wright, interview with Leonard Francis, *Fat Leonard*, podcast audio, October 5, 2021, https://fatleonard podcast.com/episodes/.

23. Jesse Hyde, "Fat Leonard's Crimes on the High Seas," *Rolling Stone*, March 11, 2018, https://www.rollingstone.com/politics/politics-news/fat -leonards-crimes-on-the-high-seas-197055/.

24. Craig Whitlock, "The Man Who Seduced the Seventh Fleet," *Washington Post*, May 27, 2016.

25. Hyde, "Fat Leonard's Crimes."

26. Greg Moran, "Jury Convicts Four Former Navy Officers in 'Fat Leonard' Bribery Trial," *San Diego Union-Tribune*, June 29, 2022.

27. Sam LaGrone, "Paying the Price: The Hidden Cost of the 'Fat Leonard' Investigation," *USNI News*, January 24, 2019; U.S. Department of Justice, Southern District of California, "Marine Corps Colonel Pleads Guilty in International Navy Bribery and Fraud Scandal," press release, September 3, 2021; U.S. Department of Justice, Southern District of California, "Former U.S. Navy Captain Pleads Guilty as the Seventh Fleet Navy Bribery Trial Approaches," press release, February 2, 2022.

28. John M. Richardson, "Message to Naval Flag Officers and Senior Executive Service," May 2016, http://cimsec.org/wp-content/uploads/2016/07 /CNO-PFOR.pdf.

29. Craig Whitlock, "Two Admirals Face Probe in Navy Bribery Scheme," *Washington Post*, November 8, 2013.

30. J. M. Richardson to Secretary of the Navy, "Accountability Action Relating to Glenn Defense Marine — RADM Timothy M. Giardina, USN," December 11, 2014, http://www.sailorbob.com/files/Fat%20Leonard/CDA%20Infor mation%20-%20Washington%20Post%20FOIA%20-%20reduced%20for %20web.pdf.

31. David B. Larter, "Navy Rebukes 3 Admirals for Accepting Dinners, Gifts," *Navy Times*, July 18, 2015.

32. Craig Whitlock, "Admiral Reprimanded for Drunken, Naked Escapade at Florida Hotel," *Washington Post*, December 7, 2015.

33. John M. Richardson, "Message to Naval Flag Officers and Senior Executive Service," May 2016, http://cimsec.org/wp-content/uploads/2016/07/CNO-PFOR.pdf.

34. U.S. Department of Justice, Southern District of California, "U.S. Navy Admiral Sentenced for Lying to Feds About His Relationship with Foreign Defense Contractor in Massive Navy Bribery and Fraud Investigation," press release, May 17, 2017; Craig Whitlock, "Admiral's Illicit History with 'Fat Leonard' Goes Back 20 Years, Prosecutors Say," *Washington Post*, April 19, 2017.

35. U.S. Department of Justice, Southern District of California, "U.S. Navy Admiral Sentenced"; Whitlock, "Admiral's Illicit History."

36. U.S. Department of Justice, Southern District of California, "U.S. Navy Admiral Sentenced."

37. U.S. Department of Justice, Southern District of California, "U.S. Navy Admiral Sentenced"; Craig Whitlock, "Admiral's Illicit History."

38. U.S. Department of Justice, Southern District of California, "U.S. Navy Admiral Sentenced."

39. U.S. Department of Justice, Southern District of California, "U.S. Navy Admiral Sentenced."

40. U.S. Department of Justice, Southern District of California, "U.S. Navy Admiral Pleads Guilty to Lying to Feds About His Relationship with Foreign Defense Contractor in Massive Navy Bribery and Fraud Investigation," press release, June 9, 2016.

41. U.S. Department of Justice, Southern District of California, "U.S. Navy Admiral Pleads Guilty."

42. Craig Whitlock, "Navy Admiral Pleads Guilty in 'Fat Leonard' Corruption Scandal," *Washington Post*, June 9, 2016.

43. U.S. Department of Justice, Southern District of California, "U.S. Navy Admiral Sentenced"; Craig Whitlock, "Navy Officers Convicted of Corruption in 'Fat Leonard' Scandal Haven't Lost Their Pensions," *Washington Post*, March 18, 2017.

44. U.S. Department of Justice, Southern District of California, "U.S. Navy Admiral Sentenced"; Craig Whitlock, "Navy Officers Convicted."

45. Craig Whitlock and Tony Perry, "Former Admiral Sentenced to 18 Months in 'Fat Leonard' Case," *Washington Post*, May 17, 2017; Craig Whitlock, "Admiral's Illicit History."

46. Whitlock and Perry, "Former Admiral Sentenced"; Justin Watson, "US Navy Admiral Sentenced to 18 Months in 'Fat Leonard' Bribery Scandal," *Navy Times*, May 17, 2017.

47. Whitlock and Perry, "Former Admiral Sentenced."

48. Whitlock and Perry, "Former Admiral Sentenced."

49. U.S. Department of Justice, Southern District of California, "U.S. Navy Admiral Sentenced."

50. U.S. Department of Justice, Southern District of California, "U.S. Navy Admiral Sentenced."

51. U.S. Department of Justice, Southern District of California, "U.S. Navy Admiral Sentenced."

52. Craig Whitlock, "Navy Repeatedly Dismissed Evidence that 'Fat Leonard' Was Cheating the 7th Fleet," *Washington Post*, December 27, 2016; Craig Whitlock and Kevin Uhrmacher, "Prostitutes, Vacations and Cash: The Navy Officials 'Fat Leonard' Took Down," *Washington Post*, September 20, 2018; David B. Larter, "Navy Rebukes 3 Admirals for Accepting Dinners, Gifts," *Navy Times*, July 18, 2015.

53. Whitlock, "Navy Repeatedly Dismissed Evidence"; Whitlock and Uhrmacher, "Prostitutes, Vacations and Cash."

54. Commander, Military Personnel Detachment, Office of Naval Reactors, Department of Energy to Navy Inspector General, "Adverse Information ICO RADM Terry B. Kraft," February 13, 2015, http://www.sailorbob.com/files/Fat%20Leonard/CDA%20Information%20-%20Washington%20Post%20FOIA%20-%20reduced%20for%20web.pdf.

55. Marty Graham, "Three U.S. Navy Admirals Censured in Bribery Scandal," *Reuters*, July 20, 2015.

56. Commander, Military Personnel Detachment, Office of Naval Reactors, Department of Energy to Navy Inspector General, "Adverse Information ICO RADM Terry B. Kraft."

57. Christopher P. Cavas, "3 Admirals Censured in 'Fat Leonard' Scandal," *Defenses News*, February 10, 2015.

58. Craig Whitlock, "Three U.S. Naval Officers Censured in 'Fat Leonard' Corruption Probe," *Washington Post*, July 17, 2015; Whitlock and Uhrmacher, "Prostitutes, Vacations and Cash."

59. U.S. Department of Defense, Office of Naval Inspector General, *Report of Investigation, Senior Official Cases: 201202138, Alleging Violation of Joint Travel Regulations by RADM Mark F. Heinrich, CAPT (RDML Select)*

David R. Pimpo and CAPT (RDML Select) Donald L. Singleton; Craig Whitlock, "Navy Rebukes Three Admirals for Taking Questionable Trip to Britain," *Washington Post*, February 7, 2014.

60. Whitlock, "Navy Rebukes Three Admirals."

61. Jeanette Steele, "Admiral Loses Star in 'Fat Leonard' Scandal," *San Diego Union-Tribune*, July 20, 2015; Graham, "Three U.S. Navy Admirals Censured"; Cavas, "3 Admirals Censured"; David B. Larter, "Navy Rebukes 3 Admirals for Accepting Dinners, Gifts," *Navy Times*, July 18, 2015.

62. Commander, Military Personnel Detachment, Office of Naval Reactors, Department of Energy to Navy Inspector General, "Adverse Information ICO RADM David R. Pimpo," February 13, 2015, http://www.sailorbob.com/files /Fat%20Leonard/CDA%20Information%20-%20Washington%20Post%20 FOIA%20-%20reduced%20for%20web.pdf.

63. Cavas, "3 Admirals Censured."

64. Craig Whitlock, "'Fat Leonard' Probe Expands to Ensnare More Than 60 Admirals," *Washington Post*, November 5, 2017.

65. Larter, "Navy Rebukes 3 Admirals."

66. Whitlock, "Man Who Seduced the Seventh Fleet"; Tim Prudente, "Former Naval Academy Superintendent: Underpaying for Gifts Was an Unintentional Mistake," *Capital Gazette*, November 29, 2015.

67. Whitlock, "Man Who Seduced the Seventh Fleet."

68. Steele, "Admiral Loses Star."

69. Commander, Military Personnel Detachment, Office of Naval Reactors, Department of Energy to Navy Inspector General, "Adverse Information ICO RADM Michael H. Miller, USN," February 13, 2015, http://www.sailorbob.com /files/Fat%20Leonard/CDA%20Information%20-%20Washington%20Post% 20FOIA%20-%20reduced%20for%20web.pdf.

70. Steele, "Admiral Loses Star."

71. Prudente, "Unintentional Mistake."

72. Commander, Military Personnel Detachment, Office of Naval Reactors, Department of Energy to Naval Inspector General, "Adverse Information ICO RADM Timothy M. Giardina, USN," February 13, 2015, http://www.sailor bob.com/files/Fat%20Leonard/CDA%20Information%20-%20Washington %20Post%20FOIA%20-%20reduced%20for%20web.pdf.

73. J. M. Richardson to Secretary of the Navy, "Accountability Action Relating to Glenn Defense Marine—RADM Timothy M. Giardina, USN," December 11, 2014, http://www.sailorbob.com/files/Fat%20Leonard/CDA%20Information%20 -%20Washington%20Post%20FOIA%20-%20reduced%20for%20web.pdf.

74. Commander, Military Personnel Detachment, Office of Naval Reactors, Department of Energy to Naval Inspector General, "Adverse Information ICO RADM Timothy M. Giardina, USN."

75. Steve Liewer, "DNA Evidence Links Fired Offutt Admiral to Fake Poker Chips," *Omaha World-Herald*, November 22, 2014.

76. Iowa Division of Criminal Behavior, "Section 5 — Gaming History of Timothy Giardina," https://bloximages.newyork1.vip.townnews.com/omaha .com/content/tncms/assets/v3/editorial/5/b3/5b3580cc-726f-11e4-af23-d706785 bee85/5470cc252431f.pdf.pdf.

77. Iowa Division of Criminal Behavior, "Recorded Interview Timothy Giardina," transcript, June 18, 2013, https://bloximages.newyork1.vip.town news.com/omaha.com/content/tncms/assets/v3/editorial/5/b3/5b3580 cc-726f-11e4-af23-d706785bee85/5470cc252431f.pdf.pdf.

78. Liewer, "DNA Evidence"; Steve Liewer, "Ex-StratCom Deputy Commander Says He Regrets Not Defending Himself over Fake Poker Chips," *Omaha World-Herald*, February 20, 2014.

79. Robert Burns, "Admiral Denies Role in Counterfeiting Casino Chips," FederalNewsNetwork.com, November 24, 2014, https://federalnewsnetwork .com/government-news/2014/11/admiral-denies-role-in-counterfeiting-casino -chips/; Liewer, "DNA Evidence."

80. Robert Burns, "Gambling Admiral Linked to Fake Poker Chips," *Navy Times*, November 22, 2014.

81. U.S. Navy, "SECNAV Censured Three Naval Officers," press release, June 20, 2018; Dan Lamothe, "Navy Officers Censured for Bringing 'Embarrassment' on the Service in 'Fat Leonard' Scandal," *Washington Post*, June 20, 2018; Geoff Ziezulewicz, "SECNAV Censures Three More Navy Officers in 'Fat Leonard' Scandal," *Navy Times*, June 25, 2018.

82. Lamothe, "Navy Officers Censured."

83. Ziezulewicz, "SECNAV Censures Three More."

84. Lamothe, "Navy Officers Censured."

85. Kristine Goodrich, "Two Brothers, Both Decorated Navy Commanders, Returning to Civilian Life," *White Bear Press*, November 5, 2014.

86. Whitlock and Uhrmacher, "Prostitutes, Vacations and Cash"; Craig Whitlock, "Navy Censures Retired Admiral for Taking Gifts from 'Fat Leonard,'" *Washington Post*, November 29, 2017.

87. Ben Werner, "Retired Admiral Censured in Ongoing 'Fat Leonard' Investigation," *USNI News*, November 29, 2017; emphasis added.

88. Werner, "Retired Admiral Censured."

89. Gidget Fuentes, "Retired Flag Officer Who 'Abused His Position to Benefit Himself' Censured in Fat Leonard Scandal," *USNI News*, December 14, 2018.

90. Craig Whitlock, "Trump Nominee Sunk by 'Fat Leonard' Corruption," *Washington Post*, November 26, 2018.

91. Lagrone, "Paying the Price."

92. Whitlock, "Trump Nominee Sunk."

93. Fuentes, "Retired Flag Officer Censured"; Geoff Ziezulewicz, "Navy Releases New Details on Retired Admiral and Former Trump Nominee's 'Fat Leonard' Censure," *Navy Times*, December 14, 2018; Andrew Dyer, "Retired Admiral and Former Trump Nominee Was a 'Top Shelf' Friend to 'Fat Leonard,'" *San Diego Union-Tribune*, December 14, 2018.

94. Ziezulewicz, "Navy Releases New Details"; Dyer, "Retired Admiral and Former Trump Nominee."

95. Ziezulewicz, "Navy Releases New Details."

96. Fuentes, "Retired Flag Officer Censured."

97. LaGrone, "Paying the Price"; Fuentes, "Retired Flag Officer Censured."

98. Craig Whitlock, "How 'Fat Leonard' Bribed the Navy to Get U.S. Diplomatic Immunity," *Washington Post*, June 17, 2017; Kristina Davis, "Former Captain Gets Prison in 'Fat Leonard' Navy Bribery Scandal," *San Diego Union-Tribune*, June 16, 2017.

99. Commander, U.S. Fleet Forces Command to Naval Inspector General, "Adverse Information ICO RDML Adrian Jansen, USN," February 17, 2017, http://www.sailorbob.com/files/Fat%20Leonard/CDA%20Information%20-%20 Washington%20Post%20FOIA%20-%20reduced%20for%20web.pdf.

100. Commander, U.S. Fleet Forces Command to Commander, Navy Personnel Command, "Nonjudicial Punishment Report ICO RDML Adrian J. Jansen, USN," February 24, 2017, http://www.sailorbob.com/files/Fat%20Leonard /CDA%20Information%20-%20Washington%20Post%20FOIA%20-%20 reduced%20for%20web.pdf.

101. Commander, U.S. Fleet Forces Command to Naval Inspector General, "Adverse Information ICO RDML Adrian Jansen, USN."

102. Commander, U.S. Fleet Forces Command to Naval Inspector General, "Adverse Information ICO RDML Adrian Jansen, USN."

103. Commander, U.S. Fleet Forces Command to Commander, Navy Personnel Command, "Nonjudicial Punishment Report ICO RDML Adrian J. Jansen, USN."

104. "Fil-Am Woman Takes Command of US Navy Region Southwest," *U.S.A. Inquirer*, March 1, 2017, https://usa.inquirer.net/1898/fil-woman-takes -command-us-navy-region-southeast.

105. Gina Tabonares-Reilly, "Pinay Takes Helm of U.S. Naval Command," *Philippine Star*, October 26, 2014.

106. Carl Prine, "Before She Handled SEAL War Crimes Cases, One-Star Was Tied to 'Fat Leonard,'" *Navy Times*, August 5, 2019.

107. Prine, "One-Star Was Tied to 'Fat Leonard.'"

108. Prine, "One-Star Was Tied to 'Fat Leonard.'"

109. Sam LaGrone, "Former Navy Intelligence Chief Ted Branch Cleared in 'Fat Leonard' Case," *USNI News*, September 22, 2017.

110. Craig Whitlock, "Two Admirals Face Probe in Navy Bribery Scheme," *Washington Post*, November 8, 2013.

111. Craig Whitlock, "The Admiral in Charge of Navy Intelligence Has Not Been Allowed to See Military Secrets for Years," *Washington Post*, January 28, 2016.

112. Craig Whitlock, "Former Navy Intelligence Chief Took Lavish Meals and Gifts from 'Fat Leonard' but Is Cleared of Consorting with Prostitutes," *Washington Post*, March 12, 2018.

113. Whitlock, "Former Navy Intelligence Chief."

114. Whitlock, "Former Navy Intelligence Chief."

115. Whitlock, "Former Navy Intelligence Chief."

116. Whitlock, "Admiral in Charge of Navy Intelligence."

117. Norman Polmar, "Navy Needs New Intel Bosses Now," *Navy Times*, September 19, 2015.

118. Whitlock, "Admiral in Charge of Navy Intelligence."

119. Hope Hodge Seck, "Navy Intel Chief Calls Loss of His Security Clearance 'Insulting,'" Military.com, February 18, 2016, https://www.military.com /daily-news/2016/02/18/navy-intel-chief-calls-loss-of-his-security-clearance -insulting.html; David B. Larter, "Navy Withdraws Intel Boss Nominee, Furthering Uncertainty," *Navy Times*, April 1, 2016.

120. Hyde, "Fat Leonard's Crimes."

121. LaGrone, "Former Naval Intelligence Chief Cleared."

122. Whitlock and Uhrmacher, "Prostitutes, Vacations and Cash"; Whitlock, "Former Navy Intelligence Chief."

123. U.S. District Court, Southern District of California, "Indictment: U.S.A. v. David Newland, Enrico Deguzman . . . Bruce Loveless . . . Robert Gorsuch," filed March 10, 2017, 69.

124. Stephen Kenny and Christopher Drew, "Contracting Case Implicates 2 Admirals," *New York Times*, November 8, 2013; Whitlock, "Two Admirals Face Probe."

125. Cid Standifer, "Timeline: The 'Fat Leonard' Case," *USNI News*, March 16, 2017.

126. U.S. District Court, Southern District of California, "Indictment: U.S.A. v. Newland et al.," 17. Years later, Hornbeck was relieved of command of a destroyer squadron when the Navy learned of his "inappropriate personal relationship" with another officer's wife. In retirement, he was arrested for driving while intoxicated and crashing his car into cornfield. See Craig Whitlock, "Navy Has Spike in Commanding-Officer Firings, Most for Personal Misconduct," *Washington Post*, June 17, 2011; Jennifer Doherty, "Capt. in 'Fat Leonard' Scandal Charged with Drunk Driving," www.Law360.com, August 19, 2020, https://www.law360.com/articles/1302768/capt-in-fat-leonard-scandal-charged-with-drunk-driving.

127. U.S. District Court, Southern District of California, "Indictment: U.S.A. v. Newland et al.," 23–24.

128. U.S. District Court, Southern District of California, "Indictment: U.S.A. v. Newland et al.," 34.

129. U.S. District Court, Southern District of California, "Indictment: U.S.A. v. Newland et al.," 4, 16.

130. Tom Wright, interview with Leonard Francis, *Fat Leonard*, podcast audio, October 5, 2021, https://fatleonardpodcast.com/episodes/.

131. U.S. District Court, Southern District of California, "Indictment: U.S.A. v. Newland et al.," 34–35.

132. U.S. District Court, Southern District of California, "Indictment: U.S.A. v. Newland et al.," 35–36.

133. U.S. District Court, Southern District of California, "Indictment: U.S.A. v. Newland et al.," 35–38.

134. U.S. District Court, Southern District of California, "Indictment: U.S.A. v. Newland et al.," 37–38.

135. U.S. District Court, Southern District of California, "Indictment: U.S.A. v. Newland et al.," 38–39; Lauren Ritchie, "Indicted Navy Captain Wants Federal Prosecutors to Drop Charges," *Orlando Sentinel*, March 4, 2019.

136. U.S. District Court, Southern District of California, "Indictment: U.S.A. v. Newland et al.," 38–40.

137. U.S. District Court, Southern District of California, "Indictment: U.S.A. v. Newland et al.," 41.

138. U.S. District Court, Southern District of California, "Indictment: U.S.A. v. Newland et al.," 41.

139. U.S. District Court, Southern District of California, "Indictment: U.S.A. v. Newland et al.," 41–42.

140. U.S. District Court, Southern District of California, "Indictment: U.S.A. v. Newland et al.," 43.

141. U.S. District Court, Southern District of California, "Indictment: U.S.A. v. Newland et al.," 43–44.

142. U.S. District Court, Southern District of California, "Indictment: U.S.A. v. Newland et al.," 44; Craig Whitlock, "Leaks, Feasts, and Sex Parties: How 'Fat Leonard' Infiltrated the Navy's Floating Headquarters in Asia," *Washington Post*, January 31, 2018.

143. Whitlock, "Admiral in Charge of Navy Intelligence."

144. Eric Lichtblau, "Admiral and 8 Other Navy Officers Indicted on Bribery Charges," *New York Times*, March 14, 2017.

145. U.S. Attorney's Office, Southern District of California, "U.S. Navy Admiral Plus Eight Officers Indicted as Part of Corrupt Team That Worked Together to Trade Navy Secrets for Sex Parties," press release, March 14, 2017.

146. U.S. District Court, Southern District of California, "Indictment: U.S.A. v. Newland et al.," 11, 16.

147. U.S. District Court, Southern District of California, "Indictment: U.S.A. v. Newland et al.," 76–77.

148. U.S. District Court, Southern District of California, "Indictment: U.S.A. v. Newland et al.," 72–73.

149. "Judge Releases Retired Admiral in Bribery Case," *Washington Times*, March 14, 2017.

150. Giovanni Russonello, "Stephen Colbert Is Missing Out on Perfectly Good Sex Scandals," *New York Times*, March 23, 2017.

151. U.S. Department of Justice, U.S. Attorney's Office, Southern District of California, "Chief Warrant Officer Pleads Guilty in International Navy Bribery and Fraud Scandal," press release, August 31, 2021; U.S. Department of Justice, U.S. Attorney's Office, Southern District of California, "Marine Corps Colonel Pleads Guilty in International Navy Bribery and Fraud Scandal," press release, September 3, 2021.

152. U.S. Department of Justice, U.S. Attorney's Office, Southern District of California, "U.S. Navy Commander Pleads Guilty in the Run Up to the Seventh Fleet Navy Bribery Trial," press release, January 26, 2022; U.S. Department of Justice, U.S. Attorney's Office, Southern District of California, "Former U.S. Navy Captain Pleads Guilty as the Seventh Fleet Navy Bribery Trial Approaches," press release, February 2, 2022.

153. Moran, "Jury Convicts Four Former Navy Officers."

154. Whitlock, "Man Who Seduced the Seventh Fleet."

155. Michael M. Gilday, "CNO Message to the Force: We Must Be Protectors and Exemplify Our Values," December 2, 2019, https://www.navy.mil/Resources/Blogs/Detail/Article/2268212/cno-message-to-the-force-we-must-be-protectors-and-exemplify-our-values/.

156. U.S. Department of Defense, Office of Inspector General, *Investigation Involving Major General Stephen M. Goldfein, U.S. Air Force, Vice Director, Joint Staff*; "Pentagon Says Contract Was Tainted," *New York Times*, April 18, 2008; U.S. Air Force, "Air Force Secretary Takes Action on DOD IG Report," press release, October, 8, 2009, https://www.af.mil/News/Article-Display/Article/118898/air-force-secretary-takes-action-on-dod-ig-report/.

157. Craig Whitlock, "Key Army Commander Accused of Steering a Contract to Ex-Classmates," *Washington Post*, June 21, 2015.

158. Kevin Lilley, "2-Star General to Retire after Reprimand in Bliss Deal," *Army Times*, June 22, 2015.

Conclusion

1. "President Trump's Rose Garden Speech on Protests," transcript, CNN.com, June 1, 2020.

2. Woodward and Costa, *Peril*, 94.

3. Goldberg, "James Mattis Denounces President Trump."

4. Leonnig and Rucker, *I Alone Can Fix It*, 171.

5. Woodward and Costa, *Peril*, 98.

6. Woodward and Costa, *Peril*, 106.

7. Milley, "2020 Class Graduation Address."

8. Leonnig and Rucker, *I Alone Can Fix It*, 187–88.

9. Leonnig and Rucker, *I Alone Can Fix It*, 188.

10. Bender, *"Frankly, We Did Win This Election,"* 159.

11. Esper, *Sacred Oath*, 3–4, 334–39.

12. Esper, *Sacred Oath*, 338.

13. Bender, *"Frankly, We Did Win This Election,"* 158; Leonnig and Rucker, *I Alone Can Fix It*, 158–59.

14. Leonnig and Rucker, *I Alone Can Fix It*, 212; Esper, *Sacred Oath*, 441–50.

15. Leonnig and Rucker, *I Alone Can Fix It*, 183; Esper, *Sacred Oath*, 486, 494, 645.

16. Leonnig and Rucker, *I Alone Can Fix It*, 189.

17. Leonnig and Rucker, *I Alone Can Fix It*, 487.

18. Leonnig and Rucker, *I Alone Can Fix It*, 361; Esper, *Sacred Oath*, 654.

19. Woodward and Costa, *Peril*, 150–51.

20. Woodward and Costa, *Peril*, 152.

21. "Remarks by General Mark A. Milley at the Opening Ceremony for the National Museum of the United States Army," *Joint Staff Public Affairs*, November 11, 2020; Milley, "Address at the Opening."

22. Leonnig and Rucker, *I Alone Can Fix It*, 360.

23. Leonnig and Rucker, *I Alone Can Fix It*, 363–64.

24. Leonnig and Rucker, *I Alone Can Fix It*, 365–66.

25. Leonnig and Rucker, *I Alone Can Fix It*, 437.

26. Leonnig and Rucker, *I Alone Can Fix It*, 366, 383.

27. Leonnig and Rucker, *I Alone Can Fix It*, 469.

28. Leonnig and Rucker, *I Alone Can Fix It*, 473–74.

29. Karl, *Betrayal*, 299; U.S. Department of Defense, Office of Inspector General, "U.S. Capitol Campus on January 6, 2021"; Earl G. Matthews, "The Harder Right: An Analysis of a Recent DoD Inspector General Investigation and Other Matters," December 1, 2021, https://www.politico.com/f/?id=0000017d-8aca-dee4-a5ff-eeda79e90000.

30. Woodward and Costa, *Peril*, xiv, xix, 151.

31. Leonnig and Rucker, *I Alone Can Fix It*, 486.

32. Leonnig and Rucker, *I Alone Can Fix It*, 492.

33. Woodward and Costa, *Peril*, xxi.

34. Leonnig and Rucker, *I Alone Can Fix It*, 498–99.

35. Robert Draper, "Michael Flynn Is Still at War," *New York Times*, February 6, 2022; Aaron Blake, "Michael Flynn, and Trump's Lasting Elevation of the Fringe," *Washington Post*, June 3, 2021; Howard Altman and Davis Winkie, "This Retired Three-Star Falsely Claims US Soldiers Died Attacking a CIA Facility in Germany Tied to Election Fraud," *Military Times*, December 1, 2020; Brannon Howse, "3-Star General McInerney Calls for Martial Law, Tribunals & Investigation of Treason," World View Weekend Broadcast, November 30, 2020, https://www.worldviewweekend.com/tv/video/exclusive-3-star-general-mcinerney-calls-martial-law-tribunals-investigation-treason; Earl G. Matthews, "Full Transcript of Bombshell Interview: Gen. Michael Flynn, Gen. Thomas McInerney with Brannon Howse — Identity of Kraken Revealed," December 1, 2020, https://eraoflight.com/2020/12/01/full-transcript-of-bombshell-interview-gen-michael-flynn-gen-thomas-mcinerney-with-brannon-howse-identity-of-kraken-revealed/.

36. Thomas, "Four Stages of Moral Development."

37. Ludwig and Longenecker, "Bathsheba Syndrome," 265–73; Bottom-lee, "Building Leaders' Moral Courage."

38. Mill, *On Liberty*, 17.

39. Adams, *Education of Henry Adams*, 147.

40. Cabell, *First Gentleman of America*, 85.

41. George Patton to Beatrice Patton, August 22, 1943, in Blumenson, *Patton Papers*, 335.

42. In a thoughtful essay, Major Peyton C. Hurley recommends that the military (particularly the U.S. Army) should investigate senior leader misconduct as "accidents" because official accident investigations focus on why something went awry with the goal of preventing future failure. See Peyton C. Hurley, "Sword of Damocles: A Framework to Identify the Causes of and Preventative Measures for Leader Misconduct," *Military Review* (September 2018): 1–8.

43. Williamson and Sinnreich, *Past Is Prologue*, 27.

44. Mill, *On Liberty*, 17.

45. Berger, "Commandant's Planning Guidance," 22; Paul Szoldra, "Marine Commandant to Leaders: Quit the 'Soft Relief' of Fired Officers," *Task & Purpose*, October 23, 2020.

46. Voth and Xu, "Encouraging Others," 1.

BIBLIOGRAPHY

Acheson, Dean. *Present at the Creation: My Years at the State Department*. New York: W. W. Norton, 1969.

Adams, Henry B. *The Education of Henry Adams*. New York: The Modern Library, 1931.

Allen, Thomas B., and Norman Polmar. *Rickover: Father of the Nuclear Navy*. Sterling, VA: Potomac Books, 2007.

Allison, John M. *Ambassador from the Prairie; or, Allison Wonderland*. New York: Houghton Mifflin, 1973.

Ambrose, Stephen E. *Eisenhower: Soldier and President*. New York: Simon & Schuster, 1991.

Annual Reports of [Nelson A. Miles] the Major-General Commanding the Army to the Secretary of War. Special Collections, University of Washington.

Aspin, Les. "Joint Ethics Regulation (JER)." DoD Directive 5500.7-R. August 30, 1993. https://www.esd.whs.mil/Portals/54/Documents/DD/issuances /dodm/550007r.pdf.

Austin, Lloyd J., III. "Statement on the Conclusion of Independent Review Commission." June 22, 2021. https://www.defense.gov/News/Releases /Release/Article/2667381.

Bacevich, Andrew. *Breach of Trust: How Americans Failed Their Soldiers and Their Country*. New York: Metropolitan Books, 2013.

Barnett, Thomas P. M. "The Man between War and Peace." *Esquire* (March 11, 2018): 144–53.

Bartsch, William H. *December 8, 1941: MacArthur's Pearl Harbor*. College Station: Texas A&M University Press, 2012.

Beach, Edward L. *Salt and Steel: Reflections of a Submariner*. Annapolis, MD: Naval Institute Press, 1999.

Beck, Robert L. *Inside the Tailhook Scandal: An Aviator's Story*. Meadville, PA: Fulton Books, 2016.

Bender, Michael C. *"Frankly, We Did Win This Election": The Inside Story of How Trump Lost*. New York: Grand Central Publishing, 2021.

Berger, David. "Commandant's Planning Guidance: 38th Commandant of the Marine Corps." August 2, 2021. https://www.marines.mil/News/News -Display/Article/2707972/2019-commandants-planning-guidance/.

Birtle, Andrew J. "PROVN, Westmoreland, and the Historians: A Reappraisal." *Journal of Military History* 72, no. 4 (October 2008): 1213–47.

Blair, Clay, Jr. "The Man in Tempo 3." *Time*, January 11, 1954. http://content .time.com/time/subscriber/article/0,33009,819338-1,00.html.

Blumenson, Martin, ed. *Patton Papers: 1940–1945*. New York: Da Capo Press, 1996.

Bottomlee, James David. "Building Leaders' Moral Courage to Defeat the King David Syndrome." Strategy Research Project, Carlisle Barracks: U.S. Army War College, 2012. https://apps.dtic.mil/sti/pdfs/ADA589035.pdf.

Bradley, Omar N. *A General's Life: An Autobiography*. With Clay Blair. New York: Simon & Schuster, 1983.

Brands, H. W. *The General vs. the President: MacArthur and Truman at the Brink of Nuclear War*. New York: Anchor Books, 2016.

Brinkley, Douglas. *The Reagan Diaries*. New York: Harper Collins, 2007.

Brown, Fred. *History of the Ninth Infantry, 1799–1909*. New York: Donnelly, 1909.

Bruno, Thomas A. "The Violent End of Insurgency on Samar, 1901–1902." *Army History* (Spring 2011): 30–46.

Bullis, R. Craig, and George Reed. *Report to the Secretary of the Army: Assessing Leaders to Establish and Maintain Positive Command Climates*. Carlisle Barracks, PA, February 2003.

Byrne, Malcolm. *Iran-Contra: Reagan's Scandal and the Unchecked Abuse of Presidential Power*. Lawrence: University Press of Kansas, 2017.

Cabell, James Branch. *The First Gentleman of America*. New York: Farrar and Rinehart, 1942.

Cantonwine, Paul E., ed. *The Never-Ending Challenge of Engineering: Admiral Hyman Rickover in His Own Words*. La Grange Park, IL: American Nuclear Society, 2013.

Carpenter, Frank G. "Uncle Sam's Pirates." *Timely Topics* 7, no. 11 (November 14, 1902): 168–69.

Carter, Jimmy. *Why Not the Best?* New York: Bantam Books, 1976.

Chaffin, Tom. *Pathfinder: John Charles Fremont and the Course of American Empire.* New York: Hill and Wang, 2002.

Clapper, James R. *Facts and Fears: Hard Truths from a Life in Intelligence.* New York: Viking, 2018.

Collins, J. Lawton. *War in Peacetime: The History and Lessons of Korea.* New York: Houghton Mifflin, 1969.

Conti, Marco, and Thomas C. Oden, eds. *1–2 Kings, 1–2 Chronicles, Ezra, Nehemiah, Esther.* Westmont, IL: IVP Academic, 2008.

Cooper, Charles G. "The Day It Became the Longest War." *Proceedings of the Naval Institute* (May 1996): 77–80.

Crowe, William J., Jr. *The Line of Fire: From Washington to the Gulf, the Politics and Battles of the New Military.* New York: Simon & Schuster, 1993.

Davidson, Phillip P. *Vietnam at War: The History, 1946–1975.* New York: Oxford University Press, 1991.

Degler, Carl N. "A Southern Eccentric." *Reviews in American History* (September 1980): 339–43.

D'Este, Carlos. *Eisenhower: A Soldier's Life.* New York: Henry Holt and Company, 2002.

Draper, Robert. "Michael Flynn Is Still at War." *New York Times Magazine*, February 4, 2022. https://www.nytimes.com/2022/02/04/magazine/michael-flynn-2020-election.html.

Draper, Theodore. *A Very Thin Line: The Iran-Contra Affairs.* New York: Hill and Wang, 1991.

Dubik, James M. "Taking a 'Pro' Position on Principled Resignation." *Armed Forces & Society* (August 15, 2016): 17–28.

Duncan, Francis. *Rickover and the Nuclear Navy: The Discipline of Technology.* Annapolis: Naval Institute Press, 1990.

———. *Rickover: The Struggle for Excellence.* Annapolis, MD: U.S. Naval Institute, 2001.

Dyer, John P. *From Shiloh to San Juan: The Life of "Fighting Joe" Wheeler.* Baton Rouge: Louisiana State University Press, 1992.

Eisenhower, Dwight D. *At Ease: Stories I Tell to Friends.* Garden City, NY: Doubleday, 1967.

Eisenhower, John S. D. *Agent of Destiny: The Life and Times of General Winfield Scott.* Norman: University of Oklahoma Press, 2015.

Ellsberg, Daniel. *Secrets: A Memoir of Vietnam and the Pentagon Papers*. New York: Penguin Books, 2003.

Esper, Mark T. *A Sacred Oath: Memoirs of a Secretary of Defense during Extraordinary Times*. New York: William Morrow, 2022.

Evans, Stephen S., ed. *U.S. Marines and Irregular Warfare, 1898–2007: Anthology and Selected Bibliography*. Quantico, VA: Marine Corps University, 2008.

Feight, Andrew. "General Jacob H. Smith and the Philippine War's Samar Campaign: American Imperialism at the Washington Hotel." *Scioto Historical*. Accessed January 20, 2021. https://sciotohistorical.org/items/show/109.

Felice, William F. *How to Save My Honor: War, Moral Integrity, and Principled Resignation*. Lanham, MD: Rowman & Littlefield, 2009.

Ferrell, Robert H., ed. *Off the Record: The Private Papers of Harry S. Truman*. Columbia: University of Missouri Press, 1997.

Frank, Jeffrey. *The Trials of Harry S. Truman: The Extraordinary Presidency of an Ordinary Man, 1945–1953*. New York: Simon & Schuster, 2022.

Ford, Worthington Chauncey, ed. *The Writings of George Washington*. 14 vols. New York: G.P. Putnam's Sons, 1889.

Friedman, Leon. *Law of War: A Documentary History*. New York: Random House, 1972.

Fritz, David L. "Before the 'Howling Wilderness.'" *Military Affairs* (December 1979): 186–90.

Fry, Joseph A. *Debating Vietnam: Fulbright, Stennis, and their Hearings*. Lanham, MD: Rowman & Littlefield Publishers, 2006.

Gallery, Dan V. "If This Be Treason." *Collier's* (January 21, 1950): 15–16, 45.

Gates, Henry Louis, Jr. *Thirteen Ways of Looking at a Black Man*. New York: Vikings Books, 1997.

Gates, Robert M. *Duty: Memoirs of a Secretary at War*. New York: Alfred A. Knopf, 2014.

———. *From the Shadows: The Ultimate Insider's Story of Five Presidents and How They Won the Cold War*. New York: Simon & Schuster, 1996.

Gelb, Leslie. *The Irony of Vietnam: The System Worked*. With Richard K. Betts. New York: Brookings Institution Press, 1979.

Gellman, Barton. "What Happened to Michael Flynn?" *The Atlantic*, July 8, 2022. https://www.theatlantic.com/ideas/archive/2022/07/michael-flynn-conspiracy-theories-january-6-trump/661439/.

Gilday, Michael M. "CNO Message to the Force: We Must Be Protectors and Exemplify Our Values." December 2, 2019. https://www.navy.mil/Resources

/Blogs/Detail/Article/2268212/cno-message-to-the-force-we-must-be
-protectors-and-exemplify-our-values/.

Gilliland, C. Herbert, and Robert Shenk. *Admiral Dan Gallery: The Life and Wit of a Navy Original*. Annapolis, MD: Naval Institute Press, 1999.

Goldberg, Jeffrey. "James Mattis Denounces President Trump, Describes Him as a Threat to the Constitution." *The Atlantic*, June 3, 2020. https://www .theatlantic.com/politics/archive/2020/06/james-mattis-denounces -trump-protests-militarization/612640/.

Grunder, Garel A., and William Livezey. *The Philippines and the United States*. Norman: University of Oklahoma Press, 1951.

Halberstam, David. *The Best and the Brightest*. New York: Random House, 1972.

Hamilton, Lee H., and Daniel K. Inouye. *Report of the Congressional Committees Investigating the Iran-Contra Affair, with Supplemental, Minority, and Additional Views*. Washington, DC: Government Printing Office, 1987.

Haque, Adil Ahmad. *Law and Morality at War*. New York: Oxford University Press, 2017.

Harte, Julia. "U.S. Military Personnel Have Been Convicted of $50 Million Worth of Crimes in Iraq and Afghanistan." The Center for Public Integrity. May 5, 2015. https://publicintegrity.org/national-security/u-s-military -personnel-have-been-convicted-of-50-million-worth-of-crimes-in-iraq -and-afghanistan/.

Hastings, Michael. "The Runaway General." *Rolling Stone*. June 22, 2010. https:// www.rollingstone.com/politics/politics-news/the-runaway-general-the -profile-that-brought-down-mcchrystal-192609/.

Herman, Arthur. *Douglas MacArthur: American Warrior*. New York: Random House, 2016.

Herring, George C. *America's Longest War: The United States and Vietnam, 1950– 1975*. New York: McGraw Hill, 2001.

———. *From Colony to Superpower: U.S. Foreign Relations since 1776*. New York: Oxford University Press, 2008.

Hill, Anita. "Opening Statement: Sexual Harassment Hearings Concerning Judge Clarence Thomas." October 11, 1991. https://cpb-use1.wpmucdn .com/blogs.uoregon.edu/dist/7/11428/files/2015/06/Hill-Opening -Statement-1991-1zxyhrw.pdf.

Hoover, Herbert. *The Memoirs of Herbert Hoover*. Vol. 2, *The Cabinet and the Presidency, 1920–1933*. New York: MacMillan, 1952.

———. *The Memoirs of Herbert Hoover*. Vol. 3, *The Great Depression, 1929–1941*. New York: MacMillan, 1952.

Huggins, Stephan. *America's Use of Terror: From Colonial Times to the A-Bomb*. Lawrence: University Press of Kansas, 2019.

Humphrey, David C., Ronald D. Landa, and Louis J. Smith, eds. *Foreign Relations of the United States, 1964–1968*, Vol. 2, *Vietnam, January–June 1965*. Washington, DC: Government Printing Office, 1996.

Hyde, Jesse. "Fat Leonard's Crimes on the High Seas." *Rolling Stone*. March 11, 2018. https://www.rollingstone.com/politics/politics-news/fat-leonards-crimes-on-the-high-seas-197055/.

Inskeep, Steve. *Imperfect Union: How Jessie and John Fremont Mapped the West, Invented Celebrity, and Helped Cause the Civil War*. New York: Penguin Press, 2020.

James, D. Clayton. *The Years of MacArthur*. Vol. 1, *1880–1941*. New York: Houghton Mifflin, 1970.

———. *The Years of MacArthur*. Vol. 3, *Triumph and Disaster, 1945–1964*. New York: Houghton Mifflin, 1985.

Janosi, F. E. de. "The Correspondence between Lord Acton and Bishop Creighton." *Cambridge Historical Journal* 6 (1940): 307–21.

Jennings, John M., and Chuck Steele, eds. *The Worst Military Leaders in History*. London: Reaktion Books, 2022.

Johnson, Timothy D. *Winfield Scott: The Quest for Glory*. Lawrence: University Press of Kansas, 2015.

Jones, Gregg. *Honor in the Dust: Theodore Roosevelt, War in the Philippines, and the Rise and Fall of America's Imperial Dream*. New York: Penguin Books, 2013.

Jones, Howard. *My Lai: Vietnam, 1968, and the Descent into Darkness*. New York: Oxford University Press, 2017.

Karl, Jonathan. *Betrayal: The Final Act of the Trump Show*. New York: Dutton, 2021.

Karnow, Stanley. *Vietnam: A History*. New York: Penguin Books, 1984.

Karpinski, Janis. *One Woman's Army: The Commanding General of Abu Ghraib Tells Her Story*. New York: Miramax, 2006.

Kearns Goodwin, Doris. *Team of Rivals: The Political Genius of Abraham Lincoln*. New York: Simon & Schuster, 2005.

Kellerman, Barbara. *Bad Leadership: What It Is, How It Happens, Why It Matters*. Cambridge, MA: Harvard Business Review Press, 2004.

Kennedy, Claudia J. *Generally Speaking: A Memoir by the First Woman Promoted to Three-Star General in the United States Army*. New York: Warner Books, 2001.

Kenney, George C. *The MacArthur I Know*. Duell, Sloan & Pearce, 1951.

Kramer, Paul A. *The Blood of Government: Race, Empire, the United States, and the Philippines*. Chapel Hill, NC: University of North Carolina Press, 2006.

Laing, Kelly L. "Leadership in Command Under the Sea." Air Command and Staff College, Maxwell Air Force Base. November 29, 2012. https://apps .dtic.mil/sti/pdfs/ADA539143.pdf.

Laver, Harry S., and Jeffrey J. Matthews. *The Art of Command: Military Leadership from George Washington to Colin Powell*. Lexington: University Press of Kentucky, 2017.

Leary, William M., ed. *MacArthur and the American Century: A Reader*. Lincoln: University of Nebraska Press, 2001.

Lehman, John. *Command of the Seas*. Annapolis, MD: Naval Institute Press, 2001.

LeRoy, James A. *The Americans in the Philippines: A History of the Conquest and First Years of Occupation*. Boston: Houghton Mifflin, 1914.

Liman, Arthur L. *Lawyer: A Life of Counsel and Controversy*. New York: Public Affairs, 1998.

Limneos, Samuel. "Death from Within, the Destruction of the Far East Air Force: Strategy vs. Feasibility." *Army History* (Summer 2017): 6–29.

Linn, Brian McAllister. *The Philippine War, 1899–1902*. Lawrence: University Press of Kansas, 2000.

———. *The U.S. Army Counterinsurgency in the Philippine War, 1899–1902*. Chapel Hill: University of North Carolina Press, 2000.

Lipman-Blumen, Jean. *The Allure of Toxic Leaders: Why We Follow Destructive Bosses, Corrupt Politicians, and How We Can Survive Them*. New York: Oxford University Press, 2006.

Leonnig, Carol, and Philip Rucker. *I Alone Can Fix It: Donald J. Trump's Catastrophic Final Year*. New York: Penguin Press, 2022.

Logevall, Fredrik. *Choosing War: The Last Chance for Peace and the Escalation of the Vietnam War*. Berkeley: University of California Press, 2001.

Ludwig, Dean C., and Clinton O. Longenecker. "The Bathsheba Syndrome: The Ethical Failure of Successful Leaders." *Journal of Business Ethics* (April 1993): 265–73.

MacArthur, Arthur. *Annual Report of Major General Arthur MacArthur, U.S. Army, Commanding, Division of the Philippines, Military Governor in the Philippine Islands*. Volume 1: *1900–1901*. N.p.: Wentworth Press, 2016.

MacArthur, Douglas. *Reminiscences*. Annapolis, MD: Naval Institute Press, 1964.

Malcolm, Joyce Lee. *The Tragedy of Benedict Arnold: An American Life*. New York: Pegasus Books, 2019.

Manchester, William. *American Caesar: Douglas MacArthur, 1880–1964*. New York: Little Brown & Co., 2012.

Margolick, David. "The Night of the Generals." *Vanity Fair*. March 5, 2007. https://archive.vanityfair.com/article/2007/4/the-night-of-the-generals.

Mathews, Lloyd J., and Dale E. Brown, eds. *The Parameters of Military Ethics*. Sterling, VA: Potomac Books, 1989.

Matthews, Jeffrey J. *Colin Powell: Imperfect Patriot*. Notre Dame, IN: University of Notre Dame Press, 2019.

———. "To Defeat a Maverick: The Goldwater Candidacy Revisited, 1963–1964." *Presidential Studies Quarterly* (Fall 1997): 662–78.

Mayer, Jane. *The Dark Side: The Inside Story of How the War on Terror Turned into a War on American Ideals*. New York: Doubleday, 2008.

McFarlane, Robert C. *Special Trust*. With Zofia Smardz. New York: Cadel & Davies, 1994.

McManus, John C. "The Man Who Would Be President." *Military History Quarterly* (Winter 2019): 34–43.

McMaster, H. R. *Dereliction of Duty: Johnson, McNamara, and the Joint Chiefs of Staff and the Lies about Vietnam*. New York: Harper Perennial, 1998.

McMichael, William H. *The Mother of All Hooks: The Story of the U.S. Navy's Tailhook Scandal*. New Brunswick, NJ: Transaction Publishers, 1997.

McNamara, Robert S. *In Retrospect: The Tragedy and Lessons of Vietnam*. New York: Vintage Books, 1996.

McPherson, James M. *Tried by War: Abraham Lincoln as Commander in Chief*. New York: Penguin Press, 2009.

Meacham, Robert, Timothy Naftali, Peter Baker, and Jeffrey A. Engel. *Impeachment: An American History*. New York: Random House, 2018.

Means, Howard. *Colin Powell: Soldier/Statesman — Statesman/Soldier*. New York: Donald I. Fine, 1992.

Mettraux, Guenael. "US Courts-Martial and the Armed Conflict in the Philippines (1899–1902): Their Contribution to National Case Law on War Crimes." *Journal of International Criminal Justice* (2003): 135–50.

Miles, Perry L. *Fallen Leaves: Memoirs of an Old Soldier*. New York: Wuerth Publishing, 1961.

Mill, John Stuart. *On Liberty*. Edited by Alburey Castell. Arlington Heights, IL: Harlan Davidson, 1947.

Miller, Stuart Creighton. *"Benevolent Assimilation": The American Conquest of the Philippines, 1899–1903*. New Haven, CT: Yale University Press, 1982.

Miller, William Ian. *The Mystery of Courage*. Cambridge, MA: Harvard University Press, 2002.

Milley, Mark A. "Address at the Opening Ceremony of the National Army Museum." *Joint Staff Public Affairs* (November 11, 2020): https://www.american rhetoric.com/speeches/markmilleynationalarmymuseum.htm.

———. "Army Profession and Leadership Policy." AR 600-100. April 5, 2017. https://armypubs.army.mil/epubs/DR_pubs/DR_a/pdf/web/ARN3758 _AR_600-100_FINAL_WEB_.pdf.

———. "National Defense University 2020 Class Graduation Address." June 11, 2020. https://www.americanrhetoric.com/speeches/markmilleynational defenseuniversitygraduationremarks.htm.

Moore, Harold G., and Joseph L. Galloway. *We Were Soldiers Once . . . and Young: I Drang, the Battle That Changed the War in Vietnam*. New York: Random House, 1992.

Moten, Matthew. *Presidents and Their Generals: An American History of Command in War*. Cambridge, MA: Belknap Press of Harvard University Press, 2014.

Mueller, Robert S., III. *Report on the Investigation into Russian Interference in the 2016 Presidential Election*. Washington, DC: Government Printing Office, March 2019. https://www.justice.gov/storage/report.pdf.

Mueller, Tom. *Crisis of Conscience: Whistleblowing in an Age of Fraud*. New York: Riverhead Books, 2019.

Murray, Williamson, and Richard Hart Sinnreich, eds. *The Past Is Prologue: The Importance of History to the Military Profession*. Cambridge: Cambridge University Press, 2006.

Myers, Richard. *Eyes on the Horizon: Serving on the Front Lines of National Security*. With Malcolm McConnell. New York: Threshold Editions, 2009.

Nixon, Richard M. "Remarks at a Promotion Ceremony for Admiral Hyman G. Rickover." December 3, 1973. https://www.presidency.ucsb.edu/documents /remarks-promotion-ceremony-for-admiral-hyman-g-rickover.

Obama, Barack. *A Promised Land*. New York: Crown, 2020.

Oliver, Dave. *Against the Tide: Rickover's Leadership and the Rise of the Nuclear Navy*. Annapolis, MD: Naval Institute Press, 2018.

Packer, George. *The Assassins' Gate: Americans in Iraq*. New York: Farrar, Straus and Giroux, 2006.

Palmer, Bruce, Jr. *The 25-Year War: America's Military Role in Vietnam*. Lexington: University of Press of Kentucky, 2002.

Parry, Robert. *America's Stolen Narrative: From Washington and Madison to Nixon, Reagan and the Bushes to Barack Obama*. Arlington, VA: Media Consortium, 2012.

Parry, Robert, Sam Parry, and Nat Parry. *Neck Deep: The Disastrous Presidency of George W. Bush*. Arlington, VA: Media Consortium, 2007.

Pearlman, Michael D. *Truman and MacArthur: Policy, Politics, and the Hunger for Honor and Renown*. Bloomington: Indiana University Press, 2008.

Peers, William R. *The My Lai Inquiry*. New York: W. W. Norton, 1979.

———. "Summary of Peers Report." University of Missouri, Kansas City. March 1970. http://law2.umkc.edu/faculty/projects/ftrials/mylai/summary _rpt.html.

Perret, Geoffrey. *Old Soldiers Never Die: The Life and Legend of Douglas MacArthur*. New York: Random House, 1996.

Perry, Mark. *Four Stars*. New York: Houghton Mifflin Harcourt, 1989.

———. *The Most Dangerous Man in America: The Making of Douglas MacArthur*. New York: Basic Books, 2015.

———. *The Pentagon Wars: The Military's Undeclared War against the United States*. New York: Basic Books, 2017.

Persico, Joseph E. *Roosevelt's Centurions: FDR and the Commanders He Led to Victory in World War II*. New York: Random House, 2013.

Peskin, Allan. *Winfield Scott and the Profession of Arms*. Kent, OH: Kent State University Press, 2004.

Peters, William C. "Adjudication Deferred." *Nationalities Papers* 37, no. 6 (November 2009): 925–52.

Polmar, Norman, and Thomas B. Allen. *Rickover: Controversy and Genius, a Biography*. New York: Touchstone Books, 1982.

Powell, Colin P. *My American Journey*. With Joseph E. Persico. New York: Random House, 1995.

———. Officer Efficiency Report, May 1986. Papers of General Colin L. Powell (Ret.). Special Collections, National Defense University Library, Fort Lesley J. McNair, Washington, DC.

Reagan, Ronald. *An American Life: Ronald Reagan, the Autobiography*. New York: Simon & Schuster, 1990.

———. "Evil Empire Speech." National Association of Evangelicals. March 8, 1983. http://voicesofdemocracy.umd.edu/reagan-evil-empire-speech-text/.

———. "Remarks Announcing the Release of the Hostages from the Trans World Airlines Hijacking Incident." June 30, 1985. Ronald Reagan Library. https://www.reaganlibrary.gov/archives/speech/remarks-announcing -release-hostages-trans-world-airlines-hijacking-incident.

Recchia, Stefano. *Reassuring the Reluctant Warriors: U.S. Civil-Military Relations and Multilateral Intervention*. Ithaca, NY: Cornell University Press, 2015.

Reed, George E. *Tarnished: Toxic Leadership in the U.S. Military*. Lincoln: University of Nebraska Press, 2015.

———. "Toxic Leadership." *Military Review* (July–August 2004): 67–71.

Reed, George E., and R. Craig Bullis. "The Impact of Destructive Leadership on Senior Military Officers and Civilian Employees." *Armed Forces & Society* (October 2009): 5–18.

Reed, George E., and Richard A. Olsen. "Toxic Leadership: Part Deux." *Military Review* (November–December, 2010): 58–64.

Report of Maj. Gen. E. S. Otis. Special Collections, University of Washington.

Richardson, John M. "Accountability Action Relating to Glenn Defense Marine— RADM Timothy M. Giardina, USN." December 11, 2014. http://www.sail orbob.com/files/Fat%20Leonard/CDA%20Information%20-%20Washington %20Post%20FOIA%20-%20reduced%20for%20web.pdf.

———. "Message to Naval Flag Officers and Senior Executive Service." May 2016. http://cimsec.org/wp-content/uploads/2016/07/CNO-PFOR.pdf.

Ricks, Thomas E. *The Generals: American Military Command from World War Two to Today*. New York: Penguin Books, 2012.

Ridgway, Matthew B. *The Korean War*. New York: Doubleday, 1967.

Robarge, David. *John McCone as Director of Central Intelligence, 1961–1965*. Langley, VA: Central Intelligence Agency, 2015.

Rockwell, Theodore. *The Rickover Effect: How One Man Made a Difference*. Annapolis, MD: Naval Institute Press, 1992.

Roll, David L. *George Marshall: Defender of the Republic*. New York: Dutton Caliber, 2019.

Schaller, Michael. *Douglas MacArthur: The Far Eastern General*. New York: Oxford University Press, 1989.

Schott, Joseph L. *The Ordeal of Samar*. Indianapolis, IN: Bobbs-Merrill, 1964.

Schratz, Paul R. "Admiral Rickover and the Cult of Personality." *Air University Review* (July-August 1983): 96–101.

Sexton, William Thaddeus. *Soldiers in the Sun: An Adventure in Imperialism*. Harrisburg, PA: Military Service Publishing, 1939.

Silbey, David J. *A War of Frontier and Empire: The Philippine-American War, 1899–1902*. New York: Hill and Wang, 2008.

Singlaub, John. *Hazardous Duty: American Solider in the Twentieth Century*. With Malcolm McConnell. New York: Touchstone, 1992.

Smith, Jacob Hurd. *Personal Reminiscences: Three Weeks Prior, during, and Ten Days after the Battle of Shiloh*. Detroit, MI: Winn and Hammond Printers, 1894.

Snodgrass, Guy M. "Keep a Weather Eye on the Horizon: A Navy Officer Retention Study." *Naval War College Review* (Autumn 2014): 1–29.

Sorley, Lewis. *Honorable Warrior: General Harold Johnson and the Ethics of Command*. Lawrence: University Press of Kansas, 1998.

———. "To Change a War: General Harold K. Johnson and the PROVN Study." *Parameters* (Spring 1998): 98–109.

Stavridis, James. *Sailing True North: Ten Admirals and Voyage of Character*. New York: Penguin, 2020.

Stephenson, Heather. "How to Be an Ethical Leader." *TuftsNow* (November 18, 2019): https://now.tufts.edu/articles/how-be-ethical-leader.

Stoler, Mark, and Daniel D. Holt. *The Papers of George Catlett Marshall: "The Man of the Age," October 1, 1949–October 16, 1959*. Volume 7. Baltimore, MD: Johns Hopkins University Press, 2016.

Taylor, Robert J., Mary-Jo Kline, and Gregg L. Lint, eds. *The Papers of John Adams*, Volume 1: *September 1755–October 1773*. Cambridge, MA: The Belknap Press of Harvard University, 1977.

Thomas, Evan. *The Very Best Men: The Daring Early Years of the CIA*. New York: Simon & Schuster, 2006.

Thomas, Joseph J. "The Four Stages of Moral Development in Military Leaders." The Admiral James B. Stockdale Center for Ethical Leadership. United States Naval Academy. https://www.usna.edu/Ethics/_files/documents/Four%20Stages%20of%20Moral%20Development%20Thomas.pdf.

Timberg, Robert. *The Nightingale's Song*. New York: Free Press, 1996.

Tooley, T. Hunt. "All the People Are Now Guerillas." *The Independent Review* (Winter 2007): 355–79.

Truman, Harry S. *The Truman Memoirs*. Vol. 2, *Years of Trial and Hope*. Garden City, NY: Doubleday, 1955.

Turse, Nick. *Kill Anything That Moves: The Real American War in Vietnam*. New York: Henry Holt, 2013.

Ulrich, Marybeth P. "The General Stanley McChrystal Affair." *Parameters* (Spring 2011): 86–100.

United Nations. "War Crimes." https://www.un.org/en/genocideprevention/war-crimes.shtml.

United States Air Force. Inspector General of the Air Force. *Report of Investigation: Brigadier General David C. Uhrich.* September 2013. http://apps.washingtonpost.com/g/page/world/report-on-gen-david-c-uhrich/769/.

———. *Report of Investigation Lt Gen John W. Hesterman III.* February 2016. https://www.airandspaceforces.com/PDF/DRArchive/Documents/2016/January%202016/031716_Hesterman_IG_Investigation.PDF.

———. *Report of Investigation, Maj Gen Thomas J. Fiscus.* October 2004. https://web.archive.org/web/20070917024330/http://www.af.mil/library/posture/fiscusroi.pdf.

United States Army, Office of Adjutant General. *Correspondence Relating to the War with Spain and Conditions Growing out of the Same Including the Insurrection in the Philippine Islands and the China Relief Expedition, between the Adjutant-General of the Army and the Philippine Islands, from April 15, 1898, to July 30, 1902.* 2 vols. Washington, DC: Government Printing Office, 1902. https://history.army.mil/html/books/070/70-28/index.html.

United States Congress. *[Hearing on] Air War against North Vietnam before the Senate Preparedness Investigating Subcommittee of the Committee on Armed Services.* 90th Congress, 1st session. August 9–29, 1967. (Stennis Hearings.)

United States Department of the Army, Office of Inspector General. *Report of Investigation: Brigadier General Bryan T. Roberts.* September 16, 2013. https://www.governmentattic.org/13docs/ArmyOIGincsSeniorOfficials_2011-2013.pdf, pages 32–41.

———. *Report of Investigation: Brigadier General Eugene L. Mascolo, U.S. Army, Director, Joint Staff, Joint Force Headquarters, Connecticut National Guard.* December 7, 2012. https://www.governmentattic.org/13docs/ArmyOIGincsSeniorOfficials_2011-2013.pdf, pages 71–88.

———. *Report of Investigation: Brigadier General Scott "Rock" Donahue, Former Commanding General, U.S. Army Engineer Division, South Pacific, U.S. Army Corps of Engineers, San Francisco, California.* April 19, 2013. https://www.governmentattic.org/13docs/ArmyOIGincsSeniorOfficials_2011-2013.pdf, pages 3–32.

———. *Report of Investigation 13-024, BG Martin P. Schweitzer.* August 23, 2013. https://www.governmentattic.org/13docs/ArmyOIGincsSeniorOfficials_2011-2013.pdf, pages 42–50.

United States Department of Defense. *Annual Report on Sexual Assault in the Military.* May 2021. https://www.sapr.mil/sites/default/files/public/docs

/reports/AR/DOD_Annual_Report_on_Sexual_Assault_In_The_Military
_FY2020_Consolidated.pdf.

―――. *Annual Report on Sexual Assault in the Military.* September 2022.
https://www.sapr.mil/sites/default/files/public/docs/reports/AR/DOD
_Annual_Report_on_Sexual_Assault_in_the_Military_FY2021.pdf.

United States Department of Defense, Office of Inspector General. *Alleged Misconduct: Vice Admiral John D. Stufflebeem, U.S. Navy, Director, Navy Staff.*
March 19, 2008. https://media.defense.gov/2018/Aug/16/2001954997
/-1/-1/1/STUFFLEBEEM%20ROI%20BLACK%20OUT%20COPY.PDF.

―――. *Fiscal Year 2019 Top DoD Management Challenges.* November 15, 2018.
https://media.defense.gov/2018/Dec/12/2002071981/-1/-1/1/TOP%20
DOD%20MANAGEMENT%20CHALLENGES%20FISCAL%20YEAR%20
2019.PDF.

―――. *Fiscal Year 2020 Top DoD Management Challenges.* October 15, 2019.
https://media.defense.gov/2020/Mar/11/2002263093/-1/-1/1/TOP%20
DOD%20MANAGEMENT%20CHALLENGES%20FISCAL%20YEAR%20
2020.PDF.

―――. *Investigation Involving Major General Stephen M. Goldfein, U.S. Air Force,
Vice Director, Joint Staff.* January 30, 2008. https://media.defense.gov/2018
/Aug/16/2001955007/-1/-1/1/MEMO_SECAF_SMS_0408.PDF.

―――. *Report of Investigation: Brigadier General Norman Cooling, USMC.* May
24, 2019. https://media.defense.gov/2019/Jun/19/2002147137/-1/-1/1
/DODIG-2019-092.PDF.

―――. *Report of Investigation: Lieutenant General Patrick J. O'Reilly, U.S. Army,
Director, Missile Defense Agency.* May 2, 2012. https://media.defense.gov
/2018/Jul/25/2001946766/-1/-1/1/O'REILLYROI.PDF.

―――. *Report of Investigation: Rear Admiral (Lower Half) Ronny Lynn Jackson,
M.D., U.S. Navy, Retired.* March 3, 2021. https://media.defense.gov/2021
/Mar/03/2002592287/-1/-1/1/DODIG-2021-057.PDF.

―――. *Report of Investigation: Rick A. Uribe, Brigadier General, U.S. Marine Corps.*
June 14, 2018. https://media.defense.gov/2018/Jul/10/2001940716
/-1/-1/1/DODIG-2018-131%20UPDATED%202.PDF.

―――. *Report of Investigation: Tailhook 9 – Part 1: Review of the Navy Investigations.* September 1992. https://ncisahistory.org/wp-content/uploads/2017
/07/DoDIG-Report-of-Investigation-Tailhook-91-Review-of-the-Navy
-Investigations.pdf.

―――. *Report of Investigation: Tailhook 9 – Part 2: Events at the 35th Annual
Tailhook Symposium.* Washington, DC: Government Printing Office, 1993.

———. "Review of the Department of Defense's Role, Responsibilities, and Actions to Prepare for and Respond to the Protests and Its Aftermath at the U.S. Capitol Campus on January 6, 2021." November 16, 2021. https://media.defense.gov/2021/Nov/19/2002896088/-1/-1/1/DODIG-2022-039%20V2%20508.PDF.

———. *Semiannual Report to the Congress, October 1, 2021, through March 31, 2022.* https://media.defense.gov/2022/Sep/27/2003085962/-1/-1/1/SEMIANNUAL_REPORT_TO_THE_CONGRESS_OCTOBER_1_2021_THROUGH_MARCH_31_2022.PDF.

———. *Top DoD Management Challenges Fiscal Year 2018.* November 20, 2017. https://media.defense.gov/2017/Dec/01/2001850837/-1/-1/1/FY%202018%20MANAGEMENT%20CHALLENGES_508.PDF.

United States Department of Defense, Office of Naval Inspector General. *Report of Investigation: Department of the Navy/Tailhook Association Relationship and Personal Conduct Surrounding Tailhook '91 Symposium.* April 29, 1992. https://apps.dtic.mil/sti/pdfs/ADA269008.pdf.

———. *Report of Investigation: Misconduct by RADM Jeffrey A. Harley, Former President, Naval War College.* January 31, 2020. https://www.secnav.navy.mil/ig/FOIA%20Reading%20Room/201801726_ROI_HARLEY.pdf.

———. *Report of Investigation, Senior Official Cases: 201202138, Alleging Violation of Joint Travel Regulations by RADM Mark F. Heinrich, CAPT (RDML Select) David R. Pimpo and CAPT (RDML Select) Donald L. Singleton.* June 17, 2013. https://www.governmentattic.org/17docs/NAVINSGENinvsSeniorMisc_2012-2013updt.pdf.

United States War Department. *Annual Reports of the War Department, 1899–1902.* Washington, DC: Government Printing Office, 1899–1902.

———. *Articles of War.* Washington, DC: Government Printing Office, 1920.

U.S. Government. *Uniform Code of Military Justice: Revised September 28, 2018.* N.p.: independently published, 2018.

Vader, John. *New Guinea: The Tide Is Stemmed.* New York: Ballantine Books, 1971.

VanDeMark, Brian. *Into The Quagmire: Lyndon Johnson and the Escalation of the Vietnam War.* New York: Oxford University Press, 1991.

Vistica, Gregory L. *Fall from Glory: The Men Who Sank the U.S. Navy.* New York: Touchstone Books, 1997.

Voth, Hans-Joachim, and Guo Xu. "Encouraging Others: Punishment and Performance in the Royal Navy." CEPR Discussion Papers, 2020. https://papers.ssrn.com/sol3/papers.cfm?abstract_id=3560283.

Wallace, Robert. "A Deluge of Honors for an Exasperating Admiral." *Life*, September 8, 1958, 104–6, 109–16, 118.

Walsh, Lawrence E. *Final Report of the Independent Counsel for Iran/Contra Matters*. 3 vols. Washington, DC: U.S. Court of Appeals for the District of Columbia Circuit, 1993.

———. *Firewall: The Iran-Contra Conspiracy and Cover-Up*. New York: W. W. Norton, 1997.

Walters, Vernon A. *Silent Missions*. Doubleday, 1978.

Weiner, Tim. *Enemies: A History of the FBI*. New York: Random House, 2013.

White, Theodore H. *In Search of History: A Personal Adventure*. New York: Warner Books, 1979.

Wildenberg, Thomas. *Billy Mitchell's War with the Navy: The Interwar Rivalry over Air Power*. Annapolis, MD: Naval Institute Press, 2013.

Wilkie, Robert L. "Harassment Prevention and Response in the Armed Forces." DoD Instruction 1020.03. February 8, 2018. https://www.esd.whs.mil/Portals/54/Documents/DD/issuances/dodi/102003p.PDF?ver=DAAzonEUeFb8kUWRbT9Epw%3D%3D.

Witt, John Fabian. *Lincoln's Code: The Laws of War in American History*. New York: Free Press, 2013.

Wolf, Leon. *Little Brown Brother: How the United States Purchased and Pacified the Philippine Islands at the Century's Turn*. New York: History Club Book, 2006.

Woodward, Bob. *Veil: The Secret Wars of the CIA 1981–1987*. New York: Simon & Schuster, 1987.

Woodward, Bob, and Robert Costa. *Peril*. New York: Simon & Schuster, 2021.

Wortman, Marc. *Admiral Hyman Rickover: Engineer of Power*. New Haven, CT: Yale University Press, 2022.

Wright, Tom. Interview with Leonard Francis. *Fat Leonard*, podcast audio. October–November 2021. https://fatleonardpodcast.com/episodes/.

Zimmerman, Jean. *Tailspin: Women at War in the Wake of Tailhook*. New York: Doubleday, 1995.

Zumwalt, Elmo R., Jr. *On Watch: A Memoir*. New York: New York Times Book Co., 1976.

INDEX

Abu Ghraib prison (Iraq), xxi–xxii, 43–45, 135, 305

Acheson, Dean G., 72–73, 77–78

Adams, John, xx

Afghanistan war, xxviii, 45, 85–87, 90, 171–73, 210, 264

Aguinaldo, Emilio, 4, 14–15, 20, 22

Ailes, Stephen, 105

Air Force, U.S., 51, 106, 256

   Air Force inspector general (AFIG), xxv–xxvi, 140, 166–67, 248–49, 252–53

Air National Guard, U.S., xvii, xix, 52

Allen, CAPT Raymond, 227

Allen, Richard V., 183

Allyn, GEN Daniel, 292

Almquist, LTG Elmer H., 100

Armitage, Richard L., 193, 196, 346

Arms Export Control Act, 174, 189

Army, U.S., 23, 62, 88, 93, 125–26

   Army Inspector General (AIG), xix, xxviii, 139, 205, 250

Criminal Investigation Division, xviii, 43, 274

101st Airborne Division, U.S., 182

173rd Airborne Brigade, U.S., 113

V Corps, U.S., 135, 197, 201

See also Johnson, GEN Harold K. "Johnny"; Powell, GEN Colin L.; Smith, BG Jacob H.

Army National Guard, U.S., xxviii, 251–52, 257–58

Army War College, 138

Arnold, MG Benedict, xv, xxi, 2

Articles of War, U.S., 2, 30–31, 53, 62, 66

Asher, BG Robbie L., xvii

Aspin, Leslie "Les," Jr., 138, 239–40

Atomic Energy Commission, xxvi, 112, 141, 151

Austin, GEN Lloyd J., III, xxvii, 253

Bacevich, COL Andrew J., Jr., 87

Baker, Newton, 56

Eisenhower, Mary G. "Mamie," 153

Elisha (prophet), 1

Emerson, LTG Henry E. "The Gunfighter," 182

Esper, Mark T., 295–96, 299

Fahd bin Abdulaziz Al Saud (king of Saudi Arabia), 186

Fall, Bernard B., 121

Fallon, ADM William J. "Fox," 52, 86

Fast, MG Barbara, 44–45

Fat Leonard scandal, xxi, xxix–xxx, 255, 259–93, 304–5

Federal Bureau of Investigation (FBI), 88, 170, 197, 199, 204–5, 210, 255, 257

Felice, William F., 90, 134

Fetterman, VADM John H. "Jack," Jr., 221–22

Finney, RADM James H. "Jay," 241–42

Fiscus, COL Thomas J., 246–49

Fitzpatrick, Darrel, 258

Flagg, RADM Wilson F. "Bud," 240

Fletcher, ADM Frank J., 148

Flynn, LTG Michael T., 88, 170, 302

Forest, Nathan Bedford, 94

Formosa. *See* Taiwan

Fort Benning, GA, 96, 181–82

Fort Bragg, NC, 178

Fort Campbell, KY, 182

Fort Carson, CO, 183

Fort Clark, TX, 9

Fort Devens, MA, 98, 181

Fort Knox, KY, 98–99

Fort Leavenworth, KS, 55, 99–100, 105, 138

Fort McHenry, MD, 57

Fort McPherson, GA, 58

Fort Monroe, VA, 100

Fort Myer, VA, 299, 301

Fort Sam Houston, TX, 50

Fort Snelling, MN, 96

Fort William McKinley, Philippines, 96

Francis, Leonard Glenn "Fat Leonard." *See* Fat Leonard scandal

Franklin, MG Craig A., 249

Franks, GEN Tommy R., 91

Freemont, BG John C., 48–49

Fuller, MG Peter, 88

Funston, BG Frederick, 12

Gamble, LTG Duane, 139–40

Gallery, RADM Daniel V., 51–52

Garces, Adriano, 19

Garcia, Ephraim, 258–59

Garrett, H. Lawrence "Larry," III, 216, 220–22, 226–31, 236

Garrison, MG Clay, xvii

Gates, Robert M., 86–87, 192

Gaouette, RADM Charles M., 140

General Order No. 100. *See* Lieber Code

Geneva Conventions, 2–3, 5–6, 20, 25, 28, 30, 32, 35, 38

George Washington University (GWU), 182

Germany, 55, 57, 61, 65, 100, 131, 144, 181, 197–98, 201

Geronimo, 54

Gersten, COL Peter E., 252–53

Gettys, MG Charles M., 182

Giardina, RADM Timothy M., 267, 271–74

Myers, GEN Richard B. "Dick," xxiii–xxiv, 91
My Lai massacre, 42, 171

Napoleon, xv
National Security Council (NSC), xxvi, 91, 115, 183–204
National War College (NWC), 100, 183
Naval War College, xvii, 147, 219
Navy, U.S.
    Naval Criminal Investigation Service (NCIS), 261, 264, 274, 285
    Naval Investigative Service (NIS), 225–36
    Navy Inspector General (NIG), 226, 269, 280
    See also Fat Leonard scandal; Poindexter, RADM John M.; Rickover, ADM Hyman G.
Neary, MG Stephen, xviii
Nelson, MG William "Bull," 7
Newell, COL Robert, 248
New York Times, 16, 35, 37, 40–41, 43, 53, 132
Ngo Dinh Diem, 101–2
Nicaragua, xxvii, 173–74, 184–86, 197–98, 200–201, 203, 208–9. *See also* Iran-Contra scandal
Nimitz, ADM Chester W., 67, 74, 142, 150–51
Nixon, Richard M., 82, 153–54, 169, 199
North, LTC Oliver L., 173–75, 185–91, 194, 197–204, 209
North Atlantic Treaty Organization (NATO), xviii, 86, 88, 100, 210, 247

North Korea, 298. *See also* Korean War
Northrop Grumman Corporation, 256
North Vietnam. *See* Vietnam War
Norton, RDML Kenneth J. "K. J.," 274–77
Nunn, Samuel A., Jr., 228–29

Obama, Barack H., 52, 86–88, 210
obstruction of justice, xvi, xix, xxi, xxvi, 169–211, 227, 235. *See also* Iran-Contra scandal; Tailhook Association
Office of Management and Budget, 182
Oliver, RADM Dave, 143, 155, 159
O'Keefe, Sean C., 231, 235–36
Operation Illwind, 255–56, 259
O'Reilly, LTG Patrick J., 139
Otis, MG Elwell S., 11–15, 18

Pace, Frank, 74
Pace, GEN Peter, 91
Pahlavi, Mohammad Reza, 173
Palestine Liberation Organization, 185
Palmer, GEN Bruce, Jr., 11, 129–30
Parcels, RADM Paul W., 242
Patton, GEN George S., 57, 59, 304
Peers, LTG William R., 42, 171
Peers Commission, 42
Pelosi, Nancy P., 299, 301
Pence, Michael R., 88, 300
Perret, Geoffrey, 83
Perry, CDRE Matthew C., 24
Perry, William J., 245–46
Persian Gulf War, 221, 238

JEFFREY J. MATTHEWS is the George Frederick Jewett Distinguished Professor at the University of Puget Sound in Tacoma, Washington. He teaches American history and leadership and has written or edited four previous books, including *Colin Powell: Imperfect Patriot* (University of Notre Dame Press, 2019), winner of the Foreword INDIES War and Military Book of the Year Award and finalist for the Army Historical Foundation Book Award.